BETWEEN STILL AND MOVING IMAGES

Edited by

Laurent Guido and Olivier Lugon

British Library Cataloguing in Publication Data

Between Still and Moving Images

A catalogue entry for this book is available from the British Library

ISBN: 9780 86196 707 0 (Paperback)

A first French edition of this book was published, under the title *Fixe/animé: croisements de la photographie et du cinéma au XXe siècle*, by L'Age d'Homme, Lausanne, 2010.

Published by
John Libbey Publishing Ltd, 3 Leicester Road, New Barnet, Herts EN5 5EW, United Kingdom
e-mail: john.libbey@orange.fr; web site: www.johnlibbey.com
Direct orders (UK and Europe): direct.orders@marston.co.uk

Distributed in N. America by **Indiana University Press**, 601 North Morton St,
Bloomington, IN 47404, USA. www.iupress.indiana.edu

Printed and bound in China by 1010 Printing International Ltd.

Contents

Introduction

Laurent Guido, Olivier Lugon

Of the multiple unexpected consequences of the shift to digital technologies, the sudden convergence of the categories of still and moving images is without a doubt one of the deepest. Occupying distinct institutional spaces and requiring different media (with moving images making a specific equipment necessary more often than their still counterparts), these categories had up to that point been perceived as mutually exclusive. Moreover, autonomous disciplinary fields had formed around them in cultural economy and academic research. Regardless, they now seem to be but two variants in the same entity, with no stable boundary to tell them apart.

The convergence is primarily technical: the same machine may produce one and the other, the same computer screen can display either one of them, and a single key will control the progression from a state to the other, speeding up or slowing down the run of images. It is as though still images have become but a subcategory of animation, a transitional situation whose inevitable transformation is a click away. The repercussions of this new technological state of affairs are palpable in every domain, from amateur practices to the information sector. Their impact on artistic production is felt more acutely, as the two forms of images now share the same exhibition spaces and may be assumed by the same author, with no hierarchy in their respective statuses.

The advent of video had already contributed to reducing the gap between these regimes, as two events showed. In 1990, the Paris exhibition *Passages de l'image* brought within the same space "the painting-image and the duration-image".[1] That same year, Raymond Bellour – one of the curators of *Passages de l'image* – published his book *L'Entre-Images. Photo. Cinéma. Vidéo*, examining "the in-between time of still images and moving images" made visible by the emergence of video and the VCR.[2] Thinking on the possible exchanges or even on the fundamental indetermination of stillness and movement has since then expanded

1   Chevrier and David 1990, 24.

2   Bellour 1990, 10.

much beyond that territory. Over the last few years, it has spawned countless events and works celebrating the new temporal regimes implied in the general hybridization of media and moving into multiple directions. Several exhibitions or publications have reconsidered the introduction of projection and the temporal image in the space of the fine arts.[3] Others have emphasized mixed practices through case studies in the form of monographs, bringing out the cinematographic work of famous photographers or the photographic practice of major filmmakers.[4] Similarly, film retrospectives have recently examined the various degrees of presence of the photographic element in cinema.[5] More decisively still, the history and the modalities of cinema have moved outside cinematheques to integrate the institutional spaces reserved for art history[6] or have been invoked as major references for contemporary art or photography.[7] At the intersection of the two fields, new objects such as film stills have also earned a new respectability.[8] Anthologies of reference texts have appeared,[9] as have studies on the question, characterized by a very rich British production.[10]

The majority of these works or events focused on the contemporary situation, often experienced as a moment when the division between stillness and movement, revealed as artificial and unsatisfying in its duality, should be left behind and even evacuated. This point of view presents some risks, and the impression of a growing lack of differentiation justifying it warrants further questioning.

First, as far as cinema is more particularly concerned, it does not necessarily follow from the announced disappearance of celluloid film to the benefit of digital technologies that any thinking on stillness and movement has become obsolescent. Setting still film frames in motion founded the specificity of the technical

---

3   Païni, 1997; NGBK 2000; Iles 2001; Païni 2002; Hoormann 2003; Michalka 2003; Alexander 2005; Hüsch, Jäger and Knapstein 2006; Michaud 2006; Douglas and Eamon 2009.

4   For photographers, see Horak 1997; for cinema, see the examples of Abbas Kiarostami, Stanley Kubrick, Chris Marker, Johan van der Keuken, Agnès Varda, among others...

5   *Le Cinéma Photographié* (Cinémathèque Française, Sept. 2 – 19, 2009) but also, and more importantly, *Fotofilm*, a programme of about thirty short films presented on the occasion of a conference (Arsenal film theater, Berlin, Nov. 24 – 26, 2006); the films were shown again at the Cinémathèque Québécoise, 21–25 October 2009. Shortly afterwards, Gusztáv Hámos, Katja Pratschke, and Thomas Tode, who were in charge of the event, published *Viva Fotofilm – Bewegt/Unbewegt* (Hámos, Pratschke and Tode 2009). Let us also mention Diekmann 2007.

6   In Paris alone, the exhibitions *Alfred Hitchcock et l'art: coïncidences fatales* and *Jean Cocteau sur le fil du siècle* took place at the Centre Georges Pompidou in 2001 and 2003, respectively; there were also *Il était une fois Walt Disney* at the Galeries nationales du Grand Palais in 2006; *Chaplin et les images* in 2005 and *Fellini, la Grande Parade* in 2009, both at the Galeries Nationales du Jeu de Paume. The reverse movement should also be noted, with the importation of painting in the Cinémathèque française with *Renoir / Renoir* in 2005.

7   See Dubois 1999; Dufour and Toubiana 2007.

8   See Pauleit 2004; Schifferli 2007.

9   Company 2007; Leighton 2008.

10   Stewart 1999; Mulvey 2005; Green and Lowry 2006; Beckman and Ma 2008; Campany 2008. Among the many events on the subject, let us also mention the seminar "*Something between...*" *Images fixes/images mobiles: convergences, glissements, translations dans les pratiques artistiques contemporaines*, organized by Nathalie Boulouch and Valérie Mavridorakis at the Université Rennes 2 on May 3, 2007; and the colloquium *Arrêts sur images. Pour une combinaison de la photographie et du film* at the Musée du quai Branly, Paris, April 9 – 10, 2010.

apparatus of film. However, the conception of film as a juxtaposition of separate images has paradoxically never been as accessible to users of cinema as in the digital era, thanks to the "pause" function available on all DVD players. By contrast, the material conditions of the traditional cinematographic spectacle never made it possible to perceive the still film frames appearing on the projected strip concretely.

Second, this premise of a growing lack of differentiation of stillness and movement can soon lead to a new form of teleology when projected onto the past: namely, whereas moving beyond stillness through movement and speed had been the horizon of the modern historical narrative, an inevitable evolution towards their hybridization had now substituted for it. This projection may prove of limited relevance for periods when the opposition between stillness and movement had a structuring force, precisely. This collection proceeds from the reverse postulate: not only does this polarity remain relevant, but it was also integral to thinking on images during the twentieth century and to multiple discourses linking a whole range of supposed values and symbolic projections to either pole. This made interactions between stillness and movement not so much a kind of evidence as a field where tensions played out productively. Indeed, it is because they articulated entities perceived as different that interactions between stillness and movement were meaningful.

Still, these exchanges were numerous. While they involved very diverse disciplines and media, from painting to scenic arts to publishing, their most vivid expression took place in photography and cinema thanks to the paradoxical relation between the two media. In effect, these seemed to embody like no other the very principles of stillness and movement. For the most part, they also shared the same technical bases – recording on a translucent negative medium, the resort to projection, and the use of enlargement in reproduction – all of which greatly fostered their interaction. Whether they took place in the space of luminous projection or in the reproduction on paper, these encounters defined an important intermediate area, whose assignment to the worlds of still images or the moving images is far from simple. In the end, the dividing line between photography and film did not exactly match the symmetrical opposition between stillness and movement. The two media ceaselessly crossed the boundary and blended these categories: photography could be perceived as a legitimate factor in the reproduction of movement, and film as a possible repository of still images.

In this far-reaching, multiform intermediate field, two periods have already been scrutinized by scholars: the digital shift at the turn of the twenty-first century, but also the pre-cinematographic era and more particularly chronophotography. The present collection ambitions to bridge between the two, running roughly from 1900 to 2000, or the "century of film".[11] It thus extends the work presented in *Stop Motion, Fragmentation of Time*, edited by François Albera, Marta Braun,

---

11   This apt expression we borrow from the Musée suisse de l'appareil photographique in Vevey.

and André Gaudreault in 2002, which identified one of the "roots of modern visual culture"[12] in the fits and starts of chronophotography, or in the articulation of animation and immobility, of instants and durations – the very culture this volume aims to explore.

A number of principles guided its conception and that of the conference where it originated, held at the Université de Lausanne in the spring of 2007.[13] These principles involve the search for a dialogue between photography historians and film historians, equally represented in the table of contents and whom the volume equally addresses; the widening of the field of study beyond the domains of art and cinephilia to take into account the social uses of images, of popular media, and of a diversity of discursive fields, from medicine to pedagogy; and the choice of a historical approach, looking to move beyond general aesthetic considerations to deal with specific historical objects, including discourses. This approach belongs in history on several accounts. First, it casts light on the existence of editorial or discursive practices, of unknown or forgotten systems or equipments that reflect to what extent the respective apparatuses of photography and cinema crossed, sometimes to the point of hybridity. Second, it attempts to historicize the various theories and experimentations that actualized this same intermedia relation, referring it more specifically to the major aesthetic trends that defined thought on art and artistic creation in the twentieth century. Finally, it also emphasizes the importance of decisive historical shifts, from large-scale technical changes to social and political events such as the Second World War.

The book does not claim to be exhaustive with respect to exchanges between photography and cinema. Rather, it focuses explicitly on the way in which these were at stake in the structural relations between stillness and movement. Accordingly, many aspects widely discussed in previous publications, from Raymond Bellour to David Campany, have been knowingly excluded – notably what pertains to representations, whether in the figure of the photographer in cinema or the cinematographic imaginary within photography. Similarly, we have left aside the more general domain of the relations of fine arts to the cinema, as well as television or electronic media.

For all that, this necessary limitation does not entail the renunciation of a broader intermedia perspective. Many studies in this collection, dealing with very different periods, approach the relation of photography and cinema through a third term that conditions how these two means of expression interact. This additional parameter can vary greatly and be felt on very different levels. One is the presence of text, written or oral, a discursive movement that directs reading, introduces

---

12   Albera, Braun and Gaudreault 2002.

13   Organized by the department of Film Studies (Section d'Histoire et esthétique du cinéma), the conference took place from 10 May 10 to 12 May 2007. The present book represents a slightly amended version of it, as a few additional texts have been included in the print version. The conference was made possible through the generous support of the Swiss National Science Foundation and the Réseau Cinéma CH. We would like to thank them here, as well as Claus Gunti for his support in putting together the event.

meaning, or more simply temporalizes a frozen image, just as it takes part in cinematographic duration, like sound effects or music. Throughout the volume, the relation between photography and cinema also takes the form of a mediation by various kinds of artistic expressions such as painting, dance, or comics, as well as some fundamental scientific or philosophical models (psychoanalysis occupies an important place, for instance). Lastly, the different objects examined in the book demonstrate the major role of "all-encompassing" media that make the circulation of images possible: the book, the exhibition, the projection or… the film strip itself!

The collection is organized in five Sections, which follow a chronological and thematic order and each have their own introduction. The first goes back over the philosophical, psychological, or aesthetic debates that enrolled photography and cinema at the turn of the twentieth century, and the way the two media simultaneously modeled conceptions of movement, duration, and the moment. The second section examines the many ways in which photography and cinema concretely crossed in the practices of some cameramen and resulted in mixed media forms, some of which no longer exist. The third looks more specifically at how print media brought together cinema and photography, especially during the interwar period. The fourth section is devoted to the decades following World War II and explores the multiple uses of the freeze frame in cinema, in particular its relation – individual as well as collective – to memory, history, and trauma. Finally, the closing section deals with the many forms assumed by the sequence in the visual culture of the last decades of the century.

Bibliography

Albera, Braun and Gaudreault 2002: *Arrêt sur image, fragmentation du temps. Aux sources de la culture visuelle moderne / Stop Motion, Fragmentation of Time. Exploring the Roots of Modern Visual Culture*, eds. François Albera, Marta Braun, André Gaudreault (Lausanne: Payot, 2002).

Alexander 2005: Darsie Alexander, *Slide Show. Projected Images in Contemporary Art* (London: Tate Publishing, 2005).

Beckman and Ma 2008: *Still Moving: Between Cinema and Photography*, eds. Karen Beckman and Jean Ma (Durham: Duke University Press, 2008).

Chevrier and David 1990: Jean-François Chevrier, Catherine David, "Actualité de l'image", in *Passages de l'image*, eds. Raymond Bellour, Catherine David, Christine van Assche, exhibition catalogue (Paris: Musée national d'art moderne, Centre Georges Pompidou, 1990).

Bellour 1990: Raymond Bellour, *L'Entre-Images. Photo. Cinéma. Vidéo* (Paris: La Différence, 1990).

Campany 2007: *The Cinematic*, ed. David Campany (London: Whitechapel/Cambridge, Mass.: The MIT Press, 2007).

Campany 2008: David Campany, *Photography and Cinema* (London: Reaktion Books, 2008).

Diekmann 2007: "Fotografie im Dokumentarfilm", ed. Stefanie Diekmann, *Fotogeschichte*, 27:106 (Winter 2007).

Douglas and Eamon 2009: *Art of Projection*, eds. Stan Douglas and Christopher Eamon (Ostfildern: Hatje Cantz, 2009).

Dubois 1999: *L'Effet-Film, matières et formes du cinéma en photographie*, ed. Philippe Dubois, exhibition catalogue (Lyon: galerie Le Réverbère II, 1999).

Dufour and Toubiana 2007 : *L'Image d'après. Le cinéma dans l'imaginaire de la photographie*, ed. Diane Dufour et Serge Toubiana, exhibition catalogue (Paris: Cinémathèque française, Magnum; Göttingen: Steidl, 2007).

Green and Lowry 2006: *Stillness and Time: Photography and the Moving Image*, eds. David Green and Joanny Lowry (Brighton: Photoworks/Photoforum, 2006).

Hámos, Pratschke and Tode 2009: *Viva Fotofilm – Bewegt/Unbewegt*, eds. Gusztáv Hámos, Katja Pratschke and Thomas Tode (Marburg: Schüren, 2009).

Hoormann 2003: Anne Hoormann, *Lichtspiele. Zur Medienreflexion der Avantgarde in der Weimarer Republik* (Munich: Wilhelm Fink Verlag, 2003).

Horak 1997: Jan-Christopher Horak, *Making Images Move. Photographers and Avant-Garde Cinema* (Washington/London: Smithsonian Institution Press, 1997).

Hüsch, Jäger and Knapstein 2006: *Beyond Cinema. The Art of Projection*, eds. Anette Hüsch, Joachim Jäger, Gabriele Knapstein, exhibition catalogue, Hamburger Bahnhof Berlin (Ostfildern: Hatje Cantz Verlag, 2006).

Iles 2001: *Into the Light. The Projected Image in American Art 1964–1977*, ed. Chrissie Iles, exhibition catalogue (New York: Whitney Museum, 2001).

Leighton 2008: *Art and the Moving Image. A Critical Reader*, ed. Tanya Leighton (London: Tate Publishing, 2008).

Michalka 2003: *X-Screen. Filmische Installationen und Aktionen der Sechziger- und Siebzigerjahre*, ed. Matthias Michalka, exhibition catalogue, Museum Moderner Kunst Stiftung Ludwig Wien (Cologne: Walther König, 2003).

Michaud 2006: *Le Mouvement des images*, ed. Philippe-Alain Michaud, exhibition catalogue (Paris: Centre Georges Pompidou, 2006).

Mulvey 2005: Laura Mulvey, *Death 24 x A Second* (London: Reaktion Books, 2005).

NGBK 2000: *Dia/Slide/Transparency. Materialen zur Projektionskunst*, ed. NGBK, exhibition catalogue (Berlin: NGBK, 2000).

Païni 1997: *Projections. Les transports de l'image*, ed. Dominique Païni, exhibition catalogue (Paris: Studio national des arts contemporains Le Fresnoy/Hazan, 1997).

Païni 2002: Dominique Païni, *Le Temps exposé. Le cinéma de la salle au musée* (Paris: Cahiers du cinéma, 2002).

Pauleit 2004: Winfried Pauleit, *Filmstandbilder. Passagen zwischen Kunst und Kino* (Frankfurt: Stroemfeld Verlag, 2004).

Schifferli 2007: Christoph Schifferli, *Paper Dreams. The Lost Art of Hollywood Still Photography*, with an introduction by David Campany (Göttingen: Steidl, 2007).

Stewart 1990: Garrett Stewart, *Between Film and Screen: Modernism's Photo Synthesis* (Chicago: University of Chicago Press, 1999).

Section I
Founding Debates

Introduction:
The Paradoxical Fits and Starts of the New "Optical Unconscious"

Laurent Guido

Two techniques for the recording of images left a deep mark on the early twentieth century: instantaneous photography and cinema. Like many modes of transportation and communication also involved in the general process of industrialization, these two media contributed towards of novel conceptions of space and time. The opening essays of this collection aim to examine the intellectual debates that arose from the sudden emergence of technological and scientific modernity from a historical standpoint, looking more specifically at the issue of movement. They take as their point of departure the philosophy of Henri Bergson in order to discuss Gilles Deleuze's decisive rereading of it with respect to the history of cinema, and to better grasp the internal articulations and the cultural implications of a thought that exerted much influence on the aesthetic ideas of its time. The importance of Bergson's writings on movement cannot be overstated when it comes to the general questions raised in this volume (the double dialectical relation between stillness and movement, and photography and cinema, since in these pages film appears first and foremost owing to its "photographic" dimension). Indeed, the philosopher refers to the "cinematographic model" in a famous passage of *Creative Evolution* only to stigmatize a rational and scientific horizon that founds its interpretation of mobility on a succession of frozen sections, like the film frames lined up on the strip projected on the cinema screen.

This node of stillness and movement at the very heart of the cinematographic medium has its origin in the technique of chronophotography. The object of a craze in the last quarter of the nineteenth century, chronophotography stood at the intersection between photography and cinema, in a sense. On the one hand, it represented a particular application of instantaneous shots that rested on the very fast capture of images. On the other hand, it laid down the essential conditions for the emergence of cinema, which was founded on the sequencing of successive photographs made possible by the pace of chronophotography. As

Maria Tortajada writes, "it is from within cinema in its chronophotographic stage that the opposition between stillness and movement began to consolidate, with photography being *related to movement* while it was itself *identified as still*". With respect to this singular articulation, and despite their obvious relations to stillness and movement, respectively, photography and cinema found themselves not so much in conflict as in a relation between media where a strong structural interdependence accounted for reciprocal exchanges and influences. Bergson aimed his criticism at this dimension of the cinematographic apparatus, which the first two contributors have chosen as their focus. Maria Tortajada begins with the assessment of Bergson's argument to consider the question of the "photographic" in the nuances of the philosopher's reasoning, an examination that leads her to look beyond *Creative Evolution* and the "cinematographic model" to highlight another articulation between stillness and movement, i.e. the "photographic metaphor". For his part, Tom Gunning gives an account of some social and cultural responses to the succession of emerging techniques for the recording of images. Instantaneous photography inaugurated the possibility of perceiving movements invisible to the eye, moments initially confined to the field of theoretical speculations before scientific tools revealed them on a large scale. It unveiled the transient, the fleeting, the ephemeral, the ordinary, where the classical aesthetic of a Lessing demanded the chosen, emblematic, pregnant moment. In its elaboration and apprehension as an absolute experience of movement (more specifically, human movement), how did early cinema negotiate the tension caused by the sudden circulation of frozen moments born of the arbitrary and the unexpected? To answer the question, Gunning points not only to artistic, but also to spectacular directions through which the experience of an immersion within the inner duration extolled by Bergson as a perfect and undividable mobile continuity could play out anew.

In the first years of the century, the issue did not solely involve new visual techniques. Debates around still representations of movement obviously extended to the field of visual arts, more particularly through the call for an aesthetic capable of meeting the new conditions of modernity. Anton Giulio Bragaglia, for instance, endorsed the Bergsonian condemnation of cinema as an extension of the chronophotographic analysis in his essay *Fotodynamismo futurista* (1913). In his view, the machine generated but successive states of movement, offering only an unsatisfactory reproduction, at once fragmentary and discontinuous. Still, the Futurist photographer did not deny the considerable influence of the technique – through the international repercussions of Muybridge's, Marey's, or Anschütz's serial images – on many artists attached to the obsessional figuration of speed characteristic of "modern life", including with visual solutions striving to represent movement in still form. Asserting the primacy of the "*dynamic sensation* itself" over "a fixed *moment* in universal dynamism",[1] the

---

1   Reproduced in French in Giovanni Lista, *Futurisme. Manifestes. Proclamations. Documents* (Lausanne: L'Âge d'homme, 1973) 163.

precepts of the *Technical Manifesto of Futurist Painting* (1910) were embodied in Giacomo Balla's paintings (*Dynamism of a Dog on a Leash, Girl Running on a Balcony, Rhythm of the Violonist...*), among others. These attempts partook of a more general context of affirmation for the pictorial decompositions of human movement, as with Frantisek Kupka (the *Study for Woman Picking Flowers* series, 1910–1911) and Marcel Duchamp (*Nude Descending a Staircase*, 1911–1912).

Explicitly influenced by Bergson, but really reusing arguments already expounded in the aesthetic debates caused by the advent of instantaneous photography thirty years earlier,[2] Bragaglia dismissed all the juxtapositions of still snapshots, deeming them incapable of faithfully reproducing the "continuous and constant stream" defining the "pure" mobility theorized by Bergson. Like Umberto Boccioni, he feared that the diagrammatic aspect of Balla's "pictorial exercises" and their excessive obviousness would result in an absurd "Futurist canon".[3] In his own photographs (*Changing Positions*, 1911; *Young Man Swinging*, 1912; *The Roses*, 1913), the photographer strove to represent gestures in the form of an uninterrupted line[4] so as to avoid the impression of jerky rhythm associated with chronophotographic works.

"Stopping Life", or Movement Frozen

In keeping with these considerations, the first theoreticians of cinema frequently made clear their contempt for any still representation of mobility. A rhetoric of specificity characteristic of a founding, militant approach permeates their aesthetic discourse. Film is considered as the absolute form of expression of movement, and its photographic dimension is often relativized and relegated to a secondary, subaltern position. This idea notably oriented the comparative thought of French film critics and theoreticians. In 1911 Ricciotto Canudo reduced photography to "a weak and quite mechanical image of painting",[5] while in 1920 Louis Delluc insisted on distinguishing it completely from the *photogénie* film should aim at: "No more photography! Cinema! All the resources of photography and the ingenuity of of those who revolutionized it will come to serve – but what a sumptuous servitude and devotion! – the fever, the sagacity, the rhythm of cinema".[6] Taken outside the passing of its time, a film loses its literal

2   In his *Esthétique du mouvement* (Paris: Alcan, 1889), Paul Souriau thus advocated the artistic imitation of gaps in human perception against the perfection of images invisible to the eye revealed by instantaneous photography.

3   Anton Giulio Bragaglia, "Che cos'era la fotodinamica," *Novella* (March 3, 1925): 25. Quoted in Giovanni Lista, *Cinema e fotografia futurista* (Milan: Skira, 2001) 158.

4   See Patrick de Haas, *Cinéma intégral. De la peinture au cinéma dans les années vingt* (Paris: Transédition, 1985) 22.

5   Ricciotto Canudo, "La naissance d'un sixième Art. Essai sur le cinématographe" ["The Birth of a Sixth Art. Essay on the Cinematograph"], *Les entretiens idéalistes*, 25 October 1911, reprinted in *L'Usine aux images* (Paris: Séguier-Arte, 1995) 40.

6   Louis Delluc, *Photogénie* (Paris: Ed. de Brunoff, 1920), reprinted in *Le Cinéma et les Cinéastes* (Paris: Cinémathèque française, 1985) [*Ecrits cinématographiques*, vol. I] 36.

meaning entirely, as Elie Faure wrote: "Stop the most beautiful film you know, make of it at any moment an inert photograph, and you will not obtain even a memory of the emotion that it gave you".[7] As to Germaine Dulac, in the mid-1920s she could identify in photography only the unfortunate "static element" of film,[8] its elementary "means of expression", in the same way as pen and ink for "thought".[9] This general hostility results from a process of eclipsing or suppressing the paradox at play in the very technical foundations of the film apparatus.

To be sure, this exclusive view of film as the specific expression of mobility does not deny the irrefutable, that is, the presence of stillness at the very core of the basic machine of cinema despite its invisibility during projection. Yet the acknowledgment is invariably tied to "static" forms of expression (painting, sculpture...), which film is supposed to prolong, or rather, transcend *through* the addition of movement. In accordance with an expression sanctioned by the aesthetic discourses of the 1910s and 1920s, film was often perceived as a "plastic art in movement". For Canudo, cinema did indeed beget "a succession of lifelike gestures, attitudes, figurations, taking the *tableau* from the space of its immobility and permanence to the time where it appears and undergoes changes".[10] The term "tableau" ("painting" or "tableau"), which then referred to the picture frame as well as to a certain type of theatrical representation, makes it possible to apprehend the pair stillness/movement at an acceptable threshold of intelligibility. It signals the permanence, within aesthetic debates, of a traditional conceptual horizon that retains most of its foundations in spite of a necessary adaptation to the new technical conditions inherent to modernity.

The assessment coexists with the persistence, among the first theoreticians of film, of another classical conception founded on the relation between stillness and movement. Situated at a different level than the stances mentioned above, it consisted in assessing the aesthetic nature of a form of expression based on its degree of permanence and involved more particularly artistic modes founded on movement (dance, theatre ...) but deemed too ephemeral or variable in their actualizations. From such a perspective, notions of immobility and fixation assume a positive role in the enthusiastic discourses of critics and theoreticians on cinema in the early 20th century. For Canudo, art is thus defined essentially by the "stylization of life into stillness", the fact of "*immobilizing* the essence of things and their universal meanings",[11] or to "fix life's elusiveness and synthesize

7   Elie Faure, "The Art of Cineplastics", *French Film Theory and Criticism 1907–1939*, vol. I (1907–1929) Richard Abel, ed. (Princeton: Princeton University Press, 1988) 265.

8   Germaine Dulac, "Photographie – cinégraphie", *Stéréo-Revue* (25 October 1926), reprinted in *Ecrits sur le cinéma (1919–1937)* (Paris: Paris Expérimental, 1994) 79.

9   Germaine Dulac, "The Essence of the Cinema. The Visual Idea", in *Film Theory. Critical Concepts in Media and Cultural Studies*, Philip Simpson, Andrew Utterson, and K.J. Shepherdson, eds. (London: Routledge, 2004) 57–62, 59.

10   Canudo, "La naissance d'un sixième Art": 33, 40.

11   Canudo, "The Birth of a Sixth Art", in *French Film Theory and Criticism 1907–1939. A History/Anthology*, vol.

its harmonies".[12] This ambition accordingly carries with it another paradoxical relation between stillness and movement, one that approaches movement itself as a closed, frozen, and synthetic structure. In Canudo's words, film also accomplishes the "dream [...] of capturing the representation in sequence of a series of *tableaux* succeeding one another",[13] of "arresting forever the very movement of life",[14] "the fleeting aspects of life" with "mechanical precision".[15] For the critic, film brings a resolution to the tension between mobility and immobility since it records movement, brings it the stability, the ever similar outlines which in his eyes define any artistic production.

This praise of "fixation", however, never calls into question the view of cinema as the emblematic art of movement, widely held in the early 20th century. This exclusive appropriation has as a consequence to push back in the shadows the photographic instant which lies at the very heart of the projection of moving images on a screen. To bring to a close the discussion around the comparison between cinema and other plastic arts, and the place assigned to photography in this ambivalent relationship, Germaine Dulac states for instance that the superiority of film over the visual arts that preceded it did not in the least rest on the freezing by photography of "the single instant of a gesture", which still points to painting or sculpture, but indeed to the fact that it "completes it and follows it in its evolution", that is, manages in the end to "reproduce visually a movement in its total period". Still, this particular consideration of cinematographic movement as setting in motion what is immobile leads Dulac to admit in the same text that indeed, "the sensitivity of photographic images each recording a stage in the movement" makes it possible, by the multiplicity of such images, "to reconstitute the entire movement".[16] As Jean Epstein writes in his turn in *L'Intelligence d'une machine* (1946), film does rely on the prodigious power to transform "a discontinuity into a continuity", or more precisely to achieve the "synthesis of discontinuous and immobile elements into a continuous, mobile whole".[17] In the same, important work, Epstein justifies the unfailing commitment of the French theoreticians of his generation to Bergson's philosophy, even though it holds cinema as a model of knowledge specific to scientific rationality, and accordingly unable to grasp the moving flow of consciousness. The filmmaker resolves the

I (1907–1929), ed. Richard Abel (Princeton: Princeton U.P., 1988) 61, 62. [Translator's note: this English translation, which may have been done from an earlier version of Canudo's text than the French translation, is used only for the passages that match the French source used by the author of the article. To avoid any confusion, the French title has been maintained as the source reference for all translations from the French version.]

12 Ricciotto Canudo, "Reflections on the Seventh Art" [1922], *French Film Theory and Criticism 1907–1939*, vol. I (1907–1929) Richard Abel, ed. (Princeton: Princeton University Press, 1988) 293.

13 Canudo, "La naissance d'un sixième Art": 37.

14 Ricciotto Canudo, "Musique et cinéma. Langages universels", *Comœdia* 3176 (August 26, 1921): 74.

15 Canudo, "Reflections on the Seventh Art": 302.

16 Dulac, "The Essence of the Cinema. The Visual Idea", *Film Theory* 58.

17 Jean Epstein, *L'Intelligence d'une Machine* (Paris: Jacques Melot, 1946), reprinted in *Ecrits sur le cinéma*, vol. I (Paris: Cinéma club/Seghers, 1974) 259.

contradiction in two steps. He begins with the admission that the material discontinuity that typifies the frames laid out on the film remains inextricably linked to the basic mechanisms of the camera and the projector. In his view, only still photographic images, immobile sections clearly distinct from one another may be found there: "the figures of each image in a film, projected in succession on the screen, remain as perfectly immobile and separate as they were ever since they appeared on the sensitive layer. However, Epstein adds an important qualification to this: the discontinuity that characterizes the cinematographic machinery does not include the perception by the spectator of the views projected on the screen. The idea had already been put forward by Rudolf Arnheim in a 1933 essay: "the displacement of the film strip in the camera and in the projector is not experienced directy by the audience. It is simply the mechanical means of creating the illusion of motion on the screen."[18] In rather similar terms, Epstein sees the existence of a real movement in the mind of the spectator, not in the technical apparatus of cinema. In his opinion, attending a film screening is akin to the absolute experience of inner duration advocated by Bergson: "the setting in motion and merging of these forms occur, not on the film nor in the lens, but only in humans themselves. Discontinuity becomes continuity only after entering the spectator." In Epstein's view, cinema thus substantiates the existence of a "mobile continuity formed only of discontinuous immobilities, in what may be called its slightly deeper reality".[19]

Towards the "Kaleidoscopic" Model

The theoreticians of the interwar period did not consider the cinema based on its technical foundations, but on the psychological bases it appealed to and through which it could express the very movement of inner thought promoted by Bergson. Even though it was belittled, the articulation in film of stillness and movement never ceased to be an issue in the theoretical, aesthetic, and cultural debates stirred by the apparition of the cinematographic phenomenon. Tom Gunning points to such ambivalence as he questions the role played by the emergence of cinema in the historical reception of instantaneous photography. On the one hand, he mentions the fact that, for many contemporaries, film brought the linearity of movement to the new photographs, which more often than not would be apprehended as improbable or absurd despite their undeniable inscription of a reality imperceptible to the human eye. On the other hand, Gunning underscores the use of the same paradoxical intersection in various avant-garde practices during the 1920s, which ran the whole gamut between distancing themselves from the film apparatus and playfully celebrating the spectacular and spellbinding powers of cinema. In this regard, the questions

---

18   That is why "the beat of the intermittent motion in the camera and the projector has no bearing upon the aesthetic rhythm of the picture". Rather, this rhythm is related to the different types of mobility involved in the filming of objects and the editing of images together. Rudolf Arnheim, *Film as Art* (Berkeley, Los Angeles: University of California Press, 1957) 181.

19   Epstein, *L'Intelligence d'une machine* 261, 263.

raised in the field of art overlapped with the respective domains of photography and cinema, which were yet to follow their own, separate tracks.

Painter Marcel Gromaire identified such a trend within the common production of the 1920s. In his view, the film, making visible the multiple, unsuspected facets of any everyday object, demonstrated its formidable potential to creators: "Considered successively from all sides, bathing in different lights, dissected in slow motion, placed in various environments, it becomes a subject of astonishment as its deeper reality is revealed to us".[20] The approach echoes not only the deconstruction of perspective space already exemplified by the methods of Cubism, but also the photographic experimentations carried out in the sphere of the Bauhaus during the same period (Herbert Bayer, T. Lux Feininger...). The "new vision" characteristic of modern life sought a heightened dynamism in the shots, the search for unusual, unorthodox angles as well as a maximal resort to close-ups, reflections, mirrors, special lenses, distortions... These many techniques were then juxtaposed, strung together, or superimposed in collages or sequences, as attested in Franz Roh's or Werner Gräff's manifestos, Alexander Rodchenko's theoretical writings, and more generally the case studies appearing together in section III.

Admittedly, film may produce equivalents for these various processes by dividing the frame (split screen, multiple exposures, or even blurs), but most filmmakers approached the question of parceling out through editing, notably offering in succession the different aspects of a same object evoked by Gromaire (the Eiffel Tower in René Clair's *Paris qui dort* in 1924, for instance),[21] which painting or photography chose to present in a single image. Besides the permanent tension between abstraction and figuration, or the exhaustion of the various dimensions of visual rhythm, the approach of avant-garde filmmakers systematically integrated a degree of reflexivity on the pair stillness – movement at the core of the film apparatus. As is evident in the notebooks (in particular the "shooting scripts") of Abel Gance, Marcel L'Herbier, Jean Epstein, or Germaine Dulac, they were interested in the film frame because it allowed them to determine the exact length of each shot within a larger concern for cinematographic rhythm. Indeed, these calculations took as their basic unit the photographic "images" succeeding each other on the film strip.[22]

20 Marcel Gromaire, "Le cinéma actuel et ses deux tendances" ["The Two Tendencies of Current Cinema"], *Les Cahiers du mois* 16–17 (1925): 206–207.

21 Léon Pierre-Quint, "Signification du cinéma", *Les Cahiers du mois* 16–17 (1925): 169–170.

22 See Laurent Guido, *L'Age du Rythme* (Lausanne: Payot, 2007) 117, 454. In this respect, Man Ray's provocative nonchalance contrasts with the precision of these timed arrangements, which foreshadowed the productions of "metric" cinema some thirty years later, with Peter Kubelka (*Adebar*, 1957, *Schwechater*, 1958, and *Arnulf Rainer*, 1960) or Werner Nekes and Dore O. (*Jüm Jüm*, 1967). In his *Self-Portrait* (1963), Man Ray writes that he made *Le Retour à la raison* the night before its first screening, randomly throwing pins and thumbtacks on strips of film covered with pepper and salt before exposing them to white light for one or two seconds, as he did with still rayographs. He admits to having no idea as to the effect of the operation once the film was projected. To these images he added a few more sequences shot with the camera to make the film last longer. See Man Ray, *Self-Portrait* (London: Bloomsbury, 1988) 260.

During the 1920s, some of these experimentations focused on the figuration of the fragmented and discontinuous character of the mechanical perception issuing from modernity. It was notably the objective of the various actualizations of the kaleidoscope in film (the kaleidoscope being another metaphor used by Bergson to describe how knowledge operates[23]), discussed by Abel Gance[24] as well as Jean Epstein. In 1925, Epstein recounted his walking down a staircase in a hotel, with mirrors placed along the way producing multiple images of him, mobile reflections that evoked "cinematographic projections". Each mirror offered a new vision of the body, like different images appearing in succession:

> Each turn surprised me from a new angle. There were as many different, autonomous positions between a three-quarter portrait and a portrait in profile as there are tears in the eye. Each of these images lived but one moment, vanishing as soon as it was glimpsed, already other. My memory alone caught one on their infinity and let two of out three slip away. And there were the images of images. A third image would be born out of second images. A descriptive algebra and geometry of gestures would emerge.[25]

Surprise and singularity constantly renewed, the infinite multiplication of points of view at a furious pace, the inability of perceiving subjects to apprehend the very images of their body – wrenched from the invisibility that usually made them inaccessible to the human look, but exposed too quickly and suddenly to be genuinely perceived by the eye: the description evidently attempts to define the sudden manifestation of countless, proliferating occurrences of stillness – represented by the thousands of distinct images impressed on film – within a continuous, "cinematographic" type of movement.

In Epstein's text, the activity of the mind struggles to contain the (over-)flow of time. Memory appears as deeply inadequate to store information comprehensively, since it manages to hold only a few geometric sections fragmenting the body of the walker in infinite variations. Accordingly, the emphasis is essentially on the mental process resulting from a movement generated out of immobility: ceaselessly following one another, still images are supposed to merge ideally in the perfect continuity of perceived mobility, when in fact they never stop "resurfacing" in an uncontrollable manner. In its "kaleidoscopic" dimension at least, the relation of cinema to the operations of the psyche constitutes one of the

---

23 That is, a succession of positions consisting in shifting from "arrangement to rearrangement". Henri Bergson, *Creative Evolution* [1907], trans. Arthur Mitchell (New York: Henry Holt and Company, 1911) 330.

24 Abel Gance views cinema as a "mirror" in which our image is "multiplied, transformed, transported into worlds of movements which gush forth at every minute from our own world, with as much variety as that offered by the figures of a kaleidoscope, and infinitely." Abel Gance, "Nos moyens d'expression. Extraits de la Conférence faite par Abel Gance à l'Université des Annales le 22 mars 1929" ["Our Means of Expression. Excerpts from the Lecture Given by Abel Gance at the Université des Annales on March 22, 1929"], in *Cinéa-Ciné pour tous* 133 (May 15, 1929): 7-8.

25 J. Epstein, "Le regard du verre" ["The Look of Glass"], *Les Cahiers du mois* 16–17 (1925), reprinted in Epstein, *Ecrits sur le cinéma* 135–136.

main lines of thinking on stillness and movement, as demonstrated in many contributions to this book (see section 4).

The Snapshots of the Psychic System

Historically, the question of movement extended to the thought on psychic processes through the several definitions of the unconscious that appeared in France at the turn of the twentieth century. In *Creative Evolution* Henri Bergson views the "unconscious" as a space where the individual may "drive back" almost the whole past, with consciousness keeping "only that which can cast light on the present situation or further the action now being prepared – in short, only that which can give *useful* work".[26] In his lecture "The Perception of Change" (1911) Bergson still considers the mechanical means of recording images as mere factors of illusion and refuses to conceive of the accumulation by memory of "memories like so many photographic plates from which we afterward develop proofs, or like so many phonograms destined to become sounds again". If that were the case, the visual recollection of a thing, at "the slightest movement of the object or the eye", would involve "not one image but ten, a hundred, a thousand images, as many and more as on a cinematographic film", and even "millions" of "different images".[27]

In her epistemological reflection on the singular status of the film frame as a constitutive element of cinema, on a par with movement, Maria Tortajada looks back on an earlier text by Bergson, *Matter and Memory* (1896), and more particularly a passage which brings up new shooting techniques. While Gilles Deleuze derived his well-known notion of "mobile section" from the same text and thereby reconciled cinema and Bergsonism, Tortajada admits at once the existence of two rather distinct "theoretical moments". Indeed, before condemning the "cinematographic model", Bergson had turned to photography in itself as a positive *metaphor* of pure perception in which fundamental matter was captured as an uninterrupted sequence of interdependent images. For Bergson, taking new techniques of vision into account was thus grounded in a consideration of consciousness and memory.

At the crossroads between media history and science history, two fields that both met with drastic changes at the end of the nineteenth century, Mireille Berton examines the same intersecting paradigms of photography and cinema. However, her primary material involves texts on the psychic system, and more specifically on subjects who, undergoing neuroses or pathological dysfunctions, experienced the sudden apparition of more or less static or eventful images. The study brings out a number of "ideas" of stillness and movement arising from extreme states

---

26 Bergson, *Creative Evolution* 5.

27 Henri Bergson, "The Perception of Change", lectures given at the University of Oxford on May 26 & 27, 1911, reproduced in *Henri Bergson. Key Writings*, Keith Ansell Pearson, John Mullarkey, eds. (London, New York: Continuum, 2002) 263.

referred to "a semiotics of disruption in the function of the real" and involving "two fundamental tropes": "unimpeded automatism and intense focalization". On a discursive level, the torments of the subjects were apprehended with the help a vocabulary akin to that of the new techniques for the recording and projection of images. From then on, relations with the two media of photography and cinema became more or less explicit. Some of the "pathogenous mental image[s]" considered by Berton include for instance the issue of attention with Theodule Ribot, the *idée fixe* with Pierre Janet, or – more directly associated with cinema – the psychic acceleration with Henri Piéron.

Relating photography, cinema, and the psychic system is largely justified by a tradition in critical thought that saw the new visual techniques as the emblems of scientific modernity and, consequently, as the privileged signs of the irrepressible anxiety and deep traumas involved in the technological transformations that occurred throughout the nineteenth century. Walter Benjamin pointed out their main aspects, in particular in "On Some Motifs in Baudelaire". In the study, he takes care to distinguish between Bergsonian *duration* and the conception of memory to which he refers for his part: defined as "involuntary", memory sees its "range" extended by the "techniques inspired by the camera and subsequent analogous types of apparatus". He also evokes the consequences of the instant shutter release of the camera, liable to give "the moment a posthumous shock, as it were", and characteristic of the new, fragmented sensorial experience peculiar to modern urban life.[28] It is in "The Work of Art in the Age of Mechanical Reproduction", however, that Benjamin establishes a relation between the unveiling of the physical world by cinema and the insights of Freudian psychoanalysis. Through the capture and analysis of multiple details indiscernible to the eye, the camera widens the scope of human knowledge for the writer, in the same way as the revelation of imperceptible realms where the deepest psychic mechanisms operate: "an unconsciously penetrated space is substituted for a space consciously explored by man". Many such remarks seem to apply to instantaneous photography or chronophotography rather than to cinema, reduced to the means (close-up, slow motion...) that make it relevant with respect to the subliminal and the infinitesimal. This is the case when Benjamin mentions the new possibility of perceiving, in the walk of a person, "the fractional second of a stride":

> Here the camera intervenes with the resources of its lowerings and liftings, its interruptions and isolations, its extensions and accelerations, its enlargements and reductions. The camera introduces us to unconscious optics as does psychoanalysis to unconscious impulses.[29]

This reference to traumatology constitutes one of the main lines in the thought

---

28 Walter Benjamin, "On Some Motifs in Baudelaire", *The Writer of Modern Life: Essays on Charles Baudelaire*, ed. Michael W. Jennings (Cambridge: Harvard U.P., 2006) 202, 191. Benjamin quotes a sentence by Baudelaire to define the experience of shock as "a kaleidoscope endowed with consciousness". (191)

29 Walter Benjamin, "The Work of Art in the Age of Mechanical Reproduction", [1935–39] in *Illuminations*, ed. Hannah Arendt, trans. Harry Zohn (New York: Harcourt, Brace, and World, 1968) 236–237.

on the place of photography within the cinematographic context (see section 4). The corpus considered in the first section, the artistic ideas and production of the early 20th century, shows for its part modes of representation associated with intermediate states of consciousness and split identities. These are marked by a constant hesitation between invisible interiority and outside materialization, or between the psychic modes of attention and distraction. These tensions and interstitial areas, where the reciprocal relation between stasis and movement ceaselessly reappears, were of primary importance for the aesthetic of Surrealism as it attempted to put them into play or even bring them to a resolution. As Samantha Lackey shows, the Surrealists' predilection for forms of "automatic" creation led their consideration of photography and cinema to intersect. The interrelation between stillness and movement aroused the interest of these poets and artists as part of experiences aimed at producing the "paradoxical effect" where the "convulsive beauty" defined by André Breton originated. One of the most blatant actualizations of this quest was indeed founded on the paradoxical basis of the film apparatus. Besides a series of still images from 1928 associated with Surrealism (a somnambulist Desnos photographed by Man Ray; the reuse of ambivalent photographs of hysterical subjects from La Salpêtrière, who unconsciously thwarted the institutional logic of the clinic), Samantha Lackey also brings out the peculiar interlocking of stillness and movement in a Man Ray film, *Retour à la raison* (1923). Some images in this short film frustrate the traditional points of reference of cinema at once, since they result from the luminous impression of various objects (drawing pins and coiled springs, for example) directly on pieces of film, without the use of a camera. Once projected, the succession of film frames no longer fulfils its common function, i.e. animation out of the frozen phases of a given movement. Instead, it consists of "a series of discontinuous still images of the same object[s]" whose undeniable indexical value opens but imperfectly onto iconic recognition. As we have already seen, *Retour à la raison* is part of a set of practices quite characteristic of the interwar film avant-gardes. In the same way as the rhythmic manipulation of images, the fragmentation of represented objects, or the multiplication of points of view, references to the animation of the immobile were extremely frequent in artists' films (Fernand Léger's 1924 *Ballet mécanique* or Hans Richter's 1928 *Vormittagspuk* dealt literally with the conception of a plastic art in movement, using editing to move different geometric forms and everyday objects around). As shown explicitly in René Clair's films (*Entr'acte*, *Paris qui dort*, or *Le voyage imaginaire*, all made between 1924 and 1926) and in the wild "poems-scenarios" by Surrealists Philippe Soupault and Pierre Albert-Birot,[30] this trend reformulates within the field of art some visual principles exploited before in the context of early cinema (in particular for the comic series made in France in the years

---

30 Pierre Albert-Birot, *Cinéma. Drames Poèmes dans l'espace composés en 1919* (Paris: Sic, 1920), reprinted in *Cinémas* (Paris: Editions Jean-Michel Place, 1995). Philippe Soupault, "Note 1 sur le cinéma" (1918) ; "Poèmes cinématographiques" (1917–1925) and "Le cœur volé" ["The Stolen Heart"] (1934), reprinted in *Ecrits de cinéma 1918–1931*, texts presented by Odette and Alain Virmaux (Paris: Plon, 1979).

1905–1915), with the dynamic use of stopping the camera, multiple exposure, quick and slow motion, reverse motion, looping, etc. All based on the manipulation of the film frame as interstice, these effects refer to one of the trends in the "attractions" characterizing the emergence of cinema: emphasizing the film apparatus to spectators fascinated by the illusionistic possibilities of the projector of moving images. Samantha Lackey sees a productive idea in this specific dimension of the first cinematographic spectacles when it comes to examining the "series of fragments" presented in *Retour à la raison*: the juxtaposition of such salient moments produces a series of successive shocks in which the hiatus stillness/movement crystallizes in an emblematic manner.

Besides these different techniques exploiting the multiple potentialities of the film frame, some others, even more direct, made possible the sudden appearance of a still image in the middle of a film in the form of a freeze frame (a film frame, repeated on the film, producing the impression of its stillness) or the insertion of a (filmed) photograph. Considering the relations between photography and cinema in *Film als Kunst* (1932), Rudolf Arnheim pointed out the feeling of uncanniness ("whole seconds in an oppressive immobility") caused by the insertion of a still image in a film, identifying the source of this tension in the gap between the sudden immobility of the object perceived by the look and the time of the screening, which in the meantime keeps flowing.[31] The critic brings up the paradoxical aspect of this situation, where a photographic image shows its stillness all the better as it directly confronts cinema. In his view, this is attested by a sequence from the urban symphony *Menschen am Sonntag* (*People on Sundays*, Robert Siodmak *et al.*, 1929 – a film shot through and through by the question of the image become a mass image, in all its forms, postcards, posters, photographs of stars…). In the film, several freeze frames successively still the movement of some protagonists captured by the camera of a beach photographer (Fig. 1).[32] To Arnheim, the effect seems comparable to the brutal action of a magic wand that would condemn a human being to the "oppressive immobility" of a sudden petrification. He insists on the difference between this type of freeze frame and the work of an actor who would voluntarily freeze his gesture, opposing the determined pose of the comedian to the "absurd momentary phases" produced by the photographic lens when it is not subservient to the will of the subject whose attitude it captures.[33] This reference to the contingency of instantaneous photographs does not simply repeat – in a more ironic and pessimistic tone than

31   "A still photograph inserted in the middle of a moving film gives a very curious sensation; chiefly because the time character of the moving shots is carried over to the still picture, which therefore looks uncannily petrified". Rudolf Arnheim, *Film as Art* (Berkeley, Los Angeles: University of California Press, 1957) 118.

32   Interspersed with close shots on the photographer settling the sitting, the sequence first shows for each subject (a determined social type) moving images followed by a frozen image. The same idea is then presented in a reverse order (the subject is first shown still, then in movement) before brief cinematographic portraits succeed one another in rapid succession. A last series of still images then responds to this apparent "triumph" of the "living" portrait obtained with the camera: a series of photographic postcards representing the mawkish poses of stereotypical heterosexual couples.

33   Arnheim, *Film as Art* 118.

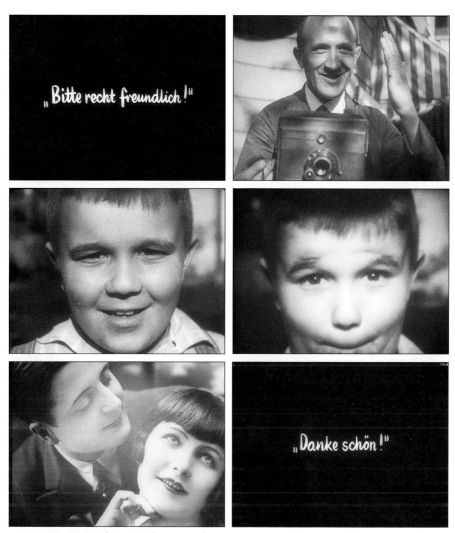

Fig. 1. People on Sunday *(Menschen am Sonntag), Robert Siodmak et al., 1929*

Epstein's – the staging of human beings deprived of any control over the mechanical device recording their movements. In Arnheim's argument, these arbitrary and random sections in the movement are first and foremost disturbing, or even outright comical. In his contribution to the volume, Tom Gunning approaches the freeze frame from that same angle, since in his view film seems to be playing out anew some of the absurdity initially perceived in instantaneous photography. For Gunning, the freeze frame "stages, displays the qualitative change from still image to movement, and the moment of amused astonishment it engenders testifies again to the power this transformation entails". He backs this idea with a famous sequence from Dziga Vertov's 1929 *Man with a Movie*

Fig. 2. Madame Du Barry, *Ernst Lubitsch, 1919*

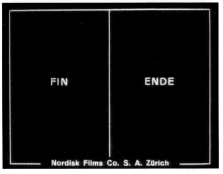

Camera, one of the most extraordinary demonstrations of such a displacement within the film apparatus itself. In the passage in question, the image of a horse, suddenly frozen, is followed by other freeze frames, then by the presentation of the physical film strip itself, down to single film frames. Handled by a film editor also appearing in the film, the still image soon comes back to life. Often commented by specialists of the relations between cinema and photography (Raymond Bellour, Philippe Dubois, Garrett Stewart, David Campany…), the sequence evinces the double temporality constitutive of cinema. Yet it also emphasizes the strangeness of the "photographic" part normally repressed by cinema in its indivisible infrastructure, as Laura Mulvey recently pointed out. Abruptly revealing this process of repression, the freeze frame does in a sense exhibit the deadly dimension inherent to all films, insofar as their apparent vitality only sets the immobile traces of a vanished time back into motion artificially and mechanically.[34] The figure was used in cinema early on, from the startling final close-up on the severed head of the main character of *Madame DuBarry* (Ernst Lubitsch, 1919, Fig. 2)[35] to the whole revolutionary activity of the Soviet nation coming to a halt in *Three Songs of Lenin* (Vertov, 1934). In the latter film, the fatal consequences of the death of the first Communist head of state are underscored by the shot of a moving train that suddenly freezes, marking the beginning of a series of various still images of dense crowds and industrial machines. In this regard, *Man with a Movie Camera* appears as one of the first actualizations of a display of the machinery of film through the freeze frame which, as appears further in this volume, assumed a programmatic value for film creation in the second half of the 20th century.

---

34   Laura Mulvey, *Death 24x A Second* (London: Reaktion Books, 2005) 13–16.

35   This conclusion appears on the print held by the Cinémathèque Suisse in Lausanne.

1

The "Arrested" Instant: Between Stillness and Motion

Tom Gunning

In his 1907 work *Creative Evolution*, philosopher Henri Bergson undertook his famous description of movement and his critique of the way understanding normally pictures this phenomenon as a succession of static states, declaring, "every attempt to reconstitute change out of states implies the absurd proposition that movement is made out of immobilities".[1] The dichotomy that Bergson sets up here between "states" or "immobilities" on the one hand, and "change" or "movement", on the other needs to be separated from historically previous dichotomies it seems to resemble, such as Lessing's distinction between the "single moment" to which the visual artist is restricted, compared to the succession of actions that the poet can portray.[2] Bergson's conception of movement could remain as elusive to a poet as to the painter or sculptor, if the attempt to convey movement relied simply on the succession of otherwise immobile images. One could say that movement for Bergson can never properly be conceived as the product of accumulation or succession, but rather constituted a different mode of being, a different state or quality.

But Bergson is concerned not simply with representing movement or even, as he puts it, understanding motion. Representation and understanding of movement generally do proceed through a succession of "immobilities", and for Bergson this constitutes their limitation. In order to grasp what Bergson calls the "reality" of movement one must take up another position, one "within" that reality: "The obscurity is cleared up, the contradiction vanishes, as soon as we place ourselves along the transition, in order to distinguish states within it by making cross cuts therein in thought. The reason is that there is more in the movement than the series of states, that is to say the possible cuts – more in the movement than the series of positions, that is to say, the possible stops." [3]

---

1   Henri Bergson, *Creative Evolution*, trans. Arthur Mitchell (Lanham: University Press of America, 1983) 308.

2   Gotthold Ephraim Lessing, *Laocoon: An Essay on the Limits of Painting and Poetry*, trans and ed. Edward Allen McCormick (Baltimore: John Hopkins University Press, 1984) 19–25.

Famously, to illustrate this illusory conception that understanding promotes of movement as the product of a succession of immobile states, Bergson resorted to the relatively recent invention of the cinematograph. The strip of cinematographic film consists of static images arranged in succession. Simply observed, the strip of film remains merely that – a series of immobile images. "In order that the pictures may be animated", Bergson observes, "there must be movement somewhere. The movement does indeed exist here; it is in the apparatus."[4] It is this mechanical separation between the images and the source of movement in the apparatus that constitutes for Bergson the limits of our ordinary understanding of movement: "Instead of attaching ourselves to the inner becoming of things, we place ourselves outside them in order to recompose their becoming artificially".

I want to take the dichotomy Bergson sets up between movement as a succession of states and movement conceived from "within" its reality as a way of discussing the evolution of the experience of movement in the late nineteenth century through instantaneous photography and early cinema. Bergson's condemnation of the ordinary understanding of movement and his call for a new experience of movement as a mode of becoming has been read all too literally by people who should know better (including fine film theorists like Mary Ann Doane and philosophers such as Giles Deleuze) as a condemnation of cinema itself as a means of representation. Bergson's enthusiasm for such cinematic techniques as time-lapse photography makes clear that rather than presenting a determinist view of the structure of the apparatus it is the spectator's relation to the image of movement that would determine cinema's relation to the reality of movement.[5] But the historical relation of Bergson's cinematic metaphor to actual technological innovation in still and motion photography merits further exploration. As opposed to the carefully chosen climatic single moment recommended by Lessing to artists, late nineteenth century photographic "snapshots" offered a very different conception of both time and representation than the traditional arts –, one whose visual absurdity, I would claim, helped Bergson rethink the nature of movement as more than a succession of instants.

As historians of photography have recently stressed, the inventors of photography in the early nineteenth century sought to fix an image that was already familiar in its mobile form for centuries in the camera obscura.[6] For Niépce, Daguerre and Fox Talbot photography sought to capture this image, and especially, since the possibility of creating an image through light-sensitive crystals had already been observed for decades, of fixing that image, not letting its sensitivity to light turn it eventually into a mottled dark mass. Thus photography

3   Bergson, *Creative Evolution* 313–314.

4   Bergson, *Creative Evolution* 305.

5   See Bergson's reaction to time lapse films of the growth of flowers reprinted in Frank Kessler, ?"Henri Bergson und die Kinematographie", *Kintop* 12 (2003): 12–16.

6   See, for instance, Michel Frizot (ed.), *A New History of Photography* (Cologne: Konemannn, 1998).

sought a victory over time, change and decay, simultaneously fixing the transient image that played within the camera obscura in a single unmoving image, and then preserving that image from chemical deterioration, a deterioration caused by the very sensitivity to light that made the image possible in the first place. Further, early photography required a long exposure rate that initially limited its possibilities of depiction to unmoving elements, still life arrangements, buildings, and monuments, or even traditional works of art, paintings and sculptures. Only the static object could maintain the staying power to impress the relatively insensitive plate. Thus the temporality of early photography was cumulative rather than instantaneous, an aspect that Walter Benjamin claimed gave early photographic portraits a contemplative dimension.

But aspirations towards instantaneity soon obsessed photographers with the ambition of constantly reducing the exposure time necessary by increasing the sensitivity of the photographic plate. By the 1860s the photographic "snapshots" that Bergson used as a metaphor for our generalized images of the static moments that "make up" a movement, actually became a technical possibility. The photograph could present an image snatched from a continuous movement, such as pedestrians strolling on a city street. The instant, previously only an abstract philosophical conception of an indivisible atom of time, now took on visible form. But a positivistic desire to see an instant of motion in a manner impossible to the human eye, soon pushed the photographic ideal of the instant to a new threshold. Muybridge's image of horses stopped in full gallop, suspended above the ground, offered not only an image impossible for the human eye to see, but rendered visible evidence of a previously unseen event. The photograph, through its mastery of the instant, seemed to no longer offer itself simply as a means of recording the act of seeing, but became a means of discovery, a nineteenth century extension of vision into the domain of the unseen aspects of time, paralleling the 17th century use of the new optical devices of microscope and telescope to visualize the unseen dimensions of space.

Thus although Bergson traces what he calls the cinematographic illusion of the intellect back to the Classical philosophy of the Eidos, in fact the snapshot offers a very different concept of both vision and the instant, one that is unintelligible outside a series or the implication of an ongoing action. Indeed, upon its appearance the photographic snapshot was widely condemned by those who hoped to place photography within the realm of the traditional arts, because it lacked precisely the timeless qualities of the ideal, especially the ideals of grace or repose. Clearly at antipodes to the carefully chosen emblematic moment in the evolution of an action that Lessing saw as the goal of the visual arts, the snapshot captured any instant whatever. "This single moment". Lessing claimed, "if it is to receive immutable permanence from art, must express nothing transitory".[7] But the snapshot often expressed precisely nothing but the transitory. Further,

7   Lessing, *Laocoon* 20.

for most viewers instantaneous photographs of motion suspended in midair, resembled a moment of fantasy and, due to its very apparent but contradictory realism, a palpable absurdity. In snapshots the movement of bodies appeared ungainly rather than graceful, comic, rather than idealized.

But perhaps more than anything else, and here a Bergsonian element enters into instantaneous photography, such images of suspended action appeared incomplete. To think of the image separated from the flow of time out of which it had been snatched was comical, precisely in the sense that Bergson himself explored in his famous 1901 essay on Laughter, where he claimed, "The attitudes, gestures and movements of the human body are laughable in exact proportion as that body reminds us of a mere machine".[8]. What appears in the suspension of motion was not the action of bodies, but the interruption of action supplied by the machine, whose very improbability triggers the impulse to laugh. A human body behaving like a machine, Bergson claimed, invariably makes us laugh. Thus the absurdity of a body in an instantaneous photograph testifies to the way the suspension of time and movement into a immobile image partakes of the machine, not the human and that in fact the recognition of the humour involved in such images, on the popular level at least, testifies to an intuitive grasp of Bergson's conception of movement.

The snapshot resulted from a technological improvement of still photography, an increased sensitivity that allowed the exposure time to be sliced to instants so brief even Zeno might not conceive of them. A leading photographic supply company in France, the Lumière company, realized that such instantaneous exposures could delight the newly enlarged field of photographic amateurs. Such new photographers rushed to obtain the new hand cameras and loaded them with Lumière's Etiquette Bleue extra rapid dry plates in order to entertain (or embarrass) friends and family with these comic snapshots. Around the same time the scientific instantaneous exposures of Muybridge and Marey dedicated to the analysis of motion had inspired American inventor Thomas Edison to envision a motion picture camera that could "do for the eye' what the his previous invention the phonograph "did for the ear" – record sensual information in time as it unfolded. Equally aware of Marey's experiments and of the new found commercial passion for instantaneous photography, the Lumières realized they could coat the new celluloid roll film with the faster film emulsions they had developed for dry plates, and devise a motion picture camera dedicated, not to freezing motion, but to capturing its unfolding. The Lumière's invention (whose name, the Cinématographe, supplied the term Bergson used for his model of (mis) understood movement) in a sense undid the violence the snapshot had done to the full and continuous unfolding of movement that Bergson celebrated. Movement itself could now be filmed and displayed.

If the Cinématographe reconstituted the movement frozen in instantaneous

---

8   Henri Bergson, *Laughter*, in *Comedy*, ed. Wylie Sypher (Garden City: Doubleday, 1956) 79.

photography, why did Bergson use it as an illustration of the traditional limited understanding of movement? The answer is both simple and complex. Bergson's condemnation of the cinematographic illusion (pace Doane and Deleuze) did not target the cinema, but rhetorically used the mechanics of the cinematograph to illustrate a misconception of movement he did condemn. The illustration consisted of two comparisons, as we saw, the filmstrip that captured a continuous movement through a series of still images, a succession of snapshots, as Bergson describes it. This strip in itself has no movement, only a succession of immobile states. The movement, as Bergson says, comes from elsewhere, from the apparatus, i.e the cinema projector that must be cranked into motion in order to impart a mechanical rapid rhythm of replacement to the images, thereby creating an appearance of movement.

Bergson's comparison of the limited understanding of movement to the cinematograph draws on, first, its accumulation of still images in a successive strip and secondly the exteriority of the motion given to the images, a mere mechanical impetus, not inherent in the images themselves. But the viewer of a projected film sees an image moving on the screen, not a strip of static images or a machine imparting motion; ordinarily she experiences neither of these aspects. Thus it is the mechanics of the cinematograph that Bergson critiques, not necessarily the spectator's experience of the moving image on the screen (which he does not really discuss in detail, the Cinématographe serving basically as an illustration or metaphor for a way of understanding movement).

If we shift focus to the moving image on the screen, the cinema may indeed provide precisely the experience of movement that traditional understanding occludes. Revealingly, early descriptions of the cinematic image frequently referred not simply to moving images, but to images "dancing" on the screen. The experience of the continuity of gestures implied in the figure of the dance would seem to argue that at least one of the fascinations for the first cinema viewers (and I would go so far as to argue the dominant one) was precisely an experience of movement, as cinema served in its first years primarily as a device that could uniquely focus on this Bergsonian experience. The subjects of early cinema in the 1890's reveal a fascination with movement in itself that I believe should be viewed not simply as the demonstration of a technical accomplishment, but precisely as an aesthetic focusing on movement as a spectacle worthy of attention. Thus the hundreds of early films of dances demonstrate the fit between subject and device: dancing images showing images of dancing. Most early films can be viewed as contemplations of the event of movement, whether that of trained bodies (dancers, acrobats, knock-about comedians, animals acts) or of the aleatory movements of everyday life (city crowds, children playing, the motion of waves.) While the chronophotographs of Muybridge and Marey, parsing movements into separate analysable phases for the purpose of scientific measurement and observation, certainly posited a viewer who remained outside of movement, I believe the cinematic gawker watching the movement captured and presented before her on the screen could take up a position within the movement, gaining that sense Bergson celebrated, "He who installs himself in Becoming sees in duration the very life of things, the fundamental reality". [9]

But what about the essentially mechanical nature of the cinema that seems to be inherent in the motion of the apparatus itself, both camera and projector? Are we to believe that it becomes fully sublated into the capturing of motion evident in a film of a serpentine dance? Does this synthetically produced movement affect one the same way that movement does in life? I confess to still being engaged and even a bit confused by this question which pivots between the role of cinema as a nearly transparent transcription of some elements of reality and it's obvious role as a medium through which things are in some sense represented. How radically different the cinema's mode of mediation is from other media constitutes the contested ground of film theory.

I approach the question historically and in terms of film practices. The fascination of movement in early cinema cannot be questioned, and this fascination finds its most extreme form, in perhaps the most resilient genre of early cinema, the phantom ride. The phantom ride placed the motion picture camera on a moving vehicle, usually a train, but not infrequently a trolley car, a boat, or an automobile. The film then captures the vehicle's movement through space, usually progressing down a track or street. I believe the experience of this moving image still exerts a fascination a century later. The relentless penetration of the receding distance seems to me at antipodes to the understanding that pictures movement as a series of immobilities. Instead, a sense of flight, of passage, of constant change and transformation fills the screen and enthralls the viewer. As a viewer I feel swept into this image, endowed with a movement that propels me through space. But given that the source of movement here, remaining unseen and off screen, behind the viewer as it were, comes from a motorized vehicle, does this present a contradiction to Bergson's attack on the mechanical aspect of the understanding of movement that he terms the cinematographic illusion? I think the question, while natural, involves a mistake. Bergson does not attack mechanical movement, but rather a mechanical model for our understanding of movement. Aesthetically speaking I would claim the power of the phantom ride comes from placing us directly in the center of this new mechanical propulsion, so central to the experience of movement in the twentieth century.

But in fact cinema's mechanical operation, parsing movement into separate immobile images also allows other possibilities. If the single still frame remains invisible in the normally projected film, its possibilities could be said, as Garrett Stewart has claimed in his book *Between Film and and Screen*, to haunt the cinema, or at least certain filmmakers. [10] This spectre often takes the technical form of the

9   Bergson, *Creative Evolution* 317.

10   Garrett Stewart, *Between Film and Screen: Modernism's Photosynthesis* (Chicago: University of Chicago Press, 1999).

Fig. 1. The Man with a Movie Camera (Chelovek s kinoapparatom*), Dziga Vertov, 1929.*

provocatively named "freeze frame". The product of repeatedly printing a single frame so that it lasts on the screen long enough to be perceived, the freeze frame would seem to subject cinematic movement to a mechanical strangling, reducing it again to a state of immobility.

I do not claim to know Bergson's reaction to this technique, or even that he would concern himself with these issues of cinematic aesthetics. However, from a perspective that claims movement cannot be reduced to the accumulation of still images, in other words cannot be experienced as a quantitative phenomenon, but rather as a qualitative one, I believe the freeze frame can play an extremely Bergsonian role. The unmoving film frame, at least in most of its uses, does not so much seem to analyse motion, break it down into its elements, as to transform it, to "freeze it" invoking in its interruption of movement the absurdity and humorous effect of instantaneous snapshots. Movement suddenly vanishes and the image takes on a wholly different aspect. Indeed the freeze frame stages, displays, the qualitative change from still image to movement, and the moment of amused astonishment it engenders testifies again to the power this transformation entails.

Obviously the freezing of action cannot convey a movement as it exists in actual duration. In contrast to the participation in movement that I claim the cinema can convey through the moving image, the freeze frame suddenly kicks the viewer out from that form of viewing. Instead, the freeze frame creates in the viewer a sense of mechanical exteriority and an awareness of the source of movement in the apparatus, precisely those qualities of the cinematic illusion that Bergson contrasted with the lived experience of movement. Undoubtedly this is partly why such a technique can be compared to a Brechtian alienation effect. But while this is one effect of the freeze frame, one might point out that in what may be the most complex use of this technique in film history, Dziga Vertov's *Man with a Movie Camera*, also reveals another dimension. Vertov's editing patterns contextualize the film's switches from still to moving images partly in terms of a revelation of the mechanical processes of film editing and projection in ways that recall a Brechtian alienation effect. But he also allows their presentation to celebrate the delight and wonder they cause, registered especially in the reaction of children to this cinematic magic show. While a materialist like Vertov might have dismissed Bergson's understanding of movement, nonetheless as a filmmaker he plays precisely with the surprise and amusement this qualitative transformation generates.

Thus the opposition between movement and stillness, between duration and suspension, between the flow of action and the freezing of an apparent pose that instantaneous or motion photography made possible provided a rich and varied series of devices for modernist representation. André Breton, in a text illustrated with photographs by Man Ray, including this instantaneous freezing of movement, announced his ideal of "convulsive beauty". Avoiding both the classical description of beauty as repose, but also perhaps also consciously avoiding the embrace of Bergsonian movement by the French avant-garde of the teens and twenties, Breton proposed images that contain a tense dialectic between these two qualities.

> The word "convulsive" which I use to describe the only beauty which should concern us, would lose any meaning in my eyes were it to be conceived in motion and not at the exact expiration of this motion. There can be no beauty at all, as far as I am concerned – convulsive beauty – except at the cost of affirming the reciprocal relation linking the object seen in its motion and in its repose.[11]

Breton later glosses his term by a series of oxymoron: "Convulsive beauty will be veiled-erotic, fixed-explosive, magic-circumstantial, or it will not be".[12]

Like Vertov, Breton celebrates the astonishment, the derangement the switch from movement to stillness, or their simultaneous evocation as in Man Ray's

---

11   André Breton, *Mad Love*, trans. Mary Ann Caws (Lincoln: University of Nebraska Press, 1987) 10, photograph reproduced on p. 20.

12   André Breton, *Mad Love* 19.

photograph, can trigger. But rather than invoking the organic motion Bergson valorized, Breton's beauty is convulsive – apparently subject to fits. Instead of the organic movement of the body Breton focuses on pathological movement, the convulsions of hysteria, the neurological disease that Breton and the Surrealists pronounced the greatest poetic discovery of the 19th century. Curiously, neurologist Charcot's "invention" of hysteria in the late nineteenth century utilized and encouraged important innovations in both instantaneous and serial photography that decomposed the hysteric fits into frozen images. But here our discussion of the adventures of the fixed-explosive, the mutual implication of still and moving images loops back into the complexity of a modern rationalization of the body and a science of visual observation that Bergson was reacting against as well as participating in.

2

Photography/Cinema: Complementary Paradigms in the Early Twentieth Century

Maria Tortajada

Introduction

The dyad stillness/movement encapsulates the confrontation or the connection between two modes of representation – or, better still, between two dispositives of vision.[1] The contrast between photography and cinema parallels that between the still image and the moving image. While the association has now become commonplace, it is by no means natural and is the byproduct of a historical configuration that formed around 1900, in direct relation with the emergence of cinema.

Speed, with the movement it expresses, occupied a nineteenth century sensitive to what constituted its modernity before they ushered in a new century. To grasp the obviousness of this statement, one only needs to read Verne, Wells, Jarry, Fénéon, and many others who made speed the object of their chronicles or fictions. The appeal for contemporaries of fast vehicles, these jewels of technical innovation and industry, is a well-known fact; so is the fascination, tinged with dread, for the accidents caused by the same vehicles in cities then undergoing changes. In this context, the knowledge of movement and its representation may well have been seen as a social issue, as the place of instantaneous photography from the 1880s on illustrates: an iconography of transiency and high speed, full of leaps, falls, and accidents, gradually spread into the mainstream. Similarly, but on another front, the scientific development of chronophotography had as its object the study of movement – notably animal locomotion, with Marey's work – in a specific application of the technique of the snapshot.

To calculate the speed of a moving object as well as the power or the labour needed

---

[1] By "dispositive", we are referring to anything that allows spectators to attend to a representation, from machines to machinery, from production to monstration to reception, from techniques to practices to institutional constraints. Technical determinations are a part of it, as are codes of representation.

for its movement, chronophotography decomposed movement. To explain speed through speed, or through terms involving the same notion, would have been tautological. In that respect, the decomposition of movement was precisely one of the major responses to the question of speed at the turn of the century. It occurred within the field of science, yet it also echoed social practices founded on the play with movement, its composition, and its reconstruction – with well-known nineteenth-century optical toys, from praxinoscopes to zootropes, that depended on the persistence of vision. Chronophotography itself developed in other directions than just science with Edison, Anschütz, and in a more ambivalent manner with Muybridge.[2] As it happens, this response to the question of speed and movement conditioned the emergence of cinema and one application of the photographic snapshot.

The relation between stillness and movement as a specific articulation between photography and cinema was first thought in this cultural framework: movement and speed were explained through the decomposition of movement, itself the condition of possibility for the reconstruction of movement as a moving image. The relation was to expand in a set of concepts that could structure the space of representations according to a defining feature of each dispositive taking the question of movement as a reference. The way in which cinema and photography were tied to or interacted with each other could not be understood at once as a confrontation. If there was such a thing as an "idea of cinema" at the chronophotographic stage, it could not be articulated to an "idea of photography" within the terms of stillness and movement in their current, common formulation. With regard to the period around 1900, the issue is not so much how cinema "contrasted" with photography, but rather how it "moved out of it" and "made use of it".

The cinematographic dispositive may be defined through its ability to reconstruct movement from still images. It partakes of chronophotography, for it is within chronophotographic practices that the synthesis of cinematographic movement was made possible, technically and conceptually. Yet chronophotography as a process consisted first and foremost in breaking down the movement of an object through a series of instantaneous photographs. As a technology, cinema cannot be dissociated from photography historically. Furthermore, while chronophotography was from the outset an application of instantaneous photography, it also re-appropriated it: the photograph became the single frame, an instantaneous image produced as part of a series and at regular intervals, the result of the decomposition of movement and the condition of possibility for its synthesis. Cinema could be said to "contain" photography among its constituent elements. The link between photography and cinema is both historical and structural.

---

2   See Marta Braun, *Picturing Time: The Work of Etienne-Jules Marey* (Chicago, London: University of Chicago Press, 1992) 228–262.

To raise the issue of the movement of cinema away from photography does not amount to assuming a genealogy between photography and cinema, but leads instead to think on the nature of the particular type of photograph that is the single frame. Indeed, the epistemological status of cinema also involves the "explanation" of its "own" still image. The technical shift from the "single" instantaneous photograph to the photograph produced serially and at regular intervals should be examined, but so should the conceptual changes associated with it. Instantaneous photography remains localizable within cinema, as no one will question the fact that the single frame is indeed a photographic snapshot. Yet it may well be – and that is what we would like to demonstrate here – that photography is no longer photography when it enters cinema. It could also be that at least two ideas of instantaneous photography coexist: with and without cinema. The technical principles underlying the snapshot remain rather constant, while the context of thinking, experimentation, actual use, or discursive finality in which it is situated all evolve.

It is as though cinema and photography had been separated through the opposition between stillness and movement, which sets them up against each other as referring to a specific category of images. So much so that cinema and photography function as a double paradigm where each is defined through differentiation from the other. The notion that cinema is characterized by the moving image has prevailed over that which places the emphasis on the single frame, once privileged by Roland Barthes.[3] Examples of this dominance may include André Bazin, who opposed photography and cinema to the benefit of the latter, for its ability to capture movement; Christian Metz, who in his semiological period founded the illusion of reality on the movement of the film image, which he viewed as "real", after all,[4] comforted on that account by Edgar Morin in his *The Cinema*, or the *Imaginary Man*.[5] Gilles Deleuze was to confirm the prerogative of the film image in discerning, in what he called "the movement-image", the expression of Bergsonian duration in its potential for change – even if the movement-image is not exactly the equivalent of the moving image.

Many of these examples show the contiguity between an ontological approach towards the image and the emphasis on movement, in which Henri Bergson played an important part historically. Everything happened as though the depre-

---

3   Roland Barthes, "The Third Meaning. Research Notes on Some Eisenstein Stills" [1970], *A Barthes Reader*, ed. Susan Sontag (New York: Hill and Wang, 1983) 317–333.

4   "Because movement is never material but is always visual, to reproduce its appearance is to duplicate its reality. In truth, one cannot even "reproduce" a movement; one can only re-produce it in a second production belonging to the same order of reality, for the spectator, as the first." Christian Metz, "On the Impression of Reality in the Cinema" [1965], *Film Language: A Semiotics of the Cinema*, trans. Michael Taylor (Chicago: University of Chicago Press, 1990) 9.

5   "But projection only puts the finishing touches to the work of movement. Movement is the decisive power of reality: it is in it, through it, that time and space are real. / The conjunction of the reality of the movement and the appearance of the forms brings about the feeling of concrete life and the perception of objective reality." Edgar Morin, *The Cinema, or the Imaginary Man*, trans. Lorraine Mortimer (Minneapolis: University of Minnesota Press, 2005) 118–119.

ciation of the single frame had been "programmed" in the early twentieth century thanks to some interpretations of Bergsonism. In the process, cinema found its "other", photography, all the more different as it shared the same basic principle – a chemical process capable of recording an image of reality.

The construction of the double paradigm stillness/movement hinged on the historical and structural intricacy of photography and cinema at its chronophotographic stage, a moment in which each dispositive was being defined or redefined. Bergson's thought at the turn of the century was itself a step in this construction, which is why we will develop a reflection on the status of the instantaneous photographic image, a condition of possibility for the moving image of cinema, starting from the work of the philosopher.

We will not perform an exegesis of Bergson here; nor will we put forth a philosophical discourse. The coherence of Bergson's work is of interest to us only insofar as it allows us, within the theoretical demonstration, to define discursive areas around local purposes. We would like to bring out the presuppositions of Bergsonian discourse about dispositives of vision, which means that the function of these dispositives and the concepts associated with them first have to be defined.

Photography in Cinema: The Single Frame

Despite what the Bazinian reading of Bergsonism might suggest, Bergson himself took a particular interest in the single frame, which he called a photograph. He gave the cinematograph a central place in his 1907 *Creative Evolution*. The cinematographic reference appears in the title of the fourth and last chapter, and Bergson proposes that the cinematograph is a strong modelization of what he was to refer to as an illusion, "the cinematographical mechanism of thought".[6] A detailed explanation of the cinematographic model appears in the conclusion to the philosopher's thoughts on evolution, life, and the way intellectual knowledge operates, a knowledge Bergson opposes to intuition. The model thus attains a prime position, as it is presented as a "speaking" synthesis, a formula capable of summarizing the analysis of scientific knowledge. Science, like knowledge, language, and perception betray the essence of reality, which is all duration and flow, as they divide it up in instants, immobilities, or forms. The cinematographic dispositive, analysed in the detail of its mechanical operations, provides an example: how does it proceed to record a marching regiment, Bergson asks? Its method is

> to take a series of snapshots of the passing regiment and to throw these instantaneous views on the screen, so that they replace each other very rapidly. This is what the cinematograph does. With photographs, each of

6   Henri Bergson, *Creative Evolution*, trans. Arthur Mitchell (New York: Henry Holt and Company, 1911) 296.

which represents the regiment in a fixed attitude, it reconstitutes the mobility of the regiment marching.[7]

The cinematograph breaks down the movement of the regiment in a series of instantaneous photographs – the single frames juxtaposed to one another. The photographic snapshot such as is found on the film strip, in its plural and serial form, thus carries with it – and this is important – the negative power of the cinematographic model because it denies the dynamics of life. Several expressions in Bergson's writing refer to these immobile units extracted from movement: "instantaneous cuts",[8] "views taken",[9] "stable views",[10] which all involve photography, and which Bergson always uses in the plural.

To what instances of movement are the immobile sections contrasted with, in the example at hand?

(1) The movement of the moving object (the regiment) in reality. Its nature is important: the regiment is treated as a body subject to a translation along a path, which a march involves by definition. The cinematographic system is always analysed by Bergson in relation to this type of spatial movement.

(2) The movement projected on the screen, which he considers to be fake. Why is that the case?

(3) The movement pertaining to the dispositive, the machine, adding to the photographic snapshots, is responsible – with them – for the illusion produced:

> It is because the film of the cinematograph unrolls, bringing in turn the different photographs of the scene to continue each other, that each actor of the scene recovers his mobility; he strings all his successive attitudes on the invisible movement of the film.[11]

Bergson was to associate "the invisible movement of the film" with abstract movement, which he criticized. Invisibility, it appears, implicitly leads to abstraction. Let us note that, while Bergson writes of the distortion of real movement by projected movement, he does not found the illusion on a representational logic of imitation but on a logic of dispositive: the making of the moving image is what poses problems and causes the distortion.

The analysis of the cinematograph shows that Bergson's thought as a whole rests on the opposition between the continuity of a movement associated with duration and the immobility of sections, whether photographic, conceptual, linguistic, or

---

7   Bergson, *Creative Evolution* 331.

8   Bergson, *Creative Evolution* 272–273.

9   Bergson, *Creative Evolution* 219.

10   Bergson, *Creative Evolution* 328–329. The expression "instantaneous visions" appears in Matter and Memory: "If we went no further [than the theory of pure perception], the part of consciousness in perception would thus be confined to threading on the continuous string of memory an uninterrupted series of instantaneous visions, which would be a part of things rather than ourselves". Henri Bergson, *Matter and Memory* [1896] (London: George Allen; New York: Macmillan, 1912) 69.

11   Bergson, *Creative Evolution* 332.

formal. Such opposition may seem perfectly apt to structure our double paradigm photography/cinema. However, the double paradigm sets dispositives up against each other by qualifying the nature of the representation: the image is said to be still or moving. In Bergson's logic, the essential relation lies elsewhere.

The movement that served as reference at the moment when this type of relation began to crystallize was not that of the projected image, which was secondary, but that of the moving object. Bergson criticizes the process of breaking down movement, an element that leads us to think, like Anson Rabinbach, that behind Bergson's cinematograph lies chronophotography.[12]

Certainly, these instantaneous sections refer to photography which, as we know, rests on a still image. Yet what interests Bergson is not to oppose it to a moving image, but to show that it distorts the movement of the moving object to the point of freezing it.

This kind of distinction may be better understood in its context of demonstration, the reference to the cinematograph. Bergson soon turns to the commentary of Zeno's paradoxes, in particular that of the arrow whose movement is also a movement of translation. The paradox goes as follows: since a moving arrow successively occupies at least two instants, in each of these instants the arrow is still. And since its path may be broken down in a series of mathematical points (these moments when the arrow is not moving), the arrow may be considered still all along its path.[13]

Bergson counters the assertion: movement cannot be broken down and comes all in one. Stillness is a theoretical or scientific abstraction: only transitions exist. This fundamental example, along with others we will not comment on here, adds to the cinematographic model. The single frame appears like one of these still moments. Yet in Zeno's paradox no "representation",[14] no recording, no reconstruction of movement, no moving image may be found – only the moving object and its stations, which Bergson compares to immobile sections in photography as well as in mathematical points. The philosopher is not so much interested in the relation between still image and moving image as between the movement of the object and the freezing of the same movement through the snapshot. While Bergson occasionally refers to the stillness of the image,[15] he does so with respect

12   Anson Rabinbach, "Time and Motion: Etienne-Jules Marey and the Mechanics of the Body", in *The Human Motor. Energy, Fatigue, and the Origins of Modernity* (Berkeley: The University of California Press, 1992) 84–119.

13   Bergson, *Creative Evolution* 335–337.

14   This would be the case in Zeno's paradox, from Bergson's point of view. Let us note that instants, points on the trajectory which mathematical thinking isolates, could not "freeze", strictly speaking, the movement of the moving object. They are substitutes for the movement which mathematical reasoning uses. Alexandre Koyré based his refutation of the Bergsonian commentary on this point, among others. See "Remarques sur les paradoxes de Zénon" (1961), *Etudes d'histoire de la pensée philosophique* (Paris: Gallimard, 1971) 17–20.

15   He thus wrote that the faculty of understanding could be exerted on "the image supposed to be fixed of the progressing action". Bergson, *Creative Evolution* 273.

to movement in reality. The expression "still image" is not ruled out, but it finds a rather particular "explanation" – in the epistemological sense of the term.

By way of recapitulation, let us say that the cinematographic model places instantaneous photography within the series, plurality, the decomposition of movement (as with chronophotography), to oppose it to the movement of the moving object. Photography corresponds to a station. Its theoretical function is to refer to the instant, which Bergson criticizes, rather than to duration. From this standpoint, François Brunet's thesis that photography played a negative role for the philosopher makes sense.[16] The observation can but refer to the historical context of the photographic snapshot at the end of the nineteenth century, a time when photography in its very precision appeared as a distortion of the experience of movement.[17] The debates caused by the snapshots of a galloping horse by Muybridge in the late 1870s, which called into question the practice of painters, attest to this.[18]

Photography without Cinema: Instantaneous Photography

Still, photography arguably assumes another form in Bergson's discourse, outside the cinematographic model and in a function that does not bear such negative connotations. It partakes of a different coherence, which to be sure is related to the one I have outlined so far: indeed, there is no contradiction in Bergson with regard to the use of photography as a reference. Two theoretical moments situate photography in two different logics, even though they are connected in the Bergsonian system through the notion of perception.

What is surprising, in the light of what has just been said, is that in what we call the photographic metaphor, outside the cinematographic model, photography is associated with movement.[19]

Everything hinges on the presentation of pure perception, an essential theoretical

---

16 François Brunet, *La naissance de l'idée de photographie* ["The Advent of the the Idea of Photography"] (Paris: PUF, 2000) 298–302.

17 On this aspect, André Gunthert writes that "with falls and leaps, awkward bodies, strange contortions, comical positions on photographs that are all the more immobile as they should have been more in movement, the revelation of the unintentional and the pure apparition of the accidental cause an unexpected shock". André Gunthert, "Entre photographie instantanée et cinéma: Albert Londe" ["Albert Londe, Between Instantaneous Photography and Cinema"], *Le cinéma et la science*, ed. Alexis Martinet (Paris: CNRS éditions, 1994) 67.

18 This is illustrated by the different stances taken by Eugène Véron (*Aesthetics*, 1878), Paul Souriau (*The Aesthetics of Movement*, 1889), or Robert de la Sizeranne (*Les questions esthétiques contemporaines*, 1904), among others. See Braun, *Picturing Time* 272 et seq.

19 The status of model has to do with the structuring role and the generalizable character Bergson grants the cinematograph. Used in the headings, it represents a paradigm capable of describing science, perception, and language. The use of photography we are about to examine is different. It is a metaphor, or a comparison, very developed and often repeated perhaps, but which explains a specific phenomenon, notably perception. It does not refer to a set of operations that may be generalized and is not meant to describe other comparable phenomena.

stage which was to allow Bergson to explain how memory works in the first chapter of *Matter and Memory* (1896). This theory of perception takes its place in a global project, "to define the function of the body in the life of the spirit".[20] Bergson starts from a definition and a conception of matter. As it happens, for the philosopher, the matter in question is the image. Matter and Memory puts forward this new, very original concept as photographic metaphors begin to appear.

"Image", it should be noted, is not synonymous with "representation" in the sense of substitute, as the theory of representation may define it based on the notion of mimesis. Images are matter itself.[21] This assertion, because it seems so paradoxical a priori, may seem disconcerting: matter, "physical reality", is defined by one of the characteristics which, as a rule, it gains through perception and the visible quality that appears to a perceiving subject. In fact, Bergson adopts a realist position, considering that matter exists in itself prior to any perceiving subject. In his view, the paradox finds its solution within the theory of images coupled with that of pure perception. Bergson constructs a theory of knowledge in which the relationship between subject and world is as continuous, direct, and immediate as possible. The solution consists in setting perception as part of the very essence of beings and things, which he does by calling matter "image".[22]

So objects, like our bodies, are images. As it happens, these images interact with one another. Bergson imagines a universe caught in an endless system of exchanges and relations, which is all movement, and writes that each image "is continued in those which follow it, just as it prolonged those which preceded it".[23] One should picture a kind of radiation of each and every thing towards all other things in the world: each object, through its luminous energy, is in contact with all the bodies in the world. In *Matter and Memory* images-bodies evade a mere spatial description that would place them in juxtaposition to one another. The idea, rather, is that of encompassment through radiation. To illustrate the interactions and the movements of matter, Bergson often takes up the same two

---

20 Bergson, *Matter and Memory* 234.

21 Matter is "an aggregate of images", Bergson writes early in his work, later reiterating the assertion: "…by positing the material world we assume an aggregate of images, and moreover […] it is impossible to assume anything else. No theory of matter escapes this necessity. Reduce matter to atoms in motion: these atoms, though denuded of physical qualities, are determined only in relation to an eventual vision and an eventual contact, the one without light and the other without materiality. Condense atoms into centres of force, dissolve them into vortices revolving in a continuous fluid: this fluid, these movements, these centres, can themselves be determined only in relation to an impotent touch, an ineffectual impulsion, a colourless light; they are still images. It is true that an image may be without being perceived; it may be present without being represented; and the distance between these two terms, presence and representation, seems just to measure the interval between matter itself and our conscious perception of matter". Bergson, *Matter and Memory* 26–27.

22 On the subject, see Henri Hude's particularly illuminating work *Bergson*, vol. 2 (Paris: Editions universitaires, 1990) 62–68.

23 Bergson, *Matter and Memory* 27.

explanatory models, the atom and the field of forces. Images act upon one another through all the points that constitute them.[24]

How do we as beings make contact with the world? The fundamental point is that humans, like objects, are matter. A first step consists in the translation of the infinitesimal dynamic model of atoms into a scale relevant for perception and the human action that prolongs it, for humans are indeed bodies. Yet Bergson actually has consciousness in mind, which also implies the temporality of memory. Before he reaches that point, Bergson defines several types of perception, from pure perception to concrete perception.

Perception is the first stage in the relation of humans to matter, and thus to the ceaseless movement of images that constitute it. Bergson theorizes that there is such a thing as instantaneous perception, which he calls pure perception: it does not exist in actuality, he writes, for there is no actual perception without memory and time.[25] Still, the theory of pure perception is needed for an understanding of the Bergsonian system as a whole.

Perception cannot be explained by locating the constitution of images in the brain, a place where mental images, for instance, would synthesize. For Bergson, the brain does not have the ability to create images, for these are matter. Images are in the world; to capture images, perception has to take place in the midst of things: it is to be understood as a particular instance of the generalized exchange occurring within matter. In perception, a living body retains only a part of the matter image – that which it needs for its action. Perception rests on selection, retaining the qualities, the surface, the "external crust"[26] of objects, thereby constituting a representation, defined as a partial image-body, with limits set by perception itself. There is no difference of kind between matter and representation, as between the sign and the object it represents, but a difference of degree: representation is matter, with something missing.[27] The fact that the definition is completely a-semiological is hardly debatable.

What is of particular interest to us here is the movement of matter perception is involved in. What distinguishes every present, real image

---

24   Still, the atom may also appear as an example of the model of knowledge Bergson criticizes: "That which usually hinders this mutual approach of motion and quality is the acquired habit of attaching movements to elements – atoms or what not, – which interpose their solidity between the movement itself and the quality into which it contracts. As our daily experience shows us bodies in motion, it appears to us that there ought to be, in order to sustain the elementary movements to which qualities may be reduced, diminutive bodies or corpuscles. Motion then becomes for our imagination no more than an accident, a series of positions, a change of relations; and, as it is a law of our representation that in it the stable drives away the unstable, the important and central element for us becomes the atom, between the successive positions of which movement then becomes a mere link". Bergson, *Matter and Memory* 269.

25   Bergson, *Matter and Memory* 24–26.

26   Bergson, *Matter and Memory* 28.

27   "But between this perception of matter and matter itself there is but a difference of degree and not of kind, pure perception standing towards matter in the relation of the part to the whole". Bergson, *Matter and Memory* 78.

is the necessity which obliges it to act through every one of its points upon
all the points of all other images, to transmit the whole of what it receives,
to oppose to every action an equal and contrary reaction, to be, in short,
merely a road by which pass, in every direction, the modifications propa-
gated throughout the immensity of the universe.[28]

This is generalized movement – but not so much the movement of a moving
object, as in the cinematographic model, as a movement of action-reaction,
spreading "in every direction" and lacking the simplicity of the mere trajectory,
according to Bergson. It may be compared with other types of elementary
movements, those of reality itself: vibration,[29] oscillation or palpitations.[30] In
Matter and Memory as in *Creative Evolution*, Bergson defines these movements
with great precision by contrasting them with a conception which, looking
exclusively to space, focuses on changes in the location of moving objects and on
series of positions. We can obviously recognize the cinematographic model in the
description.

Matter and Memory is a gigantic theater of movement. Matter, like images, is
movement. Gilles Deleuze did not fail to emphasize this in his rereading of
Bergson, granting as he did a particular importance to this opening chapter of
Matter and Memory. He made it the foundation of the movement-image, and what
he called "mobile sections", devised out of Bergson's concept of image. To
Deleuze, they were the elementary component of cinema.

And what is the metaphor chosen by Bergson to explain pure perception and
account for matter? Photography, precisely. Deleuze could afford to overlook this
fact simply because he did not have any interest in the epistemological function
of dispositives of vision.

The famous passage in which Bergson first elaborates on the photographic
metaphor aims to explain the way perception operates:

> The whole difficulty of the problem that occupies us comes from the fact
> that we imagine perception as a photographic view of things, taken from a
> given point with a special apparatus such as the organ of perception – a
> photograph which would then be developed in the brain-matter by some

28   Bergson, *Matter and Memory* 28.

29   Subchapter IV in chapter IV announces in its title that "Real movement is rather the transference of a state
     than of a thing". Bergson thus poses the hypothesis he is about to demonstrate: "But this is just the question:
     do real movements present merely differences of quantity, or are they not quality itself, vibrating, so to
     speak, internally, and beating time for its own existence through an often incalculable number of moments?"
     Bergson, *Matter and Memory* 268. See also pages 269–272.

30   "Whether we see in it vibrations or whether we represent it in any other way, one fact is certain, it is that
     every quality is change. In vain, moreover, shall we seek beneath the change the thing which changes: it is
     always provisionally, and in order to satisfy our imagination, that we attach the movement to a mobile. The
     mobile flies forever before the pursuit of science, which is concerned with mobility alone. In the smallest
     discernible fraction of a second, in the almost instantaneous perception of a sensible quality, there may be
     trillions of oscillations which repeat themselves. The permanence of a sensible quality consists in this
     repetition of movements, as the persistence of life consists in a series of palpitations." Bergson, *Creative
     Evolution* 301.

unknown process of chemical and psychical elaboration. But is it not obvious that the photograph, if photograph there be, is already taken, already printed in the very heart of things and at all the points of space? No metaphysics, no physics even, can escape this conclusion. Build up the universe with atoms: each of them is subject to the action, variable in quantity and quality according to the distance, exerted on it by all material atoms. Bring in Faraday's centers of force: the lines of force emitted in every direction from every center bring to bear upon each the influences of the whole material world. Call up the monads: each, as Leibniz would have it, is the mirror of the universe. Everyone, then, agrees on this point. The thing is, if we consider a given place in the universe, we can say that the action of all matter passes through it without resistance and without loss, and that in it the photograph of the whole is translucent: missing behind the plate is the dark screen on which the image could come out. Our "zones of indetermination" play in some sort the part of the screen. They add nothing to what is there; they merely allow the real action to pass through and the virtual action to remain.[31]

What stands out in photography, from Bergson's point of view? Without denying the chemical process and the camera obscura, he leaves them aside as irrelevant and pays attention to the photographic image itself insofar as it is "already taken". The place where it is developed matters little: his new model does not take it into account here, as he focuses on the print, the positive image. He keeps off his contemporaries' uses of the photographic paradigm as a figure of interiority, where interiority was represented by the unseen process of production of the image. In fact, Bergson disputes the use of photography as a metaphor of the psychic process of the constitution of images at the same time as he denies the brain the ability to produce any.[32]

Not only the image is already "printed", it also has a second, crucial characteristic, its translucence. The print on glass plates of the nineteenth century could be a point of comparison for the image and the light passing through it which Bergson has in mind. This type of image was used for different kinds of projections, the magic lantern for example, as well as for stereoscopic prints. The photographic snapshot is not directly referred to in this case: photography is associated indirectly with instantaneity, through the comparison with perception. Indeed, instantaneity is a characteristic of pure perception, the theoretical construction which Bergson deems necessary to the understanding of his system. This example also takes us rather far away from the chronophotographic series of the cinematographic model: here Bergson is dealing with photography alone.

What exactly does it stand for, in Bergson's view? One answer could not possibly summarize it, for the excerpt presents two states of photography. First, there is the "photograph (...) already taken, already printed in the very heart of things",

---

31 Bergson, *Matter and Memory* 31–32. Our emphasis. Translator's note: the original English translation makes Bergson's original French text barely intelligible at several points in this quoted passage and has been significantly amended to better convey the meaning of its source.

32 On these questions, see Philippe Ortel, *La littérature à l'ère de la photographie* ["Literature in the Age of Photography"] (Nîmes: J. Chambon, 2002) 324–329; and François Brunet, *La naissance de l'idée de photographie* 292–294.

that is, before any perception by a living being. The example of atoms is there to convince us that photography refers to matter. It is an equivalent of the matter-image, the body-image when its translucence allows rays of lights to pass through it. If perception is "in the things themselves", then we can consider, following Bergson, that a form of immanent "perception" defines matter.[33]

The explanation of perception by a living being only comes afterwards: photography refers to what is perceived, to representation only through the subterfuge of a "dark screen" which blocks the rays of light traveling through the universe, thereby selecting an aspect of the image already taken in the body-matter and making it appear. Bergson links the screen with our "centers of indetermination", which are responsible for perception. Which photographic technique uses a dark screen to which a translucent image would be applied? If we turn to strictly photographic techniques, some manufacturing processes for contact prints do go through the application of the negative on a dark surface.[34] The fact remains nonetheless that the translucent image which serves as a metaphor in the first state of the comparison is a print (a positive), not a negative. Bergson's text hints at another option, which takes us out of photographic processes proper. If translucent photography is matter, it seems that a likely way to make it visible would be through a process analogous to that of the camera obscura, which has the image of reality form onto the dark wall where the rays of light hit. Bergson's explanation of the process of perception is founded on the movement of light and appears a few pages before the explicit introduction of the photographic metaphor. The passage repeats in some way the one that interests us here:

> When a ray of light passes from one medium into another, it usually traverses it with a change of direction. But the respective densities of the two media may be such that, for a given angle of incidence, refraction is no longer possible. Then we have total reflexion. The luminous point gives rise to a virtual image which symbolizes, so to speak, the fact that the luminous rays cannot pursue their way. Perception is just a phenomenon of the same kind. That which is given is the totality of the images of the material world, with the totality of their internal elements. But if we suppose

33   "In one sense we might say that the perception of any unconscious material whatever, in its instantaneousness, is infinitely greater and more complete than ours, since this point gathers and transmits the influences of all the points of the material universe, whereas our consciousness only attains to certain parts and to certain aspects of those parts". (Bergson, *Matière et mémoire* 30–31) See also Henri Hude's explanation in *Bergson* 64–65: "There is, then, by nature, a direct contact between each being in this world and all others. Let us also assume that such contact is always already pure perception. Still, conscious perception is not present everywhere. How can the passage from pure perception to conscious perception be explained?" This passage is not at stake in the passage relevant to us, for consciousness implies memory. Here the two states of photography do not take into account the temporal dimension which memory introduces.

34   Albert Londe explained that it consisted in taking the negative, developed but not fixed, and "to expose it on a dark background with a bright, diffuse light to attack silver salts not yet reduced in the negative, which as a whole should make for a good positive, by difference with the sensitive salts of the plate in their totality". *La photographie moderne*, 2nd edn. (1888; Paris: Masson, 1896) 459, 490. In describing the method to "obtain directly a large-format, positive contact print from life", Londe does not mention any cases that would start from the positive.

centres of real, that is to say of spontaneous[,] activity, the rays which reach it, and which interest that activity, instead of passing through those centres, will appear to be reflected and thus to indicate the outlines of the object which emits them. [...] Perception therefore resembles those phenomena of reflexion which result from an impeded refraction; it is like an effect of mirage.[35]

Describing the passage of light through bodies, then its complete reflexion, Bergson comes to define the two stages of the photographic metaphor. In short, photography – in its translucent state as a print – is matter before it is an equivalent of perception by a living being. It becomes a representation when it "comes out" of a dark background – when, perceived by a living being, it becomes but a selection performed on matter.

The association of photography with matter as Bergson defines it is essential to our argument, for if photography refers to the image-matter, then one might as well say that as an image it is intrinsically linked to movement, as the recurring comparison with the dynamics of atoms underscores. Not the movement of a moving object, but the movements of action-reaction, vibration, and oscillation, which are distinctive features of matter.

We have so far simply outlined the place of photography within the question of movement. A further step would involve showing that photography also partakes of a dynamic system at the level of the operations of memory and is thus involved in other types of movements. Still, the present example does enough to bring out the radical distinction between the two uses of photography, whether in the photographic metaphor or within the cinematographic model (Table 1).

Table 1

Photography	In the photographic metaphor	In the cinematographic model
Notions	Instantaneity (indirect association) Translucent print Dark screen Singular use (vs series)	Instantaneous views
		Plurality of images, juxtaposition in space, series (single frames), chronophotographic logic
	= Movement (matter)	**= Stillness**
Movement	**Action-reaction** (matter)	**Translation of a moving object**

Photography thus appears in two different theoretical contexts, either as a metaphor in the theory of images and pure perception, or as a component of the cinematographic model to expose the mechanistic illusion, and particularly how science and perception function. A common point is that, in both theoretical moments, photography is connected to perception. In the first case, however, it

---

[35] Bergson, *Matter and Memory* 29–30.

refers to pure perception – a theoretical requisite for Bergson – and to matter, all of which is movement. In the second case, it refers to perception even though perception is considered from a negative angle, as what distorts the very essence of reality, which is duration. The conceptual cluster associated with photography is very different in these two cases: what is of particular interest to us here is that photography is movement when associated with matter, but it is stillness when perception is analysed as an illusion.

In the end, two photographic paradigms coexist for Bergson: one in the photographic metaphor, the other in the cinematographic model, the latter being a stage towards the double paradigm that was to oppose photography and cinema as still image and moving image (Table 2).[36]

Table 2

Photography and movement	Photography	Referred to...
Photographic metaphor	Photography = Movement Matter Perception	–
Cinematographic model	Photography = freezing the moving object (still image)	Movement of the moving object
Double paradigm constituted	Photography = still image	Cinema = moving image

The photographic metaphor stands poles apart from the photographic image as defined in the stillness/movement paradigm. A photograph is indeed a still image, materially and technically, and could as such be opposed to the moving image. Yet concepts associated with it do not take this characteristic into consideration. The reverse happens, in fact: photography is not referred to a movement that would be exterior to it since, referring to matter, it is movement.

It is from within cinema in its chronophotographic stage that the opposition between stillness and movement began to consolidate, with photography being related to movement while it was itself identified as still. This movement, however, was first and foremost that of the moving object, not that of the image projected on a screen. Indeed, what interested Bergson the most was the movement of reality, which chronophotography distorts by breaking it down.

The double paradigm truly materialized from the moment when the photographic image was related to another movement, which was then privileged: the synthetic movement associated with cinema.

---

36   It should be mentioned that the opposition is not between Matter and Memory and Creative Evolution. Both models of photography had already appeared by 1896. We will later return to this question.

3

A subjectivity torn between stasis and movement: Still image and moving image in medical discourse at the turn of the 20th century

Mireille Berton

This study, which attempts to relate the history of media to the history of sciences, falls within the scope of a broader research on the role of audiovisual media in the construction of a body of knowledge pertaining to medicine and related disciplines such as psychology. The epistemological implications of practices and knowledge founded on the application of photography and cinema to the various taxonomies of the visible world have already been the object of a sizeable literature.[1] Accordingly, what I propose instead is to examine the ways in which the photographic and cinematographic paradigms have been used in a series of texts that reflect a specific image of the psyche. Indeed, medicine – vying with philosophy for the prerogative of the so-called scientific psychology – had diagnosed new neuroses by the end of the 19th century. It was thus able to produce a genuine social discourse on psychic morbidity as the sign of a crisis in a human civilization alienated by the effects of modernity.

Within such a dark vision of the world, saturated with "anxiety-inducing predi-

---

1   Thierry Lefebvre, Jacques Malthête and Laurent Mannoni, eds., *Sur les pas de Marey : science(s) et cinéma* ["In Marey's Footsteps: Science(s) and Cinema"] (Paris: L'Harmattan/SEMIA, 2004); François Albera, Marta Braun, and André Gaudreault, eds., *Arrêt sur image, fragmentation du temps/Stop Motion, Fragmentation of Time* (Lausanne: Éd. Payot, 2002); Christian Pociello, *La science en mouvements: Étienne Marey et Georges Demenÿ (1870–1920)* ["Science in Movements: Etienne Marey and Georges Demenÿ, 1870–1920"] (Paris: PUF, 1999); Roland Cosandey and François Albera, *Cinéma sans frontières 1896–1918* ["Cinema without Borders, 1896–1918"] (Lausanne: Éd. Payot; Quebec: Nuit Blanche Éditeur, 1995); Michel Frizot, *Avant le Cinématographe, la Chronophotographie : temps, photographie et mouvement autour de É.-J. Marey* ["Before the Cinematograph: Chronophotography. Time, Photography, and Movement around E.-J. Marey"] (Beaune: Les Amis de Marey/Ministère de la culture, 1984); Georges Didi-Huberman, *Invention of Hysteria: Charcot and the Photographic Iconography of the Salpetriere* (Cambridge: MIT Press, 2003) [1982].

cates" ("prédicats anxiogènes"),[2] cinema and photography provided rhetorical
and epistemological tools which made it possible to explain the psychic activity
of a perceiving subject. The said subject then became the productive site for and
the receptor of atypical perceptive phenomena such as the sudden subjection to
the apparition of still as well as moving images (but also to the perception of
sounds, and sometimes even tactile sensations). The psychic system was thought
of as a machine capable of accumulating sensory impressions and reactualizing
them owing to some hallucinatory, oneiric, or anxious episode. It thus appeared
to combine a system of perception and representation intersecting the functional
logic of both technologies.

My hypothesis is that modernity, through photography and cinema, provided
medical discourse with an idea of still images and moving images which, in their
hypertrophied version (extreme stillness and mobility), constituted a semiotics
of disruption in the function of the real.[3] The crisis of the subject, variously
articulated by such twentieth-century discursive formations as Lacanian psychoanalysis, accordingly appears like a possible repercussion of this codification of
subjectivity and its reassessment in the light of modernity.

Stasis and flux

At the turn of the 20th century, commentaries on modernity and its different
effects regularly mentioned cases of patients whose psychic and perceptive system
had been seriously disrupted. This restructuring process at work in perception
could be measured among healthy perceiving subjects (city dwellers) as well as
sick ones (neurasthenics or hysterics). It was problematized in terms that articulated in various ways two opposed, apparently contradictory states or moments,
stillness and mobility, which involved vision, perception, and thought alternately. Accordingly, these discourses make it possible to bring to light two
extreme models of subjectivity actualized in notional pairs such as atrophy and
hypertrophy, absorption and distraction, insensitivity and irritability, inhibition
and automatism. The twin paradigms of hypnosis (divided between anesthesia
and perceptive over-acuity) and hysteria (divided between paralysis and convul-
sion) spectacularly corroborate these dualisms.[4] Perceptive disorders thus seem
to fall along an axis running between two types of psychic conditions – one where
forces of association predominate (attention, tension, resistance, wholeness,
immobility, stability), and another where forces of dissociation prevail (distraction, relaxation, suggestibility, lability, multiplicity, transitivity).

2   Marc Angenot, *1889. Un état du discours social* ["1889: a Snapshot of Social Discourse"] (Quebec: Le
    Préambule, 1989) 34.

3   In Pierre Janet's sense, namely, as a dysfunctional relation to reality or, to put it in Freudian terms, as a
    dysfunction of the reality principle.

4   On the "twinship" of hypnosis and hysteria, see Pierre-Henri Castel, *La Querelle de l'hystérie* ["The Dispute
    over Hysteria"] (Paris: PUF, 1998).

It appears very tempting, that being the case, to see a symmetry between the dual paradigm of stasis and flux and that of photography and cinema – and to attempt and connect them, following the assumption that medical discourse itself considered the techniques as the epitomes of fixity and movement, respectively. Still, the two apparatuses seem to have been approached as the sites of a subjective absorption, ambivalent in its effects, related to both paralysing captivation and dissolving stream. Cinema and photography could potentially weaken attention, will, and memory, causing various forms of perceptive instability detectable in the subjects of neurosis as well as in the subjects deemed vulnerable, such as children and women. However, while both cinema and photography were able to account for the dynamic model of the psychic system, shot through as it was by fields of opposite forces, their models were often apprehended through their individual components as well as according to concepts or ideas exclusively associated with them.[5] Photography and cinema could thus function without distinction, providing either the explanatory principle of a psychic phenomenon (in the theories of hallucination, for instance) or the objects, parts, and specific effects needed for a piecemeal approach. Photography was then often associated with mnesic images, while cinema tended to be attached to delirious images. The present analysis rests on the examination of a corpus of sources constituted from a larger research on the relations between the cinematographic apparatus and the sciences of the psyche at the turn of the 20th century.[6] It makes it possible to draw up the inventory of a series of actions performed by the psyche, some shared by both apparatuses, some others the prerogative of only one of them. For its part, photography exposes or records, fixes, preserves, focuses, haunts, freezes, or produces hallucinations whereas cinema exposes, thinks, dreams, projects, traumatizes, excites, or produces hallucinations. I should mention at this point that, while theories of the psyche generally referred to both models (with that of cinema appearing in its pre-cinematographic variations before 1900), the distribution of these occurrences involved slightly different domains. While the cinematographic model garnered the favours of the theories of dreams and consciousness, the photographic model seems to have been preferred in essays bearing on memory and attention. Systems of production or reproduction of icons in general (painting, panorama, magic lantern, etc.) appear to have entered massively the conceptual and didactic apparatus of the sciences of the psyche. This may be explained by the figurative capacities of apparatuses enrolled in the

---

5 My methodology rests on the founding principles of the epistemology of cinema put forth by Maria Tortajada and François Albera in "L'Épistémè "1900"", in *Le Cinéma, nouvelle technologie du XXᵉ siècle/ The Cinema, A New Technology for the 20th Century* [proceedings of the 2002 Domitor International Conference on Early Cinema] eds. André Gaudreault, Catherine Russell and Pierre Véronneau (Lausanne: Payot, 2004) 45–62.

6 This article is part of a doctoral thesis currently in progress titled "Le dispositif cinématographique comme modèle épistémologique dans les sciences du psychisme au tournant du XXᵉ siècle. L'invention du sujet moderne" ["The Cinematographic Apparatus as Epistemological Model in the Sciences of the Psyche at the Turn of the 20th Century. The Invention of the Modern Subject"], under the supervision of Professor François Albera.

service of theories that granted the image a fundamental position, with the mind seen as a machine ceaselessly expressing its various contents in visual terms.

Théodule Ribot and the mental image

As François Brunet underscores in his book on the idea of photography, the technology truly became a commonplace in social, cultural, and scientific discourse as early as the mid-nineteenth century, lending itself particularly well to thinking on the functioning of the psyche.[7] The modern, metaphorical use of photography as an automatic system for the production of shots emerged around 1880. Distinct from a classical mode that centered around the mimetic valency (a common trope since around 1850), this use coincided with the advent of neurasthenia, a nosological entity grouping together an infinite variety of symptoms linked to unbalance in psychological operations tied to concentration, memorization, or the action of the subject.

Théodule Ribot, the founder of scientific psychology in France, took much interest in disorders affecting memory, will, and attention, and he synthesized and actualized the totality of available knowledge on these disorders.[8] While willingly exercizing one's capacity of attention was the privilege of an elite gifted with a level of intelligence lacking among "degenerates",[9] it nevertheless presented itself as a momentary, intermittent, fixed, and fundamentally punctual state that took the form of an obnubilation of the mind freezing the course of thoughts. Indeed, according to Ribot, the mental life of a fit man consists in "a perpetual coming and going of inward events, in a *marching by of sensations, feelings, ideas, and images*, which associate with, or repel, each other according to certain laws", like a "mobile aggregate which is being incessantly formed, unformed and re-formed".[10] The statement calls to mind the theories of the English associationist school, notably represented by Alexander Bain. Bain postulated that the mind comprised psychological data, simple (sensations) as well as complex (voluntary actions), combined according to a set of precise laws, conditions, and causes.[11] All events pertaining to consciousness associated in accordance with a causal logic linking psychological states to one another, a state always being the product and the result of a previous state. Ribot viewed attention as a kind of freeze frame, which he called monoideism. Coming to interrupt a continuous and chaotic

7   François Brunet, *La naissance de l'idée de photographie* ["The Advent of the Idea of Photography"] (Paris: PUF, 2000).

8   Théodule Ribot, *The Psychology of Attention* (Whitefish, Montana: Kessinger Publishing, 2006) [1889].

9   The term was disseminated by Bénédict-Augustin Morel in France and was frequently used at the time to refer to marginal populations in general. See *Traité de dégénérescences physiques, intellectuelles et morales de l'espèce humaine et de ses causes qui produisent ces variétés maladives* ["Treatise on Physical, Intellectual, and Moral Degeneration in the Human Species, and on the Causes That Produce These Various Pathologies"] (Paris: Baillière et Fils, 1857).

10   Ribot, *The Psychology of Attention* 3. My emphasis.

11   Alexander Bain, *The Senses and the Intellect* (Whitefish, Montana: Kessinger Publishing, 2004) [1855].

psychic flux (polyideism), it thus appeared as "the momentary inhibition [...] of this perpetual progression".[12]

While polyideism and monoideism naturally alternated in the mind of a sane individual, the morbid states of attention led to an atrophy or a hypertrophy of the faculty of attention, exacerbating the intensity of these variations usually tied "to the law of rhythm".[13] The pathology was therefore always heralded by a sudden freeze or by a rush in the process of thinking. Ribot introduced all the agents playing a part in the projection of images in a passage on mania, which is characterized by a lack of attention that takes the form of a rapid association of ideas and images against which the subject is powerless. He referred to the attention-related excess as a "general and permanent over-excitation of the psychic life":

> The state of consciousness *is immediately projected outwards.* [...] sensations, images, ideas, feelings *follow each other* with such astonishing rapidity that they scarcely attain to the condition of complete consciousness, and so that frequently the bond of association uniting them is totally undiscoverable to the *spectator.* Or in the very words of one of these maniacs, "It is really frightful to think of the extreme rapidity with which ideas succeed one another in the mind". To recapitulate, we find here, in the mental order of things, a disordered flow of images and ideas; in the motor order, a flux of words, shouts, gesticulations, and impetuous movements.[14]

The maniac subject thus turned into a kind of machine producing in an automatic and irresistible manner images projected outside of oneself in the form of essentially motor and verbal releases. This type of description certainly does not allow us to assume the existence of a psychic screen on which the byproduct of such an inner agitation would appear. By contrast, such an assumption appears quite reasonable with another case of mania, that of a young law student obsessed by the fluctuations of the stock exchange and who "at last retained permanently before his eyes the image and picture of the bank-notes themselves, in all their varieties of form, size, and colour. The idea, with its incessant repetitions and intensity, *came to assume a force of projection that made it equivalent to reality.* Yet he himself had ever the full consciousness that the images floating before his eyes were merely a freak of his imagination."[15] The passage implies the presence of a virtual screen upon which the tormented mind projects its obsession. As though placed in front of the eyes of the perceiving subject, the screen receives a series of endogenous images through an exogenous projective process, as the subject expels the product of his affliction. This clearly involves the paradigm of an apparatus for the projection of – presumably moving – images. Still, questioning

---

12 Ribot, *The Psychology of Attention* 4.

13 Ribot, *The Psychology of Attention* 9.

14 Ribot, *The Psychology of Attention* 96. [My emphasis] The excess of attention paradoxically results in a stagnation of attention, a sort of paralysis that prevents consciousness from channeling and organizing what is perceived, leading to an expression of thinking both disorderly and anarchical.

15 Ribot, *The Psychology of Attention* 82. My emphasis.

as to the nature of these images described as diverse, repeated, and ceaseless is not exhausted, as it seems difficult to clear up the ambiguity on the localization of movement. Is it in the image itself, *between* images succeeding one another according to a logic of successiveness or superimposition, or both?

Generally, the image for Ribot was always the reactivation of a perceptive stimulus that took a hallucinatory turn in proportion to the intensity of the force that had presided over the impression upon the psyche of traces of the perceptive act. The process of projective emission was directly correlated to the hold of an obsession transformed into a hallucination, the consciousness of illusion notwithstanding. It thus remained tied to the idea of a psychic dissociation between seeing and knowing, a regime of belief that also shaped a number of traditions in spectacle over the 19th and the 20th centuries. At the time, Ribot insisted that "the image is not a photograph but a revival of the sensorial and motor elements that have built up the perception",[16] that is, not a mere copy of what was perceived and which as such would always lack the vividness of the original impression. These reservations towards the photographic metaphor, often used at the time to refer to the capacity of the psyche to retain the perceptive impressions issuing from the outside world, do not sound unlike comments by Hippolyte Taine on the plainly automatic character of a technique seemingly limited to unartistic redundancy and machine-produced mimeticism.[17] The photographic model nevertheless pervaded a theory of the image that could be summarized in a formula later corroborated by psychophysiology as well as the psychoanalysis of perception: seeing is always seeing again.

Idée fixe and psychic automatism

For philosopher and psychiatrist Pierre Janet, who taught at the Collège de France, the *idée fixe* – or hypertrophy of attention – took the form of hallucinations and machine-like acts, pointing to an altered state of consciousness, which dissociated itself from the self to grow "in an automatic and independent manner".[18] He found that his patient Marcelle, a young woman suffering from abulia (a state of mental weakness) as well as *idées fixes*, swung from so-called crises of "cloudiness", with ideas and images passing through her mind in a chaotic way, to "clear instants" – clear-headed parentheses temporarily breaking the trance characteristic of the cloud.[19] These crises of ideas, which were also crises of images, threw "the patient in a sleeping state punctuated by dreams", cutting her

---

16   Ribot, *The Psychology of Attention* 48.

17   Taine made a clear distinction between photography and painting: in his view, photography produced a mechanical image of the real while painting tended to imitate a reality but preserved a ratio of invention and creativity which the operation of the photographic camera would always lack. Hippolyte-Adolphe Taine, *The Philosophy of Art* (New York: Holt and Williams, 1867) 36–40.

18   Pierre Janet, *Leçons au Collège de France (1895–1934)* ["Lectures at the Collège de France, 1895–1934"], Encyclopédie Psychologique series (Paris: L'Harmattan, 2004) 49.

19   Pierre Janet, *Névroses et idées fixes* (Paris: Félix Alcan, 1898).

off completely from the outside world. They were "accompanied with sheer hallucinations"[20] and visual in nature, streaming through a mind forced to attend to a spectacle at once fast, iterative, and unavoidable. As often stated in medical discourse, the hallucination produced a very "vivid" and "intense" image, at once "precise", "detailed", "perfect", and "stable" – qualifying adjectives that could equally apply to the photographic and cinematographic images.

The study of psychic dysfunctions also made it possible to emphasize two fundamental tropes, unimpeded automatism and intense focalization. On the one hand, the perceiving subject may fall prey to an irrepressible production of images appearing either in the form of an uninterrupted and overpowering stream of images or as the apparition of a single image soon superimposed with a new image and gradually covered over by it. On the other hand, the mind of the patient may be equipped with "a mechanism of excitability that reinforces images", in Charles Richet's expression,[21] a mechanism particularly developed among subjects suffering from *idées fixes*. According to Ribot, unbridled monoideism led to the concentration of consciousness on an image or a cluster of images, a phenomenon akin to astonishment and surprise and which he explained in terms of a brutal and impetuous image breaking the natural flow of the stream of consciousness: "The state of surprise or astonishment is spontaneous attention augmented", Ribot wrote, and that notably involves "the augmentation of nervous influx in consequence of the impression [...] Surprise, and in a higher degree astonishment, is a shock produced by that which is new and unexpected [...] and in its strong form, it is a commotion. Properly speaking, it is not so much a state, as an intermediate condition between two states, an abrupt rupture, a gap, an hiatus".[22]

In both cases, the pathogenous mental image appears as an excessive image – excessively mobile in some cases, excessively immobile in others. The abnormal mobility of the neurotic psyche thus encompasses states of stasis as well as states of feverishness, a fundamental duality accounted for by the law of association by contrast, according to which opposed facts of consciousness combine in a determinist logic.[23] For many doctors the law explained the cyclothymia of neurotics, whose overworked brains ceaselessly shuttled back and forth between phases of excitement and depression. The thermodynamic model of human psychology put forth by Charles Féré demonstrated that the "degree to which the subject is vibratile"[24] depended on such alternation. In an overworked brain, excitation

---

20   Janet, *Névroses et idées fixes* 18.

21   Charles Richet, *Essai de psychologie générale*, 4th edn. (Paris: Félix Alcan, 1901) 7.

22   Ribot, *The Psychology of Attention* 23–25. The psychological notion of the augmentation of attention, widespread in the sciences of the psyche, was to be reinterpreted in filmic terms by psychologist Hugo Münsterberg, who in 1917 explicitly associated attention with the close-up in photography and cinema. See *The Photoplay: A Psychological Study and Other Writings*, ed. Allan Langdale (London: Routledge, 2002).

23   See for instance Frédéric Paulhan, *L'activité mentale et les éléments de l'esprit* ["Mental Activity and the Elements of the Mind"] (Paris: Félix Alcan, 1887).

thus caused fatigue, which in turn was transformed into overstimulation.[25] The aberrant fixation on an image caused the perceiving subject to plunge into a state that was both its inverse and its complementary reverse, thereby revealing their reciprocal, periodic, and syntagmatic perpetuation. The association between stillness and movement thus concerned not only the agitation of nervous bodies at once unfocused and petrified,[26] but also the idiosyncratic excitability of their psychic system.

Trauma and cinematographic stream

The film apparatus subjects the spectator to a spectacle both all-powerful and irrefragable and is in that respect comparable to the many devices meant to take over from a failing or refractory perception, as Jonathan Crary has demonstrated.[27] The dread of a consciousness slipping into marginal states, perceptible in a medical discourse whose theoretical, clinical, and therapeutic instruments it exceeded, echoed the concerns raised by the deleterious effects cinema was assumed to have on its audience. Indeed, while cinema may be approached as a disciplinary apparatus, it was also a place of alternative scopic regimes.

The cinematographic paradigm was widely used in the theories of dreams and of their possible pathologies (insomnia, hypnosis, somnambulism) as well as in the psychopathology of traumas. So was the photographic paradigm as a consequence, since the lexicon of cinema includes it: each time, then, a whole interdiscursive chain formed by their technical contiguity was put into play. A good example of such paradigmatic solidarity is an article by Dr. Laupts, "Le fonctionnement cérébral pendant le rêve et le pendant le sommeil hypnotique" ["The Operations of the Brain during Dreams and Hypnotic Sleep"],[28] in which the notions of impression, fixation, blur, sharpness, and tableau may be found next to those of streams of visual or sound images, impressions during sleep, images "following each other and running into each other",[29] "transforming very rapidly".[30] Photographic and cinematographic images with their main characteristics gradually appear in the description of the typical dream of the high-strung patient, whether hypnagogic or clear-headed: sharpness, hallucinogeny, fleeting or intermediate states of consciousness.

24   Charles Féré, *Sensation et mouvement. Études expérimentales de psycho-mécanique* (Paris: Félix Alcan, 1887) 126.

25   On the alternation between irritation and inhibition, see also Jean Soury, rev. of *I Fenomeni di contrasto in psicologia*, by Dr. Sante de Sanctis (Rome, 1895), *Annales médico-psychologiques* 4 (1896): 148.

26   Albert Londe's photographs both challenged and confirmed this, as André Gunthert's research has shown. See André Gunthert, *Albert Londe*, Photo Poche series (Paris: Nathan, 1999); "Entre photographie et cinéma: Albert Londe", in *Le Cinéma et la Science*, ed. Alexis Martinet (Paris: CNRS Éditions, 1994) 62–69; Denis Bernard and André Gunthert, "Albert Londe, l'image multiple", in *La Recherche Photographique* 4 (May 1988): 7–15.

27   Jonathan Crary, *Suspensions of Perception: Attention, Spectacle, and Modern Culture* (Cambridge, Mass.: MIT Press, 1999).

28   Dr. Laupts, *Annales médico-psychologiques* 2 (1895): 354–375.

29   Laupts, *Annales médico-psychologiques* 358.

30   Laupts, *Annales médico-psychologiques* 359, note 1.

Before 1900 direct references to cinema remained hypothetical, notably with regard to the use of the term "stream" ("défilé") and its probable origin in the magic lantern. A few years later, these references had become quite explicit in an article by physiologist and psychologist Henri Piéron on the speed of psychic processes.[31] The phenomenon at stake occurred following poisonings or accidents in which the subject came within a hair's breadth of death and saw the outstanding episodes of his/her life unfold as though in speeded-up motion – an acceleration which the subject interpreted as such in retrospect:

> Why does the acceleration appear to be more important than it actually is? First, because some images are rich and take time to narrate and describe; second, and mainly, because a *cinematographic stream* takes place. Images have clear outlines: they are *cinematographic tableaux* and abruptly succeed one another, without a bridge or a transition between them […] and afterwards, and even at the time, there is a tendency to fill in the gaps, or at least to consider them filled. As a few salient episodes of a life pass through the mind, it appears as though this life in its entirety has unfolded without anything missing, as in a *genuine cinematograph*. And even when the said reconstruction is impossible, given the fact that images have nothing in common, their number will be noted, whereas a single image undergoing distortion, even when it features an equal number of transformations, will always appear to be but a single image. It is the observers themselves who consider it multiple, as they turn their attention to processes of association.[32]

The imagination of the still and the moving image, in conjunction with that of the single and the multiple image (whose distinction seems blurred by the metamorphoses of what is perceived), mingle again in this case. The notion of "cinematographic tableaux" undoubtedly refers to the aesthetics of early cinema, characterized by the primitive mode of representation as defined by Noël Burch: autonomy of the image, gaps in the narrative structure, lack of a logical spatiotemporal articulation between shots.[33] In a regime of representation in which theatricality, monstration, and punctual events predominate over narrativity and vectoriality, the fixity of a tableau appears quite relative. It points to the self-sufficient dimension of each shot – a tableau working like a stage on which the various important phases of the subject's past play out recursively.

What stands out in medical discourse is the recurrent idea that the mentally ill subject turns into a machine, producing and sometimes projecting still and/or moving images. Hysterics and neurasthenics were notably considered as such – doctors then used the expression "hysterigenous machines"[34] – as they ceaselessly translated their inner impressions into representations. The parallel between psychic disorders and the (audio)visual apparatuses of modernity finds an appar-

---

31   Henri Piéron, *Revue philosophique* 28.1–6 (January–June 1903): 89–95.

32   Piéron, *Revue philosophique* 95. My emphasis.

33   Noël Burch, *Life to those Shadows*, trans. Ben Brewster (London: BFI, 1990).

34   See for instance Paul-Émile Lévy, "Traitement psychique de l'hystérie. La rééducation" ["The Psychic Treatment of Hysteria: Therapy"] in *La Presse médicale* 34 (29 Apr. 1903): 333–336; Alexandre Cullerre, "Hypnotisme et suggestion", in *Annales médico-psychologiques* 18 (1903): 253.

ent confirmation in the alarmist discourses directed at cinema from the 1910s on. Indeed, concerns about the damage caused by cinema as a pastime do not seem to have taken hold in the community of social and mental hygienists until the second decade of the 20th century. Film spectators, as the healthy counterparts to neurotics, were deemed particularly susceptible to the fast stream of enlarged, projected images and to the violence and vividness of some motifs or narratives. Accordingly, while experts listed the harmful physiological, psychological, and emotional consequences of film screenings, they backed up their clinical observations according to a conception divided between intense focalization on a "frozen" image and fast-paced attention to a continuous stream of images.

In 1911 an Italian psychiatrist, Giuseppe d'Abundo, mentioned the various possible dangers of cinema for structurally fragile individuals.[35] In his view, such a hallucinogenous machine could destabilize overly emotional and excitable subjects and lead to a confusion between images and reality which could have repercussions in the patient's life during the day or at night. A symbol and product of modernity, cinema thus shaped a psychophysiological posture – during the screening, but also after the event, as the trauma was (re-)lived later – and epitomized the contradictions inscribed in the perceptive system and its various dysfunctions. Using the metaphor of the cinematographic apparatus, the doctor considered that film images were stored in a part of the psychic system, then revived during dreams and other intermediate states (hypnagogic images, fits of hysterics, vigilant hallucinations, etc.). Moving images then appeared in an unpredictable, involuntary, and sudden manner before the eyes of the patient. The doctor also noted that the subject often remembered but a striking detail from the film – a detail which assumed outlandish and gigantic proportions once transposed in the realm of hallucination or reminiscence, while retaining its intensity and repetitiveness. D'Abundo thus described hallucination as an eminently suggestive scenario whose photographic trace remained in the visual cortical area, and which may be easily summoned up in the form of a projection at once "imitative, striking, and exaggerated in appearance". The text is remarkable for its redundancy, as it is engorged, literally as well as metaphorically, with both cinema and photography. It summarizes a number of points broached so far with respect to the paradigms of still and moving images. Both pressing and stupefying, imaginary and more than real, shifting and univocal, indiscernible and incredible, the cinematographic image seems ideally suited for the agitated, forceful, and disconcerting world of psychopathology.

---

35   Giuseppe D'Abundo, "Sopra alcuni particolari effetti delle proiezioni cinematografiche nei nevrotici" ["On a Few Particular Effects of Film Screenings upon Neurotics"] in *Rivista italiana di neuropatologia psichiatria ed elettroterapia* (Oct. 1911), published in *Bianco e Nero* 550–551 (March 2004–Jan. 2005): 61–65. Translator's note: the passage was translated from the French, after the author's initial translation from the Italian.

The dread of the subjective split

The dual paradigm of stasis and flux ran equally through the medical discourse on mental and nervous diseases and the discourse on cinema as a potentially pathogenic agent. Cinema and photography allowed to describe the functional modes of perceptive disorders in detail because both apparatuses were clearly referred to as emblems of modernity in social discourse, intellectual as well as general. In return, discursive formations related to the study of the psychophysiological reception of films largely tapped into the topical pool of specialized medical knowledge, which comprised analyses issuing mostly from psychologists or psychiatrists. Photo-cinematographic apparatuses and psychic systems thus traded their respective models. Such reversible modelization shows an interstitial space at the crossroads of the history of sciences and the history of techniques of representation, in which the principles of a theory of images that was to influence the 20th century as a whole were forged.

Still, the issue of the difference between photography and cinema, and its necessarily restrictive corollary of still and moving images, remains current. My tentative answer would be that, while photography allows to figure the work of a psychic system busy managing an economy of relationships between conscious and unconscious, cinema tends to deal with multisensorial shocks undergone by the psyche under the pressure of new living conditions. The photographic apparatus is rather well-suited in clarifying a play of lights and shadows taking place on the intimate scene of the mind; cinema accords better with a neurotic psychic system, at once hallucinogenic and hypnotic, and at odds with an outside environment notable for its aggressive potential. At any rate, the photographic model was approached relatively neutrally in texts of the period – or was at least considered independently from psychopathological etiologies, which indicates that it was largely accepted as a modern technology. By contrast, the cinematograph and its novelty raised concerns as to mental and social repercussions. More than photography, then, it seems to me that cinema (but also radio and television later) became a point of fixation for a host of anxieties on the susceptibility of the subject to suggestion and manipulation – a fact attested by the extraordinary growth of a literature on the psychology and sociology of crowds as well as on criminal anthropology at the turn of the 20th century.[36]

Film spectators and neurotics as hypnotic subjects were but possible incarnations of such a fear of a subjective split, both uncontrolled and uncontrollable since they were the easy preys of a stream of images and sounds of which they had no real command. While medicine investigated intrapsychic dissociations which shattered subjective certainty (and social relations), the cinematograph put forth, in the form of both a scientific attraction and an entertainment – an experimental lab of sorts which could gauge the ascendancy of what was perceived over the perceiving subject, as well as the effects of a dissolution of the self that threatened

---

36 See for instance the works of Gustave Le Bon, Gabriel Tarde, Sigmund Freud, and Cesare Lombroso.

the principle of reality. Bearing out this hypothesis is the fact that consciousness was often described by medical and paramedical discourse as the mere spectator of a scene taking place out of its reach: with this split, the subject appeared deeply self-alienated.[37] The whole history of the sciences of the psyche at the turn of the 20th century, haunted right through by the specter of the double and multiple personality, raises a series of questions – questions that exceed by far the small circle of specialists, if we consider their later, significant echoes in the cultural, social, and political arenas.[38]

---

37   See for instance Charles Richet, *Essai de psychologie générale* 161.

38   On this issue, see Stefan Andriopoulos, *Possessed: Hypnotic Crimes, Corporate Fiction, and the Invention of Cinema*, trans. Peter Jansen (Chicago: University of Chicago Press, 2008).

4

'A series of fragments': Man Ray's
Le Retour à la raison (1923)

Samantha Lackey

M an Ray showed his first solo film short *Le Retour à la raison at the Théâtre Michel in Paris on July 6, 1923 at the* dada *Soirée du Cœur à Barbe.* According to his account the film was greeted with derision and catcalls from the audience. However, as Man Ray noted in his autobiography (in a moment of candour rare for a dadaist) this reception was due in part to his technical inadequacies with film stock – the reel of film broke at least twice during the showing.[1] The apocryphal story of the film's creation relates how it was made last-minute at the behest of Tristan Tzara who had informed Man Ray that a small film by him had already been included in the programme of the evening. In response Man Ray hastily composed a work consisting of certain pre-filmed images (including a field of daisies, a nude torso moving in front of a window and images of revolving objects: an egg box and a paper spiral) and new footage – a development of his photographic rayograph process whereby objects were placed directly on the celluloid and then exposed to light, effectively producing a negative shape of the object on the film.[2]

Generally, it is true to say that the subsequent reception of the film has stressed its role within the Dada movement and its import as an innovative early work of anti-diegetic, abstract, avant-garde cinema. With the exception of the insightful publication, *Man Ray directeur du mauvais movies*, which presented the film as resisting singular meaning, critics have posited Man Ray's involvement in film as quite simply symptomatic of an attempt to extend photographic or object based experiments, or as a form of film poetry.[3] Rather than dismiss these readings out

---

1   Man Ray, *Self-Portrait* (1963), London, Bloomsbury, 1988, pp. 212–213.

2   Man Ray's description of the film is at odds with the extant version and there is some confusion as to the actual content of the film. Within this essay I will be referring to the version released on video to accompany the seminal exhibition mounted by the Centre Georges Pompidou in 1998, Man Ray: directeur du mauvais movies.

3   See Jean-Michel Bouhours and Patrick de Haas, eds., *Man Ray directeur du mauvais movies*, Paris, Éditions du Centre Pompidou, 1997, Steven Kovács, *From Enchantment to Rage*, New Jersey, Associated University Presses, 1980 and Carl Belz, 'The Film Poetry of Man Ray', in *Man Ray*, exhibition catalogue, Los Angeles, Institute of Contemporary Arts, 1960, pp. 43–52.

of hand I hope, in this essay, to suggest that the film can be more productively contextualised as an element of the nascent conceptualisation of surrealism. Furthermore, I will suggest that the continued preoccupation by the surrealists, most particularly André Breton, with the representation of arrested movement, both in language and image is revealing of the changing approaches and fortunes of the movement and its correlative – automatism.

Surrealism, automatism, medium

Writing in 1924, in the First Manifesto of Surrealism, André Breton famously placed automatism at the heart of surrealist practice in his definition of surrealism as:

> SURREALISM, *n.* Psychic automatism in its pure state, by which one proposes to express -- verbally, by means of the written word, or **in any other manner** -- the actual functioning of thought. Dictated by thought, in the absence of any control exercised by reason, exempt from any aesthetic or moral concern.[4]

This proximity of surrealism to automatism proved notoriously problematic, its practice subject to a barrage of criticism from both within, and without, the movement. This disparagement was largely orientated around the question of authenticity and the impossibility of expressing 'the actual functioning of thought' without some form of authorial intervention. Of course, fifty years later, this problem was recognised as contributing significantly, and positively, towards the disruption of Enlightenment epistemologies in Roland Barthes' recognition of surrealist automatism's contribution towards 'the desacralization of the image of the author ... by entrusting the hand with the task of writing as quickly as possible what the head is unaware of'.[5] Twenty years after this intervention, the post-war reception of automatism into postmodernism was sustained by the publication of a lecture by the art-historian Rosalind Krauss. Entitled, *'A voyage on the north sea.' Art in the Age of the Post-medium Condition*, her account sought to explore the ubiquity of installation art via the historical conditions of its development. Emerging from the North American appropriation of certain aspects of surrealism as prefiguring the dismantling of rationalist assumptions of Western thought, Krauss' revisionist account of the film-related work of Marcel Broodthears critically resuscitated the topic of automatism.

In her description Krauss undertook two particular theoretical routes that intersect with the conceptual matrices of still and moving: firstly she attempted to replace the term medium with that of automatism, and secondly she focused attention on the role of film in the dissolution of medium specificity. Krauss

---

4   André Breton, 'First Manifesto of Surrealism'(1924), in *Manifestoes of Surrealism*, trans. Richard Seaver and Helen R. Lane, Michigan, The University of Michigan Press, 1972, p. 26.

5   Roland Barthes, 'The Death of the Author', in *Image, Music, Text*, trans. Stephen Heath, London, Fontana Press, 1977, p. 144.

acknowledged the motivation behind her thwarted, intentional, omission of the term medium within the body of the essay, as an attempt to sidestep the ideologically loaded, Greenbergian, connotations of the word. Of course, in the use of the word 'automatism' she was also aware, she wrote, of the word's own implications; those of the automatic, mechanical sense of a camera, the connotation of autonomy and 'the Surrealist use of "automatism" as an unconscious reflex'.[6] This emphasis on the importance of automatism as a term still carrying a theoretical currency flags up for the reader some kind of productive, critical, 'automatic', relationship between automatism, surrealism and film that signals a surrealist prescience regarding the role of film in the dissolution of medium specificity.

Indeed, the surrealist Max Morise had, in 1924, embedded these connections (albeit somewhat latently) within surrealist doctrine in the pages of *La Révolution surréaliste*. Within his speculative exploration of the possible paths for visual automatism he identified the essential criteria of the representation of 'the rapid succession of images, the flight of ideas' as 'a fundamental condition of every surrealist manifestation':

> It seems that no painter has yet managed to give an account of a series of images, for we cannot stop with procedures of the primitive painters who represented on differing places of their picture the successive scenes they imagined. The cinema – a perfected cinema which would let us bypass technical formalities – opens a path towards the solution of this problem.[7]

It is significant that Krauss had chosen to think the plurality of contemporary artistic practice firstly back through surrealism, and secondly through a parallel instance of medium disruption in the invention of the portapak, the lightweight inexpensive video camera that opened up the possibility of film work to multiple artists. These artists also participated in the Anthology Film Archives, a regular film screening of European (surrealist), Russian, early avant-garde films, and works by Keaton and Chaplin in New York in the late 60s. In her account, the disruptive influence of these films was primarily assimilated in to the forms of structuralist film-making. However, she also advanced the theory that the work of Broodthaers took on a complementary use of these early films, responding to their very openness. He, she explains, understood,

> 'this medium [of film] in the light of the openness promised by early film, an openness woven into the very mesh of the image, as the flickering irresolution of the illusion of movement produced the experience of sight itself as dilated: a phenomenological mixture of presence and absence, immediacy and distance ... the filmic apparatus presents us with a medium whose specificity is to be found in its

6   Rosalind Krauss, '*A Voyage on the North Sea' Art in the Age of the Post-Medium Condition*, London, Thames & Hudson, 1999, p. 5.

7   Max Morise, 'Enchanted Eyes' (1924), in Mary Ann Caws, ed., *Manifesto: A Century of Isms*, Lincoln and London, University of Nebraska Press, 2001, p. 479.

condition as self-differing. It is aggregative, a matter of interlocking supports and layered conventions.'[8]

An openness, I would argue, that acknowledges the support of the still photo-graph within the moving image. Furthermore, this emphasis on the importance of the openness and interstitial status of the nascent film form speculatively suggested to me that the "machinations" of surrealist visual production could benefit from an interrogative approach to their relationship to other kinds of image-making – a kind of backward-looking reassessment of the surrealist filmic project.

Presence and absence: Early film to surrealist film

Another point for thinking back from surrealist film is offered in Tom Gunning's ground-breaking account of the relationship between avant-garde film and early film in which he suggested that certain strategies of display and spectatorship were common to both.[9] In addition to his innovative thinking regarding film it is also important to note that both his work, and that of Krauss, signal a recent critical turn that invokes early film as significantly related to surrealist practice and to the perceived postmodern claim for the disruption of specificity. It is not the intention, however, of this essay to build a teleological argument. Rather, this initial dependence on secondary sources proposes a speculation that beyond these theoretical claims there lays a ground of valid surrealist interrogation of these issues.

Gunning described the mutual tropes of avant-garde and early film under the term 'cinema of attractions', itself appropriated from Sergei Eisenstein's use of the descriptor 'attraction' in order to describe, initially, a demanding, exhibition-ist form of theatre and then the montage technique of a skilfully edited collision of shots, both of which resulted in the subjection of the audience to 'sensual or psychological impact'.[10] The 'cinema of attractions' was, and continues to be, a form of filmmaking orientated around the display of filmic properties and the solicitation of spectator attention. Common examples of devices used to draw attention to the defining quality of the film, the possibility of demonstrating movement, included the use of camera trickery, slow-motion and fast-forward. Further than that, the early film often took as its subject the moving vehicle, the train arriving at the station, the funfair or travelogues filmed from cars, planes and trains.

8   Krauss, 1999, p. 44.

9   Tom Gunning, 'The Cinema of Attractions. Early Film, Its Spectator and the Avant-Garde' (1986), in Thomas Elsaesser (ed.), *Early Cinema. Space – Frame – Narrative*, London, BFI Publishing, 1999, pp. 56–62. A more detailed account of 'the cinema of attractions' is given by Gunning in 'An Aesthetics of Astonishment: Early Film and the (In)Credulous Spectator' (1989), in Linda Williams (ed.), *Viewing Positions. Ways of Seeing Film*, New Brunswick, Rutgers University Press, 1997, pp. 114–133.

10   Sergei Eisenstein, 'The Montage of Attractions' (1923), in Richard Taylor (ed.), *Sergei Eisenstein, Writings 1922–34*, London, BFI Publishing, 1988, p. 35. As cited by Gunning, 1999, p. 59.

According to Gunning the solicitation of the spectator was achieved through methods which played on a knowing viewer who was already familiar with a wide variety of optical devices and aware of the type of spectacle with which they were to be presented with (he contests for example the myth that the audience for *Arrivée d'un train à La Ciotat* would have been unable to discern between filmic representation and reality). Thus, the early film show often emphasised devices that would highlight the impact of first presentation; a common tactic was to hold the initial image of the film still as if it were a slide projection and supersede it with the moving image. Additionally the film showing was often accompanied with a lecture, delivered alongside and creating a sense of expectation. Here, 'the impact derives from a moment of crisis, prepared for and delayed, then bursting upon the audience'.[11] A further harnessing of the spectator was identified in the model of early film that used as its structure a series of small shocks which direct attention and rouse the audience from a position of distraction and which Gunning described as revolving 'around the act of display and the anticipations that can be heightened by delaying or announcing it (or both) and its inevitable disappearance'.[12] In referring to this Gunning used the phrase, 'Now you see it. Now you don't', in order to characterise this succession of instants that are implicated in the cinema of attractions' temporal construction.

What is interesting in Gunning's account is the way this phrase 'now you see it, now you don't' is reminiscent of those accounts of the psychological investigations that attempted to demonstrate through differing modes of attention (hypnosis, hysteria, automatism) the existence of a stratified consciousness. What I wish to emphasise here is the surrealist recognition of a complex chain of relationships between the proving, experiencing, or accessing of a subconscious and the potential for a visual representation of this in the filmic or photographic register. The prescient surrealist acknowledgement of the impossibility of a single authorial voice and a stable subjectivity intersected with both their awareness of late nineteenth century attempts to account for modern experience, characterised by the fragmentary, the fleeting and the subjection of the self to series of shocks and the Bretonian-directed desire to resolve fractures within privileged moments of everyday experience: the marvellous, the found object, Convulsive Beauty.

Between still and moving image

In the Manifesto of Surrealism, in an attempt to explore the possibilities of visual automatism, Breton related an experience that appeared to exist *between* the states of attention and distraction. He wrote of a moment that was *neither sleep, nor wakefulness* when he perceived a clearly articulated phrase that was something

---

11   Gunning, 1997, p. 121.

12   Tom Gunning, '"Now You See It, Now You Don't": The Temporality of the Cinema of Attractions', *The Velvet Light Trap*, no. 32, Fall 1993, p. 9.

like: 'There is a man cut in two by the window'. This phrase was accompanied by the 'faint visual image of a man walking cut half way up by a window perpendicular to the axis of his body'.[13] Although Breton identified this as an image of a rare sort, this apparent singularity should be read as referring to the particulars of the image, rather than the imaging process itself. Indeed in the late nineteenth century entire investigations had been dedicated to the study of images that appeared at that same interstitial moment that temporarily possesses consciousness.[14] Accounts of this state of *demi-sommeil* related the difficulty of maintaining the image, past an instantaneous snapshot, speaking instead of a succession of such visions, which appear, exist and are then withdrawn. Continually thwarted in attempts to maintain hold of the imagery of the unconscious, the spectator of night visions and the spectators of early film are caught in the same position. An account of these dream phantasms from 1886 (from a book held in Breton's library) describes this exact process:

> For many years I have been accustomed to seeing multitudes of faces as I lie awake in bed, generally before falling asleep at night, after waking up in the morning or if I should wake in the middle of the night. They seem to come out of the darkness as a mist, and rapidly develop into sharp delineation, assuming roundness, vividness and living reality. Then they fade off only to give place to others, which succeed with surprising rapidity and in enormous multitudes.[15]

As soon as a resolution of the image was achieved, it disappeared to be replaced with another; but one that was still conceived within a proto-cinematic framework. While many claims have been made for the effects of new technologies on issues of subjectivity and perception it is clear, at the very least, that the arrival of the cinema coincided with attempts to elucidate the existence of layers of consciousness and writers often fell on cinematic-type analogies to explain them – the role of the screen in both the projection of film and the description of the subconscious providing one such example.

What I would like to propose is that *Le Retour à la raison* operates in a manner resonant with these descriptions of flickering images, of stasis and movement, attention and distraction, vacillating between internal image and external manifestation. Approximately half of the film is taken up by the curious movement of rayographs; these particular images are made from the indexical traces of salt and pepper, drawing pins, coiled springs and nails, and the proliferation of the shapes

13 André Breton, 1924, p. 22.

14 In particular I am thinking of Eugène B.Leroy's *Les Visions du Demi-Soleil*, Auguste Liébault, *Du sommeil et des états analogues considérés au point de vue de l'action du moral sur le physique*, Paris, V. Masson, 1866 and Auguste Liébeault, *Le sommeil provoqué et les états analogues*, Paris, Doin, 1889.

15 Gurney, Myers and Podmore, *Phantasms of the Living. Vol. 1*, London, Tribner and Co., 1886, p. 473. The legitimacy of placing this quote in the same discursive field as the discussion of the *demi-sommeil* state is somewhat confirmed by the presence of the French translation of the work, *Les Hallucinations télépathiques*, Paris, Félix Alcan, 1891, in Breton's library. See *André Breton, 42, Rue Fontaine*, Paris, Calmels Cohen Book Catalogue, 2003, n.p.

left by the multiple objects on the film stock give the appearance of dancing, ghostly objects which disrupt conventional vision and metamorphose in the blink of an eye from one object to another. The other shots in the film are cut in quickly and without diegetic logic. They include: shots of a fairground; a calligraphic poem; a field of daisies; an egg box revolving on a string; a work of art, *Dancer/Danger*, with smoke blowing across it and conclude with a truncated revolving female torso, dappled by the shadows cast by a window blind.

Each time one of the micro-sets of images threatens to assert a sense of their own sensibility, of pattern, identification and aesthetic appeal they change to the next. This mode of cinematic temporality operates as a whole to position the work as a short film of attractions, a series of small jolts, described by Man Ray himself as, 'a series of fragments ... with a certain optical sequence that makes up a whole that still remains a fragment'.[16] – 'now you see it, now you don't'.

From still to moving

Yet, *Le Retour à la raison*'s relationship to the visual field and the production of the image is more complex than a fragmentary aesthetics of appearance and disappearance and this complexity, I think, arises out of the creative methodology of the rayographic section of the film which explicitly produces the illusion of movement from the still image. If, as it is claimed by Man Ray, the filmstrip was stretched out on the floor, the drawing pins, salt, pepper and coiled springs placed on top of it and then exposed to light – then what we see is not the illusion of movement caused by the running together of 24 frames per second, but rather a series of discontinuous still images of the same objects which, when placed in immediate proximity, produce fragments of film which operate to disorientate because their discontinuous nature as still images suggests the impossibility of experiencing the images as a direct representation of filmed reality and thus disrupt any theory of sustained cinematic identification or stable subjectivity.

This ability of the cinema as a whole to replicate, or produce particular states of mind in the spectator was recognised by many early theorists, including the young poet Louis Aragon. His early film criticism provides a useful example of this intersection of the psychological and the film. In 1918 he wrote the essay, 'Du Décor', published in the specialist magazine *Le Film*, as a celebration of the new medium which combined the germs of a surrealist theory of film with a clear influence from contemporary filmic discourse. His thesis found its rationale in the absolutely contemporary nature of the medium and its ability to stand in for and depict 'the modern'. Intrinsic to this argument was the transformative power of the cinema:

> Poets without being artists, children sometimes fix their attention on an object to the point where their concentration makes it grow larger, grow so much that it

16   Man Ray quoted in Frank Stauffacher , ed., *Art in Cinema*, New York, Arno Press, 1968, p. 25.

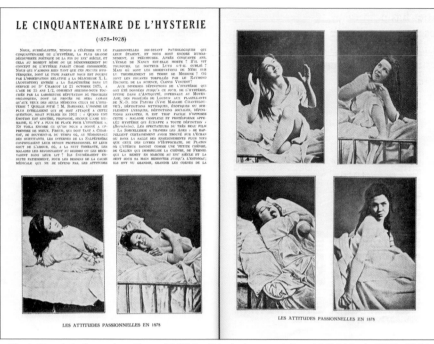

Fig. 1. *"Les Attitudes passionnelles en 1878"*, La Révolution surréaliste *11 (15 March 1928): 20-21.*

completely occupies their visual field, assumes a metaphysical aspect and loses all relation to its purpose ... Likewise on screen objects that were a few moments ago sticks of furniture or books of cloakroom tickets are transformed to the point where they take on menacing or enigmatic meanings. The theatre is powerless where such emotive concentration is concerned.

To endow with poetic value that which does not yet truly possess it, to wilfully restrict the field of vision so as to intensify expression: these are the properties that help make the cinematic décor the adequate setting of modern beauty.[17]

This description of the powers of cinema linked together the modern, the visual field and film's ability to focus the concentration of the spectator upon an object. The objects described by Aragon were detached from their usual patterns of signification and reinstated as part of those filmic processes which direct and control, not only the visual, but also the psychological.

How then do we position *Le Retour à la raison*, produced as it was in 1923, between Aragon's primary investigations into film and Breton's culmination of his early theory and ambition in the pages of the *First Manifesto of Surrealism*?[18] As Dawn

17   Louis Aragon, 'On Décor'(1918), in Richard Abel, *French Film Theory and Criticism, 1907–1939, Vol I*, Princeton, Princeton University Press, p. 166.

18   For a fascinating account of Man Ray's relationship to surrealism and to film and the object that touches

Ades has pointed out the period between 1919 and 1924 remains largely under-researched; tellingly titled the *mouvement flou* by Aragon, it lacked intellectual cohesion and defined aims.[19] One thing is certain, however; those artists and writers involved were attempting to come to grips with the possibilities of the external expression of internal models.[20] In turning to the literature of dynamic psychiatry and early psychology in the work of F.W.H. Myers, Théodore Flournoy, Pierre Janet, Hippolyte Taine and William James, the members of the group were determined to key into the changing conceptions of the subliminal. Following the success of Breton and Philippe Soupault's experiments with automatic writing in *Les Champs magnétiques* (initially published in the pages of the review *Littérature* in 1919) the group also experimented with hypnotic trance and the potential for different forms of automatist production. The resemblance between the subliminal space of the dream and the cinema screen and the latter's attendant possibilities for moving between the analogous states of attention and distraction are well known from Breton's later description of his and Jacques Vaché's visits to the cinema where the two men dropped in to a film, staying only until bored at which point they would rush off to another.[21] Yet, this early 'surrealist' engagement with film exceeded this characterisation through an engagement with types of popular filmmaking, the writing of film scenarios and, most importantly as a conceptual model for describing the works being produced in this period of the early twenties. Take, for example, Breton's introduction to Max Ernst's first exhibition in Paris in 1921. In his effusive appreciation of the works Breton repeatedly invoked the filmic and did so within the context of the contemporaneous scientific dissolution of stable conceptions of space and time. The cinema was, it seems, inextricably linked to the relation of representation to movement; 'Today', he wrote, 'thanks to the cinema, we know how to make a locomotive *arrive* on canvas', thus intimating the importance of the relationship between movement and stasis. Ernst, through his work, Breton suggested, provided a new encounter with the 'innermost depths of our internal life', in his resolve to replace still life with the projection of 'the most captivating film in the world'.[22]

Although there is, to my knowledge, no evidence to suggest that Man Ray was directly involved in the experiments with automatism or the *époque des sommeils*

on many of the same issues as this essay see Ramona Fotiade, 'From Ready-made to Moving Image: The Visual Poetics of Surrealist Cinema', in Graeme Harper and Rob Stone, eds. *The Unsilvered Screen: Surrealism on Film*, London, Wallflower Press, 2007, pp. 9–22.

19 Dawn Adés, 'Between Dada and Surrealism: Painting in the *Mouvement flou*', in Terry Ann R.Neff, ed., *In the Mind's Eye: Dada and Surrealism*, exhibition catalogue, New York, Abbeville Press, 1985, p. 24

20 Adés identifies the main participants in this period of the *mouvement flou* as: Louis Aragon, Jacques Baron, André Breton, René Crevel, Robert Desnos, Paul Eluard, Max Ernst, Max Morise, Benjamin Péret and Roger Vitrac.

21 André Breton, 'As in a wood' (1951), in Paul Hammond, ed. *The Shadow & Its Shadow: Surrealist Writings on the Cinema*, San Francisco, City Lights Books, 2000, p. 73.

22 André Breton, 'Max Ernst' (1921), in André Breton, *The Lost steps*, trans. Mark Polizzotti, Lincoln & London, The University of Nebraska Press, 1996, p. 61.

his proximity to the proto-surrealist group is attested to through the repeated inclusion of his photographs within the pages of *Littérature* and Breton's description of his rayographs within the pages of his 1924 anthology, *The Lost Steps*. As such it is possible to attribute to his works a degree of awareness regarding the discourses surrounding automatism and the role that his own works might play. Although connections must be made tentatively, Man Ray's own production repeatedly played into the paradox of the still visual manifestation of the automatist train of thought. However, there is a detectable shift in the works which were integrated into the official elaboration of Surrealism proper. *Le Retour à la raison*, the collages of Max Ernst and, indeed, Max Morise's early description of the problematic of automatism, as predicated unsuccessfully on 'a succession of images' all demonstrated the still image (or object) projected into movement. In fact, Man Ray's subsequent film, *Emak Bakia* (1926), through the inclusion of a chronophotographic-type figure jumping into the air explicitly pointed to the proto-cinematic technologies from which this motif derives. Alternatively a later engagement with images that operate between still and moving operated conversely to demonstrate the moving image, stilled.

From moving to still

Examples of this are to be found in two of the most celebrated surrealist texts: André Breton's *Nadja* and Breton and Aragon's commemorative article 'Le Cinquantenaire de l'hystérie'.[23] Published in 1928, both were illustrated with excerpts from a series of photographic images. Among the various illustrations of *Nadja* rests Man Ray's photographic strip of the poet and critic Robert Desnos awaking from a somnambulist experiment into automatism within which he accessed variously the personalities of Marcel Duchamp, Breton and/or the deeper reaches of his own consciousness. The appropriated 'hysterical' photographs published on the pages of *La Révolution surréaliste* were also a series, this time of the *attitudes passionnelles*: the paradigmatic visual exemplar of hysteria taken under the direction of Charcot at the Salpêtrière (Fig. 1). Although the importance of hysteria as both a psychoanalytic and an artistic model exceeds the limitations of this essay and has been recently examined in detail by a number of eminent scholars, its appropriation by the surrealists is illuminating of the subject in hand; as Mattais Winzen has succinctly pointed out, 'Characteristic of the clinical picture of hysterical fits, as it was outlined more than a century ago, is the heavy contrast between the urge to move and factual paralysis'.[24] Thus, both these series of images show the capture of a still image, removed from movement, not for the purposes of reconstitution of that movement but, as I would argue,

---

23   André Breton, *Nadja*, Paris, Gallimard, 1928. Louis Aragon and André Breton, 'Le Cinquantenaire de l'hystérie', in *La Révolution surréaliste*, no. 11, 15 March, 1928, pp. 20–22.

24   Mattaias Winzen, 'Hystericized Spaces', in *Die verletzte Diva: Hysterie, Körper, Technik in der Kunst des 20. Jahrhunderts*, p. 155.

visible evidence of a fractured identity and subjectivity, whether in the hysterical expression of repressed trauma normally hidden under the surface, or the assertion that Desnos, while ostensibly in repose, is 'performing miracles with his eyes closed'.[25] The idea that the photograph, or the point of motion stilled, can provide access to a materialisation of the strata of states of consciousness opens up the suggestion of a sustained and now more nuanced surrealist analogy between the mechanics of representational technologies: the photograph and the film – and the operations of the mind.

André Breton famously concluded his novel *Nadja* with the declaration that 'beauty will be CONVULSIVE or not at all'.[26] This statement was arrived at through one of the Hegelian dialectical oppositions so familiar from his writing, whereby he attempted to express 'a certain attitude ... with regard to beauty' and which is 'neither dynamic nor static'. Continuing in this vein he wrote:

> Beauty is like a train that ceaselessly roars out of the Gare de Lyon and which I know will never leave, which has not left. It consists of jolts and shocks, many of which do not have much importance, but which we know are destined to produce one Shock which does.[27]

Here are the familiar touchstones of my argument: the train at the station, the repetition of movement stalled, the experience of shock and the possibility of one particular shock, moment, or stillness to access, perhaps, 'the actual functioning of thought.'

It is of little surprise that the two images that Breton subsequently chose to illustrate this 'convulsive beauty' were also tied into these concepts. Writing again on the subject of the convulsive in his novel of 1937, *L'Amour Fou*, he lamented the impossibility of 'not having been able to furnish, along with this text, the photograph of a speeding locomotive abandoned for years to the delirium of a virgin forest'– such an image was published without attribution in *Minotaure* in 1937.[28] This, he suggested, would have perfectly supplied an illustration for 'convulsive beauty' which he describes as losing:

> any meaning in my eyes were it to be conceived in motion and not at the exact expiration of this motion. There can be no beauty at all, as far as I am concerned – convulsive beauty – except at the cost of affirming the reciprocal relations linking the object seen in its motion and its repose.[29]

This form of automatism, this point of access to a particular moment, was exemplified for Breton in another of Man Ray's photographs, published in

25 André Breton, 'The Modern Evolution', in *The Lost Steps*, trans. Mark Polizzotti, Lincoln and London: University of Nebraska Press, 1996, p. 125.

26 André Breton, *Nadja* (1928), trans. Richard Howard, London, Penguin Books, 1999, p. 160.

27 Breton, 1928, pp. 159–160.

28 André Breton, *Mad Love*, (1937), trans. Mary Ann Caws, Lincoln and London, University of Nebraska Press, 1987, p.10. The photograph was published in *Minotaure*, vol. 10, Winter 1937, p. 34.

29 Breton, 1937, p. 10.

L'Amour Fou and titled *Fixed Explosive*. This 'convulsive' photograph of a fla-
menco dancer, her hands in the air, recalls the hysterical poses of Charcot's
subjects and points to a body caught in the photographic technology of representation.

In this I must acknowledge a debt, again, to Rosalind Krauss who cogently
claimed photography to be at the heart of surrealist practice through its engagement with the fixed-explosive; photography's integral ability to arrest nature.[30]
But this does not seem to adequately account for the role of film in relation to
the surrealist movement (as she came to acknowledge in her aside regarding
automatism that formed the basis of introduction to this essay). The fortunes of
automatism waned in the late 1920s and early 30s in favour of the theses of
Convulsive Beauty and Objective Chance. With the new insistence on a surrealist
interaction with everyday experience the self-referential explorations of automatism manifested in the trance, the séance and Man Ray's film were no longer
appropriate. Instead a new tension between still and moving was inaugurated.
This change is signalled in the works chosen by Breton to represent his new
conceptual paradigms for surrealism. It does not, however, invalidate the charge
that all the interchangeable operations between stasis and motion within surrealist production drew attention to an awareness of the impossibility of representing a stable, unified subjectivity in the face of the experiences wrought by
modernity – the knowledge of a stratified consciousness – and were exemplified
through a radical engagement with new technologies of representation: the
photograph and the film.

30   Rosalind Krauss, 'The Photographic Conditions of Surrealism', *October*, vol. 19, Winter, 1981, pp. 3-34.
     Hal Foster's psychoanalytical reading of Convulsive Beauty has also been of great influence; Hal Foster,
     Compulsive Beauty, Cambridge, MIT Press, 1993.

Section II
Crossings Between Media

Introduction:
Between the Photograph and the Film Frame

Olivier Lugon

With the advent of cinema, the moving image – whose existence, under very different forms, already spanned several centuries at that point – became identified with a dominant model for the next hundred years: the simulation of a continuous movement whose implementation itself relied on a series of invariable technical principles (the unidirectional linear run, standardized speed, and the regular succession of contiguous units). Still, before the cinematograph, animation had by no means been limited to this illusionistic mechanics of fluid movement: it had at its disposal looped repetition, sudden apparition and disappearance, manual modulation of speeds and directions. The point with many optical toys was thus to marvel not so much at the animation of a motif as at that of images themselves, and attention focused as much on operating these toys as on looking at some representation of movement. Film undoubtedly led to a growing uniformity in these practices, depriving the spectators of any control over the animation of images, which took place in their back and soon retreated to the separate space of the booth, to some degree without their awareness. The constitutive units in the production of the illusion disappeared as such in the very emergence of the spectacle (it is surprising in that regard that the strip of film frames, by definition the invisible object of the cinematographic spectacle, eventually became its dominant graphic symbol). The run could no longer admit of variations in direction or speed, or of modulations in the gaps between images.

The Multiple Forms of Film

Yet the development of the flexible and translucent celluloid strip in the 1880s was not in itself the vehicle for this homogenization. At the moment of its inception, its main contribution to the field of photography had to do with the massive increase in the sensitive surface available for recording. The gain later translated in many different ways and brought about radically different modes of recording and representing time. First, as exploited by George Eastman, film contributed to the expansion of amateur practice and souvenir photos: the accumulation of autonomous moments, isolated from the continuity of lived experience and celebrated in their very exceptionality, summed up life through a set of salient points not contiguous in time. Almost simultaneously, Jean Damoizeau used it to create panoramic 360° photography, founded on the circular scanning of space. In this case, even though the image assumed the appearance of single snapshots, it was actually woven with duration as time had been registered from one end of the negative to the other in the course of the rotation of the camera. The horizontal unfolding of the negative thus bears the passage of time, but a time impressed on the film without the least skip, the least jerk, the least phase, in a faultless continuity that makes it imperceptible to the eye. Finally, the cinematograph, a third way to exploit the film strip as a recording surface, was to cross the first two models: a succession of distinct moments, each of which making up a unit on the film strip, close enough nevertheless to be recorded, then reproduced in a perfect spatiotemporal continuity.

The film strip alone was thus able to bring together the passing of time and the mechanical run in multiple ways and to articulate very diverse relations between instant and duration. Besides, these different uses did not consolidate into partitioned fields of activity. They mixed within the practice of many cameramen, and their encounter could occasionally give rise to new hybrid forms, intermediate media themselves very diverse. The present chapter is devoted to these crossings.

That photography and film never ceased to be found together in practice is obvious. At first, no user of the cinematograph was not also a photographer, and in the first years of the medium, the same cameraman could be sent on a campaign to shoot still images as well as filmed sequences. Even as the two domains grew increasingly autonomous, many careers kept straddling them, including within a Modernism concerned with the specificity of media. From Paul Strand to László Moholy-Nagy, from Helmar Lerski to Henri Cartier-Bresson, from Robert Frank to William Klein, many great names in modern photography did in fact oscillate between still and moving images,[1] just as many filmmakers, from Chris Marker to Abbas Kiarostami to Agnès Varda and Johan van der Keuken developed a parallel photographic work. In the past few decades, these passages have become general with the spread of postmodern discourses, the growth of electronic media, and the increasing openness of contemporary art to moving images. Studying these two areas separately is therefore no longer an option, and Clément Chéroux advocates such a hybrid history through his example of Georges Méliès.

---

1   On the subject, see Jan-Christopher Horak, *Making Images Move. Photographers and Avant-Garde Cinema* (Washington, London: Smithsonian Institution Press, 1997).

Indeed, Chéroux shows how Méliès, like other pioneers of the new cinematograph, could only have been affected by his amateur practice of photography and particularly by the success in amateur circles at the turn of the century of "photographic recreations", a whole range of amusing tricks, playful distortions, and various manipulations of the medium. Many of these played with superimposition and consisted in making several shots with the same plate, thereby juxtaposing disconnected moments in a kind of immobilized animation: two characters posing separately are reunited in the same image, another enters a conversation with himself, etc. According to Chéroux, many of Méliès's cinematographic tricks (from the simulation of specters to beheadings) originated less in the scenic forms of conjuring, that is, in the fluidity of stage arts, than in such complex play with still images. Within this framework, the various elements of the Mélièsian fantastic – doubles, substitutions, and disappearances of all kinds – are founded on the perpetuation, in the new art of the simulation of continuous movement, of effects specific to the photographic image, to the temporal disjunctions or clashes linked to the capture of separate moments.

Even after the advent of cinema, other forms of animation or coordination of separate instants were thus able to live on beyond, or even within the illusion of continuity. Similarly, Kim Timby and Valérie Vignaux point out the existence of "para-cinematographic" media forgotten today and which, while seeking to exploit the success of cinema, somewhat deconstructed it and emphasized those of its aspects related to jerks, skips, and intervals. Far from considering these as pale imitations, debased or poorer versions of "genuine cinema", the two authors mention how the force of attraction of these media may have lain in the fact that they *were not* cinema, precisely, and reintroduced still images, pulsation, and modulation at the heart of the continuous run of film, drawing on the richness of the intermediary zone between stillness and movement.

Kim Timby unearths a singular form of photography famous in the 1910s and 1920s, the line-screen animated portrait. In the tradition of the lamellated or notched images of the seventeenth and eighteenth centuries, it consisted in interlacing thin strips from three images into a single sheet of paper. The person handling it could make each of them appear in turn in the frame that held the line-screen. By contrast to cinema, animation did not depend on the linear run of a strip of film but relied instead on the alternation between a limited number of states in the form of a still image – a photograph that could ceaselessly change while remaining still. As with many "pre-cinematographic" optical toys, spectators were responsible for operating this little paper machinery through the action of their thumb, and thus for enjoying the ever-renewed resumptions and halts of movement. Two very different definitions of moving images emerge from the corpus of portraits analysed by Kim Timby. In some cases, the represented character does appear to begin a minimal gesture repeated ad infinitum: the motif seems to move. Yet in other instances, alternation involves heterogeneous portraits such as those of the leaders of the Triple Alliance, which for obvious reasons cannot produce any natural succession. The image is still moving for all that, but it is the apparatus rather than the motif that seems to assume the movement. It is *between* the images that things move, and the entertainment of beholders comes from this always slightly shaky "in-between" more than from the represented movement per se.

With the Pathéorama still film, Valérie Vignaux demonstrates that the film strip itself did not have as its sole function the illusion of a continuous movement. As we have seen, celluloid film was not even specially developed to that end. It was primarily a storage surface, whose forward movement the cinematograph subjected to a radical acceleration. This resulted in an archival paradox, the imperceptibility as such of stored images. Nevertheless, the conception of film as an addition of autonomous images lived on: film continued to appear as an improvement over photography, multiplying its descriptive power through the profusion of images accumulated in the course of shots, and later through their enlargement at the time of projection. This quantitative dimension played a major role in the early considerations on the documentary function of the film strip and led to the invention of a "cinema" of sheer storage, the microfilm. The description given by two of its promoters in 1907 underscores the power of multiplication inherent to film:

> A 165-foot roll of film may now be stored in a small tin can 6 inches in diameter and 1 inch deep. 5,000 views are reproduced on the roll, each of which may be projected on a screen of up to 170 sq. feet. The little can may thus hold in the tiniest volume the material needed to project, endlessly and repeatedly, 860,000 sq. ft of photographic documents![2]

Each and every one of the thousands of film frames may thus be seen as a singular document to study separately. In the shift to the film strip, the photographic medium was in the end submitting as much to the modern logic of quantitative optimization as to the concomitant demand for speed.

Still many other films were shot without looking to produce the least movement, among them Oskar Messter's extraordinary serial images (*Messter-Reihenbilder*) during the First World War (Fig. 1).[3] These "films" of aerial observation meant only for paper prints constituted a genuine landscape chronophotography. At stake was not the decomposition of movement, but an improved form of cartography which made it possible to cover with increased effectiveness large portions of territory. The objective was to scan continuously and automatically swaths of land several miles in length, through long series of shots taken in rapid-fire

2   Robert Goldschmidt and Paul Otlet, "Sur une forme nouvelle du livre. Le livre Microphotographique" ["On a new form of the book. The photomicrographic book"], *Bulletin de l'Institut international de Bibliographie* 12:1-3 (1907): 69.

3   On the subject, see Wolfgang Mühl-Benninghaus, "Messters Beitrag zum Ersten Weltkrieg", and Tiziana Carrozza, "The Eye Over the Hill: Aerial Photography Up to the First World War", *KINtop 3* (Basel, Frankfurt, 1994): 103–115 and 117–128, respectively; and Martin Loiperdinger, *Oskar Messter, Filmpionier der Kaiserzeit*, KINtop Schriften 2 (Basel, Frankfurt: Stroemfeld/Roter Stern, 1994).

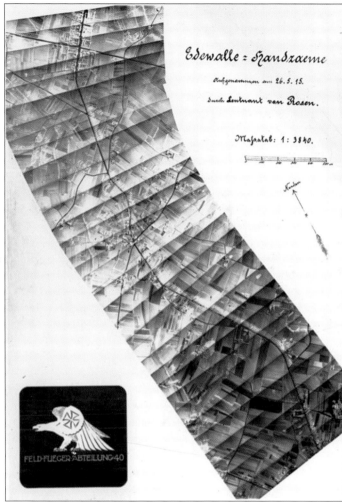

*Fig. 1. Oskar Messter's serial images (*Messter-Reihenbilder)* in the Edewalle-Handzaeme area, taken by lieutenant von Rosen, 1915 (German Federal Archives).*

succession and at such a speed that no gap would appear between shots. The resulting views even had to overlap enough that, once printed on paper and examined with a stereoscope, their optical superimposition would produce a three-dimensional effect – turning chronophotography into a modality of stereoscopy. The pace was thus not determined by the twenty four images per second necessary for the illusion of movement, but by the need to set the interval between shots, and therefore the speed of both the plane and the camera, on the observer's interocular distance. To put it plainly, this was a pace "synchronized" with the body of the beholder and whose adjustment had to provide a sense of volume, rather than movement.

Many other apparatuses produced film in order to exploit primarily the film frame. In the 1920s, some of the professional photographers practicing "surprise

photography" with passers-by used film to capture people on the run and then
tried to sell them the print of a short sequence of their passage, in an attempt to
create a hypothetical market for printed film frames.[4] The distinction between
photograph and film frame could at times be so thin that, decades before
dual-mode digital cameras, some manufacturers tried to market cameras capable
to produce either one. That was the case of the Autocinephot (1919) or the Debrie
Sept (1923), which made it possible to use the same 35-mm film on different
modes: film, photography, or an intermediate setting, a rapid-fire succession of
still images.

In the same period Charles Pathé tried to exploit just this intermediate zone
between photography and film frame with his "Pathéorama still film", whose
history Valérie Vignaux recounts. As the name indicates, the film was not used
to simulate movement, but to serve as a medium for a sequence of still images
joined on the same film according to a narrative thread. It was a modernized
version of the magic lantern performance, as it were – with a cinematic dimension, since its very medium carried the linear continuity of the narrative and that
its subject was often a cinematographic work. Indeed, many of these films aimed
to summarize a whole film, to provide "a summary of sorts" in a few dozen images.
A set of random film frames sampled from the continuous flow of images on the
film, quite often salvaged from scraps left over by the production, were thus raised
to the rank of unlikely pregnant moments, an impossible status they gained with
the support of accompanying oral commentaries and intertitles. However, the
film strip could also comprise a selection of photographic views transferred on
film, on the model of the collection. Indeed, Valérie Vignaux points out the
importance of the Pathéorama in the shift from the lantern's glass plate to the
slide on film, whose precursor would be the "still film". If we follow this
genealogy, the lighter 24x36 mm slide and the art of the slideshow, very lively in
the second half of the 20th century (see section 5), may be considered as deriving
from cinema as much as from the lantern show.

Projections

As appears here, the film strip – a medium shared by photography and cinema
for most of the 20th century – operated as a privileged agent in exchanges between
the two media (see also Michel Frizot's contribution in chapter 3). The same goes
on the side of projection through light. What brought the study of photography
and the study of cinema so far apart is perhaps not so much the opposition
between stillness and movement as one of its material foundations, the caesura
between paper image and light image. From the moment the history of photography ceases to be reduced to the history of prints, and the vast field of projected
photography is taken into account, boundaries become more permeable and the

---

4   See *Street & Studio. An Urban History of Photography*, ed. Ute Eskildsen, with Florian Ebner and Bettina
     Kaufmann (London: Tate Publishing, 2008) 32.

very stillness of the photographic image less absolute. Indeed, any image could be said to be moving as soon as it is projected, since it can appear or disappear in front of the viewer. It then ceases to belong to the permanence of the object-image to exist as a duration, to become active and living in a way, to assume the force of an event. Most importantly, from that point on such an image carries in itself the potentiality of an unfolding, an evolution, a metamorphosis. An intermediate dimension between space and time, free from a still medium, fluctuating, light introduces temporality and "animation" at the center of the still image.

The richness of the non-cinematographic moving projection has been abundantly emphasized in recent studies on the magic lantern and "pre-cinema". What characterizes most of these histories, however, is their adoption of 1895 as a horizon, and often as a limit, as though the multiple forms of projection found their outcome, their raison d'être in the cinema and disappeared in it. Nothing could be farther from the truth. The projection of still images was probably never as present and rich as during the 20th century, in particular in the years that immediately followed the advent of the new medium, then in the 1960s – the hour of glory of the slideshow, not to mention its electronic rebirth at the turn of the 21st century. Not only did the lantern projection live on after the birth of cinema, it also kept crossing its path as part of mixed programmes in exhibitions, fairs, conferences – and in teaching, as Christel Taillibert underlines in her examination of interwar debates on educational methods.

Indeed, due to the reluctance of the teaching profession towards the cinematographic spectacle, the idea of a combined use of still and moving images took on importance during the period. As Christel Taillibert explains, the mix assumed a number of forms: the succession within the same lesson of projected plates and films, the transfer of some film frames on a print medium, but also such proposals as freezing the frame in the course of the screening or studying the films frame by frame – all of them methods difficult to implement with film, but which ended up prevailing with the expansion of video, DVDs, and Power-Point presentations. What was at stake in all cases was – in the name of pedagogy and a proper assimilation of knowledge – to reintroduce stillness, reflexive pauses, and concentration within the elusive continuity of film, and at the same time to return the teacher to an active position in front of the uncontrollable run of the cinematographic machine. In the end, Taillibert explains, the distribution of still images paradoxically benefited from the efforts to promote cinema in schools more than cinema itself.

1

The Great Trade of Tricks: On Some Relations Between Conjuring Tricks, Photography, and Cinematography

Clément Chéroux

In the first years of the cinematograph, the technical processes used to create an illusion, reconstruct imaginary scenes, invent chimeras, transport the spectator in unlikely places – in short, to fool the audience – were referred to under the generic term of "tricks". The word belongs to the vocabulary of theater. "In theater, the word "trick" refers to any arrangement or mechanism used to move sets and execute changes visually, and to any means used to make an object appear or disappear. The trick is a form of material realization of illusion", Max de Nansouty explained in 1909 in a book titled *Les Trucs du théâtre, du cirque et de la foire* ["Tricks in the Theater, the Circus, and the Fair"].[1]

Whether in "*trick* views" or "*trick* films", the repeated use of the word in early discourses on cinema immediately situates the invention within the tradition of stage arts, indicating more precisely its relation to a category of spectacles where illusion prevails, conjuring tricks. In his *Lexique français du cinéma des origines à 1930*, Jean Giraud thus wrote: "Trick: masculine noun, theater, conjuring", soon adding, "at first the word essentially applied to magic tricks and conjuring tricks".[2] In a conference published in the early 1910s under the title "Trucs et illusions, applications de l'optique et de la mécanique au cinématographe", E. Kress also noted that "the cinematograph has simply followed the path opened up by conjuring".[3]

The relationship between film tricks and white magic lasted long after the early 20th century. In most of the texts consulted in the preparation of this historiog-

---

1   Max de Nansouty, *Les Trucs du théâtre, du cirque et de la foire* (Paris: A. Colin, 1909) 37.

2   Jean Giraud, *Le Lexique français du cinéma des origines à 1930* (Paris: CNRS, 1958) 202.

3   E. Kress, "Trucs et illusions, applications de l'optique et de la mécanique au cinématographe", *Conférences sur la cinématographie*, vol. 1 (Paris: Comptoir d'édition de *Cinéma-Revue*, undated) [1912], republished in "Pour une histoire des trucages", ed. Thierry Lefebvre, *1895, revue de l'association française de recherche sur l'histoire du cinéma* 27 (September 1999): 12.

raphic essay – technical articles, testimonies from professionals, history books, or even more theoretical essays – the cinematographic trick is systematically considered, if not conceived, in its relation to conjuring. The world of conjuring, whether it involved cards, objects, bunnies pulled out of hats, or magic wands, seems to have been one of the main topoi in the historians' reading of tricks in early cinema. That many film pioneers – Walter R. Booth in England, Leopoldo Fregoli in Italy, and of course Georges Méliès in France – also performed as conjurers undoubtedly made the association easier.

Among the first cameramen who were also magicians, Méliès occupies a privileged place. The scope of the work, the number of preserved films and documents make his a particularly favorable case in studying the correlation between conjuring tricks and film tricks. Méliès himself did acknowledge on several occasions the importance of the ties between his trick films and his activity as a director of the Théâtre Robert-Houdin, one of the Meccas of magic in Paris. In a letter published after his death in *L'Escamoteur*, a journal dedicated to conjuring, he explained: "My [film] career is so closely connected to my career at the Théâtre Robert-Houdin that it would be vain to try and separate them. For it is, all in all, my familiarity with tricks, my passionate love for the fantastic which determined my calling as 'magician of the screen', as I am called."[4]

This assertion of an affinity between magic and cinema, which recurs over and over in Méliès's statements, also played a decisive role in his critical reception. The majority of his exegetes analysed his filmic prowess through the sole prism of his knowledge as a conjurer. In 1945, in the first monograph devoted to Méliès, Maurice Bessy and Lo Duca pointed out that Méliès had grown a passion for magic at London's Egyptian Hall in 1884. After training himself, he gave a few performances before acquiring the Théâtre Robert-Houdin in 1888. There he developed and performed his most remarkable tricks: "Cagliostro's Mirror", "The Polish Swing", "The Persian Stroubaika", "The Recalcitrant Beheaded Man" and a few others. "From the beginnings of the cinematograph", Bessy and Lo Duca explained, "the new invention was featured in the evening shows at the Théâtre Robert-Houdin; but since Méliès always had to put his personal touch on everything he became involved in, he then came up with a type of special effects utterly different from what existed then. [...] Georges Méliès the cinegraphist borrowed from Georges Méliès the conjurer".[5]

In the various books they devoted to Méliès, film historians Georges Sadoul and Jacques Deslandes both wrote at length on the tenuous link between the magic tricks he created for his theater on the boulevard des Italiens and some of his trick films.[6] The following generation of historians confirmed this affinity. In a

4   Georges Méliès, excerpt from a letter published in *L'Escamoteur* 8 (Jan. 1948), reproduced in Jacques Deslandes, *Le Boulevard du cinéma à l'époque de Georges Méliès* (Paris: Les éditions du Cerf, 1963) 30–31.

5   Maurice Bessy, Lo Duca, *Georges Méliès, mage* ["Georges Méliès, Magus"] (Paris: Jean-Jacques Pauvert, 1961) 25.

1997 article, Italian Antonio Costa stated for instance that "the most typical aspect of Méliès's cinema came out of a cinematographic reproduction of tricks performed at the Théâtre Robert-Houdin".[7] As to Jacques Malthête, the film-maker's great-grandson who did much to advance Méliès studies, he wrote: "Méliès, who was first and foremost an illusionist, conceived his trick films as genuine stage numbers for his magic theater, where they were screened regularly. The themes that were cinematographed were thus those of the theater of conjuring tricks. […] In fact, cinematography was for Méliès just another way to practice conjuring."[8] The book he co-edited with Laurent Mannoni in 2002 is indeed titled *Méliès, magie et cinéma* and includes an important contribution by film producer Christian Fechner, who also happened to be a specialist of Robert Houdin and was himself a conjuring world champion several times.[9] Anglo-saxon historiography adopted a similar perspective. In their research, Paul Hammond or John Frazer in the 1970s, and more recently Tom Gunning or Elisabeth Ezra have also situated "Mélièsian trick-mania" in the direct lineage of conjuring.[10]

The art of conjuring thus seems to have constituted the privileged historical model in considering Méliès's tricks in particular and tricks in early cinema in general. I obviously do not intend to dispute this discursive association here, as it appears perfectly founded historically and particularly obvious in Méliès's case. Rather, I mean to demonstrate that the world of magic was not the one and only referential horizon of the first trick performers, and that they occasionally tapped into other technical domains for specific expertise. Méliès himself admitted to the fact, stating in a 1926 *Ciné-Journal* article:

> In the many columns written about me in all languages, I have quite often read that the dexterity I had gradually attained in cinematographic tricks I owed to my practice of conjuring. How wrong! Certainly, conjuring had given me a taste for invention and tricks. But how different [are] the methods of these two arts![11]

6   See Georges Sadoul, *Georges Méliès* (Paris: Editions Seghers, 1961); *Lumière et Méliès* (Paris: Lherminier, 1985); and "L'époque Méliès (1897–1902)", *Histoire Générale du cinéma, les pionniers du cinéma (de Méliès à Pathé)*, vol. ii (Paris: Denoël, 1947) 19–237. See also Jacques Deslandes and Jacques Richard, "L'œuvre de Georges Méliès" ["The Work of Georges Méliès"], *Histoire comparée du cinéma. Du cinématographe au cinéma, 1896–1906*, vol. ii (Tournai: Casterman, 1968) 395–499.

7   Antonio Costa, "Pour une interprétation iconologique du cinéma de Méliès: "vues dites à transformations" et trucages" ["For an Iconological Interpretation of Méliès's Cinema: So-called "Transformation Views" and Tricks"], *Georges Méliès, l'illusionniste fin de siècle*, eds. Jacques Malthête and Michel Marie (Paris: Presses de la Sorbonne nouvelle, 1997) 175.

8   Jacques Malthête, "Quand Méliès n'en faisait qu'à sa tête" ["When Méliès Did as He Pleased"], in Lefebvre, "Pour une histoire des trucages": 23.

9   See Christian Fechner, "Le Théâtre Robert-Houdin, de Jean Eugène Robert-Houdin à Georges Méliès", *Méliès, magie et cinéma*, eds. Jacques Malthête and Laurent Mannoni (Paris: Paris Musées, 2002) 72–113.

10 Paul Hammond, *Marvellous Méliès* (London: Gordon Frazer, 1974); John Frazer, *Artificially Arranged Scenes: The Films of Georges Méliès* (Boston: G. K. Hall and Co., 1980); Tom Gunning, " "Primitive" Cinema: A Frame-up? Or the Trick's on Us", *Cinema Journal* 28:2 (Winter 1989): 3–12, and "Attractions, truquages et photogénie: l'explosion du présent dans les films à truc français produits entre 1896 et 1907", *Les Vingt premières années du cinéma français* ["The First Twenty Years of French Cinema"], eds. Jean A. Gili, Michèle Lagny, Michel Marie, Vincent Pinel (Paris: Presses de la Sorbonne nouvelle - AFRHC, 1995) 177–193; Elisabeth Ezra, *Georges Méliès, the Birth of the auteur* (Manchester: Manchester University Press, 2000).

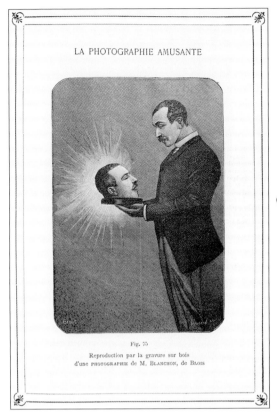

Fig. 1. "La photographie amusante" (Entertaining Photography), La Science en famille, revue illustrée de vulgarisation scientifique, *vol. II, 1888: 145 (private coll., Paris).*

These "various methods" were detailed by Méliès in a letter published in 1925 by film historian G.-Michel Coissac. He listed six of them: first, the "stop or substitution trick;" the techniques of conjuring, of course; the "theatrical machinery;" "chemistry;" "pyrotechnics;" and finally, "photo- graphic tricks".[12] In the enumeration, only the first trick, which consists in stopping the camera and replacing the subject with another before resuming shooting, was a genuine cinematographic innovation. All other tricks were borrowed from an extra-cinematographic expertise known by Méliès through his previous activities.[13] Indeed, a number of documents on the Théâtre Robert-Houdin show that Méliès already exploited conjuring tricks, theatrical machinery, chemistry, and pyrotechnics

11   Georges Méliès, "En marge de l'histoire du cinématographe", *Ciné-Journal, le journal du film* 889, (10 September 1926) 9.

12   Georges Méliès, letter to G.-Michel Coissac, reproduced in Coissac's *Histoire du cinématographe* (Paris: Cinéopse, Gauthier-Villars, 1925) 379.

13   This distinction is based on a categorization proposed by Christian Metz in "Trucage et cinéma" ["Special Effects and Cinema", 1971], *Essais sur la signification au cinéma*, vol. II (Paris: Éditions Klincksieck, 1972) 173–192. Metz distinguishes between what he calls "cinematographic tricks", which pertain to a technique specific to cinema, and "profilmic tricks", which are, in his own words, "tricks" analogous, basically, to those of conjurers".

Fig. 2 (left). Foy and Baillot, Un coup de pompe, S.V.P. *(Pump me up, please, please), gelatin silver print, 1899, published on the cover of Photo* Pêle-Mêle, *8 August 1903 (Coll. Christophe Gœury, Paris).*
Fig. 3 (right). Frédéric Laporte, double portrait, gelatin silver print, 1886 (© Société française de photographie, Paris).

there.[14] As to the sixth category of tricks, which I will proceed to analyse in depth, it belonged to a photographic tradition already fifty years old when Méliès took it over.

Indeed, photographic tricks existed since the 1840s. They were then used occasionally in very specific applications such as the combination on the same image of several people who had not been able to pose together, or the correction of a light differential too important through the reassembly of negatives with different exposures. They became much more widely used with the growth of amateur photography in the 1880s. From that time on, popular periodicals such as *La Nature*, *L'Illustration*, or *La Science en famille* had their readers play with photography by making dexterity drills and easy tricks available to them (Fig. 1). A first collection wholly consisting of such entertainment, Albert Bergeret and Félix Drouin's *Les Récréations photographiques*, was published in 1890 and reedited in 1891 and 1893.[15] The success of this inaugural book prompted a multiplication of similar publications. In 1894, E. Ogonowski and Violette's *La Photographie amusante* appeared, and in 1904 C. Chaplot published *La Photographie récréative et*

---

14 See Fechner, "Le Théâtre Robert-Houdin", *Méliès, magie et cinéma* 72–113.

15 Albert Bergeret, Félix Drouin, *Les Récréations photographiques* (Paris: Charles Mendel, 1890).

Fig. 4. Anon., Gentlemen of the Jury,
gelatin silver print, left part of a
stereoscopic print, 1897 (private coll.,
Paris)

fantaisiste. Recueil de divertissements, trucs, passe-temps photographiques ["Recreation and Fantasy Photography, a Collection of Photographic Entertainment, Tricks, and Activities"], a second edition of which appeared in 1908.[16]

It is rather difficult to provide a quick and synthetic description of these works. Their construction does not seem to be based on any internal logic, except perhaps the accumulation of all possible and conceivable processes. For instance, they show how to make photograms by laying out small objects on the very surface of the sensitive paper, to stage tableaux and keep a record of them through photography, or to put together imaginary scenes thanks to photomontage. They also invite amateurs to enhance ordinary objects with photographs and to make photographic parlour games (card games, snakes and ladders, lotto sets, checkers, etc.). They encourage them to distort their image by taking pictures of themselves in front of mirrors at fun fairs, using the optical aberrations of short-focal-length lenses or unusual points of view (high-angle and low-angle shots), or even melting the photographic gelatine by subjecting it to intense heat. In this heterogeneous hodgepodge of suggestions for amusement, one systematically recurs in the collections: it consists in having people pose in front of a black backdrop and having them adopt different but correlated attitudes to record them on the same negative. The technique offers a wide array of amusing situations: a fellow

16   E. Ogonowski, Violette, *La Photographie amusante* (Paris: Société Générale d'Éditions, undated [1894]); C. Chaplot, *La Photographie récréative et fantaisiste. Recueil de divertissements, trucs, passe-temps photographiques* (Paris: Charles Mendel, undated [1904]). On the subject, see also Clément Chéroux, *Une généalogie des formes récréatives en photographie (1890–1940)*, doctoral thesis under the supervision of Philippe Dagen, Université de Paris 1, 2004.

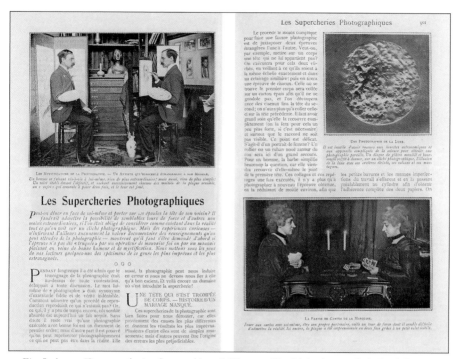

Fig. 5. Anon., *"Les supercheries photographiques"* (Photographic tricks), photographs by Paul Gruyer, Lectures pour tous, *1901–1902: 900–901 (private coll., Paris).*

playing chess against himself, another one fighting a duel with his double, a conductor working with musicians who look suspiciously like him, twins giving each other a light, etc. (Figs. 2–4).

The publication in Europe and in the United States of about fifteen books enumerating the various opportunities for playing with photography, as well as the regular appearance of entertainment columns in specialized periodicals, make it possible to assess the extent of the recreational phenomenon in the amateur community at the turn of the century. The relatively important number of extant "recreation photographs" in family collections today even supports the claim that recreational photography was widely practiced at the time. In the early 20th century, the visibility of these images spread beyond the private sphere of amateur photography, as they appeared extensively in the illustrated press (Fig. 5) and were distributed as postcards by industries seeking to attract customers with their visual appeal (Fig. 6). Albert Bergeret, the author of the first book on recreation photography on 1890, became one of the main French publishers of fantasy postcards at the beginning of the century, largely tapping into the stock of entertainment developed during the previous decade.

If recreational iconography was known to both amateur photographers and a mainstream audience, it would be a stretch to imagine that the film profession may not have known about it. In fact, Alice Guy writes in her autobiography that

Fig. 6. Société industrielle de photographie,
Salomé. Le bourreau la lui remet *(Salome: the
headsman gives it to her), gelatin silver print on
postcard, 1904 (Coll. Gérard Lévy, Paris)*

at Gaumont (where she worked as a director), photography specialist Frédéric
Dillaye, well-known at the time for books that made photography as art and as
technique accessible to the general public, explained to her how tricks worked.[17]
A number of cameramen of early cinema had themselves been photographers,
whether professional or amateur. That was the case for Emile Cohl, for example,
who opened a portrait studio in Paris in 1884. Besides the traditional output, he
appears to have made a few recreational photographs, as attested in a double
portrait of Henry Gauthier-Villars, also known as Willy.[18] These competences
were no doubt helpful when, in his own words, he became a "trickster"[19] for
Gaumont in 1908.

Méliès also practiced photography as an amateur, though the fact is a lot less
known than his passion for magic. Indeed, in the biography she devoted to him,
his granddaughter Madeleine Malthête-Méliès mentions that he took up photog-

---

17 Alice Guy, *The Memoirs of Alice Guy Blaché* (Methuen, N.J.: Scarecrow Press, 1986) 26.

18 See François Caradec, *Feu Willy, avec et sans Colette* (Paris: J.-J. Pauvert, Carrere, 1984), iconographic
supplement after page 160. On Emile Cohl's photographic activity, see Clément Chéroux, "La photographie
n'est pas un fromage" ["Photography Is Not a Cheese"], *1895, revue de l'association française de recherche sur
l'histoire du cinéma* 53, special issue on Emile Cohl, ed. Valérie Vignaux (December 2007): 99–108.

19 Emile Cohl, "Oui, je suis le père du dessin animé" ["Yes, I Am the Father of Animated Film"], *Paris-soir*
15 September 1934, quoted in Donald Crafton, *Emile Cohl, Caricature, and Film* (Princeton: Princeton
University Press, 1990) 92.

Fig. 7. Un homme de têtes *(The Four Troublesome Heads, 1898)*, L'Homme-Orchestre *(The One-Man Band, 1900)*, L'Homme à la tête en caoutchouc *(The Man with the Rubber Head, 1901)*, L'Illusionniste double et la tête vivante *(The Triple Conjurer and the Living Head, 1900)*, *Georges Méliès*

raphy in the late 1880s, that is, precisely at the moment a recreational use of the medium was developing: "When he stayed at home, Georges headed for the attic, but this time it was not to practice conjuring tricks. Indeed, several months before, he had discovered photography and it had become another one of his passions".[20] A few separate photographs and a small vacation album preserved at the Cinémathèque française and in a private collection are the remaining evidence we still have of this activity of amateur photographer.

Given his passion for photographs as well as tricks, Méliès could not ignore recreational photography, especially not at a time when amateurs were more and more numerous to practice it, when books multiplied, and postcard publishers and the mainstream press published them in plenty. When, in his letter to Coissac already cited, Méliès evoked "photographic tricks", he was certainly referring to recreations. In fact, the close examination of some of his films – *Un homme de têtes* [*The Four Troublesome Heads*, 1898], *Evocation spirite* [*Summoning the Spirits*, 1899], *L'homme-Orchestre* [*The One-Man Band*, 1900], *L'homme à la tête en caoutchouc* [*The Man with the Rubber Head*, 1901], *La danseuse microscopique* [*The Dancing Midget*, 1902], *Le Mélomane* [*The Music Lover*, 1903], *Un peu de feu, S.V.P.* [*Every Man His Own Cigar Lighter*, 1904],[21] for instance, does reveal that the tricks he resorted to pertained to the techniques of recreational photography more than to those of conjuring (Figs. 7–9).

20 Madeleine Malthête-Méliès, *Méliès l'enchanteur* (Paris: Ramsay, 1995) 89.

21 I am using the dating established by Jacques Malthête and Laurent Mannoni in *L'Œuvre de Georges Méliès* (Paris: La Cinémathèque française, Éditions de la Martinière, 2008).

Fig. 8. Anon., double portrait of Georges Méliès, film still from Un peu de feu S.V.P. (Every Man His Own Cigar Lighter), gelatin silver print, 1904 (Cinémathèque française/Centre national de la cinématographie, Paris).

Fig. 9. G. Méliès, L'Homme à la tête en caoutchouc (The Man with the Rubber Head, 1901), crayon and ink drawing on paper, 1901 (Cinémathèque française/Centre national de la cinématographie, Paris).

To understand this, it is necessary to compare the ways to achieve a few visual effects common to recreational photography and conjuring. Two examples will do. To produce the apparitions of ghosts or wandering spirits supposedly returned from the kingdom of the dead, magic theaters placed a slanted two-way mirror that allowed the main scene to be seen while reflecting a strongly lit ghost-like figure located in the backstage area. Conjurer Henri Robin, for instance, used this stratagem in the early 1860s in his phantasmagoria shows on the boulevard du Temple (Fig. 10).[22] To obtain a similar effect, books of photographic

22   On Robin's ghosts, see Henri Robin, "Histoire des spectres", *L'Almanach le Cagliostro* (1864): 13–20, and "Les spectres dévoilés", *L'Almanach le Cagliostro* (1865): 20; Laurent Mannoni, "La lanterne magique du boulevard du crime. Henri Robin, fantasmagore et magicien", *1895* 16 (June 1994): 5–26; Christian Fechner, *La Magie de Robert Houdin, "Une vie d'artiste". Essai biographique*, vol. ii (Boulogne: Editions FCF, 2002) 150–187, 218–222, 265–271.

Fig. 10. Robin, "Les spectres dévoilés - Disposition du théâtre Robin pendant les spectres" (Revealing Ghosts - Robin Theatre by the staging of the ghosts), print by Bertrand, L'Almanach le Cagliostro, 1865: 30 (private coll., Paris).

recreations offered a much easier trick to execute: the mere superimposition of two different views on the same negative (Fig. 11). In their book, Bergeret and Drouin wrote:

> Do you want to enliven any landscape with a ghost? There is nothing easier. Take a photograph of a cemetery, for example. [...] As you come back to the studio, cover a willing ghost with white sheets and, placing him before a black backdrop, take a photograph on the same plate, getting as close as possible to the ghost you have thus come across.[23]

Fig. 11. Anon., Spectre (11 heures du soir) *(Ghost, 11 pm), gelatin silver print, right part of a stereoscopic print, ca. 1890 (Musée Nicéphore Niépce, Chalon-sur-Saône).*

---

23 Bergeret, Drouin, *Les Récréations photographiques* [1893 edition] 195.

Fig. 12. Le Repas
fantastique
(A Fantastic Meal),
G. Méliès, 1900.

Fig. 13. Gaston
Tissandier, "Le décapité
parlant" (The speaking
beheaded), print by
Gilbert, Les
Récréations
scientifiques ou
l'enseignement par le
jeu, Paris, G. Masson,
1881: 129 (private coll.,
Paris).

Though obtained through a distinct technical process, the result of the recreation was perfectly similar to the effect produced by conjuring. Upon examination, it appears clearly that the transparency of ghosts in Méliès's "haunted films" was produced through superimposition on a black backdrop much more than through a two-way mirror (Fig. 12). Incidentally, the second solution would not have been without raising serious problems with exposure or focus. To make ghosts appear, Méliès thus manifestly privileged the technique of recreations over conjuring tricks.

So it went for another visual effect shared by both recreational photography and conjuring. In one of his books of scientific popularization, Gaston Tissandier describes the famous magic trick of "the living beheaded" as follows (Fig. 13):

Fig. 14. Anon., double portrait, gelatin silver print, ca. 1890 (Musée Nicéphore Niépce, Chalon-sur-Saône).

Visitors took a peek into a small room which they could not enter, and where a three-legged table stood; atop the table was a human head, laid on a sheet at the center of a tray. The eyes were moving and the head could speak. It undoubtedly belonged to a man whose body could absolutely not be seen. Spectators thought they saw an empty space below the table, but the body of the individual who was sitting there was concealed by two silvered mirrors set at a 45-degree angles from the right and left walls. The whole thing was arranged so that the image of these walls would coincide with the visible part of the background wall.[24]

With photography, a similar effect could be obtained through a much simpler technique (Fig. 14). Bergeret et Drouin suggested yet again to resort to superimposition on a black backdrop to enjoy a recreation also called "the living beheaded".[25]

Méliès was familiar with this magic trick, which he had himself staged at the Théâtre Robert-Houdin with mirrors and cases in an 1891 show titled *The Unwilling Beheaded*. However, in reproducing it for one of his films, he opted for the technique of recreational photography. Directed in 1898, *Un homme de têtes* (*The Four Troublesome Heads*) features a strange barker (played by Méliès himself), who can have his own head multiply in as many replicas and does his utmost to

---

24   Gaston Tissandier, *Les Récréations scientifiques, ou l'enseignement par le jeu* (Paris: G. Masson, 1881) 134.

25   Bergeret, Drouin, *Les Récréations photographiques* [1893 edition] 183–184.

Fig. 15. Un homme de têtes *(The Four Troublesome Heads),* G. *Méliès, 1898*

have them sing together after aligning them on a table. The first third of the film includes a detail of particular interest. After having the head talk and sing on the table in the tradition of beheading tricks, Méliès kneels down and moves underneath the table (Fig. 15). The movement, which could pass as yet another prank, is in fact a rhetorical nod addressed to the spectator, to the connoisseur of magic tricks, or even to the future historian. Méliès thereby indicates that he was not using the customary case of magicians, but relied instead on a new form of illusion – a double exposure with a black backdrop inspired by photographic recreations, which at that point had become part of cinema's array of tricks.[26]

These two examples – among many others – demonstrate that, while Méliès remained deeply attached to the tradition of conjuring, his great classic tricks, his compulsory figures, or his stereotyped world, he had by then moved to give them life through other tricks which had less to do with conjuring tricks than with new visual technologies. The spirit of magic was still there, but found a new expression *through* modern images. Méliès's passion did not disappear somewhere between the theater on the boulevard des Italiens and the Montreuil studio: rather, it was transformed. On the stage of the Théâtre Robert-Houdin, magic was an indivisible whole: the subject of the show and its technology were one. Magic remained the subject of many of Méliès's trick films, but the technique changed. In *Un homme de têtes* (1898), *Évocation spirite* (1899), *L'enchanteur Alcofribas* (same title in English, 1903), *Les Cartes vivantes* (*The Living Playing Cards*, 1905), to mention but a few, the point is indeed to show a conjurer performing a trick. However, in obtaining these effects, the magician traded his usual stratagems for those of photo-cinematography. Méliès's films have all the appearances

---

26 Méliès repeated the same gesture in several other films such as *Le Chevalier mystère* (*The Mysterious Knight*, 1899). In an interview he was kind enough to give me, Jacques Malthête pointed out that the gesture was sometimes mentioned in the script, which indicates its importance.

of filmed magic tricks, but in actuality they involve "cinemagic" tricks. The trick is no longer in the trick itself, but in the film – or, to put it differently, cinema itself has become the great trick.

I want to emphasize again that the issue at hand here is not to deny or diminish the role played by conjuring in the elaboration of a Mélièsian filmic imaginary, but to show that his world was the product of intricate connections between crafts in which recreations had their importance. Indeed, by way of conclusion, I have to wonder about the almost complete lack of references to recreations in Méliès's critical fortune. The historians who evoke them in dealing with his trick films are in fact rare. Deslandes is the most terse of all. In one sentence, he explains that Méliès "made his own processes such as superimposition, well-known to photographers".[27] Sadoul was slightly more verbose on the subject, writing in his *Histoire générale du cinéma*:

> It was also in 1898 that Méliès used three new tricks for the first time: superimposition, multiple exposure, and masks. All three processes were borrowed from photographic technique and appeared in quick succession in the Star Film catalogue. This appears to demonstrate that Méliès had just procured a photography manual and was applying all the tricks described in it. Méliès most likely took inspiration from an American book, *Magic Stage Illusions and Scientific Diversions including Trick Photography*, published at the very beginning of 1898 by Albert A. Hopkins.[28]

The copious 500-page volume which Sadoul refers to does include a chapter on photographic recreations, but it is first and foremost an encyclopedia of illusionism that features all the tricks used in conjuring shows.[29] Sadoul thus understood very well the importance of photographic recreations. Still, the historian symptomatically brings up a book on conjuring, and an American book at that, even though several collections of recreations were available in French in Méliès's time, and despite the fact that the French press also published some regularly over the period.[30]

Sadoul's telling omission attests to the little interest of early film specialists for photographic tricks. The following generations of historians or critics, in France as well as internationally, did not pay any more attention to them. Recreations are evoked here and there in the studies of early cinema, but they are generally lost in the flood of references to conjuring. Indeed, the extent of the neglect leads to wonder whether film historians, to borrow a psychoanalytic term particularly appropriate here, might not have *repressed* the photographic, in a genuine unease

---

27 Deslandes, Richard, "L'œuvre de Georges Méliès", *Histoire comparée du cinéma* 465.

28 Sadoul, *Histoire Générale du Cinéma* 52.

29 The book cited by Sadoul had in fact been published in London the year before. Albert A. Hopkins, *Magic Stage Illusions and Scientific Diversions Including Trick Photography* (London: Sampson Low, Marston and Company, 1897).

30 Sadoul also fails to mention the fact that the engravings illustrating Hopkins's chapter come for a large part from articles on photographic recreations published in *La Nature* in the late 19th century.

when it came to contemplating photography as a historical predecessor of cinema, producing a lineage outside its original milieu. It thus appeared more legitimate for the trick film to come down from conjuring shows than to be the natural child of recreational photography. This says a lot on the difficulty to think early cinema beyond theater, staging, and spectacle, and to approach it as a radically new form of representation issuing from technologies of analogic recording – all in all, as a modern image.

It also sheds light on how much catching up the history of photography has to do in certain areas. Indeed, to this day, only two historical articles have been devoted to photographic recreations.[31] Their place in specialized publications at the turn of the century, at least as important as that granted to art or documentary photography, seems inversely proportional to the number of pages devoted to them nowadays in history books. It is now a little known, ill-identified and, to top things off, not very accessible corpus. Accordingly, how could film historians gauge the importance of recreations as a phenomenon when even photography experts do not know about it? Only a combined effort by photography and film historians would make it possible to understand the decisive role played by recreations in the development of an early fantastic cinema. Only a cross analysis of these recreational practices will allow us to understand the great trade of tricks at the turn of the century, an important moment in the exchange between photography and cinematography.

Acknowledgements: I wish to thank Olivier Lugon and Laurent Guido warmly for inviting me to expand on my research for the doctoral thesis on photographic tricks and examine its implications in the field of cinema on the occasion of the conference *Fixe/animé, croisements de la photographie et du cinéma au XXᵉ siècle / Still/Moving, Crossings Between Photography and Cinema in the 20ᵗʰ Century*. I also want to express my gratitude to Laurent Mannoni, Jacques Malthête, and Valérie Vignaux for their advice, help, or guidance in the exploration of this vast historical field.

31   Nicolas Villodre, "Les Récréations photographiques à la fin du xixᵉ siècle", *Photographies* 8 (September 1985): 106–109; Clément Chéroux, "Les récréations photographiques, un répertoire de formes pour les avant-gardes", *Études photographiques* 5 (Nov. 1998): 72–96.

2

"Cinema in a Single Photo": The Animated Screen Portrait of the 1910s

Kim Timby

One of the most intriguing intersections between cinema and photography is the animated line-screen portrait manufactured during the 1910s and the 1920s. For example, a rather ordinary looking head-and-shoulder portrait of a man is framed by a postcard format passe-partout (Fig. 1). When the mount is bent back and forth along the right edge marked "Remuez douce-ment ce bord" [gently move this edge], the specificity of the photograph is revealed: its subject becomes animated. He rolls his eyes, making exaggerated facial expressions as his hair flips from side to side (Fig. 2). The sequence has no particular beginning or end: whatever the direction in which the mount is bent, the same animation takes place at different speeds, depending on how fast the device is handled. Several poses blend as they switch from one to the other, making the object fascinating to play with.

Such screen photographs are a rich example of the intermediate zones between still and moving images. Indeed, these portraits may be considered as both: they visibly transform, producing the illusion that their subjects move – yet they assume the appearance of standard photographs that one can hold in one's hand, their multiple images cleverly concealed. The quotation used in my title will serve as a guide for exploring the cultural meaning, but also the theoretical significance, of these hybrid photographs. The Parisian studio that created the image described above touted the technique as "cinema in a single photo".[1] This slogan is significant on two accounts. First, it indicates to what extent the *cinema* structured the existence of such moving images – providing a first clue for the examination of their social and aesthetic importance in France. Even more telling perhaps is the way in which this bold advertisement encapsulates the technical specificity of such images with respect to cinema or other forms of animation: indeed, they feature an illusion of movement in what appears to be *a single*

---

1   "Photographie/animée (La),/Invention sensationnelle./Le cinéma dans une/seule photo./Bergeron, Ferreté & Cie,/r. Martel, 8. [T] Bergère 41.01." (Didot-Bottin business directory, 1918 and 1919, in the listings for Photographers).

Fig. 1 (above). Ferreté & Cie, animated line-screen portrait, ca. 1918-1921.
Fig. 2 (below). Details from Fig. 1.

photograph. We will see that animated screen portraits were a playful and accessible item in the early twentieth century that benefited from public fascination for the nascent seventh art, but that they were also more than that. Not simply poor imitations of images on the silver screen, *belle époque* animated screen photographs emerge as particularly rich precisely because of their liminal nature, as both still and moving images.

Cinema …

Historical contextualization is essential to understanding the importance of animated line-screen photographs.[2] In the commercial and playful form represented by the small image shown above, the process seems to have been invented

Fig. 3. *Felsenthal & Sons (?), animated line-screen advertisement, ca. 1914–1918.*

in the United States. It was patented there by Alexander S. Spiegel between 1905 and 1911, first in association with drawings, then photographs.[3] The idea quickly reached France, where it was patented again by Spiegel between 1908 and 1915, then from 1915 to 1917 by other inventors, who sometimes mentioned the work of their American forerunner[4] – an indication that they were familiar with his images, probably already in circulation in France at the time. Patents and business directories, as well as the fashion and hairstyles of the people photographed, all indicate that animated photography was popular on both sides of the Atlantic during the World War I era. Some published views display political personalities of the time, and an American image used as an advertisement even refers explicitly to the war (Fig. 3). Labeled "The Triple Entente", it alternates between the portraits of different heads of state; the caption transforms it into a dated advertisement: "MIDDLETONS ARTURA SHOES ARE ALWAYS IN THE FRONT

2   For an introduction, see my article "Images en relief et images changeantes. La photographie à réseau ligné" ["Stereoscopic Images and Changing Images. The Case of Line-Screen Photography"], *Études photographiques* 9 (May 2001): 124–147. This research is developed in my doctoral thesis, "Images en relief et images changeantes: l'invention et la commercialisation de la photographie à réseau en France, 1896–1980". Diss. École des hautes études en sciences sociales, Paris, 2006.

3   Patents 944 385, *Picture Post-Card or Display Device*, 15 March 1909; 946 407, *Picture Post-Card or Display Device*, 15 March 1909; 1 066 766, *Process and Apparatus for Making Composite-Picture Slides and the Like*, 20 November 1911. The dates cited here are those of the patents' filing; the same patents were often mentioned according to their issuance date on the images sold (cf. Fig 1). See also patent 829 492, *Display Device*, 29 November 1905. All patents cited in this text may be consulted online at http://ep.espacenet.com, or at the closest national patent office (in France, the Institut national de la propriété industrielle).

4   Ivan-Louis Andrieux and Edmond-Clément Papeghin, French patents 480 717, *Châssis photographique à plaque mobile* ["Photographic frame for mobile plate"], 19 January 1916; and 483 190, *Carte-support pour photographies animées* ["Support card for animated photographs"], 14 March 1916.

*Fig. 4. Anon., animated line-screen view
of a flapper, 1920s.*

RANKS/DO WE HAVE TO GO TO WAR TO GET YOUR BUSINESS?", "WAR/NO NEED TO
WORRY/... IF YOU ARE WEARING ... MIDDLETONS/ARTURA SHOES". The production
of animated portraits continued during the 1920s, not so often in the form of
private portraits, it seems, than in that of smaller commercial views (half-postcard
sized) such as a one of a flapper who moves her arms when the edges of the mount
are pressed from side to side (Fig. 4).

Another form of animated line-screen photography also existed during the
period. Instead of the light materials used in the portraits we have just seen, these
images were on glass. This made them heavier and more cumbersome, but also
more vivid, as they could be lit from behind. The animated effect was produced
when viewers tilted the image or changed their angle of observation. Eugène
Estanave, a mathematician and the first to work on animated screen photography
in France, created such images on glass from 1906 in the laboratory of the
physicist Gabriel Lippmann at the Sorbonne.[5] This particular form of animated
photography also seems to have appealed to a few advertising specialists, who
used it to create large images that animated for passers-by (and that were surely
designed for display in store windows). One photograph of this sort from the
1920s, measuring 35 x 28 cm, shows a woman wearing glasses (Fig. 5). Viewed
from one angle she looks at the viewer, and from another she looks down, reading
a book. A text changes to herald the qualities of "Telegic/Le bifocale invisible"
(Telegic/The Invisible Bifocal Lens): "Rajeunit le visage/vue parfaite, loin et

5   On Estanave, see my article, "Images en relief et images changeantes", as well as Michel Frizot, "Line Screen
      Systems" in *Paris in 3D, from Stereoscopy to Virtual Reality, 1850–2000* (London: Booth-Clibborn; Paris:
      Paris-Musées, 2000) 152–157.

Fig. 5. Animated Picture Products Co., animated line-screen advertisement, 1920s, seen from two different angles

près/avec le même verre" (Makes your face look younger/perfect eyesight, from a distance and close up/with the same lens).

Whether on paper or glass, these animated photographs were contemporaneous with the first decades of cinematography, and this art was clearly an important factor in the fascination they elicited in the early twentieth century. Screen photography's ties with the cinema are revealed by numerous clues, not the least of which the vocabulary used to describe it. While most of the time screen photographs were simply referred to as "animated photographs" (an expression also used in association with the first screenings of the Cinematograph[6]) or as "changing images", sometimes cinema was explicitly cited. Animated screen photography was, as we have seen, "cinema in a single photo" and, according to Estanave, involved "an embryonic cinematographic movement".[7] It was an image that moved *like at the movies*.

The influence of the cinema is also evident in the successful commercial practices surrounding animated screen photography. The process's first big success was in the domain of personalized portraits. At least two sources for the production of

---

6   This is the case, for example, in the title of the article referenced in note 12 or on the well-known poster showing spectators looking at a man jumping over a horse on the screen, on which the following may be read: "GRAND SUCCÈS DU JOUR/LE CINÉMATOGRAPHE/LA PHOTOGRAPHIE ANIMÉE/ PAR LE/ CINÉMATOGRAPHE/DE A & L. LUMIÈRE" ["Great success of the day/The Cinématographe/Animated photography/by A & L Lumière's Cinématographe"].

7   Eugène Estanave, "Photographies à couleurs changeantes" ["Photographs with changing colours"], in *Comptes rendus de l'Académie des sciences* ["Reports of the Academy of Sciences"] 152 (1911): 1158–1159.

Fig. 6. Anon., flip-book with a portrait of a man, ca. 1910-1930

such portraits existed in Paris in the neighbourhood of the Grands Boulevards, where many movie theatres and screening venues were also located: one was to be found at 12 boulevard des Italiens, at the corner of the passage de l'Opéra (probably at Midget's, the only photographer at this address in business directories of the period); another one was at 8 rue Martel, north of the boulevard de Bonne Nouvelle (location of Bergeron Ferreté & Cie, the authors of the image featured in Fig. 1, from roughly 1918 to 1921). The boulevards were therefore not only a place to go to the movies: they also catered to a demand for smaller, personalized animated images. In the 1910s, this leisure district concentrated all sorts of animated spectacles, energized by the craze for cinematography. Another popular item was the flip-book, which gave an impression of animation when its pages were flicked through rapidly. One specimen from the time showing the portrait of a man (Fig. 6) strings together several actions over forty-two images: the subject turns his head, moves a cigarette away from his lips, looks up, then smiles and turns his face towards the camera, smoothes his hair with his hand, turns so as to appear in profile, then looks at the camera again before raising his hand and ending with a laugh. Cameras designed for the production of such personalized flip-books were marketed at professional photographers. A 1911 Gaumont catalogue shows that the attraction was present on the Boulevards and recounts how it came into fashion:

> As soon as the cinematograph that we still know today appeared under the auspices of the Lumière brothers, people became preoccupied with bringing

Fig. 7. Anon., animated line-screen view of a man on the phone, 1920s, details.

into every home a convenient, easy-to-use and cheap device that would make it possible to enjoy the synthesis of movement allowed by the cinematograph. Boulevard peddlers started selling small album-notebooks: the fast, regular flipping of pages under the thumb gave the retina the illusion that the image pasted onto them came to life.[8]

We can infer from this that immortalizing one's own movements in a screen portrait was, in a certain sense, a way of associating oneself with the cinema. During the 1910s, people clearly wanted to see themselves represented as if in a movie theater: animated, in a rectangular frame with round corners (like on a movie screen),[9] and making faces.

And faces they made. The strongest sign that animated photography tapped into the craze for cinema is the iconography of these popular views, which borrowed tropes from the medium. Great facial expressivity was part of the aesthetics of silent cinema, in which exaggerated expressions were common and often framed in close shot (and could even comprise an entire movie).[10] It was also part of the representation of cinematography in still images at the time, as can be seen in countless promotional photographs. Such facial expressivity was commonly found in animated screen photographs, like the one of the character with tousled hair (Figs. 1, 2). Animated portraits were always close-up views (a rare occurrence in classic studio portraits of the time) and drew on a limited but interesting range of effects: a wink, rolling eyes, a smile, the variation in the angle of a smoker's cigar, a restless moustache, a raised eyebrow, a stray lock of hair, etc. Published

---

8   Comptoir général de la photographie and Société des Établissements Gaumont, *Tarif général des appareils, fournitures et nouveautés photographiques* ["General catalogue of cameras, supplies, and novelties"], Paris, January 1911, 50.

9   Round corners appear in various representations of projection screens and film screenings of the time. See for instance illustrations in *Pathé, premier empire du cinéma* ["Pathé, the First Empire of Cinema"], ed. Jacques Kermabon (Paris: Éditions du Centre Pompidou, 1994) 197, 199, 200, 203, 204, 206, 209, and 271.

10   On the evolution of gestural expressivity during the silent period, see for instance the contributions of François Albera, Frank Kessler, and Sabine Lenk in *L'expression du sentiment au cinéma* ["The Expression of Feeling in the Cinema"], Claude Murcia et Gilles Menegaldo, eds. (Poitiers: La Licorne, 1996).

Fig. 8. Anon., animated line-screen view of a couple, 1920s, details.

views, of which multiple copies were manufactured, often featured even more spectacular gestures. On such image (Fig. 7) is quite entertaining to manipulate. A man shouts into a telephone handset, his forehead furrowed, then twists his wide-open mouth in an attitude of astonishment, purses his lips, and rolls his eyes, looking up. Another staple was the use of subjects from the vaudeville or the music hall worlds, associated with cinema (albeit probably already in a nostalgic way in the 1920s): a flapper dancing, a made-up subject wearing a wig, a barrel organ player, etc. Another example of a published image (Fig. 8) presents a slightly different iconography, also with strong cinematographic connotations: the close framing of a couple in three stages of an embrace. In one view the woman appears cheek to cheek with her lover, eyes and face turned towards the viewer; in the following one, she turns in the direction of her lover to meet his lips, while still looking at the viewer; in the third view she lowers her eyes, tilting her head back to receive a kiss.

Animated screen portraits are thus indeed *"cinema* in a single photo", as the advertising slogan that serves as our main thread claimed. They are not just animated views, as could be produced prior to 1895, but a sort of reduced version of the public's image of cinematography during the 1910s and the 1920s: an animated device sold near movie theaters presenting close-ups of expressive faces, spectacular characters, or other connoted iconographies.

... in a single photo

While "cinema" points to the referent of the animated screen photograph and helps us understand its place within popular culture, the second part of the slogan we have been examining – "in a single photo" – directs our attention to the originality of the technique in the history of images, and to its ambivalence as both a still and a moving image. Animated screen photography relies on the succession of individual, similar views, just like cinema and the apparatuses that preceded it starting in the 1830s (phenakistiscope, zootrope, praxinoscope, etc.).

However, when invented, it differentiated itself from existing animated images through the use of a new technique that allowed it to combine multiple views into what appeared to be *a single image*.

Further elements regarding the physical construction of animated photographs will help us understand their specificity then analyse their modernity through ties to other contemporary technologies. Animated portraits produce an illusion of movement by interlacing thin strips from three images. It is as though each view had been cut into thin vertical bands, then the three combined using every third strip from each. This operation was performed photographically, most of the time with a special frame devised for the process.[11] The frame contained a "screen" of vertical opaque parallel lines which was pressed against the negative. Between exposures, the lined screen was moved by a fraction of a millimeter over the negative to expose different zones of the sensitive surface one after the other. In this way, three photographs taken one after the other (they were poses, not snapshots of a continuous movement) could be interlaced in a single negative. To obtain an illusion of animation from this negative, one simply needed to print it, then to cover the positive image with a light plastic screen with lines identical to those used in the camera; when the screen was moved over the interlaced images, they appeared in succession through its black lines. In commercial forms of the process like Fig. 1, the screen placed over the image was attached to the side flap of the mount, which when bent pulled and pushed on it, making it slide over the image. The composite portrait could also be printed on transparent film and glued behind the window of the mount (as in Fig. 4), with a printed paper screen of black lines glued to the back of the mount behind it; when an uneven, alternating pressure was applied to the lateral edges of the mount, the photographic layer slid back and forth over the screen background and the image appeared to animate. When glass was used, the composite image and the screen were either printed on two different plates, mounted one on top of the other at a slight distance from each other, or on opposite sides of the same plate of glass. Viewers simply had to change their angle of observation to see the different images appear in succession through the screen. The nature of the construction of animated screen photographs (particularly those on paper) explains why they were in practice limited to three poses, despite their cinematographic claims. This facilitated the differentiation of the interlaced photographs, but above all was a good compromise between a satisfying animated illusion and excessive darkening of the final image: each subsequent image interlaced meant making the screen's opaque lines wider, in order to hide the strips of all but one of the images at any given time.

---

11   U.S. patent 1 066 766 (by Spiegel); French patents 480 413, Alexander S. Spiegel, Robert Glendenning, and Gabriel Felsenthal, *Chambre photographique pour portraits animés* ["Camera for animated portraits"], 8 December 1915; 480 717, Ivan-Louis Andrieux and Edmond-Clément Papeghin, *Châssis photographique à plaque mobile* ["Mobile-plate photographic frame"], 19 January 1916; and 483 610, Bergeron, Ferreté & Cie and P. Duchenne, *Châssis porte-plaques universel pour photographies animées* ["Universal plate-holding frame for animated photographs"], 27 November 1916.

The way animated screen photography operates shows how physically different it is from other types of animated images. Several views are presented to the viewer in swift succession, as with other systems, and the clever juxtaposition of different poses may bring to mind well-known photographic and cinematic techniques (double exposure, tricks based on substitution). But it was new to interlace thin strips of several images so as to combine them into a *single*, apparently unique, image. This technical specificity of screen photography is at the root of its ambivalence between still and moving. In apparatuses such as the flip-book or the zootrope, the multiple images required for the illusion are in plain sight: their existence and their differences may be observed while the set of images is at rest. So it goes with cinema: while most contemporaries never had the chance to examine personally a film strip outside screenings, in the early years of cinematography illustrated periodicals published examples of sequences from these films in the form of series of still images.[12] Line-screen photography caused an epistemological break in the domain of moving images by interlacing individual views needed for the production of the illusion, thus making it impossible to see them separately, one beside the another. There was movement without the movement of the film through the projector. A "cinematographic" effect was presented in the guise of a standard photograph.

The ambivalence of screen photography, which conceals the multiple views on which it depends for its operation, had repercussions outside the technical sphere of its existence. Its liminal nature greatly contributed to its appeal, and therefore to its commercial success. Since individual views could be distinguished only by animating the image then stopping the movement at different stages, the desire was strong to explore the object in detail so as to penetrate its mystery. The way the process is presented in the postcard format is particularly attractive. Such images are designed to be held and animated by their intended viewer, who soon notices that a certain type of manual activation sets the image in motion. The viewer is the master of the unfolding of the animation – of its start and stop, but also its speed. The instruction "gently move this edge" is easily overlooked (though in the end a slow, gentle manipulation of the object produces the most convincing impression of movement). With a touch of assiduity, freezing the animation at different points makes it possible to count the three poses that give life to the subject when seen in succession. This isn't always a simple task, however, for the views blend unevenly when changing from one to the other and can be difficult to distinguish separately, leading to strange distortions, as with an early American example that has a slightly (unintended) Cubist-Futurist look (Fig. 9).[13] It is a pleasure to make the image alternate between still and moving.

---

12   For one example, see Daniel Bellet, "Le cinématographe et les photographies animées", in *Le journal de la jeunesse* (1895): 358–362.

13   Imperfections in the illusions produced by some images seem to come from flaws in the way the screen was mounted, but in other cases a gradual physical deterioration of the screen (probably made of cellulose nitrate) may be the cause.

Fig. 9. Brown's Photo Shop, animated line-screen portrait, ca. 1910–1914.

Each state becomes frustrating when too prolonged: the animation composed of only three views quickly seems repetitive; but seeing the image in a state of stillness makes it tempting to repeat the animation, so curious to observe. Between stillness and movement, understanding the operating mode of the object became a source of amusement in itself. Animated screen portraits drew their appeal not only from animation and expressive scenes reminiscent of the cinema, but also from the way they worked, which amused viewers while always eluding their grasp to some degree. It isn't uncommon to find examples that have been opened, dissected, their cardboard mount taken apart in an attempt to solve the enigma.

A sign of the intrinsic appeal of animated screen photography is its spontaneous association with advertising and other forms of public display. Large images on glass plates (like the one featured Fig. 5), which produced an illusion of change or animation when seen from different angles, lent themselves particularly well to such uses. Indeed, the system seemed to have the potential to attract curious passers-by, who would slow down to watch the repercussions of their movements on this unexpected visual creation. The American Frederic Ives, apparently the first to patent the process in 1903, immediately thought of using it for shop signs.[14] In France and Belgium, when Estanave presented his research to photography experts around 1910, they reckoned that the system could be put to "good use" in advertising ("and more particularly for illuminated advertisements"), and

---

14 Frederic Ives, U.S. patent 771 824, *Changeable Sign, Picture, etc.*, 27 October 1903 (this patent mentions a change between two different subjects, not the animation of one subject).

were reminded of signs they had seen using similar techniques to interlace several images "visible separately from distinct points of view".[15] Estanave's peers were probably referring to a much older system in which two different images were cut into strips and alternately applied on an accordion-like zigzagged surface. This type of display seems to have been part of daily life during the 1910s. The artist Marcel Duchamp, with all his interest in perception, movement, and ordinary objects, noticed it around 1912–1915 and contemplated integrating it in his work *The Bride Stripped Bare by Her Bachelors, Even* so as to present a square ("for instance") seen straight on or at an angle from a given spot. In his notes Duchamp drew a zigzag representing what he called the "Wilson-Lincoln system", adding, "i.e. like the portraits which seen from the left show Wilson seen from the right show Lincoln".[16] The idea of a changing image on a pleated surface dates back to the eighteenth century at least,[17] yet it apparently achieved particular visibility in public space in the early twentieth century, when screen photographs were spontaneously compared to it. Few concrete traces of such public uses of screen photography remain. Was it too complex to put together? Too easily damaged? Little suited to large formats? Or have the images that were produced simply been lost over time? In any case, the area in which contemporaries foresaw success for the invention was advertising, of which the place in urban life was rapidly expanding. Advertising as a profession was taking hold and its specialists were keen to identify new ways of attracting and holding the attention of passers-by in the city. Urban publicity was a rich field for visual experimentation in which questions of movement and attention, perception and attraction, were explored in very concrete ways. The intriguing, interactive ambivalence of animated screen imagery – not to mention its ability to synthesize various states of the same object – involved issues that aroused much interest in 1910.

Animated screen images feature movement in what appears to be a single photograph, which is an attractive specificity. The system may seem trivial – an amusing little game, the object of a passing fancy – yet other instances of its implementation show that its placement at the crossroads of classic photography and series of images was then at the vanguard of photographic research. Before entertaining the *flâneur* of the Boulevards in the form of animated portraits or illuminated advertisements, the interlacing of images using a line screen had

---

15 *Bulletin de la Société française de photographie* (1910): 171; Moritz von Rohr and Étienne Wallon, "Le développement de la Parallax-Stéréoscopie", in *Ve Congrès international de la photographie. Compte rendu, procès-verbaux, rapports, notes et documents* ["5th International Conference of Photography. Report, Minutes, Records, Notes, and Documents"] (Brussels: Émile Bruylant, 1912) 241–242.

16 Marcel Duchamp, *The Writings of Marcel Duchamp*, Michel Sanouillet and Elmer Peterson, eds. (1973; New York: Da Capo Press, 1989) 65. The note appeared in the *Green Box* of 1934.

17 See for example Barbara Maria Stafford and Frances Terpak, *Devices of Wonder* (Los Angeles: Getty Research Center, 2001) 225-226, as well as *Ich sehe was, was Du nicht siehst ! Sehmaschinen und Bilderwelten. Die Sammlung Werner Nekes* ["I See Something that You Don't See! Vision Machines and Worlds of Pictures. The Werner Nekes Collection"], exhibition catalogue, Bodo von Dewitz and Werner Nekes, eds. (Cologne: Museum Ludwig; Göttingen: Steidl, 2002) 239, 446–447.

been used at the turn of the century in two other areas that relied on the synthesis of multiple images: colour photography and stereoscopic photography.[18] The idea was first put forward to simplify the three-colour process, based on the recording of three photographs through three differently-coloured filters. A screen of tiny coloured elements laid on the sensitive surface made it possible to record only one photograph, which was looked at through the same screen. Marketed for the first time in 1895, the method became widespread in 1907 in the form of the well-known Autochrome process, with its screen of green, orange and violet dots. As early as 1896, under the influence of colour photography, the same trick was used to present stereoscopic photographs, which were comprised of two shots taken from slightly different positions to approximate binocular vision. A lined screen made it possible to interlace the two views and, when placed a few millimeters from the final composite image, to observe a three-dimensional illusion.[19]

The *animated* screen photography of relevance to us here appeared in the wake of these inventions. When Frederic Ives took out a patent for this system of animation in 1903, he had already been working on stereoscopic screen photography (since the previous year) and on colour screen photography.[20] Inspired by Ives, Estanave began his work on the screen process around 1905 with three-dimensional effects, just before his first experimentations with animation. Animated screen photography was thus clearly inscribed in the research of the early twentieth century, and its sphere of influence spread much beyond cinema itself to include other types of photography depending on the combination of several images. While contemporary with the cinema, it was just as significantly contemporary with the Autochrome and the first tests of three-dimensional imagery visible without a stereoscope or special glasses.

Exchanges between animated, three-dimensional and colour photography were clearly based on their shared technical foundations. And the ties between these processes were all the more tight-knit that striving for the combination of these three illusions "in a single photo" then partook of what we may call "perceptive realism". Animated screen photography touched on both a major theoretical question and an important technical challenge at the turn of the twentieth century: was it possible to bring new qualities to photography that made it more precisely imitate human perception, while at the same time maintaining the presentation of a simple traditional image? It was a dream that photography could magically imitate all the aspects of our visual perception. One animated screen photograph (Fig. 10) is a nice *mise en abyme* of the process as "cinema in a single

---

18 I further investigate these and other relations between three-dimensional photography and colour photography, founded on the use of multiple images, in my "Colour Photography and Stereoscopy: Parallel Histories", *History of Photography* 29:2 (Summer 2005): 182–196.

19 On the way the technique works, see the sources already mentioned for Estanave.

20 Ives had already earned recognition at the time for his work on half-tone engraving, whose line screen prompted his interest for screen photography.

Fig. 10. Anon., animated line-screen view of a woman with actors' portraits, 1920s, details.

photo". It shows the face of a woman looking at the portrait of a movie star. When the image is animated, the attitude of the woman changes (she smiles, raises her eyes, blows a kiss), as does the portrait pictured (three different actors appear one after another).[21] This tiny composition, with a living character and a still photograph transforming at will, has the lineaments of a utopian "integral" image – one that assumes all the appearances of the world without disclosing the artifices needed to produce such an illusion.[22] While popular images such as this one or the portraits once sold on the Boulevards can be considered pure amusements, the technique they used held utopian potentialities for specialists. Estanave even expressed the hope that colour, three-dimensional effects and animation would one day be combined in a single photograph thanks to the simultaneous use of several screens. It would have constituted one more step towards the "general problem of photography" as he defined it: "to represent through images objects as we see them".[23]

During the 1910s, animated screen photography – as a hybrid image that was both still and moving – was modern in the technical system it implemented and in the way it explored visual attractiveness. Modestly yet undoubtedly, it caught the interest of scientists, industrialists and the common man, who expressed interest in the technique by having a personalized portrait made. The production of animated portraits apparently subsided after the 1920s in Europe, although

21 These are Harold Lloyd and two actresses I have not been able to identify with certainty. The iconography of these screen images thus seems to have followed what was happening in cinema. The heyday of these images saw the phenomenon of stardom appear and develop, following the anonymity of performers in early cinema. See *Stars au féminin. Naissance, apogée et décadence du star système* ["Stars in the Feminine. Advent, Culmination, and Decadence of the Star System"] (Paris: Centre Pompidou, 2000).

22 I developed this analysis of the utopian "integral image" in my doctoral thesis and investigated its manifestations during the 1930s and 1940s in "Brave New Photography", my contribution at the conference "Literature and Photography: New Perspectives", University of St Andrews, May 2007.

23 Eugène Estanave, *Relief photographique à vision directe. Photographies animées et autres applications des réseaux lignés ou quadrillés* ["Direct Three-Dimensional Vision in Photography. Animated Photographs and Other Applications of Lined or Crosshatched Screens"] (Vitry-sur-Seine: F. Meiller, 1930) 1.

some late American examples were manufactured for fairs and exhibits until the mid-1930s. Their disappearance parallels changes in cinema, which had served as a catalyst for the craze that surrounded them. These changes only underscored the limits of the technique: after World War I, cinema definitively shed its status as a technical novelty – that of animated photography – to become the site of consolidation of other technical and aesthetic traditions and associations. In this new cultural context, interest for cinema continued and even grew, but manifested itself in other ways. The status of animated screen photography changed. It no longer interested scientists and must have appeared old-fashioned to the public, representing as it did early cinema; for all, its power of representation surely seemed disappointingly limited. Significantly, the technique no longer found an audience in the form of personalized portraits – surely an indication that its contemporaries had come to perceive it differently. "The genuine modernity of 1920s cinema [...] is that of speed [*la vitesse*]", Jacques Aumont argues.[24] The animated screen portrait, with its instructions for *gentle* handling, its reliance on a very limited number of staged poses, its jerky animation that always looped back on itself instead of moving forward towards something new, represented anything but speed. It belonged to a specific period in the history of still photography and of animated photography, a moment that revealed the hopes pinned on both techniques.

---

24   Jacques Aumont, *Moderne ? Comment le cinéma est devenu le plus singulier des arts* ["Modern? How Cinema Became the Most Singular of the Arts"] (Paris: Cahiers du cinéma, 2007) 26.

3

The Pathéorama Still Film (1921): Isolated Phenomenon or Paradigm?

Valérie Vignaux

To reflect on the intersections between photography and cinema in the 20th century, and more particularly on the relations between stillness and movement, I have chosen to focus on an object which bears a paradoxical name: the still film. Indeed, it relies as much on the stillness of the photographic image as on the run of the cinematographic print, which sets it in motion. The still film is a piece of 35-mm film, about one meter long, on which twenty images (occasionally fifty) are reproduced end to end. Devices close to the magic lantern or – later – slide projectors, made it possible to show the views on the film, while a toothed wheel allowed lecturers to move the film forward at their own pace.

The advent of the film still in the history of the projection of images has not been dated. The object was apparently invented in the early 20th century and seems to have become obsolete around the 1980s. Used in educational lectures as a medium in the transmission of knowledge, the still film replaced the glass plates widely used in projections during the 19th century and was itself replaced by slides, which freed users from the order imposed by the film strip. The quantitative importance of extant titles (several thousands have been preserved) and the fact that none of the publishers has survived make the still film a *terra incognita*. To contribute to – scarce – existing research on the still film, [1] I chose to look into the Pathéorama catalogue distributed by Pathé. The collection I had initiated as part of my activities at the cinémathèque of the city of Paris school system had yielded only four Pathéorama reels out of the thousand films that emerged out of the attics where they had been put away. From then on, I set out to gather paper archives or objects (machines and films) preserved in the collections of the Cinémathèque

---

1   Thierry Lefebvre, "Sage comme une image. L'abbé Songaylo et le Pathéorama", *1895* 21 (December 1997): 147–155; Thierry Lefebvre, "Films fixes et santé publique", *Revue d'histoire de la pharmacie* 331 (2001): 381–399; Thierry Lefebvre, "Film safety, formats réduits, films fixes", and Didier Nourrisson, "Le 7e art d'enseigner…: le film fixe", *Cinéma-Ecole : aller-retour*, ed. Didier Nourrisson and Paul Jeunet (Saint-Etienne: Presses Universitaires de Saint-Etienne, 2001) 141–150 and 151–164, respectively; and Didier Nourrisson, "Arrêt sur les images de l'alcoolisme", *A votre santé ! Education et santé sous la IVe République*, ed. Didier Nourrisson (Saint-Etienne: Presses Universitaires de Saint-Etienne, 2002) 125–136.

française, the Fondation Jérôme Seydoux-Pathé, and the Association pour la sauvegarde des films fixes en Anjou, a local organization located in the Loire valley and whose aim is to preserve still films. All this amounted to patents, ten publications or so – more often than not in the form of advertisements presenting the catalogue –, a dozen machines, and around a hundred rolls.[2] The scarcity of materials still allowed me to advance a number of methodological suggestions towards a cultural history of techniques. These propositions relate to a research on pedagogical and educational cinema in the interwar period in France, more broadly, they involve thinking the roles and the place of archives in writing the history of cinema.

The Pathéorama may be considered a phenomenal object in the sense that its main merit was its endurance. However, as François Dagognet aptly notes in his *Éloge de l'objet* ["In Praise of Objects"], "the object is a 'total social phenomenon': reading it, deciphering, on its shell or in its lines alone, the cultural traits embedded in it, are skills to be learned, just like the translation of morphologies".[3] I will thus attempt to turn the phenomenon into a paradigm, based on the remaining evidence.

The Pathéorama as Phenomenon

The device, as suggested by the successive applications for patents at the Office national de la propriété industrielle, was still a work in progress when it first appeared. When it was first mentioned on 25 March 1921 by the manufacturer, the invention was defined according to three parameters: "… a film comprising various cinematographic views […] as well as a device for directly viewing the said film and possibly for screening it".[4]

The organization of images, or the production process of the films, are described in much detail, so much so that they seem to constitute one of the main characteristics of the invention:

> The film which is the object of the invention consists in putting together a succession of various cinematographic views, related or not to the same subject and possibly separated by titles for explanation. […] The film may comprise views unrelated to one another, just as it may involve views correlated to some degree; […] these views may serve as illustrations to the main points of a cinematographic subject or scene and accordingly provide a kind of summary of them. […] Although the making of such films mainly relies on the many scraps found in the manufactures of cinematographic film […] regular films may also be used, obviously, by taking apart the views that make them up and recombining them.[5]

2   I want to thank Laurent Mannoni, Stéphanie Salmon, and Luc David for their reception and advice.

3   François Dagognet, *Éloge de l'objet : pour une philosophie de la marchandise* (Paris: Vrin, 1989) 40.

4   "Brevet n°532.804, Office national de la propriété industrielle, République française", Cinémathèque française, collection of optical devices and machines.

The description stresses out the origin of images ("the many scraps found in the manufactures of cinematographic film") and the operations of editing (since images may be combined without necessarily being correlated, in order to form a summary of sorts).

A few weeks later, on 21 April 1921, an additional clause defined the conditions of reproduction for what was from then on referred to as "film composé" ["compound film"]. According to the document, the model serving to make duplicates may be

> made of blank film on which the desired subjects are reproduced, whether chosen among images of cinematographic films or in collections of photographic views.[6]

The additional clause thus adds images from the photographic industry to "scraps" of film. The choice of the term "collection" seems to hint at the collections put together to illustrate the many lectures given all over the national territory as part of popular education since the end of the nineteenth century. The rather general wording also leaves open the possibility of building up an in-house collection of photographic views.

The next day, on 22 April 1921, the company registered the plans for the device designed for direct vision, which was made up of:

> ... a rectangular box [approximately 5.5 x 2.4 in.] with three compartments, two of which [...] serve as magazines for the film on either side, while the oblong central compartment serves as a dark room, with a glass opening to let the light shine through the film on one side, and the magnifying eyepiece on the other side.[7]

Improvements to these plans were described in a new additional clause dated August 4, 1921: the box came with a hinged lid, the ends of the film strip were held by a small metal clip, and the case had been given an appropriate curve to ease the unwinding of the film.

One year later, on 21 October 1922, the company finally registered a patent for a projection lantern named Cocorico, which allowed "all people who owned devices for the direct viewing of strips of images to instantly transform these into projection devices". The lantern, however, permitted but a screened image of modest size which, according to the catalogues, could not exceed 3 x 2.5 ft.

Why did Charles Pathé launch this device of little consequence on the market even though he was otherwise known for his pugnacity in business, a trait he also wrote about in his autobiography, *Souvenirs et conseils d'un parvenu*[8] ["Memories

5   Brevet 532–804, Cinémathèque française.

6   "Brevet n°24.748, 1ᵉʳᵉ addition au brevet d'invention n°532.804, Office national de la propriété industrielle, République française", Cinémathèque française, collection of optical devices and machines.

7   "Brevet n°534.375, Office national de la propriété industrielle, République française", Cinémathèque française, collection of optical devices and machines.

8   Reproduced in Charles Pathé, *Écrits autobiographiques*, ed. Pierre L'Herminier (Paris: L'Harmattan, 2006).

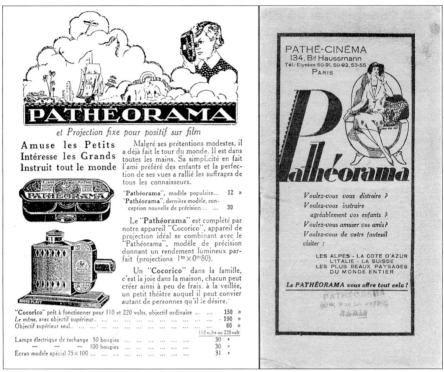

Fig. 1 (left). Advertisement for the Pathéorama, undated (© Cinémathèque française).
Fig. 2 (right). Catalogue Pathéorama, undated (© Fondation Jérôme Seydoux-Pathé).

and Advice of an Upstart"]? Available documents can probably shed light on this question.

The Paradigm of Amateur Cinema

According to the advertisements, the Pathéorama was easy to handle and may be used without difficulty by women or children. Its reasonable price made it affordable for a popular audience: the viewer was sold at a cost of about ten francs, the films cost 2.5 to 5 francs apiece, and the Cocorico projector cost 120 francs. It could also be an outward sign of wealth: the manufacturer included a luxury Bakelite model in the range of products to attract a typical young, very stylish female customer, possibly with a Pathéorama in one hand, a cigarette holder in the other, as suggested in advertisements.

This positioning on the family market places the Pathéorama in the tradition of operations imagined by Pathé to develop the private market. As early as 1912, the industrialist marketed a camera that came with a projection device using a smaller-format film (28mm), the Pathé-Kok, a name which calls to mind the Kodak amateur device distributed by Eastman. Pathé, as is well known, moni-

Fig. 3. Poster for the Pathéorama, undated (© Fondation Jérôme Seydoux-Pathé).

tored very closely the activities of the American company and, in 1926, the two companies signed an agreement to market the blank film under the name Pathé-Kodak. Still, the product was later abandoned, probably because of the Second World War, and its cost was deemed too high. In the early 1920s, Charles Pathé turned his focus back on the amateur film market. On 21 February 1921, a month before the patent application for the Pathéorama, he registered the plans for a camera and a projection device called Pathé-Baby, designed for 9.5mm film with central sprocket holes. Judging by the order of 5,000 units passed to engineer Victor Continsouza, Pathé was apparently confident of the success of the new object. A catalogue of films offering reedited versions of movies exhibited by Pathé-Consortium – feature films, documentaries, pedagogical films, but also newsreels – supplemented the Pathé-Baby. Simultaneously, on 16 September 1920, Charles Pathé called a general meeting to ratify the division of his company into two entities, Pathé-Consortium (responsible for the Pathé catalogue, production, distribution, and exhibition) and Pathé-Cinéma (in charge of the manufacture of blank film and equipment, light-format film equipment for amateurs, home cinema, or pedagogical cinema). Charles Pathé professed his lack of interest for the former, staking most of his economic interests on the latter.

The Pathéorama pertains to a number of initiatives that aimed to increase amateur practices. However, Charles Pathé necessarily had other aims, failing which the device would have been redundant in relation to the Pathé-Baby, and paling in comparison. On 16 September 1920, the industrialist made his intentions known at the general assembly that ratified the break-up between Pathé-Consortium and Pathé-Cinéma:

> We inform you that we currently have the project of a cheap, small popular cinematograph under consideration, that we believe could be used both as a toy by children and as a lecture aid in some types of teaching. […] At any rate, should this new device – whose launching we are counting on to shift our surplus production of blank film – come to fail, I still think that we would not have any difficulty using our film stock in the many possible applications of film in the replacement of photographic glass plates used in everyday photo- graphy.[9]

The Pathéorama was thus part of a commercial strategy whose objective was to substitute still images on film for views on glass plates. The 1926 Pathéorama catalogue underlined this:

> The goal our company has been pursuing is to put within everyone's means, for a modest price, a set of carefully selected views accompanied with a documented explanatory text, which could meet the same needs as photographic glass plates, commonly used yet difficult to handle because of their fragility.

The study of periodicals *Le Fascinateur* and *Cinéopse*,[10] over the period from 1901 to the 1920s, suggests – in the absence of any counterexample – that the device was the first of its kind to be marketed. It was later widely adopted by the different suppliers, who thought it better to replace the heavy and fragile glass plates with small, light, and handy film rolls. The Pathéorama popularized a technique, the reproduction of still images on film, and was to catch the interest of pedagogues using images in their work.

The paradigm of Pedagogical Cinema

Like many of his contemporaries in the early 1920s, Charles Pathé had an interest in pedagogical cinema. In 1923 the industrialist marketed a projector called Pathé-Enseignement, and in 1926 he launched a periodical titled *le Cinéma chez soi* ["Cinema at Home"], under the patronage of a committee that included the main promoters of educational cinema: Jules Breton, Minister of Hygiene and chair of the famous extra-parliamentary Bessou commission, entrusted in 1916 by Minister of State Education Paul Painlevé with the responsibility to study the means to generalize the use of cinema in education; Julien Luchaire, head of the

---

9   *Pathé, Écrits autobiographiques* 299.

10   Published by the Éditions de la Bonne Presse and run by the specialist of educational projections G.-Michel Coissac.

Institut de coopération intellectuelle; Henri Queuille, the guardian of the cinematheque of the Ministry of Agriculture; Edmond Labbé, the protector of the cinematheque of the Department of Vocational Training; and senator Joseph Brenier, head of the Office du cinéma éducateur in Lyons.[11] The inaugural editorial justified the project as follows: "Our agenda is in our title. Our audience includes families and the school system, another family."

In spite of these declarations of intent, the periodical changed layouts in June–uly 1927, barely a year later, and changed its focus:

> The contents of this journal will now be wider in range. Obviously, we will still give educational cinema much coverage [...] Our publication will remain the periodical of families and schools. However, the variety of cinematographic activities in all its forms will be more amply commented. We will cover the projects of

Fig. 4. Charles Pathé, cover of Cinéma chez soi (Cinema at Home), August-September 1926 (© Fondation Jérôme Seydoux-Pathé).

authors, the productions of studios, the creations of artists.

The more theoretical journal of the first issues – where an article by Jean Comandon on scientific cinema had appeared – was turning into a newspaper intended for the users of the Pathé-Baby. It presented these Pathé-Consortium productions liable to be distributed in lighter format and listed the latest releases. Meant for amateurs, it was also aimed at the subsidiaries that distributed devices and films across France, regularly publishing their addresses. In 1919 and 1932, advertisements for the Pathéorama still appeared in the journal.

The creation of the Pathéorama thus seems to have pursued three objectives: to create new outlets for blank film, to familiarize a non-professional audience with the projection of images, and to provide pedagogues of all kinds – mothers, teachers, or priests – with views suitable for them. The presentation of the device in the 1926 catalogue repeated the argument: "Our collection of films, which now

---

11   These personalities and commissions are discussed in detail in Valérie Vignaux, *Jean Benoît-Lévy ou le corps comme utopie, une histoire du cinéma éducateur dans l'entre-deux-guerres en France* ["Jean-Benoît Lévy or the Body as Utopia, a History of Educational Cinema in the Interwar Period in France"] (Paris: AFRHC, 2007).

*Fig. 5. Cover of the Bulletin de la Cinémathèque
Sainte-Thérèse 5, February 1934.*

counts 300 titles, constitutes a genuine encyclopedia which should be kept by its owners [...] and deserves to be looked at frequently".[12]

In the reference to the Encyclopédie, Charles Pathé situated his initiative in a movement of ideas which had emphasized the use of images in the transmission of knowledge since the Enlightenment.[13] However, the examination of the catalogue shows that the chosen categories had nothing encyclopedic to them: no scientific films are listed, to give but one example. The advertisement published in *le Cinéma chez soi* in 1929 itemizes the categories of films represented in the catalogue:

> The choice of films is very wide and includes documentary views [...], views of the colonies, of travels, as well as of the main scenes from great films. Religious films have not been forgotten [...] neither have tales for children.[14]

12   1926 catalogue, Fondation Jérôme Seydoux-Pathé.

13   See Roland Barthes, "Image, raison, déraison", *L'Univers de l'Encyclopédie*, ed. Roland Barthes, Robert Mauzi, and Jean-Pierre Seguin (Paris: Les Libraires associés, 1964), reproduced in *Les Planches de l'Encyclopédie de Diderot et d'Alembert vues par Roland Barthes*, ed. Jérôme Serri, catalogue of the exhibition at the Musée de Pontoise (Association les amis de Jeanne et Otto Feundlich, 1989).

14   *Le Cinéma chez soi* 28 (February 1929): n. p.

The Catalogue

The study of these films was carried out thanks to the documents preserved in the three institutions previously mentioned, the Cinémathèque française, the Association pour la sauvegarde des films fixes en Anjou, and the Fondation Jérôme Seydoux-Pathé. The first two hold about fifty titles each in their collection while the Fondation only holds a dozen. While the preservation of films in the collection of optical devices and machines of the Cinémathèque française seems natural, given the institution's policy of acquiring devices with matching reels when possible, the presence of the films in Anjou is more surprising. The Association was created to preserve the many extant still films locally because of the activities of a Catholic cinematheque, the Cinémathèque Sainte-Thérèse founded in 1928 by M. Mousseau with a double mission. As a distributor of equipment, it made access to the cinematograph easier in order to counter lay youth clubs, but also encouraged amateur practices of cinema. To that effect, the Cinémathèque Sainte-Thérèse created the G.A.C.C. (Groupement national des amateurs cinéastes catholiques). It also published a bulletin and catalogues presenting Pathé-Baby films that could be shown in youth fellowships – films which it gave itself license to re-edit. The Pathéorama is mentioned until 1943, but the catalogue does not appear to have been augmented since its constitution in the mid-1920s. It seems that Charles Pathé, excluded from procurement contracts for pedagogical films (a hypothesis the change in the editorial line of *le Cinéma chez soi* would also support), turned to religious congregations.

The films I have been able to examine combine forty images or so. They sometimes involve several parts titled "series", a very probable reference to the term "serial" then used in the film industry. The films for which the company was famous were adapted in two or three episodes and probably made out of the cinematographic scraps previously evoked. They include Henri Diamant-Berger's twelve-episode film *Three Musketeers* (1921), André Antoine's *The Girl from Arles* (1921), René Leprince's *l'Empereur des pauvres* ("The Emperor of the Poor", 1922), or Jean Kemm's *l'Enfant roi* ("The Child King", 1923). As to Robert Flaherty's *Nanook of the North* (55 minutes), it was condensed in three episodes of about forty images each. Some descriptive elements were left aside, intertitles were altered, but the structure and continuity of the works were evidently respected.

Besides film adaptations, which account for 29 titles out of 277 (almost 11%), the majority of the catalogue (141 titles, or 51%) is made up of documentary views, that is to say, "tourisms", "great cities", "mountain", "beaches and ports", "French colonies", but also "actualités". Subjects were organized based on existing productions such as the film made out of a "Cinégraphie" by R. Alexandre's. Still, they could also be put together with photographic views marketed by other companies or organizations: images by Le Deley, the Clichés d'Art de l'Agence économique du Gouvernement Général de l'Afrique Occidentale française (a film distributor as well), images borrowed from the Verascope Richard (better known

Fig. 6. Fragment of a Pathéorama film strip, Toby Chien garde l'auto (Toby the Dog Watches the Car), undated (© Cinémathèque française).

for its stereo photography technology), or the postcards published by l'Abeille, Librairie Blanchard, or C.A.P. Strasbourg. Very heterogeneous images are thus classified under the documentary label. Besides tourism films, the category also comprises topicals on events such as *les Fêtes de la Victoire 1919* or *L'Exposition internationale des arts décoratifs de 1925*, which could have qualified as *actualités*. The views could be edited in several films: the films *En Tunisie* and *La Vie au harem* use the same views of female faces.

Films for children (61 titles, or 22% of the total) were also made from images belonging to various modes: an imagery in the style of Epinal for an adaptation of *Le Petit poucet* (*Little Red Riding Hood*), an edit of a Roger Lortac cartoon, *Un Chien trop bien dressé* ["A Dog Too Well Trained"], or a composition from photographs for a "comic film", the only one in its section, *Toby chien garde l'auto* ["Toby the Dog Watches the Car"].

Religious films (12 titles, or 4.5% of the total) can be adaptations, such as *La Vie de Jésus* in four parts of forty images or so each (*Naissance* ["Birth"], *Enfance* ["Childhood"], *Miracles et Vie publique*, *Passion et mort*), whose author I have not been able to ascertain but which is very probably adapted from Ferdinand Zecca's *The Life and Passion of Christ* (1904); or a film titled *Lourdes ou les apparitions de la Sainte Vierge à Bernadette*, made at little cost since it was sampled from two shots only.

The examination of the Pathéorama leads to the conclusion that it appears to be a "total social phenomenon", to use François Dagognet's expression. The device confirms genealogies which located the origin of moving images in the many toys that consisted in setting them in motion. A projection lantern combined with a catalogue with encyclopedic ambitions, the Pathéorama is also a reminder that since the 17th century, the screening of images has been part of various processes in the transmission of knowledge. The device also crystallizes a change of medium in the projection of still images, from glass to film. Finally, the catalogue shows how modes of representation cohabited without conflicting in the early 20th century. Indeed, these postcards held a documentary value, displaying what remained invisible for most: the sea, the Orient, etc.

I will conclude these thoughts on an invention and a catalogue of images with the unexpected testimony of Chris Marker, a user and maker of Pathéorama films:

> It was a funny object, a small metal box [...]. If you were rich, you could insert the small box in a kind of magic lantern [...]. I had to content myself with the minimal version: placing my eye on the lens and looking. Why then [...] could I not in turn make something approaching? [...] So with scissors, glue, and translucent paper, I made a faithful copy of the real Pathéorama reel. After that, frame by frame, I started drawing a series of poses of my cat [...] inserting a few titles for the commentary. And all of a sudden, the cat joined the world of the characters of *Ben Hur* or *Napoleon*. [...] I was quite proud of the result, [but] Jonathan soon made a sobering comment to me: "You idiot, cinema is made of moving images, he said. You can't make a film with still images." Thirty years went by. Then I directed *La Jetée*.[15]

---

15 Chris Marker, "De l'autre côté du miroir", text written for the booklet accompanying the DVD edition of *La Jetée* (G.C.T.H.V., 2003).

4

The Mixed Use of Still and Moving Images in Education during the Interwar Period

Christel Taillibert

From the beginnings of cinema, moving images were seen by educationalists as a new tool that could serve their cause. A production of didactic films covering a wide range of topics soon developed parallel to a vast production of "spectacular" films, as fiction and entertainment films were then referred to. The early period of educational cinema, from the early 20th century to the turning point of World War II, is characterized by an ambiguous and complex relationship with still images. The study of contemporary writings and of the educational films themselves shows that demands and expectations in relation to didactic cinema and the creation of teaching materials resorted to elements of comparison, judgment, and analysis almost always referred to an opposition between the two types of visual media.

The Initial Reluctance of the Teaching Profession

To understand how this very original situation came to be, the strong misgivings of teachers about the integration of cinema in their practices must be taken into consideration. Their distrust mainly owed to the perceived threat of their replacement by the new pedagogical tool. As long as images were still, no matter their content, the educational role of teachers remained central in explaining, commenting, relating elements to one another. With film, it seemed, the moving image laid claim to all these prerogatives, condemning teachers to attend a lesson over which they had no control along with their pupils.

The advertisements of some producers of didactic films did nothing to allay these fears, emphasizing the "pedagogical revolution" which filmed lessons would inevitably bring about in the field of teaching. Most of these concerns were obviously unfounded, yet they endured in a diffuse form until the late 1930s in the debates stirring up the spheres of pedagogical cinema. The advocates of a didactic cinematography, who argued for the integration of these new tools in the pedagogical materials available to schools, thus set out to demonstrate the senselessness of these anxieties through a number of points.

The History of Visual Education

The first argument consisted in presenting cinema as a logical development in the evolution of didactic materials long used in schools. These traditional, widely used visual aids included models, castings, globes, wall maps, or blackboards and – more recently – photographs, slides, and stereoscopies. The cinematograph should accordingly be viewed by teachers as a continuation of and an improvement upon the visual aids already available to them. The most eloquent and conspicuous expression of this idea was the initiation and the publication of a large study, "Essay on the Historical Evolution of Visual Education", in the early 1930s.[1] It came out of the Rome International Institute of Educational Cinema, an organization created within the League of Nations and whose mission was to federate research and debates on educational and didactic cinema.[2] Through a chronological structure that runs from prehistory to modern times, the report tends to emphasize the privileged part images have always played in the transmission of knowledge, supporting its claim with texts by the greatest philosophers and pedagogues in history. The author concludes that "cinema, barely forty years old, is thus but a new means at the disposal of teaching through visual aids, which is by contrast as old as the world, one might say, and all the more necessary as it is the expression of a natural need of the human species.[3] If cinema was simply one more element in the gamut of visual aids whose effectiveness had already been tested, any fear about it thus lost its justification.

The Pedagogical Advantages of the Moving Image

The second argument advanced at the time to promote the adoption of the moving image in teaching materials involved showing the pedagogical advantages it had over other media, particularly still images. The element considered as the most evident and convincing was of course the ability of cinema to

---

1   Luisa Rossi-Longhi, "Essai sur l'évolution historique de l'éducation visuelle", *Revue Internationale du cinéma éducateur* (Rome), 77 p. The study was published in several installments from February to November 1932.

2   The Istituto Internazionale per la Cinematografia Educativa was founded in Rome by Benito Mussolini in 1928 and put under the umbrella of the League of Nations. Its core objective was to foster the production, diffusion, and exchange of educational films between countries, in keeping with the spirit of the League – the pursuit of mutual understanding and collaboration between peoples. Despite the distinct agenda of the Fascist regime itself, which saw it as a part of its diplomacy, the organization soon gained international recognition as a center for thinking and taking initiative with respect to educational cinema. It closed down in December 1937 when Italy withdrew from the League of Nations. See Christel Taillibert, *L'Institut international du cinématographe éducatif. Regards sur le rôle du cinéma éducatif dans la politique internationale du fascisme italien* (Paris: Éditions L'Harmattan, 1999).

3   *Rossi-Longhi, "Essai sur l'évolution historique de l'éducation visuelle", Revue Internationale du cinéma éducateur* (Sept. 1932): 803.

reproduce movement, as Parisian school teacher Jean Brérault fervently attested in a study devoted to the use of cinema in primary education:

> The realm of cinema – this evidence is repeated over and over nowadays – is that of movement. Still, an explanation is in order here. Movement first refers to everything that is itself moving: natural elements, living beings, machines, etc. It also involves what is naturally immobile but may be presented from a mobile point of view. This is the case for panoramic views as well as horizontal, vertical, forward, and backward tracking shots. These tracking shots, so common today, present the advantage of giving represented objects an amazing depth: they make it possible to move around them or to discover their various aspects in continuity. A mountain landscape, for instance, as seen from a car moving on a winding road, is infinitely more evocative than a still image. My pupils always greatly benefited from the screening of films such as "La Route des Alpes" or "La Route des Pyrénées", which were shot during a scenic trip in an automobile.[4]

The second element playing to cinema's advantage was its capacity to represent volumes, masses, and accordingly make the understanding of distances and dimensions easier. These advantages thus enabled the medium to be an effective help in the teaching of arts, as Henri Focillon declared at the International Conference on Didactic and Educational Cinema (Congrès International du cinéma d'enseignement et d'éducation) in 1934:

> With the three-dimensional arts, architecture and sculpture, we tend to think that the volume is only the superposition and sequence of a few profiles. We have tried to show somewhere else that profiles are countless, and that even if we were able to capture and project many of them through still images, we would still be missing a fundamental sense of the mass, the relation between parts, and the way they go together and balance one another, which a continuous sequence may render.[5]

Other arguments most frequently put forward included the ability of film, in its discursive logic, to relate isolated information, to take into consideration the specific context for each phenomenon, to create logical links, and therefore to facilitate intellectual acquisition. Finally, the last advantage which I should mention here is the possibility for cinema, thanks to the playful dimension of the screening, to make it easier for pupils to be alert intellectually and thus to withhold information. "Cinema has a considerable edge over old maps and still projections", an investigation on the relations between the teaching profession and cinema read in 1931, "that of instructing and amusing at the same time. And when you remember that children and adolescents need distraction, you have to acknowledge that the task of educating is made easier by this combination of what is useful with what is enjoyable, by this way of teaching through amusement which, while exhibiting form, interests and instructs children."[6]

4   Jean Brérault, "Utilisation du cinématographe dans l'enseignement primaire", *La participation française au congrès international du cinéma d'enseignement et d'éducation* (Paris: Comité français de l'Institut International du cinématographe éducatif, 1934) XVI-XVII.

5   Henri Focillon, "Le cinématographe et l'enseignement des arts" ["The Cinematograph and Art Education"], *La participation française au congrès international du cinéma d'enseignement et d'éducation* LV.

However, this was not a widespread opinion, and some used the same arguments at the time to prove the opposite, i.e. that cinema was by nature unfit for the needs of teaching. Bessie D. Davis, a teaching specialist in the division of film screenings at the Metropolitan Museum in New York, summed up this commonly shared idea as follows:

> For pupils accustomed to attending movie theaters, the screen is now so closely associated with the idea of entertainment and the possibility to approve or disapprove, to observe or forget in whole or in part that even at school the cinema will never appear to them as a means of study.[7]

The Complementary Functions of Still and Moving Images

While the cinematograph did indeed have unquestionable didactic advantages, the advocates of the introduction of the new tool in schools were very careful not to recommend doing away with devices involving still images or using moving images exclusively. In 1934 the International Institute of Educational Cinema issued its own conclusions on the subject: "Still and moving images are two essentially different things. Each is excellent in its sphere, but their respective usages meet completely different ends. Far from mutually exclusive, the two modes of projection are meant to supplement each other."[8] This assertion sometimes gave rise to heated debates in order to establish with precision the situations in which one or the other of these technologies was more appropriate. Some teachers even tried to propose a classification of the respective areas for which one or the other technology was better suited, based on the discipline taught, the level of study involved, and the intellectual abilities of the students under consideration. Some surveys even tried to analyse the didactic potential of these two forms of projection according to the gender and socio-professional background of the pupils.[9] Following these studies, the lists that were drawn up often contradicted one another, definitively ruling out the use of cinema in some disciplines while sanctioning it as an effective teaching auxiliary in others. During the huge conference that brought together the main international figures of educational and didactic cinema in Rome in 1934, participants attempted to bring the debate to a conclusion by putting forward a list of the disciplines from which cinema should not be excluded, but in which it should still be used cautiously: history, religion, mathematics, and modern languages were thus designated as the exclusive domains of still images.[10] This compulsive classifica-

6   "Le monde enseignant et le cinéma" ["The Teaching Profession and Cinema"], *Revue Internationale du cinéma éducateur* (April 1931): 411.

7   Bessie D. Davis, "La valeur comparée des projections fixes et des projections animées" ["The Comparative Value of Still Images and Moving Images"], *Cinéma et enseignement* (Rome: Istituto Internazionale per la Cinematografia Educativa, 1934) 176.

8   "Quelques considérations sur le film sonore et parlé" (note by the Institute), *Cinéma et enseignement* 218.

9   Giovanni De Feo, "Le monde scolaire et le film d'enseignement" ["The Teaching World and the Educational Film"], *Revue internationale du cinéma éducateur* (Aug. 1932): 696.

tion, it should be mentioned, went sometimes very far since an inventory of topics for which still images or moving images were deemed more appropriate was also done within each discipline. As an example, the Office International des Musées drew up a precise list of headings in each of its activities for which moving images should be preferred to still images (current events, to arouse the curiosity and the interest of the public; ethnographic collections, to put objects back in the context of their everyday function; the study of monuments or works of art in their artistic, historical, natural atmosphere; the stages in the production of works of art; etc.).[11]

The Pedagogy of Moving Images

Parallel to these debates meant to reassure teachers as to the continuity in their practices, a specific pedagogy for the integration of cinema in educational methods was also developed with a similar view to assuaging. Indeed, as already noted, the reluctance of teachers primarily had to with a feeling of dispossession of their pedagogical role in the face of films presented as self-sufficient. A vast work of propaganda was therefore orchestrated in order to bring out the central part the teacher still played in a lesson accompanied by the projection of moving images:

> Film may thus be used increasingly in schools, provided its role as a visual auxiliary in the work of the teacher is maintained and reinforced. A position superior to that of the teacher or the suppression of the teacher are theoretical possibilities which practical application should lead to dismiss at this time, just as it has dismissed the hypothesis of a purely mechanical education in which the cameraman may substitute for the teacher. Will this hypothesis prove true in the future? It seems unlikely when one considers the fact that any film, even the best from the point of view of teaching, will always remain cold, arid, and ineffective, if it is not made lively and understandable by the words of the individual whose mission calls upon him to observe and raise the child's soul in life.[12]

To consolidate this stand, many writings made every effort to define the role of the schoolmaster in the pedagogical process specific to teaching through film. They invariably emphasized a central element, the schoolmaster's words, which had to be safeguarded, even during the screening. The resolutions of the 1934 conference thus read,

> the use of cinema must not obstruct the educative action of the schoolmaster and the effects of his words [...] He is the one who should formulate the problem, light the way for pupils, comment on the facts, prompt and direct the child's activity. [...] The schoolmaster should be able to intervene during the screening itself to illustrate the points that call for specific information.[13]

10   "Résolutions du congrès", *La participation française au congrès international du cinéma d'enseignement et d'éducation* 23.

11   Office International des Musées, "La cinématographie au service des musées et des monuments d'art", *Cinéma et enseignement* 226–228.

12   *Cinéma et enseignement* III–IV.

Consequently, active pedagogy was mobilized in order to strengthen the key role moving images could play in education. Following its principles, which involved a constant appeal to the pupil's faculties, the schoolmaster had to avoid stating definitive conclusions on the projected images, asking instead the right questions, pointing to a few visual elements, and guiding the thought of his students *"to encourage them on the path to discovery"*.[14] Also emphasized was the fact that "the resort to film [must] not leave children to the agitation of a flow of images, but [must] instead be the opportunity to stimulate them in all forms of exercises.[15] Many descriptions of standard lessons for different teaching subjects were issued at the time to illustrate these assertions.

The Joint Uses of Still and Moving Images

Besides the central role of the schoolmaster's words in appealing to the intelligence of pupils, the other crucial element appearing in these thoughts on methodology involved the place given to still images within this use of moving images. Meeting points between usages for these two didactic instruments may be noted at several levels.

First, the importance of a recourse to the freeze frame in the course of the film screening was stressed a lot, with the goal of sustaining the pupils' attention on a specific aspect of the demonstration. "For cinema to be of appreciable help in teaching, a teacher wrote in 1931, the schoolmaster has to be able to emphasize some images as needed thanks to a device allowing him to stop the film."[16]

The possibility supposedly offered by the film projector to freeze a chosen image, providing a pedagogical alternative to the continuous run of the film strip, made it possible to combine effectively the advantages specific to either technology. High school teacher Emile Brucker perfectly summed up the situation when he wrote:

> Has the introduction of moving images made the screening of still images pointless? Dating back to the first experiments with cinema in teaching, from all directions schoolmasters have asked for the possibility of freezing the film. That shows how essential the projection of still images remains; the reason for it is obvious, since the former is fleeting and the latter alone makes it possible to keep the pupils' attention focused on a given topic.[17]

That the distinct practices related to the film image and to the still image would

13   "Résolutions finales du Congrès", *Revue Internationale du cinéma éducateur* (May 1934): 402.

14   Adrien Collette, "Les projections cinématographiques dans l'enseignement primaire" ["Film Screenings in Primary Education"], *Revue Internationale du cinéma éducateur* (December 1930): 1425.

15   "Résolutions finales du Congrès", *Revue Internationale du cinéma éducateur* (May 1934): 402.

16   "Le monde enseignant et le cinéma", *Revue Internationale du cinéma éducateur* (September 1931): 918.

17   Emile Brucker, "Le cinématographe dans l'enseignement secondaire" ["Cinema in High School Education"], in *La participation française au congrès international du cinéma d'enseignement et d'éducation* XXVIII.

be thus intertwined characterizes the way moving images were seen from a pedagogical standpoint.

Some even praised the study of films frame by frame. French schoolteacher Adrien Collette, a member of the extra-parliamentary committee on cinema in schools, wrote the following on a lesson devoted to the mechanisms of rumination:

> The examination of the film frame by frame, with the naked eye or a magnifying glass, is necessary in this lesson: it makes it possible to understand the mechanism of rumination properly; it reveals the movement of the tongue that pulls the blades of grass together before the jaws catch hold of them, as well as the lateral movement of the lower jaw while the molars break up the grass. This comparison of successive images of the film takes quite some time, but it is very evocative.[18]

The use reserved for the freeze frame came with another prerogative likely to restore still images to favour within the pedagogical use of film. It involved recommending that the teacher and the students draw sketches during or after the screening in order to reproduce on paper or on the blackboard the most significant elements in the mechanisms studied. In his 1932 report on the use of cinema by French schoolteachers, Jean Brérault declared that "the execution of sketches, during or after the projection, is a good exercise", adding, "this search for form and details is also of invaluable help for writing. It demands an effort on the part of children that contributes to the development of their personality".[19]

This similar concern with laying out essential information provided by the film on a stable medium and turning it into a still image explains the nature of debates on the need for teachers to be provided with specific opuscules for each available film. These opuscules would include not only a description of all the scenes in the film, the subtitles, or spoken commentary but also reproductions of the most significant images and diagrams. The rationale was that

> Cinema is always useful when it serves as a didactic instrument in the scientific-cultural order, but on two conditions: [...] that the pupils-viewers have at their disposal a few main photographs from the film on which they can later concentrate their thought to reconstruct the film mentally...[20]

Reflection on the pedagogical use of film thus constantly leads to the same conclusions: the need to supplement filmic material with still images.

Our last point in regard to these pedagogical uses that keep bringing together still and moving images involves the reiteration of the need to resort to the two technologies within the same lesson. Indeed, Jean Brérault – who explored the question at length – defined educational films as "documents which the school-

---

18 Collette, "Les Projections cinématographiques dans l'enseignement primaire", *Revue Internationale du cinéma éducateur* (December 1930): 1427.

19 Jean Brérault, "Ce que pensent du cinéma les instituteurs français qui s'en servent" ["What French Schoolteachers Who Use It Think of Cinema"], *Revue Internationale du cinéma éducateur* (March 1932): 253.

20 "Le monde enseignant et le cinéma", *Revue Internationale du cinéma éducateur* (April 1931): 409.

master uses to illustrate a lesson in connection with screenings of still images, observation, experience".[21] Exposing the principles on which a standard lesson should be based, the schoolteacher suggested that the following plan be adopted:

> The lesson will generally begin with explanations by the schoolmaster and the thoughts of the pupils on the still images or experiments. Already, during this initial work, there will be an attempt to evoke the moving scenes that will be shown at the end. The curiosity of the pupils will thus be stirred up and the film shown in the best conditions. The still image and the film do not conflict; they complement each other. The film projector and the slide projector should always be side by side. Each has a very specific role to play in the lesson as a whole.[22]

G.E. Hamilton (U.S.A.) corroborated this thesis, affirming in 1934 that "a lesson [should] first be illustrated with still projections, then, as much as possible, and in a more detailed manner, with stereoscopic views. Finally, one [could] provide a lively representation of the subject with the help of cinema."[23] His analysis of the evolution of visual education in his country in the first thirty years of the twentieth century is also of interest in that he observes that the introduction of cinema in teaching had had as a consequence a wider use of still images. He thus notes that textbooks have become more lavishly illustrated, that some reading manuals "take for granted the use of stereoscopic views and still images as an integral part of the reading method and the acquisition of vocabulary",[24] that schools have purchased large sets of stereoscopic views and slides, etc. Reading these observations, it thus seems as though the many debates spurring the development of didactic cinema had as their main consequence an awareness – by teachers in the field as well as by public authorities – of the need to reinforce visual aids in education. However, for reasons linked to costs, practicality, and habit, still images gained the most from this attention.

Be that as it may, a fundamental fact to take into consideration when examining the history of educational cinema over the period is that moving images were never seen as self-sufficient. Still images overwhelmingly dominated discourse, even in the case of the most fervent advocates of pedagogy through film. In terms of visual aids, the standard equipment recommended in schools thus involved:

– a standard-format film projector;

– a light-format film projector;

– one or two slide projectors;

– an overhead projector (an epidiascope) to project photographs;

---

21 Brérault, *Revue Internationale du cinéma éducateur* (Apr. 1931): XI.

22 Brérault, *Revue Internationale du cinéma éducateur* (Apr. 1931): XV.

23 G.E. Hamilton, "Le rapport entre les projections fixes et les projections animées", *Cinéma et enseignement* 169.

24 Hamilton, *Cinéma et enseignement* 164.

– finally, a projector for microphotographs.[25]

This was of course a rather utopian vision that rarely became reality in the field. Still, the enumeration shows to what extent still and moving images were considered concomitantly as far as visual aids were involved.

Moving Images … that Move a Lot

I would like to conclude with a few comments on the nature of didactic films produced over the period to try and trace some of the conclusions of these debates in their conception. Indeed, positing a logical continuity with the importance tirelessly given to still images in the use of didactic films, it would only make sense/ to expect that the films integrate "pauses" in their structure through the insertion of still images meant to focus the attention of spectators on an aspect of discourse. As it happens, however, the study of a large corpus of didactic films of the period – that of the LUCE National Institute in Rome in particular, from the creation of the institution in 1924 until the Second World War – seems to bring out a holy horror of stillness, as though the fact that it is a film implied a permanent animation of images. Thus, even when traditionally still images are incorporated in the script – diagrams, geographic maps, etc. –, at no point are they presented to the viewer without the occurrence of some movement: pointers indicate specific areas, diagrams become animated, or arrows signal elements to observe. And when images provide an object, a tool, etc., for observation, either the camera moves around it, or the object moves in front of the camera, or the background is more or less artificially animated. This frenzy in the animation of images is all the more surprising that it belies the possibility for the teacher to intervene during the screening to comment on them. According to the pedagogical precepts of the time, teachers should be in charge of pointing to some elements on the maps, commenting on the diagrams, providing the explanatory captions at the required moment, etc.

To understand this ambivalence between discourse and the actual products offered for pedagogical use, another aspect of the debates already examined should be taken into account, the necessity to rely on film only when the subject matter at hand made it an absolute necessity and when it was superior to still images in that area. Put differently, the insertion of still images in the continuity of the film was perceived as a potential new factor for rejection: indeed, how could the use of film then be justified compared with the possibilities of visual aids consisting of still images? To animate the films, sometimes to excess, thus appeared as a continuous justification of the medium itself from the viewpoint of the subject treated.

Looking at the structure of these films, a few alternatives to the stillness of images

---

25   W.W. Whittinghill, "Organisation de l'enseignement visuel dans les écoles" ["The Organization of Teaching through Visual Aids in Schools"], *Cinéma et enseignement* 181.

surface when it comes to allowing more time while maintaining a purely cinematographic language:

  – the length of some shots, which makes it possible for the eye to dwell on
  certain details without recourse to a still image;

  – the use of slow-motion, which allows to better discern observed mechanisms;

  – intertitles, which sometimes seem to function as "pedagogical pauses" to
  establish an idea, a concept and which, like still images, act as a suspension
  in the unfolding demonstration.

Even so, the relation of the films themselves to the concept of still image generally
proves extremely ambivalent. Strongly recommended in discourses and usages,
the resort to still images seems to have been completely rejected in the conception
of films. The evolution of didactic films from the early specimens to the Second
World War thus attests, against the needs expressed by educators, of a constant
search for discursive autonomy. The structure of scripts, mise en scène, the role
of intertitles, and – from the 1930s on – voice-over commentary are as many
elements designed to reinforce the effectiveness of films in transmitting information on their own. Accordingly, a number of questions remain as to the reasons
for this discrepancy, all the more since it is well-known that the spheres of
production and education were far from hermetic to each other. In all probability,
these rich and copious theoretical views, these numerous investigations and
conferences organized in the field of didactic cinema primarily aimed to appease
education professionals easily rebellious in the face of innovation and change.
These rhetorical harangues therefore had very little influence on an autonomous
production sector that operated without much concern for what were usual fears
in the teaching profession.

Section III
Cinema and the Printed Page

Introduction:
Cinema Flipped Through: Film in the Press and in Illustrated Books

Olivier Lugon

As we saw in the previous chapter, exchanges between cinema and photography could be all the richer as the two media shared a recording surface (flexible 35-mm film) and often a mode of diffusion (light projection) for a century. Yet their paths also crossed on a third "ground" involving no sensitive emulsion, the printed page. Indeed, photography had its largest circulation in a print form; and before the expansion of television, cinema's main outlet besides the theater was print publication.

Already, before the advent of the Lumière cinematograph, paper had been the privileged medium for cinematic movement, from the plates of the phenakistiscope and the zootrope to cards for Mutoscope machines to the pages of flip books. Yet even after 1895, during the hundred years that saw film dominate the production of moving images, the film image kept returning to paper. However, it did so very differently, since the point from then on was not so much to obtain movement on paper as to bring attention to the fact that it was taking place somewhere else, in the darkness of movie theaters. It did so using "relay-images", whose stillness was thus reinforced even further in the eyes of the spectator. There lies the paradox of the century of cinema: any image other than the film image came to be perceived as still, especially the ones supposedly issuing from cinema, making the period the golden age of frozen images. The symbolic primacy gained by the aesthetic of the instantaneous and "the decisive moment" in the photography of the time probably constitutes the best instance of this dialectic and of this new system of the non-moving image as frozen image.[1]

---

1   On this question, see David Campany, who articulates the issue as follows: "Stillness became definitive of photography only in the shadow of the cinema [...] It was almost as if cinema, in colonizing the popular understanding of time, implied that life itself was made up of distinct slices and that still photography had the potential to seize and extract them." David Campany, *Photography and Cinema* (London: Reaktion Books, 2008) 27.

While the printed page fostered exchanges between photography and cinema, it did so following two opposite directions. On the one hand, in the face of competition from the new cinematographic medium, attempts were made to communicate the dynamism, bursts of energy, and narrative richness cinema was then credited with to print photography through the selection of photographs and page layout. Thierry Gervais and Myriam Chermette describe this phenomenon by examining the press in the first half of the century. At stake was the compensation for the supposed deficiencies of still images to better compete with the new medium, inventing cinematographic forms for print photography. On the other hand, film images were wrenched from the volatility of projection as they were given a photographic form and provided with the stability of paper reproduction. Michel Frizot examines this aspect, assessing the possible repercussions of freezing moving images on the photographers themselves through the example of Henri Cartier-Bresson. Between these two options, some similarly sought to print film images on paper – not so much to make them still as to impart movement on them in a different way, through the means of the book and page layout. François Albera analyses a form of published cinema at once photographic and cinematic.

Printed Sequences

In the first half of the century, cinema undeniably constituted the horizon of the illustrated press and of many experimentations with the photography book. It served all the more as a model since, from the 1920s on, it enjoyed the vivid image of the youngest medium, while already benefiting from a cultural recognition which "old" photography was still struggling to attain: before photography, and in its place, in a sense, cinema had managed to become "the seventh art". While this cinematographic model constantly served as a reference, determining more precisely what it covers proves rather difficult, beyond a field of connotations confusedly tied to ideas of dynamism and cultural or technical modernity: urban intensity, popular energy, mechanical power (see introduction to section 1). Accordingly, the textual or graphic evocations offered seem almost contradictory: they refer in turns to the principle of a continuous run and the fluidity of an uninterrupted movement, to the primacy of discontinuous montage, that is, to the opposite system of the break, the shock, and the fragment, to the multiplication of points of view, or to the emotional impact of a large-format image. These diverging interpretations could translate into very diverse choices of page layout: a rapid-fire sequence of snapshots, a vertical, horizontal, or tabular strip of images, the juxtaposition of heterogeneous photographs (whether binary or multipolar), the fragmented photomontage, or superimposition.

According to Thierry Gervais, a characteristic of film did strike press magnates at the turn of the century and had an impact on the changes undergone by periodicals of the Belle Époque: the profusion of visual information it seemed capable of conveying. As Gervais puts it, "history painting faded in the face of the rise of the cinematograph" as a model of organization for the new magazines: the large synthetic compositions typical in 19th-century illustrated periodicals, which required a sustained, concentrated visual attention, gave way to a sequential multiplication of snapshots and the new primacy of a narrative succession premised on the addition of fragments and the acceleration of reading. The term "cinematography" of events referred to arrangements of multiple images that could comprise juxtaposed snapshots as well as genuine film frames. Like a film, the magazine in its totality was from then on thought of as a dynamic whole oscillating between a narrative thread and "moments" of graphic attraction. In so doing, it involved a faster reception where what was once read was now "leafed through", in a new pleasure tied to the swift succession of images.

Following this new path, the reception of information was subjected to a new system of distraction, as Myriam Chermette notes about editorial changes that belatedly reached daily newspapers in the 1930s. Exchanges developed as early as the 1910s between large-circulation newspapers and cinema, notably with cine-novels, the adaptation in serial form of films appearing simultaneously in theaters in weekly episodes. However, not until the interwar period did the cinematographic model truly make forays into the page layout of daily newspapers, with the introduction of narratives in images. Thanks to a strip of multiple snapshots, the reader was supposed to attend an "unfolding" action or phenomenon ranging from a few seconds to a lifetime. Any event or process was henceforth considered as *unfolding* in continuity, no matter the temporal intervals separating the phases of the action and its mostly uneven progress.

In these daily newspapers, as in many other publications during the interwar period, this ideal of continuity was embodied in the recurrent representation of the film strip itself, with its characteristic lateral sprockets reproduced decoratively, as a form of framing which, rather than isolating the image, opens it even further to the successiveness of the sequence. This "film strip" could thus be unrolled vertically – explicitly mimicking the film reel – or horizontally – in which case the 24 x 36 photographic roll served as a reference, even as its kinship with film equipment was underscored. In both cases, the continuity of the run of film was hinted at through a display – or the appearance thereof – a state of images to which spectators normally did not have access: the sequential recording as it exists on the film strip before its public exhibition through projection or editorial work, both of which typically reduce the profusion of moments to a single image. To do justice to the temporal density of modern images, graphic designers thus gave themselves the paradoxical mission of simulating the pre-editorial state of recording their work was supposed to conceal. Such sequential strips invaded many domains of interwar visual culture, from advertising to exhibition design (Fig. 1) to amateur photography, becoming a privileged graphic symbol of the dynamism and sensorial profusion attributed to the century. They obviously

Fig. 1. Xanti Schawinsky, exhibition Die Schule *(The School), Magdeburg, 1930.*

multiplied in publications or periodicals devoted specifically to cinema, to which Michel Frizot turns his attention.

Film Frames and Stills

Besides these graphic imitations of film, two forms of "genuine" cinema images appeared in these publications, the reproductions of film frames and stills. The former proved the rarest. Indeed, their reproduction often turned out to be poor: as "snapshots" too slow to come out sharp, film frames looked as though they were immersed in a uniform halo that paradoxically evoked the auratic blur of pictorialism more than the specific blur of movement. However, this hazy look could also turn into an advantage, allowing the informed reader to immediately identify the reproductions as film images which, more than any photograph, seemed to vibrate with a before and an after, and all the potentiality of a narrative. Much more frequent, stills also assumed a peculiar temporal density. Consisting in reenacting – or more precisely, posing – some shots of the film for the photographic camera during the shooting, they document a reality always dressed to become an image, or already an image, as it were.[2] The explicit staging they

2 On stills, see David Campany, "Posing, Acting, Photography" and John Stezaker, "The Film-Still and its Double: Reflections on the 'Found' Film-Still", in *Stillness and Time: Photography and the Moving Image*, eds. David Green and Joanna Lowry (Brighton: Photoworks/Photoforum, 2006); David Campany's previously mentioned *Photography and Cinema* (London: Reaktion Books, 2008); as well as Winfried Pauleit, *Filmstandbilder. Passagen zwischen Kunst und Kino* (Frankfurt: Stroemfeld Verlag, 2004).

involve seems to endow them with the synthetic power of the painting and the ability to transcend the status of isolated, fragmentary snapshot. The action they depict seems at once taken from real life and synthesized from a narrative development, between event and tableau. In its photographic form cinema, the medium most identified with modern speed and fleetingness, has thus paradoxically been able to give the snapshot a temporal density more typical of history painting and the representational mode of the pregnant moment.

Michel Frizot examines the implications, for the photographers themselves, of the publication of such images in the midst of "mere" photographs in periodicals that mixed them indiscriminately. In his view, the confrontation with this "cinema reduced-to-photography" constituted one of the major sources of Henri Cartier-Bresson's art and of a whole section of modernist reportage that originated in Nouvelle Photographie. As Frizot demonstrates, Cartier-Bresson himself worked with the idea of photography as "condensation", the compact form of an imaginary script which his Leica, using the same film as cinema, allowed him to develop along consecutive shots in a position of constant viewing – as with a film camera. A redefinition of instantaneous photography may thus have been invented through exposure to the other photography that was printed cinema.

Interferences and ambivalences between these two images systems – photographer's photography and cinema photography – marked many a publication in the interwar period. For instance, avant-garde cinema was most likely known to a majority of the contemporary public in photographic form through the countless reproductions published in art periodicals or cultural magazines which, as much as theaters, contributed to the circulation of its images. Works benefited from the imaginary potential of isolated photographs charged with all the mystery created by the absence of the film, but also, by contrast to a theatrical experience, from a theoretical base provided alongside the reproductions. This notably helped the circulation in Europe of Soviet production, which relied extensively on the translation of cinema into still images. Even in the USSR, the periodical *Sovetskoe Kino* ("Soviet Cinema") inaugurated a section titled "Photo in Cinema" in 1926. It featured film frames deemed worthy of photography alongside "real" photos;[3] three years later El Lissitzky reused the principle in the Soviet room of the *Film und Foto* exhibition in Stuttgart. Among the many print enlargements on paper filling the space he intermingled film images and photographers' images so closely that many commentators later equated Soviet photography with values coming primarily from Soviet cinema.

Even if it remained an isolated occurrence, the *Film und Foto* project alone embodied the liveliness of exchanges that could exist between the two arts at the very heart of a modernism aspiring to define the specificities and draw the boundaries of each medium. This was even more the case for the companion

---

3   See Osip Brik, *Sovetskoe Kino* 4–5 (1926), quoted by Margarita Tupitsyn, *The Soviet Photograph, 1924–1937* (New Haven/London: Yale University Press, 1996) 37.

Fig. 2. Franz Roh and
Jan Tschichold (ed.),
foto-auge / oeil et
photo / photo-eye
(1929): plate 76 (film
frames taken from Dziga
Vertov's Man with a
Movie Camera, 1929)

publications to the exhibition. Franz Roh and Jan Tschichold's *foto-auge – œil et photo – photo-eye*, an album aimed to establish "the essence and value of *photography*",[4] ended with a montage of film frames from Dziga Vertov's *Man with a Movie Camera*, as though the future of photography lay primarily with cinema – or at any rate in graphic forms that would take it into account (Fig. 2). In the other two books published for the exhibition, Werner Gräff's *Es kommt der neue Fotograf!* ("Here Comes the New Photographer!") and Hans Richter's *Filmgegner von heute – Filmfreunde von morgen* ("Enemy of film today – friend of film tomorrow"), exchanges between cinema and photography involved the totality of the project. The two titles were presented by the publisher as two sides of the same project, and were indeed written jointly during Richter and Gräff's winter

4   This is the subtitle to Franz Roh's introductory text, "Mechanismus und Ausdruck. Wesen und Wert der
     Fotografie" / "Mécanisme et expression. Les caractères essentiels et la valeur de la photographie" /
     "Mechanism and expression. The essence and value of photography", in *foto-auge – œil et photo – photo-eye*,
     eds. Franz Roh and Jan Tschichold (Stuttgart: Verlag Fritz Wedekind, 1929). My emphasis.

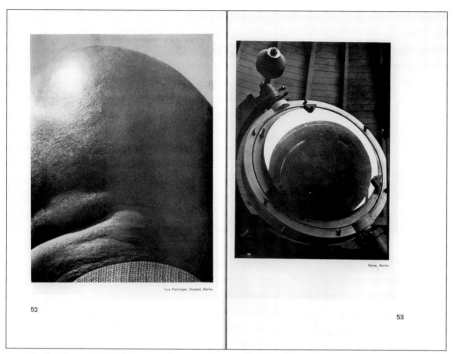

Fig. 3. Werner Gräff, Es kommt der neue Fotograf ! *(Here Comes the New Photographer!), in collaboration with Hans Richter (1929): 52–53.*

vacation together, each of them receiving credit as a "collaborator" in the other's book. Not only did the two friends work hand in hand, they also swapped photographs for their projects without scruples: film frames by Vertov or Richter, photographs from MGM, Universal, or UFA ended up illustrating the specificities of photography according to Gräff; and many photographs were made expressly by the two men to demonstrate what film was in Richter's book. They went as far as to reconstruct the supposedly historical experience of the Kuleshov effect to photograph it, with Werner Gräff taking the place of actor Ivan Mosjukin (see François Albera's essay, Fig. 20). There even is an occurrence of the same image appearing in both titles and serving to praise the specificities of the two media indifferently (Figs. 3, 4).

In the end, the modernist dogma of the specificity of the medium seems to have held moderate sway or, more precisely, to have operated selectively: while great care was taken to distinguish the new media from their non-mechanical predecessors (photography against painting, cinema against theater), criteria remained more flexible when it came to differentiate between them. The dividing line between stillness and motion proved much more porous than the boundary drawn between the mechanical and the handmade, the indexical record and the imitative representation. Photography and cinema appear as the two possible modalities of a same medium-entity verging by turns on stillness or motion.

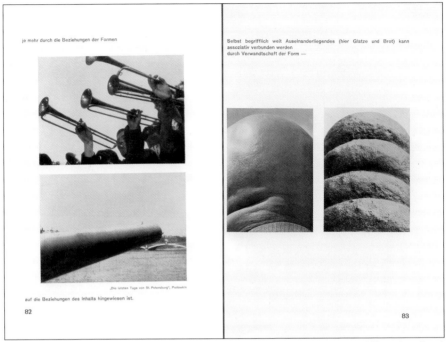

Fig. 4. Hans Richter, Filmgegner von heute - Filmfreunde von morgen *(Enemy of film today - friend of film tomorrow), in collaboration with Werner Gräff (1929): 82–83.*

The Film Book

These convergence effects are reinforced by another feature of modernism: the preeminent place of the manifesto and the legitimation by the text. Accordingly, the "meta-medium" of print and its various forms, as the repository for any art and any image, towered above all the aesthetic production of the first decades of the century. For the cinema, however, this constant return to paper also involved the impossible situation of having to exemplify its specificity as an art of movement through still images, in an apparent betrayal. François Albera reexamines this dilemma, looking at a few great modern cinema books (including Hans Richter's) and their multiple attempts to set cinematographic images into motion through the means of graphic arts and page layout. Albera points out that cinema has not been so much the art of moving images as that of images set in motion through some equipment exterior to them, and that movement could just as well originate in other types of "machineries", including the printed book. The film book could thus be thought of less as a repository of allusions to film than as a substitute of sorts for the projector. For El Lissitzky as well as Alexandre Rodtchenko and Varvara Stepanova, the book became a kind of optical toy operated by a reader who ceaselessly set it in motion in the very act of leafing through, whereas Hans Richter or Hermann Eidenbenz later looked for an equivalence to the succession of images in the simultaneity of page organization.

The latter solution implies the possibility of a graphic transcription of the cinematographic language, and accordingly of a simultaneous form of the suggestion of movement. It thus raises the more general question of the actual relations that may have existed between graphic montage and cinematographic model, and more specifically between graphic and filmic montage: could it be that the "static" organization of co-presence within photomontage, typophoto, or page layout derives from the dynamic organization of succession specific to the join in film? Is it necessarily the plastic condensation of a temporal succession? Does any photographic montage refer to cinema, as many texts of the period and retrospective studies proclaim? Historically, this is far from obvious. When Berlin Dadaists seized on the notion of "montage" in the late 1910s, producing the neologism "photomontage" out of it, it had no cinematographic connotation for them and referred strictly to an industrial mode of production based on assembling preexisting pieces. It was associated with the modern values of mechanics, functional effectiveness, impersonal gesture, but not in itself to movement or animation (and indeed, was the production through "montage" and assembly line so evidently superior to the fluid progression of traditional crafting in terms of dynamism?). In the course of the 1920s, however, after film theoreticians – more particularly from the Soviet Union – also appropriated the term, these cinematographic overtones became predominant, first in French and Russian, then, more slowly, in German and English. Around 1930, the reversal seemed complete: at that point, in the worlds of photography and a burgeoning graphic design, the model of the film, together with that of the assembly line, embodied an effective communication founded on speed. Even in the German sphere, photomontage and typophoto had come to be defined with relation to cinema at that point: Raoul Hausmann characterized photomontage as "static film",[5] César Domela wrote of it as "a transition between the single image and a succession of images (film)",[6] and brothers Heinz and Bodo Rasch affirmed that "photomontages are little movies in the surface".[7] Taking the idea literally, László Moholy-Nagy went as far as to derive a film synopsis from one of his first photomontages, "Huhn bleibt Huhn" ("Once a Chicken, Always a Chicken"), seeing it as a "visual manuscript for a film so that all of its scenes can be visualized at once".[8] So it went for typophoto, whose "synoptic" aspect he related to the "kinetic process"[9] of film and which he first demonstrated in the publication of the synopsis of a hypothetical film, "Dynamics of a Metropolis", in *Painting*

5   Raoul Hausmann, "Fotomontage", *a bis z* 2:16 (May 1931), reprinted as "Photomontage" in *Photography in the Modern Era: European Documents and Critical Writings, 1913–1940*, ed. Christopher Phillips (New York: Aperture, 1989) 179.

6   César Domela, "Les photomontages", (1931) in *César Domela. Typographie, photo-montages & reliefs*, exhibition catalogue (Strasbourg: Musée d'art moderne et contemporain, 2007) 84.

7   Heinz and Bodo Rasch, *Gefesselter Blick. 25 kurze Monografien und Beiträge über neue Werbegestaltung* (Stuttgart: Verlag Dr. Zaugg & Co., 1930) 8.

8   László Moholy-Nagy, *Vision in Motion* (Chicago: Paul Theobald and Company, 1947) 285.

9   László Moholy-Nagy, "Typophoto" (1925), in *Painting Photography Film* (Cambridge: MIT, 1969) 40.

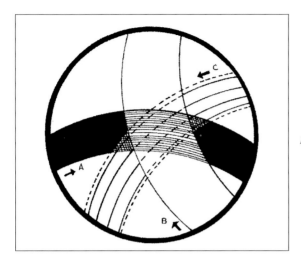

Fig. 5. László Moholy-Nagy,
"Polycinema", in Malerei
Photographie Film *(Painting*
Photography Film), 1925 (diagram
of a circular screen with three
simultaneous projections)

Photography Film in 1925. Photographic publishing was itself increasingly paired with "a book cinema", to use graphic designer Johannes Molzahn's expression. The association marked the reception of many illustrated works of the period, from Helmar Lerski to Moï Ver.[10]

From that point on, and seen through the prism of cinema, any collection of multiple images thus looked like the condensation of a run of successive moments, just as any photomontage appeared as the site of a temporal density folding duration back into the fleetingness of the instant. This Moholy-Nagy kept celebrating under the banner of "simultaneity", one of the central categories of modernism since Futurism, which may be defined as the ultimate intensification of an accelerating succession, the concentration of modern speed in the instant. From the moment when it becomes "simultaneous", the still image should accordingly no longer be understood as the absence of movement: it might in fact be its maximal acceleration. The non-moving forms of the modern image would in the end not be any less dynamic or "fast" than cinema, which in return may stand to gain from reintegrating their power. Moholy-Nagy, like Abel Gance and other contemporary artists, proposed to do just that through his idea of "polycinema", a cinema of multiple images projected side by side (Fig. 5).[11] It involved taking the principle of simultaneous montage back into filmic succession itself, confronting these two modern "speeds" of film and photomontage, sequence and co-presence, run and instantaneity within the cinematographic spectacle – or, to put it differently, reintroducing a little of the printed page within film to make it even more dynamic.

10   Johannes Molzahn, "Nicht mehr sehen ! Lesen !", *Das Kunstblatt*, 12:3 (March 1928), reprinted as "Stop Reading! Look!" in *The Weimar Republic Sourcebook*, Anton Kaes, Martin Jay, and Edward Dimendberg, eds. (Berkeley, Los Angeles: The University of California Press, 1994) 648.

11   László Moholy-Nagy, "Scheme of a Simultaneous or Polycinema" (1925), in *Vision in Motion* (Chicago: Paul Theobald and Company, 1947) 283.

1

"The little paper cinema": The transformations of illustration in *belle époque* periodicals

Thierry Gervais

During the *Belle Époque*, major French illustrated periodicals such as *L'Illustration* gave the pictorial compositions of their in-house artists prime space in their layouts (Fig. 1). Full pages or centrefolds most often showed topical illustrations done in a "classic" artistic style. To paraphrase art historian Georges Roque, the use of images in the press revealed a complex relationship to the fine arts, between "difference" and "deference".[1] Their reproduction in the thousands excluded them from the body of unique works presented at the Paris Salon, even though their graphic make-up faithfully adhered to the rules of history painting.

At the same time, new illustrated publications appeared in France and brought competition to the established illustrated newspapers. In 1898 the first issues of *La Vie illustrée* ["Illustrated Life"] and *La Vie au grand air* ["Outdoor Life"] were published (Fig. 2). While *La Vie illustrée* focused on general news, *La Vie au grand air* dealt with sports. Both used half-tone engraving to reproduce photographs – rather than engravings based on drawings – for the disemmination of images, providing their readers with a much more abundant iconography. The extensive use of photography engendered a paradigm shift: until this time, painting had inspired the draughtsman; now cinematographic forms would become the reference for page layouts.

A New Breed of Periodicals

On 20 October 1898, the first issue of *La Vie illustrée* was published under the management of Félix Juven, who appointed Henri de Weindel as editor (Fig. 3). While de Weindel's opening piece regarding the weekly's objectives was evasive,[2]

---

1 Georges Roque, "Introduction", in *Majeur ou mineur? Les hiérarchies en art*, ed. Georges Roque (Nîmes: Jacqueline Chambon, 2000) 20.

Fig. 1. "La guerre du Transvaal" (The Boer War), L'Illustration (n° 2975) 3 March 1900: 136–137.

the front page certainly set the tone. For half the price, *La Vie illustrée* featured twice as many images as *L'Illustration*.[3] Images appeared from the front page on, and their sheer number structured the organization of each issue.[4]

In his article, Henri de Weindel explained that the weekly could "be read by all eyes and *leafed through* by all hands".[5] The second part of the quote refers directly to the layout of the paper, generated by the use of images: "leafing through" a newspaper is possible only if readers can linger over elements other than text. Reducing the share of text in favour of images, *La Vie illustrée*, as an object, allowed its readers to become spectators of the news. A comparison between an issue of *La Vie illustrée* and an issue of *L'Illustration* reveals the distinctions between two newspapers that used images in divergent ways. The Dreyfus Affair

2   Henri de Weindel, Lucien Métivet, "Bloc-Notes" ["Miscellaneous Notes"], *La Vie illustrée* (n° 1) 20 October 1898: 2.

3   In 1898 a yearly subscription to *L'Illustration* cost 36 francs, as opposed to 15 francs for *La Vie illustrée*; a single issue of *L'Illustration* was sold at a price of 75 centimes, compared to 30 for the new periodical. In 1898 an average of twenty-eight images altogether appeared in an issue of *L'Illustration*, while the front page of *La Vie illustrée* regularly boasted fifty photographs or more. See Thierry Gervais, "Dessins et photographies publiés dans *L'Illustration* de 1897 à 1915" ["Drawings and Photographs Published in *L'Illustration* from 1897 to 1915"], *in L'Illustration photographique. Naissance du spectacle de l'information (1843–1914)* ["Photographic Illustration. The Advent of News as Spectacle (1843–1914)"], diss., History and Civilization, EHESS, 2007, 489–492.

4   The mention of the number of illustrations on the front page was discontinued with the January 26, 1899 issue, three months after publication began.

5   De Weindel and Métivet, "Bloc-Notes". My emphasis.

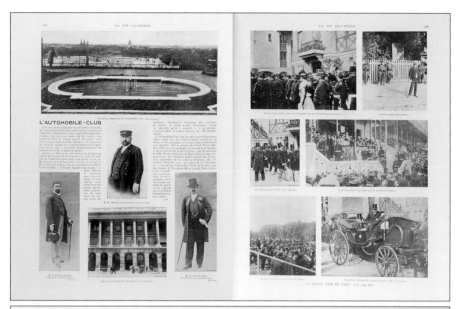

Fig. 2. La Vie illustrée *(n° 35) 15 June 1899 and* La Vie au grand air *(n° 515) 1 August 1908.*

– specifically the court-martial judgement that sentenced the captain to ten years imprisonment – was the main topic covered in both *La Vie illustrée* (14 September 1899) and *L'Illustration* (16 September 1899).[6] Thirty-five images appeared in

6   *La Vie illustrée* (n° 48) 14 September 1899: 393–408; *L'Illustration* (n° 2951) 16 September 1899: 177–192.

Fig. 3. La Vie illustrée *(n° 2) 27 October 1898: front page.*

Fig. 4 (below). "L'Affaire Dreyfus", L'Illustration *(n° 2951) 16 September 1899; "L'Affaire Dreyfus",* La Vie illustrée *(n°48) 14 September 1899.*

L'Illustration as a whole, while *La Vie illustrée* featured fifty-two images, leaving not a single page devoted to text alone (Fig. 4).

Five images illustrate the affair in *L'Illustration*, two of them woodcuts, and all involving drawing (Fig. 5). These large-format woodcuts are given prominence, postioned on the front page and in the centrefold. All represent key figures or

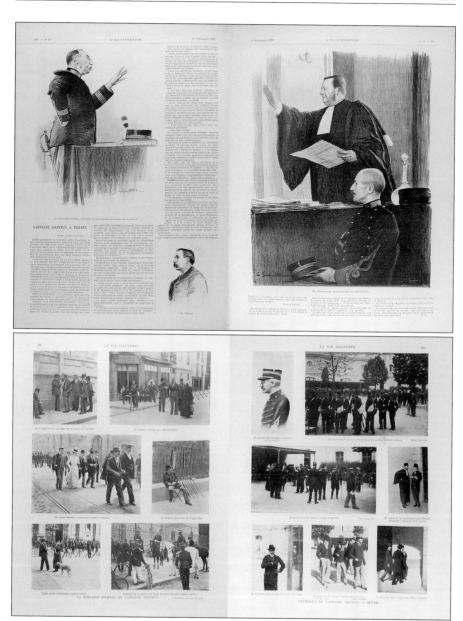

Fig. 5 (upper). "L'Affaire Dreyfus", L'Illustration (n° 2951) 16 September 1899, 177–185.
Fig. 6 (lower). "L'Affaire Dreyfus", La Vie illustrée (n° 48) 14 September 1899, 393–401.

specific scenes such as the exit of military witnesses after their depositions. The images are few in number, but they command a total of four pages.

In *La Vie illustrée*, twenty-one images report the same event: three drawings by Georges Bedon, sixteen photographs by different photographers all made in

Rennes, and two document reproductions dealing with reactions to the event in Germany. All images, regardless of their origin, are reproduced as half-tone engravings, and cover a total of six and a half pages. With an editorial content equivalent to that of *L'Illustration* (about two-thirds of a page), *La Vie illustrée* devotes fifty percent more space to images. More significantly still, the proliferation of illustrations resulting from the substantial use of photographs produced page layouts in stark contrast to those of *L'Illustration*.

The second spread features thirteen photographs taken before and after the verdict was read (Fig. 6). The left page brings together six photographs, all of them accompanied by short descriptive captions. A generic title, "The Last Day of the Dreyfus Affair", appears at the bottom. The right page follows a similar arrangement, with seven images related to "The Epilogue of the Dreyfus Affair in Rennes". Save for one portrait, all of the photographs are outdoor snapshots and present the comings and goings of important figures involved in the trial, or depict the atmosphere in the city through street scenes. Despite the temporal split that distinguishes them, both pages invite similar approaches and outlooks on the part of the readers. The stepped layout of images on the page, along with western reading practices, encourage readers to look from left to right and from top to bottom, quickly moving back and forth between the images and their captions. The spread, which uses text sparingly and, privileges illustrations, reinforces the argument in Weindel's article, that of broadening the readership to include people who want to read less or, more precisely, want *to see* the trial unfold.

A few weeks earlier, a special issue of *La Vie illustrée* on "The Dreyfus Affair in Pictures" featured similar page layouts (Fig. 7).[7] The front page announced "300 illustrations: photographs and documents" throughout the entire issue. Thirty of the forty-eight pages involved clusters of images accompanied by short captions and organized around a title, including "Trial Documents", "The Degradation, January 4, 1895" and "The First Zola Trial". Photographs and drawings were sometimes numbered to produce a narrative effect, allowing the reader/spectator to follow the progression of an episode over a page of the newspaper. *La Vie illustrée* was then part of a trend that was breaking free from such constraints as reading or pagination inherent in the illustrated weekly format in order to attract readership through visual narratives. While these kinds of layouts were not entirely new, they became widespread by the turn of the 19th century.

Various technical and economic considerations led to the reliance on photography to illustrate the pages of *La Vie illustrée* and were part of larger transformations that were steering the weekly towards new forms. The decision to increase the number of illustrations necessitated the use of small-format images rather than large illustrative compositions thereby approaching the steady succession of images recorded by the cinematograph, screenings of which were prevalent in

---

7   *La Vie illustrée* (n° 32) 25 May 1899.

Fig. 7. La Vie Illustrée *(n° 32) 25 May 1899:*
front page, 116–117, 124–125.

Paris at the time. The published photographs were always closely related to their referents, and photographers most often turned to an aesthetics of the snapshot.[8]

8   André Gunthert, "Esthétique de l'occasion. Naissance de la photographie instantanée comme genre" ["The Aesthetics of the Circumstance. Birth of the Snapshot as a Genre."] *Études photographiques* 9 (May 2001) 64–87.

The single image ceded its autonomy, becoming part of a whole. The appeal of the central spread influenced the issue in its entirety, such that each and every page aroused the interest of readers/spectators, who could thenceforth content themselves with "flipping through" a copy of *La Vie illustrée*.

The synthetic image a large, classically composed and autonomous drawing summarizing an event gave way to the analytical page, whose meaning derived from the narrative organization of a wealth of photographs. With the iconographic choice made by de Weindel's weekly, the interest shifted from individual images to the page layout as an assemblage of images. Structured around an image-laden corpus and prominent titling, pages showed a horizontal arrangement in marked contrast to the vertical rhythm of the columns of text. This break changed the presentation of information in the newspaper; the page now became a space where text and image could interact freely, beyond classical discursive rules. Though lacking in sophistication, page layouts in *La Vie illustrée* affected the way people understood and handled the weekly. The emancipation from the pictorial model, which resulted in a new print object, could also be seen at work in *La Vie au grand air*, revealing even stronger cinematographic references.

The Rise of the Art Director

The first issue of *La Vie au grand air* appeared on 1 April 1898, a few months before *La Vie illustrée*.[9] The new periodical was created by Pierre Lafitte, who went on to become a major figure in the French press during the *Belle Époque*.[10] In addition to *La Vie au grand air*, his ventures into periodicals included *Fémina*, *Musica*, *Je sais tout* ["I Know Everything"], and *Fermes et châteaux* ["Farms and Castles"], all richly illustrated and printed on coated paper. On 4 February 1899, an article entitled "Notre programme" appeared in *La Vie au grand air*.[11] After eleven issues as a monthly publication, its success now made the shift to a weekly paper possible. The issue featured sixty illustrations, all involving photography.[12] With the number and type of images it published, the sports newspaper had to find graphic solutions suited to the design of every issue, as did *La Vie illustrée*. Unlike de Weindel's weekly, however, Lafitte's sports paper looked for more complex graphic solutions and, to that effect, appointed Lucien Faure to the position of art director.[13]

9   *La Vie au grand air. Revue illustrée de tous les sports* ["Outdoor Life. The Illustrated Magazine of All Sports"] (n° 1) 1 April 1898.

10 On Pierre Lafitte's career, see Juliette Dugal, "Pierre Lafitte, "Le César du papier couché"", *Le Rocambole* 10 (Spring 2000): 12–38.

11 The editors, "Notre programme" ["Our Plan"], *La Vie au grand air* (n° 21) 4 February 1899: 244.

12 *La Vie au grand air* (n° 21) 4 February 1899: 243–254. In issue n° 59 (29 October 1899), the editorial board estimated the number of "photoengravings" in each issue to approximately sixty. See "À nos lecteurs" ["To Our Readers"] 74.

13 To our knowledge, the status and the task of art director for an illustrated periodical officially appeared for the first time on that occasion. See the editors, "Notre programme", *La Vie au grand air* (n° 21) 4 February 1899.

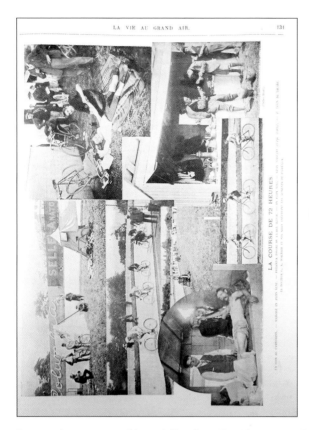

Fig. 8. La Vie au grand air *(n° 11) 1 September 1898: 131.*

By moving to a weekly publication, *La Vie en grand air* offered a more comprehensive coverage of sporting news, and drew the attention of its readers to the means by which the newspaper itself was designed. Besides mention of renowned contributors, the article referred to an interest in the cinematograph, then seen as an indication of modernity. While the use to which the medium might be put is not specified, the issues of *La Vie au grand air* that came out before World War I featured cinematographic sequences on several occasions. In 1907 readers discovered the "cinematography of the runner" through stills printed in vertical strips on the page.[14] More frequently, the weekly included chronophotographs that broke down the movement of various jumpers or the style of an athlete.[15] These layouts, while allowing for an analysis of a fleeting movement performed in a matter of seconds, proved less successful for reports of events unfolding over several hours. The cinematographic model was most prevalent in the reporting of news with a direct correlation to the duration of an event: it found its full

14 L. de Fleurac, "La cinématographie du coureur à pieds", *La Vie au grand air* (n° 454) 1 June 1907: 376.

15 "La chronophotographie du mouvement à l'école de Joinville" ["The Chronophotography of Movement at the Joinville Military School"], *La Vie au grand air* (n° 757) 22 March 1913: 214-15; "Le style dans l'effort physique", *La Vie au grand air* (n° 791) 15 November 1913: 976–77.

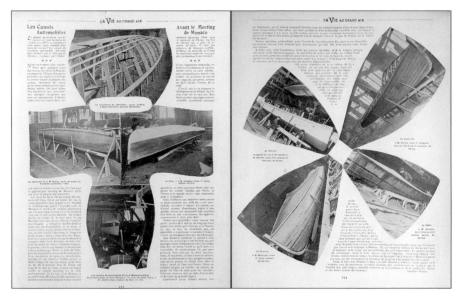

Fig. 9. La Vie au grand air *(n° 285) 25 February 1904: 153–154.*

expression in graphic design. The artistic vision developed by Lucien Faure resulted in layouts for single pages and spreads that distinguished *La Vie au grand air* from traditional illustrated newspapers, allowing readers to become informed, not by reading, but by "leafing through [an] issue".[16] After Henri de Weindel, the expression "leafing through" was adopted in the writings of Pierre Lafitte as a way to characterize the act of "reading" the periodical.

As early as 1898, entire pages of *La Vie au grand air* featured narrative combinations of images with visual effects (Fig. 8). To illustrate a bicycle race, a page from the 1 September 1898 issue included seven photographs from the event.[17] Printed sideways on the page, they meet the eye as a whole. In a composition entitled "The 72-Hour Race", rectangular and circular images are laid out edge to edge or, in some cases, overlapping.

The organization of images was variously handled and page layouts became, on occasion, quite complex, as with the 1904 presentation of "Motorboats Before the Monaco Meeting" (Fig. 9). The shape of the boats' propellers was exploited in reporting the event.[18] Photographs of the principal boats were cropped to fit the form of a single blade, while Georges Prade's text was shaped to fill the remaining space, always subservient to the form of the images. The article covers two pages, each with a differently shaped propeller. In this instance, the two pages are

16   La direction ["The Editors"], "À nos lecteurs", *La Vie au grand air* (n° 59) 29 October 1899: 74.

17   *La Vie au grand air* (n° 11) 1 September 1898: 131.

18   Georges Prade, "Les canots automobiles avant le meeting de Monaco", *La Vie au grand air* (n° 285) 25 February 1904: 153–154.

Fig. 10. La Vie au grand air *(n° 233) 28 February 1903: 135–138.*

consecutive, but do not form a spread; early on, however, the weekly also involved double-page spreads and their graphic design benefited from this larger space.

In February 1903, André Foucault recounted the final of the rugby championship (Fig. 10).[19] The four-page article is accompanied by nine illustrations: eight photographs and a drawing that fills an entire spread. Made by Tofani after a photograph, the drawing presents a break by the Racing club de France into the defence of the Stade français in a classical composition where all lines converge upon the ball. Four sentences of the caption describe less the action depicted than the reasons for using a drawing for its representation:

> May our readers see something else here than what was called a "composition" in the old illustrated journalism. This superb plate is the faithful reproduction of a photographic document. Still, due to their speed, snapshots are better suited to freezing gestures than to indicating movement. This is why we asked skilled artist Tofani to assist photography in this case, giving the scene back everything the lens had taken away from it.

Opting for photography and situating a publication within the dynamic of modern journalism meant renouncing this illustrative mode, in which drawing ceaselessly intervened to make up for the limitations of photography. In order to achieve that, *La Vie au grand air* had to develop layouts in accordance with its specific use of photographs.

---

19 André Foucault, "Le Racing champion de Paris" ["The Racing Wins Paris Championship"], *La Vie au grand air* (n° 233) 28 February 1903: 135–338.

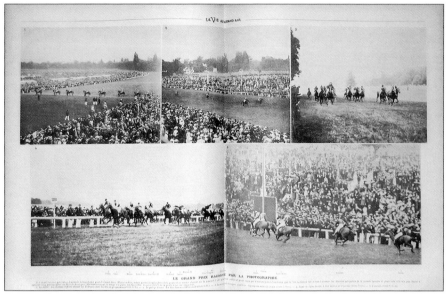

Fig. 11. La Vie au grand air *(n° 145) 23 June 1901: 356–157..*

Spreads soon featured series of snapshots depicting equestrian trials or bicycle races. The 23 June 1901 issue included a centrefold arrangement entitled "The Grand Prix as Told in Photographs" with two bands comprising five snapshots "of the various episodes of the race" (Fig. 11).[20] Captions of this kind became increasingly common and the use of photography transformed the page-spread into a narrative space, one structured as a sequence of fleeting moments recorded by photographers.[21] The "animation" conferred by Tofani on the snapshot was replaced by a written account accompanied by a succession of images. "How many [spectators], even among the most privileged, can claim to have seen the race?" In the layout of the Grand Prix horse race, the succession of published images recounted the progress of the race, and the variety of viewpoints brought a new, analytical vision of the competition that no spectator in attendance could experience. In order to report on sports news, the weekly paper embraced and exploited the characteristics of photography, in particular its instantaneity. The dynamism no longer occurred in the images themselves, but rather on the page, through the sequential arrangement of photographs.

The model and the references cited to legitimize the use of images in the press were clearly moving from the realm of the fine arts to the cinematographic world. In the 21 June 1902 issue, which featured a montage of six photographs of the Grand Prix de Paris, the title announced, "What the Lenses of *La Vie au grand air*'s Six Photographers Saw", with a caption stating that the snapshots of the race

20   *La Vie au grand air* (n° 145) 23 June 1901: 356–357.

21   See also *La Vie au grand air* (n° 250) 26 June 1903: 424–425; and issue n°403, 9 June 1906: 436–437.

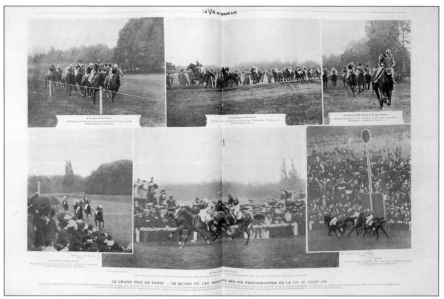

Fig. 12. La Vie au grand air *(n° 197) 21 June 1902: 408–409.*

made it possible to present readers with "a veritable cinematograph of Kizil-Kourgan's victory" (Fig. 12).[22] The relation between the spread and the cinematograph resulted from the use of photography, the multiplicity and the variety of shooting angles, and the montage that shaped the narrative of the race.

The reference to cinema was not an isolated detail in the sports weekly; it was explicitly repeated several times in titles for spreads (Fig. 13). In May 1911, the central spread proclaimed "The Cinematography of the Paris-Madrid Catastrophe" and related, in images, the aviator Emile Train's accident.[23] One year later, *La Vie au grand air* presented a montage of six photographs across a spread with the title "The Cinematography of a Flight by the Aviator Simon" appearing at the bottom (Fig. 14).[24] To distinguish itself from the traditional illustrated press, the sports weekly resolutely turned to modern cinematographic forms for the dissemination of news events.

The Spectacle of Information

Besides the Lumière brothers' "current topics" or Georges Méliès's famous reconstructed *actualités*,[25] the screening of newsreels continued to gain ground in

---

22   *La Vie au grand air* (n° 197) 21 June 1902: 408–409.

23   *La Vie au grand air* (n° 662) 27 May 1911: 332–333.

24   *La Vie au grand air* (n° 699) 10 February 1912: 93–94.

25   *Méliès, magie et cinéma*, Jacques Malthête and Laurent Manonni, eds. (Paris: Paris-Musées, 2002). See also Jean Mitry, "Le montage dans les films de Méliès", *Méliès et la naissance du spectacle cinématographique*, ed. Madeleine Malthète-Méliès (Paris: Klincksieck, 1984) 149–155.

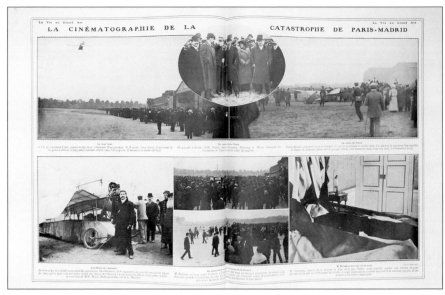

Fig. 13. La Vie au grand air *(n° 662) 27 June 1911: 332–333.*

Parisian theatres of the *Belle Époque.*[26] In 1901, the Grévin Museum launched *Le Journal lumineux* ["the luminous news"], which, as part of its programme, screened film recordings of official visits and war scenes in a 300-seat theatre. In 1907 Gabriel Kaiser could, in turn, boast that he was able to "bring very recent news and [make it] his trademark".[27] While this cinematographic genre became a component of various programmes, regular weekly *actualités* only appeared with *Pathé faits-divers* in March 1909. Soon renamed *Pathé journal*, these newsreels were shown continuously and were constantly updated from the spring of 1912 on.[28] For a price of 25 *centimes*, Pathé provided viewers with their share of gossip, sports events, or disasters, challenging the illustrated press head-on.

Pierre Lafitte was well aware of the on-going visual revolution in news. In 1907 he signed agreements with Pathé, and more specifically with Omnia, the limited company in charge of the distribution of Pathé productions. The théâtre Fémina, located on the ground floor of the Champs-Élysées building, became the Omnia-Pathé-Fémina theatre, and was used for screenings as well as live events.[29]

26 For a comprehensive history of movie theatres in Paris before the First World War, see Jean-Jacques Meusy, *Paris-Palaces ou le temps des cinémas (1894–1918)* (Paris: CNRS Éditions, 1995). Concerning the role of cinema in the visual culture of this time, see Vanessa R. Schwartz, "From *Journal plastique* to *Journal lumineux*. Early Cinema and Spectacular Reality", *Spectacular Reality. Early mass culture in fin-de-siècle Paris* (Berkeley, Los Angeles, London: University of California Press, 1998), 177–199.

27 Meusy, *Paris-Palaces* 150.

28 Meusy, *Paris-Palaces* 343.

29 Meusy, *Paris-Palaces* 147. It should be noted that these agreements are not mentioned in Juliette Dugal's article, "Pierre Lafitte, "Le César du papier couché".

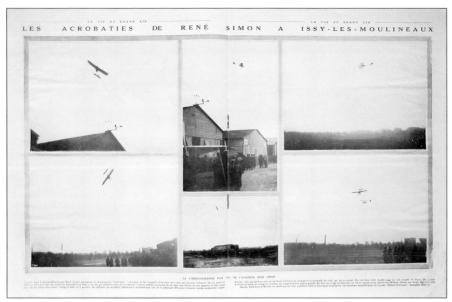

Fig. 14. La Vie au grand air *(n° 699) 10 February 1912: 93–94.*

Moreover, the bourgeoisie that *La Vie au grand air* sought as its audience, tended to favour the productions of the *société des Films d'Art*, which in addition to producing newsreels[30], adapted plays for the screen.[31] Historian Jean-Jacques Meusy cites some statements by Anatole France that appeared in *Phono-Ciné-Gazette* in 1908:

> I like the cinematograph because there I find documents on contemporary history. The unfolding "film" informs us better than the printed sheet ... Yes, I insist! ... The newspaper does not provide all these details which, in their concision, reveal the true physiognomy of things and bring out the deeper meaning of a spectacle ...[32]

The writer first confronts the two media in the domain of news and gives cinema the edge. The multiplicity of images succeeding each other in a visual stream seems to guarantee the dissemination of news. By way of this cinematographic flow, Anatole France identifies another representation of the news, one enriched with details he perceives as having even greater instructive value. Moreover, he associates the cinema's informative power with the notion of spectacle. Often forgotten in the history of the press, spectacle has to do with form and appears, in this context, as a decisive element in the transmission of information. As early

---

30   Jean-Jacques Meusy, "La non-fiction dans les salles parisiennes" ["Non-fiction Films in Parisian Theatres"], *1895* 18 (Summer 1995): 169–200.

31   Alain Carou, "Cinéma narratif et culture littéraire de masse: une médiation fondatrice (1908–1928)", *Revue d'histoire moderne et contemporaine* (Oct. – Dec. 2004): 21–38.

32   "À travers la presse. Anatole France et le cinéma" ["In the Press. Anatole France and Cinema"], *in* *Phono-Ciné-Gazette* (n°87), 1 November 1908, quoted in Meusy, *Paris-Palaces* 151 [our translation].

as 1908, the cinematographic form of news was perceived as more relevant and became an irrefutable reference for the press.

In the introductory article to the new programme for *La Vie au grand air* in 1899, it may have been too early for Lafitte to acknowledge the impact of cinema, but in 1910, in the first issue of *Excelsior*, the editor was categorical:

> With the service to and the pleasure of the general public in mind, we want to be the first to take advantage of the astounding progress made over the last decade in the typography, photographic art, and photoengraving industries. The creation of *Excelsior* is the natural outcome of such progress. [...] Thanks to these invaluable elements, *Excelsior* will be able to fulfill its ambition: to become the cinematograph of universal news.[33]

As René Jeanne and Charles Ford put it, "with cinema all-important, news no longer circulated as it used to, before the cinematograph".[34] While the two historians were referring to the content of news, they might just as well have been writing about the form of newspapers. However, it was not until the interwar period and the advent of famous magazines such as *Vu* or *Regards* that the *mise en scène* and the *mise en page* (page layout) were equated. In 1937, journalist Jean Selz explained that:

> ... the little paper cinema that is the magazine also [...] turned the *mise en scène* of its pages into a living thing, then into a speaking thing, that is, one that brought together photographic and typographic elements to produce "explosive" enough meanings such that the reader could enjoy the magazine as a spectator: without effort.[35]

Touching on the term "magazine", the author refers to contemporary weeklies, which used "processes whose dynamism and technical boldness were unknown in the press twenty-five years earlier" – that is to say, prior to the First World War. Still, the processes in question already existed, and the description given of magazine page layouts could apply to *La Vie au grand air* and its graphic constructions. Early cinematographic productions served as visual referents. Spreads featured sequences of numbered snapshots and offered the reader/viewer the account of a horse race or an aeronautical disaster in narrative form.

The cinema of the *Belle Époque* also developed more attractive forms, thus providing its audience with further surprises. Tom Gunning gave a precise description of the "cinema of attractions" over the period, pointing out that a close-up was then considered as an effect, much more "a visual moment"[36] than a narrative element emphasizing the expression of a face. The historian also

---

33   Pierre Lafitte, "Notre programme", *Excelsior. Journal illustré quotidien* ["Excelsior. Daily Illustrated Newspaper"] (n° 1), 16 November 1910: 2.

34   René Jeanne, Charles Ford, *Le cinéma et la presse* (Paris: Armand Colin, 1961).

35   Jean Selz, "Le cinéma et la mise en page" ["Cinema and Page Layout"], *Presse-Publicité* (n° 3) 28 March 1937: 8. [Our emphasis]

36   Tom Gunning, "Cinéma des attractions et modernité", *Cinémathèque* 5 (spring 1994): 130.

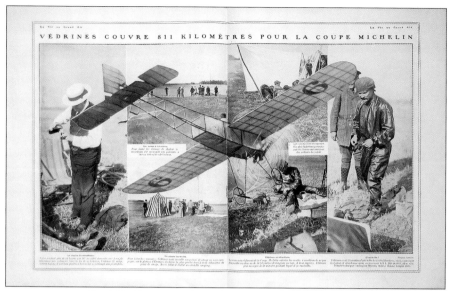

Fig. 15. La Vie au grand air *(n° 674) 19 August 1911: 556–557.*

underscored the fact that "some genres such as [...] *actualités* had close ties with these devices throughout the history of cinema",[37] and that the narrative mode often combined with that of attraction in filmic construction. Such a definition of early cinema also assumes that spectators could let themselves become absorbed into a "fictional universe", allowing them to be seduced by the novelty of an effect. Is such a dual relationship not similar to that in which readers of *La Vie au grand air* engaged as they flipped through an issue? And didn't the spread devoted to the Michelin Cup allow for both a share of narrative, with the chronological publication of images, and a share of spectacle, with its superimposition of the cut-out image of Védrine's plane (Fig. 15)?

In August 1911 Jules Védrine flew 504 miles aboard a Morane monoplane as part of the Michelin Cup competition. To cover the event, the sports weekly laid out seven photographs with short captions over four columns across the central spread.[38] The play of overlapping images and symmetry was a common device in the layouts of *La Vie au grand air*.[39] In that issue, the art director overlaid the montage with the image of the monoplane photographed from a low angle, and cropped to the edge of the aircraft. The illustrations of the original layout appear partly masked and relegated to the background by the shape of the Morane. The reading of images from left to right, spurred by the captions that underline each

37 Gunning, "Cinéma des attractions et modernité" 131.

38 "Védrine couvre 811 kilomètres pour la coupe Michelin" ["Védrine flies 504 miles for the Michelin cup"], *La Vie au grand air* (n° 674) 19 August 1911: 556–557.

39 See for instance the central spreads in *La Vie au grand air* (n° 143), 9 June 1901: 308–309; and issue n° 355, 30 June 1905: 636–637.

column, is thus disrupted by the monoplane printed in the foreground. In other words, the visual narrative of Védrine's journey is interrupted by a spectacular visual element, that of the plane itself. In the montage of the spread, the organization of images produces a narrative thread, but it also generates a spectacle whose purpose is to appeal to the readers as much as to inform them.

The editorial choices and graphic principles adopted by *La Vie illustrée* and *La Vie au grand air* indicate a renewal of the models in the French illustrated press of the early twentieth century, as history painting faded in the face of the rise of the cinematograph. Analytical layouts devised by art directors increasingly competed with the great synthetic compositions executed by artists. The use of photography was reinforced by layout work which strove to tell a story in images within a spectacular framework – an objective close to that of contemporary cinematographic productions. These changes in the treatment of information resulted in a new printed object, one quite different from the illustrated periodical. While a weekly such as *L'Illustration* was designed to be read from the first to the last page, *La Vie illustrée* and *La Vie au grand air* involved autonomous pages and spreads that made random browsing possible. During the *Belle Époque*, modern readers no longer read illustrated newspapers: they flipped through magazines.

2

From Illustrated Narratives to Narratives in Images: Influences of the Moving Image on the French Daily Press in the Interwar Period

Myriam Chermette

In the early 20th century, the relationship of humankind to the world it inhabited underwent dramatic changes: while the photographs brought back by pioneers of reportage widened the perspective, photomechanical reproduction made available for observation everyday details which until then had escaped attention. In turn, he invention of cinema drastically changed perceptions and met with great popular success. Taking heed of the taste and curiosity of the public, major companies created genuine filmed news, or "actualités filmées", within ten years of the first screenings of the cinematograph. These circulated in theaters until the 1970s.[1] In France, "current topics" – initially produced by the Lumière brothers – were gradually replaced with "actualités filmées" ("filmed news", or newsreels) distributed in Pathé and Gaumont theaters from 1908 on.[2]

These "moving photographs" had an equivalent in the press in the form of still images. Popular newspapers inserted them in their columns over the same period, a few years after magazines, and their large circulation contributed to make their use commonplace. Indeed, the main newspapers (*Le Matin, Le Petit Parisien, Le Petit Journal*, and *Le Journal*) then played a considerable role: selling millions of copies, they helped shape the tastes and opinions of the public.[3] Their monopoly on news delivery was almost complete at a time when radio and television

1 Marcel Huret, *Ciné-actualités, histoire de la presse filmée, 1895–1980* (Paris: Henri Veyrier, 1984) 168.

2 René Jeanne, Charles Ford, *Le cinéma et la presse, 1895–1960* (Paris: Armand Colin, 1961) 184. See also "Les actualités filmées françaises", *Cahiers de la cinémathèque* 66 (1997); François Ekchajzer, "Le Pathé-Journal", in *Pathé, premier empire du cinéma*, eds. Jacques Kermabon, Jacques Gerber, Sylvie Pras (Paris: Centre Georges-Pompidou, 1994) 320–331.

3 Claude Bellanger, Jacques Godechot, Pierre Guiral, Fernand Terrou, *Histoire générale de la presse française*, vol. III, *De 1881 à 1940* (Paris: PUF, 1972) 255–257.

obviously did not exist and the distribution of newsreels was comparatively limited.

Given the technical and chronological contiguity of the two innovations – newsreels and development of photography in the press – it would be fair to assume that they soon met and mixed, as was the case with the weekly press and the appearance of the magazine format.[4] However, structural differences made such crossings anything but evident. Their respective uses of images met two distinct ambitions: to illustrate a text, and to narrate in images. To answer both demands at once would have required giving up the traditional forms of the daily press, a step that major publishers, satisfied with their sales, were not ready to take. This compartmentalization was thus first contested by the initiatives of newspapermen eager for novelty. Bringing together the logics of still and moving images, they contributed to the transformation of iconography in the press.

When photography appeared in popular newspapers in the early 20th century, its function was not so different from the function of illustration assigned to drawing.[5] The front page of *Le Matin* dated 26 September 1906 (Fig. 1) is in that regard representative: it features two portraits, one of Minister of Public Works Louis Barthou and one of the Queen of Spain, next to two views of Brussels. The photographs show the faces of protagonists and the places where actions took place, but they provide no information on the weekly rest of railroad construction workers, the pregnancy of the Queen of Spain, or the crime committed in Brussels – all topics treated in the articles they illustrate.

In fact, daily newspapers at the time were first and foremost devoted to text. They were made by men of letters, journalists or writers, who saw their trade as a work of writing on and articulating current events.[6] The very nature of the photographic medium, which seems to provide a hold on reality, was at opposite extremes and added credence to the then widespread reputation of the image as "vulgar", too easily accessible. Photographs, then, only played a secondary role, all the more since the technical constraints of reproduction further added to these journalistic considerations.[7] Before the First World War, they accordingly appeared only to illustrate articles.

A more simple presentation dominated the period immediately following the conflict, and photography was even less prominent. The layout of the 1 January 1920, issue of *Le Journal* (Fig. 2) shows how: with its density, its scarce use of blank spaces, and titles lacking legibility, it is a fitting example of the daily

4   Thierry Gervais, "L'invention du magazine, la photographie mise en page dans *La Vie au grand air* (1898–1914)", *Etudes photographiques* 20 (June 2007) 51–67. See also Thierry Gervais's contribution in this volume.

5   Myriam Chermette, *Images de presse : production et usages de la photographie dans un quotidien d'information*, Le Journal *(1929–1935)*, diss., Ecole des Chartes, Paris, 2006, 162–163.

6   Christian Delporte, *Les journalistes en France, 1850–1950* (Paris: Seuil, 1990) 56–57.

7   Pierre Albert and Gilles Feyel, "Photography and the Media", *A New History of Photography*, ed. Michel Frizot (Köln: Könemann, 1998).

Fig. 1. Le Matin, *26 September 1906: front page.*   *Fig. 2.* Le Journal, *1 January 1920: front page.*

newspapers of the time. As years went by, press companies took into account evolutions in the tastes of the audience[8] or technical developments, and gradually inserted more photographs in their columns. Still, the essential was always said in the article itself. Photography came as a surplus, often as a mere accessory: a portrait or a landscape providing a representation for a figure or a place, sometimes a snapshot, an image from immediate events.[9] The headline of *Le Journal* on 28 August 1933 (Fig. 3) features a fair number of photographs, yet their function has not changed in the least. Page layout remains compact, with an organization in columns little favourable to the publication of images.

This illustrative iconography was completely at variance with newsreels, which relied on images as their essential medium. Indeed, directors of newsreels put out weekly series of short films, which until the advent of sound were accompanied with intertitles.[10] They highlighted a few topics, narrating them in images, and presented a less complete news coverage than did daily newspapers. In the

---

8 An analytical report of the editorial staff of *Le Journal* mentioned these evolutions : "…while Intelligence as a sense defined the past century, Vision undoubtedly appears as the dominant sense of our era (…). Our century has made the expression of the image easy. The progress we have witnessed in the field of the visual has contributed to the need TO SEE." Archives Nationales, collection *Le Journal*, 8 AR 279, report (1934) 5–6.

9 This brief presentation of the iconography in the daily press uses statistical analyses of the four main general newspapers, *Le Petit Parisien*, *Le Petit Journal*, *Le Matin*, and *Le Journal* between 1920 and 1940. It aims to provide general characteristics and does not preclude a more complex use of images here and there.

10 Marcel Huret, *Ciné-actualités* 28–32.

Fig. 3. Le Journal, *28 August 1933:*
front page.

newstheaters of *Pathé Journal, Gaumont-Actualités, Eclair-Journal,* and *l'Eclipse-Journal,* screenings made the public feel as though they witnessed the news, in a great proximity with the depicted facts. Anatole France captured this impression, writing:

> I like the cinematograph because in it I find documents on contemporary history. The unfolding "film" informs us better than the printed sheet ... Yes, absolutely! A paper does not provide us with the details which, in their graphic summary, still reveal the true physiognomy of things.[11]

Even if the choices made during shooting and editing did, like the writer's pen, stand between the information and the audience and gave a very indirect view of it, they were not visible at the moment of the projection. Besides, news were presented in the form of short narratives susceptible to entertain the spectator. In effect, the succession of shots and the short length given each topic left no time for the public to get bored.[12]

11   "À travers la presse. Anatole France et le cinéma" ["In the Press. Anatole France and Cinema"], in *Phono-Ciné-Gazette* 87 (November 1, 1908).

12   Newsreels then consisted of weekly shows of about ten subjects, each lasting between one and two minutes.

Fig. 4. Le capitaine Rascasse, *1925, still ("Le Journal-L'Aurore" Papers, National Library of France, Paris).*

The use of images by the daily press for illustration purposes was thus poles apart from that of newsreels, in which images told a story. If the two uses existed side by side without intersecting, some forms such as the *ciné-roman* ("cine-novel") during the silent era prove that the two media did not ignore each other and could even be combined on occasion. These films, whose action was divided into several episodes, were projected on screens at a weekly pace while the story appeared simultaneously as a serial in a major daily newspaper (*Les Mystères de New York* in *Le Matin* in 1915, or *Le Secret du sous-marin*[13] in *Le Journal* in 1918).[14] The practice, which reached France in the 1910s after meeting with success in the United States, was very successful due to the fact that it brought together the power of seduction of images and the distribution capacity of the press. It resulted in the creation of a company, the Société des Ciné-romans, which produced films as serials until the advent of sound cinema in the late 1920s.[15]

Still, this cooperation between the press and film companies did not affect compartmentalization in the use of images in the least, as each medium retained its particularities: the newspaper published the text and the cinema distributed

13 Bibliothèque nationale de France, collection *le Journal-l'Aurore*, Qe 1123, J. 198.

14 Alain Virmaux, *Un genre nouveau, le ciné-roman* (Paris: Edilig, 1983) 16.

15 René Jeanne, Charles Ford, *Le cinéma et la presse, 1895–1960* 168.

Fig. 5. Excelsior, *4 January 1913:*
front page.

the images. Even in the case of fiction films, when production companies sent the newspapers a great number of stills or photographs of actors (as with different scenes from *Le Capitaine Rascasse*, Fig. 4), newspapers published only the text, exceptionally an image or two, reserving the photographs for publicity leaflets.[16]

While mainstream newspapers, which were dominant in terms of sales and distribution, mostly confined photographs to an illustrative role, this was not the case of the French daily press as a whole. Indeed, daily newspaper *Excelsior* had a completely different ambition, to become "the cinematograph of universal news".[17] Founded by Pierre Laffitte in 1910 and subtitled *Journal illustré quotidien*, it featured a quote attributed to Napoleon next to its headline: "The most summary sketch tells me more than a lengthy report". This constituted the first initiative by one of the daily newspapers to spread the news in images on a large scale. It was directly inspired by newsmagazines: Pierre Lafitte had also partici-

16   Archives nationales, collection *Le Journal*, 8 AR 530, register of serials.

17   Pierre Lafitte, "Notre programme", *Excelsior, journal illustré quotidien* 16 November 1910: 2.

pated in the launching of *La Vie au grand air* ("Outdoor Life", 1898), *Fémina* (1903), or *Je sais tout* ("I Know Everything", 1905), and he wanted to apply the formulas and the ambitions that had made magazines successful to daily newspapers as well.[18]

To that end, *Excelsior* devoted two pages (the front page and the fifth page) to photography, not as an illustrative document but as the organization of news in images. While the layout often led to an accumulation of photographs, the editorial staff also offered headlines inspired by magazines when the themes lent themselves to it (sport, natural disasters, spectacular events suited for a visual treatment). The headline on 4 January 1913 (Fig. 5) features the high-angle photograph of a skijumper, inviting the reader to discover the point of view of the athlete; in the 22 January 1913 issue, a photograph shows the members of the Briand cabinet walking. These layouts, original in their construction, convey the idea of movement in a still medium.

Likewise, the newspaper published narratives in images, series of photographic sequences which evoked newsreels and were indeed referred to as "cinematographs". When *Mona Lisa* was stolen from the Louvre in 1911, a photographic reconstruction of the events appeared on the front page.[19] These sequences involved a succession of snapshots linked to current events and had more to do with newsreels than with the traditional photography in the daily press, which until then had mostly featured images inspired by a pictorial model (notably portraits or landscapes).[20] These posed scenes gradually came to appear outmoded and too static because of the distribution of newsreels showing politicians at work, and no longer under the spotlights of a studio photographer.

However, *Excelsior*'s innovations were not exploited, as the newspaper met with commercial failure. Without going into too much detail, its sale price – twice as high as those of its competitors – and the technical difficulties of its production, which often made it impossible to catch up with current events, did not allow the newspaper to reach a circulation comparable to that of major titles. Pierre Lafitte had to sell it in 1917 to the Dupuy group, which published it until 1940.[21] Until the early 1930s, *Excelsior* was the only illustrated daily newspaper, but the formal innovations of the early years of the century subsided, while the influence of newsreels remained limited.

Owing to this failure, the initiatives of *Excelsior* did not have any direct impact on its competitors, the major morning newspapers. Indeed, they sold hundreds of thousands of copies with an essentially illustrative use of images and therefore had no interest in appropriating an unprofitable formula. They had an opposite

18   Bellanger, Godechot, Guiral, Terrou, *Histoire générale de la presse française* 382.

19   *Excelsior* 14 Dec. 1913: 1.

20   Françoise Denoyelle, *La Lumière de Paris* ["The Light of Paris"] vol. 2, *Les Usages de la photographie (1919–1939)* (Paris: L'Harmattan, 1997) 47–48.

21   Bellanger, Godechot, Guiral, Terrou, *Histoire générale de la presse française* 383.

Fig. 6. Paris-Soir, 14 October 1934: last page.   *Fig. 7. Paris-Soir, 5 May 1937: last page .*

reaction with *Paris-Soir*, whose economic success encouraged major newspapers to change their methods[22] and legitimized possible influences between still and moving images in the daily press as a whole.

Launched in 1923, the newspaper struggled along until Jean Prouvost took it over in the early 1930s,[23] opting for a primarily visual formula initially inspired by *Excelsior*.[24] In fact, Lafitte served as an advisor to Prouvost, who reused some of his ideas such as the publication of images over one to two pages, with an adapted layout, and the use of snapshots. However, he went farther than his predecessor, imposing photography as an essential element of daily life and, to that end, mixing the logics of still and moving images. He accordingly gave photography a major role, equivalent to that of the text: reporting on current events, but only for those subjects suited for visual treatment. As with newsreels, the editorial staff selected five or six events, which indicates that they did not mean to provide a comprehensive view of the news, but would "relate [them], bring them to life by all means available: the talent of one or several reporters, the talent of photogra-

22   Francine Amaury, *Histoire du plus grand quotidien de la IIIe République*, le Petit Parisien *(1876–1944)*, vol. 1 (Paris: PUF, 1972) 289.

23   Raymond Barillon, *Le Cas* Paris-Soir (Paris: Armand-Colin, 1959) 23–51.

24   Editorial, *Paris-Soir* 2 May 1931: 1.

phers".[25] The selected topics fell into two categories: extraordinary facts, for which the public tried to grasp a reality outside their experience, and spectacular events, by definition visual (sport events, human interest stories, including criminal cases, aeronautical feats). These sometimes secondary events took on a new dimension thanks to this iconographic treatment.

To "bring it to life", the editorial staff resorted to a number of the image's possibilities: event-images for a scoop, whose very existence was widely discussed (the photographs of the assassination of King Alexander of Yugoslavia and Minister Louis Barthou on 13 October 1934); sensational images, which appealed directly to the readers' emotions by their violence; narratives in images, inspired by the moving image. The latter attempted to touch the readership like newsreels, allowing people to follow an unfolding action, the spectacle of current events, in a linear or reconstructed fashion.

These narratives comprised of a succession of photographs on the same subject were inserted in a page layout adapted to the iconographic document. Indeed, the concentration of images over two or three pages made it possible to design a more flexible layout in which the column would no longer strictly determine spatial organization. As the need arose, horizontal strips could even be splashed across the top of a page: on 14 October 1934 (Fig. 6), four such strips gave an account of the "different periods in M. Raymond Poincaré's life". From 1936 on, narratives in images were even isolated from the rest of the page by a double rule, which emphasized the photographs and suggested that they formed a whole.

The coherence of these sets was reinforced by the caption relating the images to one another and running from the first to the last, with suspension points as the only interruption between each photograph. "The Duke of Windsor, formerly Edward VIII ... has left his Austrian residence for the castle of Candé, in the Touraine region", the last page reads on 5 May 1937 (Fig. 7). The scarcity of the text in this instance calls to mind the intertitles of newsreels in silent cinema. It succinctly provides the relevant information, whereas the appeal of the narrative mainly resides in the image and what is given to see. This use of the caption (brief, quick, incisive in *Paris-Soir*) sharply contrasts with that observed in the daily newspapers of the time, with their long and specific titles and captions.[26]

To report on current events, these narratives integrate some principles of the moving images, the notion of movement and the succession of sequences. When they are in chronological order, they deal with events of varying duration, most often expressed in three or four images: a whole life on 14 October 1934 (Fig. 6), with the last page being devoted to a series of photographs on the life of Raymond Poincaré; a few decisive hours on 30 August 1933 (Fig. 8), with the arrest of a young murderess, Violette Nozière, related in five photographs (the arrest, the

25 Hervé Mille, *50 ans de photographie de presse, archives photographiques de Paris-Soir, Match* et *France-Soir* (Paris: BHVP, 1990) 16.

26 Hervé Mille, *Cinquante ans de presse parisienne* (Paris: La Table ronde, 1992) 87.

Fig. 8. Paris-Soir, *30 August 1933: last page.*   *Fig. 9.* Paris-Soir, *3 September 1933: last page.*

arrival at the police station, the search, the taking of fingerprints, the entrance in the cell); a few seconds on 17 September 1938, as a motorcyclist moves through a wall of wood and flames at 60 mph.

Chronology is not the only thread of these constructions of images, which on occasion may also serve to reconstruct the different facets of an event – again, in three of four images. On 21 September 1936, during the Spanish Civil War, *Paris-Soir* reported on the fire of the Toledo Alcazar through a gripping master view of the scene of the tragedy, combined with two closer views of the building after the fire and the neighbouring hills clouded in smoke, as though a camera-man was moving on the battlefield, getting nearer to certain details.

The resort to these photographic narratives pertains to two distinct uses. First, they illustrate: on 17 October 1936, for instance, three photographs accompany an article on Bette Cooper, who has chosen to give up her title as Miss America and turn down her crown. Second, they may be the main medium for information, and *Paris-Soir* could be particularly original in that regard. Photography then represented the different stages or aspects of an event to give the reader the impression of attending it. On 5 May 1937 (Fig. 7), a series of five images thus showed the departure from Austria and the arrival in France of the Duke of Windsor, formerly King Edward VIII, who had just abdicated so that he could

Fig. 10. Le Journal,
7 July 1934: front page.

marry a commoner. The interest of these images does not lie in the information they deliver, but in the relation they establish between the reader and current events, allowing people to follow the Duke on his journey. This type of narrative in images adds variety to the treatment of information and introduces a dimension of entertainment, like newsreels. The succession of images rests readers and allows them to follow the event without reading a precise description of it.

The editorial staff also added visual effects to these images to make them more effective with the public. These effects evoke moving images: the page layout made it possible to stress out the impression of swift succession thanks to what may be called the "film strip effect", a series of photographs – all of them the same size – printed over the white outline of a film reel unwinding horizontally or vertically. The linearity of the background linked images together; when images did not come from the same source, as with the series of Raymond Poincaré portraits on 14 October 1934 (Fig. 6), cutting out and reframing produced uniformity, aligning all photographs on the same plane.

The selection of images had the same objective. Most of the time, the chosen photographs were not the typical shots common in the daily press – master views or general views – but photographs made in the midst of the event: close-ups, views from the back, high-angle or low-angle shots breaking with the then conventional aesthetic and with classical composition while better suggesting proximity.[27] The departure of Violette Nozière's mother from the hospital on 3 September 1933 was shown in two images (Fig. 9). On the first, she may be seen leaning on a police lieutenant in long shot, while the second picture shows her entering the car in medium shot. These narratives in images, along with page layout effects and the choice of photographs, had to give readers the sense that they were experiencing current events firsthand, and even that they could imagine for themselves the continuity of movement offered by newsreels. Despite the important formal work involved in these two techniques, they produced the illusion of an immediate, off-the-cuff transmission, which could entertain the readers all the more since the selected subjects often involved spectacular events. In appealing to a mass audience, the editorial staff of *Paris-Soir* thus took inspiration from two dimensions of newsreels, their assumed proximity with current events and their ability to entertain spectators.

The success of *Paris-Soir* prompted morning newspapers to transform their iconography so as not to lose their readership.[28] Without going into particulars, an examination of the front page of *Le Journal* dated 7 July 1934 (Fig. 10) reveals how the newspaper covers in several images the "Fêtes de la Lumière et de la Vitesse" ["Celebrations of Light and Speed"] at the Bois de Boulogne. The new use does not substitute for the old one, yet it partly redefines and complements it. It confirms the preponderant role of the image in the general news press, be it in the form of narratives whose postwar posterity was limited to popular papers like *France-Soir*, or in the form of a news document.

---

27 Myriam Chermette, "Le succès par l'image ? Heurs et malheurs des politiques éditoriales de la presse quotidienne (1920–1940)" ["Success in Images? Fortunes and Misfortunes of Editorial Policies in the Daily Press (1920–1940)"], *Études photographiques* 20 (June 2007): 85–89.

28 Myriam Chermette, *Images de presse* 229–235.

3

On a Cinema Imaginary of Photography (1928–1930)

Michel Frizot

The relations between photography and cinema are very obvious yet very complex: this probably explains why they are still discussed so little. Indeed, the analyses of the past three decades have been so concerned with their inscription within semiological, stylistic, or sociological perspectives that they went for simplification without really looking at the primary material. As for me, coming to photography through the discovery of the work of Etienne-Jules Marey proved a vantage point like no other to observe the transitions between the two media. The simple idea that the film apparatus is first and foremost an improved photographic apparatus did issue from Marey, making any "film" (in the sense of a film strip) a linear set of still photographic views and any "film" (in the sense of a projection on a screen) a "moving photograph", as it was then called. However, limiting the investigation to the "cinema of pioneers" quickly leads to a self-repeating ontology. In their common history over more than a century, photography and cinema have constantly been in contact, in friction, opposite each other in very different ways that sometimes had to do with shared stakes, re-definitions of either medium, or even with the uncertainties punctuating their respective developments. What I would like to do here is collect a few ideas and observations lifted in the course of studying photography, within what may be called a "photographic economy" of cinema – more particularly in a recent study of Henri-Cartier Bresson[1] during the years 1928–1930, which confirmed some older intuitions.

The late 1920s did in fact see a remarkable convergence in the attention given to photography and cinema – a convergence epitomized in the famous 1929 Stuttgart exhibition *Film und Foto*, also known as Fifo, organized by the Werkbund. The great international event of avant-garde practices in photography and cinema, it took place just as both media were about to enjoy a new boom in the

---

1   Michel Frizot, "D'imprévisibles regards. Les leçons de photographie d'un Scrapbook" ["Unpredictable Looks. The Photography Lessons of a Scrapbook"], *Henri Cartier-Bresson, Scrapbook, Photographies 1932–1946* (Göttingen: Steidl, 2006) 31–71. I also refer the reader to that text for a number of illustrations which could not be reproduced here.

1930s: photography, with its dominance in the media, advertising, posters; cinema, with the advent of sound, the consequent changes in its narrative function and its social future, but also its perception as a "moving photograph", since photographs do not "speak"! A key moment in the distribution of Modernist influences, the Fifo may be analysed in terms of content, selection, and representativity, but even more relevant for my argument is the dissymmetry in the presentation and the reception of photography and cinema, which has to do with the system of the "exhibition". Indeed, no less than a thousand photographs were on display whereas the film programme included only fifty films or so. In the absence of the small video screens that would be available nowadays, film was also shown through the exhibition of ... photographs, either film frames or stills.[2] With screenings scheduled over only two weeks, the real impact of the films could be felt, not in the direct visibility of the works, but rather in what is referred to as media "coverage" these days, and which was the (other) major novelty at the time. Indeed, several books were published on the occasion of the Fifo, making it "exist" and giving it an international resonance: Werner Gräff and Hans Richter's *Es kommt der neue Fotograf!* ["Here Comes the New Photographer!"], Franz Roh and Jan Tschichold's *foto-auge* ["photo-eye"], and Richter and Gräff's *Filmgegner von heute – Filmfreunde von morgen* ["Fiends of cinema today – friends of cinema tomorrow"]. Countless illustrated articles also appeared on that occasion, and images (or authors) recognized thanks to their presence at the Fifo were subsequently the objects of a continued attention, as attested in the annual special issues on photography of *Arts et métiers graphiques* (first published in 1930).

This example is relevant to what interests us here for two reasons: first, cinema benefited from a translation into a "photographic" media characterized by stillness, deprived of the film strip and the film screening; second, photography, as it turned out, lent itself well to multiplication in the media through photoengraving and printing in magazines, daily newspapers, and books. The combination of these means resulted in a double alteration in the "representation" of the films: the use of a still (photographic) image which was not even necessarily a frame from the film, and an inked printing from a photoengraving, sometimes even with a brown or bluish ink characteristic of some publications. A secondary phenomenon logically amplified this mutation, which affected the reception of photography as well as that of cinema reduced-to-photography: the creation of magazines specializing in the circulation of photographic illustrations of current events (*VU*, 1928) and cinema (*Pour Vous, Cinémonde*). Many questions were to arise from this new media coverage and the modes of reception it imposed on photography and cinema.

For my part, as I was examining Cartier-Bresson's *Scrapbook* (which consists of his own selection of photographs from 1932 to 1946), I wanted to look into the origin of his practice by situating it in its artistic context and the unexpected

2   One exception: the Soviet room designed by El Lissitzky, where short strips of film were actually projected in loops in "film cupboards" in the midst of photographs.

turns of his visual training. This takes us back to 1929, a year in which there is evidence for his growing interest in photography.[3] Given that Cartier-Bresson long hesitated and wavered – at least in the 1930s – between cinema and photography, it seemed to me that his originality as a photographer had been shaped by painting, to be sure (the Lhote Academy in 1928), by the reference to Surrealism, as has often been said, but also by a close familiarity with cinema. This involved watching films, obviously, as well as consulting specialized magazines featuring film photographs, and photographs in general. Indeed, it is often forgotten, when thinking about these distant years, that a 1929 photographer would go to the movies, read magazines, art periodicals, and novels, look at illustrated books, etc., and would find in all of these more powerful or inspiring sources for a "visual" education[4] than the timid reverence towards André Breton which more easily went down in history. As it happens, Cartier-Bresson himself clearly emphasized that fact in the famous introduction he wrote for his book *Images à la sauvette* ["Images on the Sly"], later abusively dubbed "the decisive moment".[5] He begins with what constitutes his photographic creed, often repeated and reinterpreted, with a short first paragraph on his pictorial references, and then writes at the start of the second paragraph:

> Then there were the movies. From some of the great films, I learned to look, and to see. *Mysteries of New York* [1915], with Pearl White; the great films of D.W. Griffith – *Broken Blossoms* [1919]; the first films of Stroheim, *Greed* [1924]; Eisenstein's *Potemkin* [1926]; and Dreyer's *Jeanne d'Arc* [1928] – these were some of the things that impressed me deeply.[6]

That such a famous photographer would state that his look was shaped from the beginning by cinema is so rare that the admission went unnoticed. Yet besides getting an education through films seen in theaters, an experience certainly significant for any photographer, the Cartier-Bresson of 1929 – and particularly in that year – benefited from an extraordinary conjunction of literary and artistic publications. Like him, these had opted for photography shortly before, thanks to the means of photoengraving (half-tone engraving or rotogravure – rotary photogravure): *Bifur*,[7] *Jazz*,[8] *Documents*,[9] and above all a specialized periodical of

3   Cartier-Bresson considered that his first photographs fit for circulation dated back to 1932.

4   An example is given in *Scrapbook*, 40–41: Cartier-Bresson, who made photographs in Africa during his 1931 trip, may have seen Marc Allégret's 1928 *Voyage au Congo* as well as André Gide's book featuring 64 photographs in heliogravure by Allégret and bearing the same title (Paris: Gallimard, 1929).

5   Paris: Tériade, 1952. TN: *The Decisive Moment* was also the title chosen by the American publisher, Simon and Schuster (1952).

6   Henri Cartier-Bresson, "Untitled", in *The Education of a Photographer*, ed. Charles H. Traub, Steven Heller, and Adam B. Bell (New York: Allworth Press, 2006) 12–22. The information between brackets is ours.

7   Eight issues of *Bifur* were published between May 1929 and June 1931 by the Editions du Carrefour, with Georges Ribemont-Dessaignes as the editor. Michaux, Soupault, Tzara, Picabia, Leiris, Desnos, Joyce, Hemingway, etc., appeared in the pages of the periodical, whose run could reach 3,000 numbered copies.

8   *Jazz, l'actualité intellectuelle*, founded by Titaÿna, with Carlo Rim serving as the editor, published 15 issues from December 1928 to March 1930.

9   Georges Bataille was the general secretary of *Documents*, which appeared in 1929 and 1930, and again in 1933–1934.

high intellectual standard, *La Revue du cinéma* (1928–1931, published by Galli-mard. Given his proximity with literary circles (he was close friends with Crevel), Cartier-Bresson cannot have ignored these publications. Is it an effect of the Fifo, or rather a part of the climate surrounding both the advent of cinema and the development of photography as the two artistic mediums of modernity? These publications unquestionably involved an amalgam or a hybridation (or, more simply, a mix of genres?) between the "photographic photograph" and "the film photograph", and it was not always possible to distinguish between the two. Accordingly, readers could very well start looking at film frames (unless they were stills meant for lobby cards) as a photographer's pictures devoid of any reference to the film – especially in *Jazz*, which cultivated that ambiguity. This could be all the truer for a novice photographer who had made it his special knack of poking his nose into things and sense them, as this type of photography, free of the specific intentionality of the photographic approach, opened onto new possibilities. On his discovery of the advantages of the Leica in 1932, he later declared, "I would go poke my nose into things, there is no other way to put it, I would go try and sense things with the camera. What is more, I was nurtured on a whole literary and visual knowledge."[10] This visual knowledge, which I have called "the anterior look" and which determines the ability of any photographer to "sense" things, is what is in question here. Cinema, churning out as it did moving images or still images derived from films, made new photographic attitudes possible and opened an iconic horizon that did not yet belong to photography. What I am concerned with here is identifying the photographic impact of "cinema" when it is visible in the form of a photograph, and is thus identified with this category. The film image oscillates by nature between the complete pre-determination of the studio fiction film and the looser determina-tion of documentary or experimental cinema. Ambulatory photography as prac-ticed by Cartier-Bresson is full of hazards and depends solely on what may suddenly appear "in front of" the photographer, and which he may or may not be able to see and to capture. However, the rapid emergence of these photographs of a second type, which were not part of the field of photography – be it reportage or New Photography –, obviously had effects on innovative photographic prac-tices that have yet to be assessed.

André Kertész, Eli Lotar, and Germaine Krull, the three main protagonists of the beginnings of *VU* in 1928 (and therefore of the birth of reportage) share well-known connections to cinema. Krull was Joris Ivens's companion before becoming Lotar's in Paris; since 1927 Lotar had been a stills man at the very least[11] and had collaborated with Ivens on *Zuyderzee* (1929). On Kertész and cinema nothing is known, but how could he have made a portrait of Eisenstein in Paris (in 1929 as well!) if he had not seen any of the Soviet director's films? Given this understandable silence on the part of photographers on references

10   "Henri Cartier-Bresson, Gilles Mora: conversation", *Les Cahiers de la Photographie* 18 (1986): 119.

11   On Marcel L'Herbier's *L'Argent*.

which did not seem relevant to them, Cartier-Bresson's admission is all the more valuable.

Photographic Ambivalence

To make these observations on proximity meaningful, the analyst of photography needs to take a closer look. The desire to be more specific on a context and on sources leads to more fundamental questions that are also adjacent to photographic ontology. In what way are photographs "excerpted" from a film representative of that film? What do they convey of its aesthetic or simply of its narrative argument, at the very least? While these interrogations may not sound very relevant to film specialists, they take on another significance with respect to photographic studies as soon as juxtapositions and generic mixes become increasingly common. The periodicals and magazines which proliferated around 1929 constituted a place for these mixes and interferences, already very present in Moholy-Nagy's *Painting Photography Film* (1925–1927) – a book whose title is in that regard quite eloquent. All this points to the fact that the apparent explosion of photographic practices, styles, and usages rested on the unity of photography as a system, of the strip of film as a physical medium, and of photoengraving, which in Moholy-Nagy's work is common to photography and cinema. His elaborations on *typofoto* (the possibility of including photography in typography), and particularly the last part of the book, *Dynamik der Gross-Stadt. Skizze zu einem Film gleichzeitig Typofoto* ["Dynamic of the Big City. Sketches towards a Film and a Typophoto"], delimit what were to be the photography- and medium-related characteristics of *VU* in 1928. What Moholy-Nagy anticipated and put into place constituted a decisive break: from the moment photoengraving becomes the last medium and the final step in various pictorial operations (photography, film, painting), everything ultimately comes down to the materiality of the printed photograph, introducing an uncertainty as to their original structure and medium: paintings, photomontages, art or amateur photographs, as well as films in their minimal "photo" version. A fundamental consequence of the phenomenon, which spread around 1928, was a new *ambivalence* of photographic images (or of images made photographic by printing, on a par with one another). This ambivalence obviously has to do with reception: the reader-viewer no longer knows for sure in which sphere the images originated, what the process of their production has been, or which "this has been" they refer to. Also at stake is the intentionality attributed to a greater or lesser degree to any photograph by its viewers. This entails two consequences which, it seems to me, call for further scrutiny: a redefinition of the imaginary powers of photography in this printed form, which was to dominate the 1930s, and whose foundation probably still permeates our experience and thinking; and, more difficult to tease out, its backlash effect on the photographers themselves as to what was "possible" in the personalization of photographic practice, including for reportage (this was the starting point of my study on the context of Cartier-Bresson's visual knowledge in his early career).

In fact, the ambivalence of meaning, of iconic signs produced by this mix had been there for a few years, almost as a cliché in Surrealism (Man Ray had used it in a sometimes provocative spirit). *La Révolution surréaliste* (1924), which featured reproductions (mainly photographs of paintings) introduced this distortion in the meaning of photographs, the distance between interpretation and objective reference, with its cover illustrations: "La France" captions a photograph by Man Ray showing laundry drying in the wind (1 March 1926), while "Les dernières conversions" ["The Latest Conversions"] refers to an unreferenced Atget photograph of a group of people observing an eclipse (15 June 1926). *Bifur*, edited by Georges Ribemont-Dessaignes, a former Dadaist who later turned against Breton, typically included ten to fifteen plates separate from the text. It also featured this systematic poetic of the gap between short, cryptic captions and the more prosaic evidence of the subject: "Garage" alongside two hearses photographed by Kertész, "Sources" ["Springs"] for barrels of wine (Kertész, again),[12] "Anatomie humaine" for a mannequin factory (Stone),[13] "Forêt" for a stack of wood billets (Lotar),[14] "Parti du centre" ["Centrist Party" or "Starting from the Center"] for a potbellied man looking at a newsstand (Ecce Photo).[15] The photographs, which came from quite different contexts, were complemented by a few borrowings from cinema: three "excerpt[s] from a Man Ray film in the works" (Fig. 1), an "excerpt from Luis Bunuel's *Un Chien andalou*",[16] two "excerpts from S.M. Eisenstein's *The Old and the New*" next to a self-portrait as a bald man by Claude Cahun captioned "Frontière humaine". "Buster Keaton cherche sa voix" is a photograph of the actor looking fixedly at a microphone.[17] *Bifur* also published a text by Eisenstein, "The Dramaturgy of Film Form".[18]

The Hybridation of Photographs

Monthly magazine *Jazz* (1929–1931) is certainly the best example of this hybrid photographic illustration, insofar as the modernity of this "cultural" publication rested on the use of "art" photography as it emerged at the Fifo, and each issue of the periodical featured a film column by Pierre Scize. Photography, which was

12 *Bifur* 1 (May 1929).

13 *Bifur* 2 (July 1929).

14 *Bifur* 3 (Sept. 1929).

15 *Bifur* 7 (Dec. 1930).

16 *Bifur* 2 (July 1929). The Man Ray film in question would be *Les Mystères du château de Dé*, an image of which appeared on the cover of the third issue of *La Revue du cinéma* (May 1929) with the title "essay for a film in the works".

17 *Bifur* 4 (December 1929).

18 *Bifur* 7 (December 1930). With respect to the role of images, it should be pointed out that *Bifur* was primarily a review of literature and poetry. Also, around 1926, Ribemont-Dessaignes had already collaborated to *Le Film complet* (1922–1958), a magazine which novelized screenplays.

Fig. 1.
Excerpt from a Man Ray film in the
works, hors texte *plate,* Bifur 2
(July 1929).

also featured in advertisements for the first time (for the books of publisher Querelle, among others), appeared in all columns, especially regular ones (records, books, bookstores). This was a first source of ambiguity, as the question arose of what kind of photograph could give an account of (or focus on) the contents of a record or a book that did not involve any photographs. Still, in this type of magazine the prime expression of the ambivalence stillness/movement lay in the film column or in articles related to cinema. This was especially the case since a frequent topic in these pieces was avant-garde cinema, whose protagonists occupied both positions, photographer and movie maker. Man Ray, for instance, appeared in the first issue for *L'Etoile de mer* ["The Starfish"], with six photographs which do not really differ from his "actual" photographs.[19] In the second issue Joris Ivens was much in evidence with his film *The Bridge*, evoked through photographs by Germaine Krull. Besides, the periodical returned to the subject in its seventh issue (15 June 1929) with an article on Ivens written by Florent Fels, and which deals with *The Bridge* (1928), *The Breakers*, and *Rain* (both 1929). The piece introduces Ivens as a "photographer of moving photographs" [sic] and tells of his growing up in a shop selling photography equipment and accessories. According to the author of the article, Ivens "climbs on a bridge, lies in the rain, on the sidewalk, to capture a close-up of the water spraying from under a tyre, splashing a shoe. He lives only for this beloved little box of steel and crystal" (Fig. 2). The position described better fits the attitude of a photographer than that of a filmmaker, be it in the avant-garde. Of course, the photographs-illustrations produced (one of which shows Ivens filming) are in all likelihood

---

19 When it comes to stillness and movement, Man Ray alone constitutes an excellent object of study through his production of photographs out of film frames, his production of film through the use of rayographs on the film print, the presence of the film print itself in rayographs, the way in which he conceived of film and editing, etc. On this issue, see Samantha Lackey, " 'A series of fragments': Man Ray's *Le Retour à la raison* (1923)", in this volume.

Fig. 2. Joris Ivens filming, Jazz 7 (15 June 1929): 302.   *Fig. 3. Eli Lotar, "Ici, on ne s'amuse pas" (No fun being here), Jazz 11 (November 1929): 482.*

"excerpted" from the films, despite their manifest reframing. This might just be a reading resulting from our referential habits, however.

In the same issue, the film section deals with Painlevé, with *The Passion of Joan of Arc* (Dreyer), *Storm over Asia* (Pudovkin), and *Women of Ryazan*. Issue 11 gives Bunuel's *Un chien andalou* a prominent place, alongside Painlevé's *Sea Urchins*, Donald Crisp's detective film *14–101*, and Chaplin's *A Dog's Life*. Each film is "represented" through a picture, while the section itself opens with the image (signed by Sougez) of a blank film strip artistically unwound! Across all issues, it seems as though the editorial staff of *Jazz* opted for two consistent themes suitable for photographic illustration: ports and street life. Indeed, these provided multiple opportunities to play with an industrial esthetic and the upside-down perspectives of bridges and boats (chimneys, cranes, hulls, masts) in vogue in Nouvelle Photographie and its best representative in *Jazz* at the time, Germaine Krull: "Port de Londres par Mac Orlan" (1, 15 December 1928, photographs by Krull), "Port d'Amsterdam par Florent Fels" (2, 15 January 1929, seven pictures by Krull), "Hambourg par Mac Orlan" (3, 15 February 1929, two pictures by Krull, one by Lotar), "Port de Papeete" (3, 15 February 1929, pictures by Titaÿna), "Port de Paris par Louis Cheronnet" (12, 15 December 1929, five pictures by Lotar, one by Krull).

"Ici, on ne s'amuse pas" ["No fun being here"], an article by photographer Eli

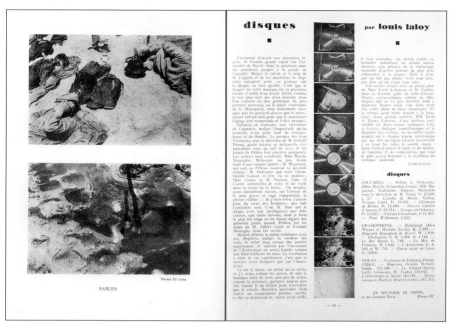

Fig. 4. Eli Lotar, *"Sables" (Sands)*, hors texte plate, Bifur 3 (September 1929).

Fig. 5. *"Un nocturne de Chopin vu par Germaine Dulac" (Chopin nocturne seen by Germaine Dulac)*, "Records" section, Jazz 12 (15 December 1929): 551.

Lotar on the draining of the Zuyderzee in the Netherlands, is particularly ambiguous. Illustrated with four photographs by Lotar (Fig. 3), it deals with the same subject as Joris Ivens's film *Zuyderzee* (1930, 40'), which Lotar co-directed and on which he was a stills photographer, as on other films before (Ivens was also one of the favourite authors of *Jazz*). This helps situate the ambivalence of these photographs – an ambivalence which appears upon careful examination: workers sleeping on a ballast embankment, two images of construction sites, "Sur la digue" ["On the Sea Wall"] and "Aux écluses" ["At the Locks"], earth being craned above a barge. None of these four unusual images belongs to the documentary rationality of reportage or to the elegance of art photography taken over by advertising. They do not even belong to a middle ground, but rather to "something else" that can only be assigned to a film posture: what appears in the camera viewfinder through a mode of attention related to the gradual scan of space, and which was not current in photography. In the first image (the workers sleeping on the ground), which has so little usual photography framing in it and seems to contradict the title of the article, the position of the bodies on the ground, the imperfect framing, which cuts across shapes without giving them any breathing room, the contrast between the shore and black clothes, all seem to come out of a cinematic shot – the kind of cinema practiced by Ivens and Lotar. A very similar photograph published in *Bifur* (3, September 1929) shows a different area in the same shot (and from the same point of view), as though the camera was scanning what lay in front of it (Fig. 4). Still, these images do have the status of photographs in this context (the upright format of the fourth excludes film as a possible source), even if they are slanted by a finality that had not yet been assimilated into the usual practices of photography, save for those of a few combining photography and cinema in their work. Cartier-Bresson was to be among them.

If Pierre Ichac's "Notes sur le chameau" ["Notes on the Camel"] (8, July–August 1929) is illustrated with seven photographs looking very much like reportage photographs, these were in fact "excerpted from films" by the same author, *Pastorale égyptienne* and *Voyage au désert* (1929). This generic mix also involves Titaÿna's "report" at the Panama canal, with the layout stacking up the six photographs as if to recreate the progression on the canal through successive still shots. In another issue (12, 15 December 1929), the record section is illustrated with a "film strip" of nine film frames titled "Un nocturne de Chopin vu par Germaine Dulac" and borrowed from Dulac's film *Disque 957* (Fig. 5),[20] mentioned on the previous page in the film section!

Some Movement, Somewhere

Another section in *Jazz* was "La Rue" [The Street"], on a par with cinema, the music-hall, and theater. Run by Carlo Rim, it appeared from the very first issue with four photographs by Atget, the hero of the young generation celebrated as early as 1926 by Man Ray, and who had passed away in 1927. In the second issue (15 December 1929), the section featured "Rue de Lappe", three photographs by Germaine Krull, which combined the then budding concept of reportage with the photographer's attentive stroll in a given place. This type of presentation could also be found in magazine *VU*, which first appeared on 21 March 1928. The street and the city were not new sites for photographic practice: they were the sites of an instinctive Nouvelle Photographie, whose ultimate objectives were the production of personal photographs and the satisfaction of the reportage's commissioners. In the same issue, "La rue chinoise par Carlo Rim" frontally represents a public execution with a saber through two series of three photographs each, one after the other, as if it were a film. These documents, "cartes postales rapportées de Canton par Titaÿna" ["postcards brought back from Canton by Titaÿna"], might even have originated in a film. "La Rue", as capitalization indicates, called for a new attention and gave rise to an ocular posture that found a practical application in photography and a metaphor in film. The metaphor may seem facile today, yet it outlines the modernity of 1929: "curious travelers carry in their memory an invisible reel on which the Street of the world winds up like a film – a film that would not only be a documentary, but a vaudeville, a tragedy just as well",[21] Carlo Rim wrote in his column. The editor of *Jazz*, who

20 *Disque 957*, 1928, 6 min., a visual symphony adapted from Chopin's Preludes 5 and 6.

21 *Jazz* 2 (15 January 1929): 82.

was about to become the editor of *VU*, also wrote, "human memory is a sophisticated camera which erects fabulous palaces on the models of our childhood, [...] which can blend two images of life into a dream image".[22] This made it possible to articulate image, film, travel, and narration for modern readers who, by definition, fed their memory out of an armchair. This memory still had to be provided or given rise to in the first place, and Carlo Rim himself wrote his column on the basis of photographs – that is, by photographic proxy, and sometimes without much of a connection to the street ... In "La photographie et la rue" (fourth issue, 15 March 1929), he briefly praised the "photographie d'art", which he saw as thwarting the designs of painting ("Daguerre seized the trompe-l'oeil and killed it"). However, he illustrated his creed with photographs celebrating these objects "making up the simple setting of our life": the Michelin tire photographed by Tabard, the strawing of Nicolas wine bottles by Draeger, and a male mannequin sitting on a bench in a shop window, the height of the modern spirit.

The photographic illustration of such an ill-defined section ("The street") manifests the perceptive and conceptual discomfort caused by the passage from stillness to movement at the heart of the cinematographic paradox, reversed by photographers into a passage from movement to stillness. Yet movement is not only a property of the "subject", of the filmed or photographed reality: the movement is also that of the machine (photographic or film camera), run by the photographer or the filmmaker ... Cartier-Bresson summed this up squarely in a late interview: "documentary is reportage with a moving machine",[23] he declared, echoing Carlo Rim's critical stance (1930):

> The snapshot forms a whole. The film is a succession of snapshots, all more or less *posed*, and which very seldom provides us with the illusion of the unexpected and the rare. Ninety films out of a hundred are never-ending poses. A photograph cannot be premeditated like a murder or a work of art.[24]

The Photographic Attractions of Cinema

With *La Revue du cinéma* (1928–1931), which defined itself as a "review of film criticism and experimentation", the aims were clearer: to give an account of experimentation in film or films by recognized authors such as King Vidor, Clarence Brown, Charlie Chaplin, Sergei Eisenstein, all deemed future classics, exclusively through photographs (supposedly) taken from the films or provided by the production to promotional ends (which included stills and photographs taken on the set as well as studio pictures of actors).[25] As I set out to peruse the

22　*Jazz* 2 (15 January 1929): 83. The latter part of the sentence refers to superimposition.

23　"Henri Cartier-Bresson, Gilles Mora: conversation", *Les Cahiers de la Photographie* 18 (1986): 121.

24　"Curiosités photographiques. De l'instantané" ["Photographic Curiosities. On the Snapshot"], *L'art vivant* 137 (1 September 1930): 694–695.

25　The advertisement for *La revue du cinéma* in the fourth issue of *Bifur* announced "film excerpts – rare photographs."

periodical,[26] in which I saw one of the most plausible sources of Cartier-Bresson's visual knowledge, I was able to see how close to the images made over the first years of the photographer's activity some published "film photographs" could seem – without Cartier-Bresson's photographs being imitations in any way. Meeting points between photography and cinema result from gaps, in photography and in cinema. Indeed, most of these films had a screenplay (except a documentary film like *Zuyderzee*, which in fact reappeared in issue 24 in 1931). In other words, unlike an "instinctive" photographer's photograph, what happens in the image, what occurs as an image, has been planned and recorded with a movie camera located in a premeditated place but has to be plausible as a situation and as gestures. In the years 1929–1930 the general framework was often that of a level of "scenographic" organization that aimed for spontaneity without belonging for all that to the realm of photography. People such as Cartier-Bresson or Lotar, whose intentions (as far as recording goes) situate them on the fence between photography and cinema, could draw on that gap to imagine a script, a pre-view of the photograph to come (or not), of the situation witnessed.

Indeed, an analysis of Cartier-Bresson's famous photographs, not as successful unique items (an interpretation he tended to substantiate in his comments) but as the results of a multiple shot (several images made in a row) proceeding from an intention, has the following implications: either the situation repeats itself, which involves a waiting posture; or the unforeseen movements are processed through a formal organization characteristic of Cartier-Bresson's images. On this *organization founded on waiting*, I refer the reader to the various examples given in my essay,[27] with the reproductions of *preserved* negatives from the same shot (up to sixteen, for "Séville, Espagne", 1933). Starting with *La Revue du Cinéma*, I pointed out a few "filmic" images that strongly hint at this potentially photographic posture: groups, for instance, are arranged with a view to obtain a maximal effect (*All Quiet on the Western Front*, Lewis Milestone, 1930; *Westfront 1918*, G.W. Pabst, 1930; or *Contre-enquête*, Jean Daumery, 1930).[28] Cartier-Bresson's fighters' scene ("Valence", 1933), four different images of which are known,[29] aimed for a similar effectiveness with tangled bodies and looks. Excerpts from José Leitao de Barros's *Maria do Mar*[30] (1930) and Murnau's *Tabu*[31] (1931) stand in this interval, between photography and narrative cinema, though not as much as Marie Dressler's inquiring side look in *Anna Christie*[32] (1930) – the close shot of a face that irresistibly brings to mind one of Cartier-Bresson's figures of

26   The periodical may be consulted at the Kandinsky library, Centre Pompidou, Paris.

27   Frizot, "D'imprévisibles regards. Les leçons de photographie d'un Scrapbook", *Henri Cartier-Bresson, Scrapbook, Photographies 1932–1946* 31–71.

28   *La Revue du cinéma*, issues 22 (May 1931), 16 (Nov. 1930), and 17 (Dec. 1930), respectively.

29   See *Henri Cartier-Bresson, Scrapbook, Photographies 1932–1946*, figures 25 and 26.

30   *La Revue du cinéma* 17 (December 1930).

31   *La Revue du cinéma* 25 (August 1931).

32   *La Revue du cinéma* 23 (June 1931): 29. The film, directed by Clarence Brown, stars Greta Garbo.

"looks" (the watch at the bullring, "Valence, Espagne", 1933), of which seven shots kept by the photographer are known.[33] In magazines, Cartier-Bresson looked at cinema images as photographs, knowing that they were possible only in a cinema situation: this encouraged him to open a photographic path into such situations or constraints, such sense of organization – produced, however, during a photographic confrontation with raw reality. In his own admission, He clearly oscillated between photography and cinema throughout the 1930s (he admitted so himself), with the same creative intentionality, the same wish to convey a vision of the world. After spending part of the year 1935 in the United States in contact with photographer and filmmaker Paul Strand, serving as an assistant to Renoir, directing two short films on the Spanish Civil War (1937–1938) and a third on the return of prisoners (*Reunion*, 1945), he all but renounced cinema after the Second World War, explaining much later: "I knew I would not do any mise en scène, probably focusing on documentary films instead, for I have no literary imagination."[34] The ability for scriptwriting was the dividing line for him, between getting imagined situations to take place (cinema) and capturing an unexpected situation as though it were part of a screenplay (photography) – as though *one* photograph condensed the material of a mini scenario (so went his theory of photography as *condensation*[35]).

Interchanged Figures

The mix of photographs in art magazines around 1930 is but one expression of the phenomena (contact, dissociation, re-association) occurring between photography and cinema at the time. In the years 1882–1889 Marey – who in turn produced photographs, sequential photographs that could be animated, and films – had, like Edison, circumscribed the common original principle: a shot with a photographic apparatus. Symptomatically, his research did in fact appear in *La Revue du cinéma* in several articles, the journal's only reference to the origins of cinema – under the auspices of slow motion and speeded-up motion.[36] The expansion of cinema at the beginning of the century resulted in other modes of contact between the cinematographic model and the photographic model serving as its foundation. One of the material elements conditioning this convergence was the use of the 35mm film strip as the medium for the photographic negative. As is well-known, the Leica camera, a "miniature" designed around this material, implemented the principle before other brands followed suit. As it happens, the Leica became widespread from 1927–1928 on (Kertész purchased one in 1928).

33 See *Henri Cartier-Bresson, Scrapbook, Photographies 1932–1946*, figure 33.

34 "Henri Cartier-Bresson, Gilles Mora: conversation", *Les Cahiers de la Photographie* 18 (1986): 120.

35 "With reportage, I tend to look for the unique photograph, namely, for condensation." "Henri Cartier-Bresson, Gilles Mora: conversation": 121.

36 "Ralenti et accéléré. Une visite à l'Institut Marey" ["Slow Motion and Speeded-up Motion. A Visit at the Marey Institute"], Paul Sabon, *La Revue du cinéma* 10 (May 1, 1930). See also issues 12 (1 July 1930) and 25 ("Le cinéma scientifique", 1 August 1931).

The fact is anything but trivial: indeed, beyond the medium itself, the physiological posture and the mental posture associated with it were altered by the Leica: an eye-level viewfinder, a reduction in the parallax of the viewfinder, allowing for precise framing, direct association between ocular vision and the viewfinder, rapid forward movement of the film. All in all, the camera encouraged the multiplication of consecutive shots a few seconds apart in a position of constant viewing and attention to what took place "before" one's eyes, a rather cinematographic posture. Henri Cartier became Cartier-Bresson with the purchase of his Leica in 1932, as he began to make photographs closer to "cinema" than to art photography or Nouvelle Photographie. It is not surprising, then, that many shots resulting in "one" (good) photograph would be retrieved, and that on occasion the succession of views[37] may even be established thanks to the numbers on the film, introduced by Perutz in 1930. Photographic contact sheets show the continuity of shots in strips of six 24 x 36mm views akin to the film fragments sometimes reproduced in illustrations. In that case, the ambivalence of the film mode was used to give the impression of a real or fictitious continuity between autonomous photographs. On the one hand, the clear display of film as a succession of photographs was accepted in order to show something else than a single image; on the other hand, the photograph placed in the proximity of other photographs contributed to a sense of temporal sequence or the suggestion of narration.

In the seventh issue of *Jazz* (15 June 1929), the section on "La Rue" bears a subtitle, "Paris jugé par un amateur d'hôtels". From the balcony of a hotel, an American observes this strange game: "two iron kiosks, hideous, stinking, obscene; some men enter, take a turn, then leave, their hand on the fly, their eyes ingenuous... (...) You are the most spiritual people on the surface of the earth, but you pee like pigs". The layout of three photographs linked up vertically as if on a film strip repeats the same scene, but with the appearance of time unfolding (Fig. 6). The "subject matter", while not very refined, is a signature for the urban modernity of 1929, to the extent that Cartier-Bresson broached it in his early career.[38] The presentation of the "strip" of film, with its photographs "stacked up" vertically, refers to the cinema – it is a figure of film – whereas the lateral (or horizontal) juxtaposition of images is the photographic version of the film strip of the Leica camera. Still, the Leica advertisement itself, in a visual slip, plays on the confusion between the medium and its imaginary reference. Admittedly the camera, with its "36 exposures without reloading", offered an uncommon continuity of shots for the time (Fig. 7).

37   *Henri Cartier-Bresson, Scrapbook, Photographies 1932–1946*, figure 19, 50.

38   "Henri Ford sortant d'une pissotière" ["Henri Ford exiting a street urinal"], 1932. The street urinal, on which posters were stuck up, also appear in "La Villette" (1932).

Fig. 6. "*La Rue par Carlo Rim*" (*The Street by Carl Rim*), photos by Latour, Jazz 7 (15 June 1929): 322.

Fig. 7. Leica advertisement, VU 277 (5 July 1933): 973.

The *all-photo* turn of illustrated magazines

In the sphere of media, and particularly among illustrated magazines, cinema and photography forged new associations. While photographic illustration had already enjoyed a boom with half-tone engraving at the end of the 19th century, the spread of rotogravure in the printing of weekly magazines ushered in a completely new order in which cinema could still be found in the form of a photographic display, in two distinct ways: the creation of specialized magazines and the articulation of photographic illustration on the cinematographic model. I have already examined the appearance of a "cultural", high-brow kind of magazine with *La Revue du cinéma*, whose format and design was close to that of *La Révolution surréaliste* or *Documents*. Yet a fair survey should also take into account more popular magazines, which approached cinema through images of stars, studio activity, the commercial promotion of films released in theatres, and its economy. *Cinémonde* was launched on 26 October 1928, whereas *Pour vous l'Intran*, the weekly film magazine stemming from *L'Intransigeant* (one of the major French daily newspapers, which already gave photography a prominent position in its pages), first appeared on 22 November 1928.[39] Both benefited from photogravure on rotary presses (rotogravure), whose accurate reproduction of half-tones perfectly suited photography. Their model was *Mon Ciné*, published

---

39   A sports weekly, *Match l'Intran*, had already appeared in 1926, also in rotogravure.

Fig. 8. *"Cinéma, ou vingt ans de vie moderne"*
(Cinema, or twenty years of modern life), Pour
Vous l'Intran, L'hebdomadaire du cinéma *1 (22*
November 1928): 11.

Fig. 9. *"Le secret du cargo" (The secret of the cargo),*
Cinémonde *18 (21 February 1929): 332.*

since 1922. *Pour vous,* with about 40 photographs over 16 pages, and *Cinémonde* (16 pages as well) obviously went through the commonplaces of film illustration, yet once again the photographs did not only refer the reader to the general subject of the film, but to a particular scene or situation (often love-related). It should be emphasized again that, *as photographs,* these images had an impact on the reception of all the photographs telescoping in all kinds of magazines, and therefore on the posture of image producers, that is, photographers. Let us mention, in the very first issue of *Pour vous,* the linear figure of film frames on a vertical strip of film, which seems to represent an expanded scanning of history (from *L'Arroseur arrosé* to *Joan of Arc*) under the title "Cinéma, ou vingt ans de vie moderne" (Fig. 8). Just as noteworthy is a one-page advertisement for *Le Secret du cargo* in the eighteenth issue of *Cinémonde*: it features eight photographs which in themselves are not very telling, but are still characteristic of the "all-photography" option adopted in visual communication (Fig. 9).

On unexplored corpuses, generally accepted ideas are in plenty and soon turn out to be ideas whose surface has just been scratched – one of them, for instance, holds that photography imposed its model, from the standpoint of "technique" and medium (the so-called "reproducibility", in effect a misnomer), through the invasion of daily newspapers and magazines. In fact, in the years 1928–1929, a moment of technical transformation for cinema, the cinema model had a backlash effect on photography – including on the types of media specific to it such as the printed photograph. The omnipresence of photography through photoengraving – in daily newspapers, magazines, and books – and its quantitative (and qualitative) explosion through rotogravure relied, more than is generally thought, on the cinema model, or rather, on the film model.[40] The publication of *VU*, "journal illustré de la semaine" (1928) provides evidence for this. The reader should first bear in mind the fact that in France *VU* was THE magazine that took the power of photography as a medium to a culmination and served as a model to many newsmagazines (general or specialized news, sports, etc.), among which *Life* (1936) and *Paris Match* later. In other words, what appeared with *VU* is but the form of photographic information we still cultivate today in many versions. As it happens, the argument on the conception of *VU* developed by its director Lucien Vogel (by no means an insignificant photographer himself), rested on the reference to cinema, apparently the epitome of effectiveness and modernism.[41] While distinguishing itself from other news outlets through the omnipresence of photography in all sections and offering "pages bursting with photographs", *VU* set as its first objective "to convey the rush of contemporary life". To that effect, it had to come as close as possible to a film, as Vogel put it in his conclusion: "animated like a beautiful movie, *VU* will be highly anticipated by its readers every week". The weekly periodicity evokes the ritual of cinema-going and the newsreels – also weekly – presented before the feature, which *VU* expressed as its "new formula: the illustrated report of world news", a characteristic aspect of the show at the movie theatre in 1928.

This proximity was corroborated by the launching of *VU* with a silent film by Edmond Gréville shown as part of the "actualités Gaumont" and titled *Un grand journal illustré moderne*. The first two intertitles state that "Today's hectic life does not leave any time for reading" / "seeing is imperative: we are in the century of images". The "hectic life" is represented in filmed shots, "images" in the pages of the first issue of *VU* being leafed through. Going through the 20 (and later 32) pages of the magazine, the specificity of *VU* – to adapt photography to the illustration of *all* sections, as announced in the profession of faith of the inaugural issue – appears clearly: photos are everywhere, from news reports to travel, "men on the earth", scientific discoveries, literary life, society gossip, sports, not to mention the "rigorous selection of photos from the best films" in the section *VU à l'écran* (which also means "seen on the screen"), written by Edmond Gréville. As if this were not enough, a weekly section was devoted to a hodgepodge of photographic "genres" under the heading "Dans le monde" ["In the World"], with titles frequently changing. To mention but one example of the photographic ambiguity of illustrated magazines as it mirrored cinema, an article appeared in the first issue of *VU* on the shooting of *Paname* (*Apaches of Paris*), adapted from

---

40   On these issues, I refer the reader to my study "Photo/graphismes de magazines : les possibles de la rotogravure, 1926–1935", proceedings of the conference *Photo/graphismes* (Jeu de Paume, Paris, 2007), http://www.jeudepaume.org/pdf/Photographisme_FR.pdf.

41   "Remarques sur un nouveau Journal illustré", *VU* 1 (March 21, 1928): 11–12.

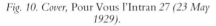

Fig. 10. Cover, Pour Vous l'Intran *27 (23 May 1929).*

Fig. 11. Cover, VU *27 (19 September 1928), Constance Talmadge, "photographie prise spécialement pour* VU *par le studio Alban" (photograph especially taken for* VU *by the Alban studio).*

Francis Carco, illustrated with five photographs by Eli Lotar extolling Parisian atmospheres at night, the over-lit set ... and the chiaroscuro resulting from the technical possibilities of photography.

Compared to the "illustrative" uses of the years 1928–1930, the primary visual consequence of such a choice was a mix of genres, on the same page or across pages. What was at once an ambivalent and clashing juxtaposition created, for the reader as well as for the producer of images, a new order for photographic "signification" (by this I do not mean objective appearance, but rather the imagination to which anyone exploring the surface of a photograph is referred to).

The cover allowed potential buyers walking by the newsstand to get an idea of the contents of the magazine or, more prosaically, was used by the editorial staff as an easy means to catch their eyes. Already, film magazines had gradually put together an illustrated media coverage specific to cinema, which privileged the close shot of a face looking straight at the readers (Fig. 10) and consisted in using studio portraits of actresses (and more rarely, of actors) to promote a movie. More often than not, the portraits were reframed to emphasize the face, and the eyes "entreating" spectators. *VU* resorted to a calculated and brilliant use of these

Fig. 12. *"Ménilmontant"*, Film-Photos wie noch   Fig. 13. *"Passion"*, Film-Photos wie noch nie
nie *(Film photos as never seen before) (1929): 108.*   *(Film photos as never seen before) (1929): 171.*

"cinema looks" that never appeared in films and were restricted to lobby cards. They constituted injunctions to "see" the character, to go see the film, and even more, to see the magazine when these entreating eyes were associated with the *VU* logo in a succession of I-see-you, you-see-me, you-see-me-looking-at-you … (Fig. 11). With a keen understanding of the power of the look and its role of intercessor – which a brand name alone cannot play –, the newsmagazine adapted the media effectiveness of the look to many other contexts, including news items on minor events (theft, crimes, etc.), as the 2006 *Regarder VU* exhibition at the Maison européenne de la photographie in Paris showed.[42]

The different ways in which photography and cinema approach the look brings this study full-circle and back to Cartier-Bresson: many of his pictures hinge on the looks exchanged by the photographer and the protagonists of his photographs, or only between these protagonists. Always, he learned much from cinema and what lies between cinema and photography, the receptive and perceptive exchanges, images blending in one another. While photographing, it

42   In one of the rooms of the exhibition, we spread the following themes over three walls: the *Le visage-expression* ["The Face as Expression"], *Le visage-faciès* ["The Face as Features"] and *Le visage-regard* ["The Face as Look"], the last two only involving *VU* covers. See images in Michel Frizot and Cedric de Veigy, *VU, The Story of a Magazine,* London, Thames and Hudson, 2009.

seems to me, he never forgot "cinema situations", whether he was looking for them or prompted them, knowing that the screenplay, which characterizes cinema, could be encapsulated in one photo. An amazing object – a book – provides an open ending to this osmotic circulation between photography and cinema, a resonance chamber of sorts for the photographic fantasy that runs through cinema. All in all, what is left of cinema when movement is taken away? Photographs which are not really photographs, photographs never seen. *Film-Photos wie noch nie*,[43] published in the year that sparked off our study (1929), categorizes over 190 pages the aesthetic novelties of cinema … in the form of photographs, 1200 of which are reproduced in the book. The photos of the films show feelings, situations, intentions never seen before in images, barely glimpsed in the moving image yet never "seen" in actuality and which, at any rate, cannot be looked at. The book, which deserves a thorough study, thus inventories – for the still and careful look – innovations introduced by cinema, visibile only in the form of photographs, classifying them page after page according to themes, famous figures, situations that made up the modernity of cinema in 1929 (Carmen, Faust, dreams of love, bullrings covered in blood, boarding schools, passion…). Each page features a cluster of images edited together, and which can accordingly only be "photomontages". There lies the ambiguity of the book, evoking as it does an imagination of the in-between whose impact, relying on cinema, can only affect photography – photographer's photographs, magazine photographs, studio photographs (Figs. 12, 13). A style which was thought to be characteristic of Nouvelle Photographie or creative reportage may have been the result, through circuitous paths, of that visibility of cinema.

---

43 *Film-Photos wie noch nie* ["Film Photos as Never Seen Before"], ed. Edmund Bucher and Albrecht Kindt (Giessen: Kindt und Bucher Verlag, 1929). A banner announces on the cover, "1200 photos of the best films from all countries".

4

From the Cinematic Book to the Film-Book

François Albera

"I do not see things as being in movement as much as I see them as a succession of still images. Add to that the peculiarity – perhaps due to a defective vision – that images persist on my retina for quite a while. At the races, for instance, I still see the horses above the fence after they have jumped. From that image I reconstruct what happened before, after."
Claude Simon (*Le Monde*, 26 April 1967)

The book holds a particular place in the variety of possible passages between stillness and movement. Mallarmé and his *Un Coup de dés* – to take an unquestionable reference – ushered it into modernity. That Mallarmé started thinking on the *mobility* of the book[1] with what he termed "the Book, in its totality", in the context of "moving images" and shortly after the advent of the cinematograph evidently owes nothing to chance.[2] To him mobility

---

1   "The book, total expansion of the letter, should derive from it directly a spacious mobility, and by correspondences institute a play of elements that confirms the fiction." "The Book: a Spiritual Instrument" [1895] in Stéphane Mallarmé, *Divagations*, trans. Barbara Johnson (Cambridge, London: Harvard University Press, 2007) 228. In a letter to André Gide, Mallarmé explained what he meant by such "play": "A certain word, in large characters, dominates on its own an entire white page and I believe I can be certain about the effect created". (May 14, 1897, in *Selected Letters of Stéphane Mallarmé*, ed. and trans. Rosemary Lloyd (Chicago: The University of Chicago Press, 1988) 223.

2   Such temporal proximity finds an expression in the response Mallarmé gave to a survey on illustrated books: "I am for – no illustration; everything a book evokes should happen in the reader's mind: but, if you replace photography, why not go straight to cinematography, whose successive unrolling will replace, in both pictures and text, many a volume, advantageously". Quoted in English translation in Jacques Derrida, *Dissemination*, introduction, notes and translation Barbara Johnson (London: Continuum International Publishing Group, 2004) 294. Original French text in Stéphane Mallarmé, *Correspondance*, Henri Mondor and Lloyd James Austin, eds., vol. IX (Paris: Gallimard, 1984) 236. Mallarmé made a concurrent statement on the "mimetic" in a letter to Gide: "[In this poem] the constellation will, fatally, assume, according to precise laws and in so far as it's possible in a printed text, the form of a constellation. The ship will list from the top of one page to the bottom of the next, etc.: for, and this is the whole point at issue [...], the rhythm of a sentence about an act or even an object has meaning only if it imitates them and, enacted on paper, when the Letters have taken over from the original etching, must convey in spite of everything some element of that act or that object." (Lloyd, *Selected Letters of Stéphane Mallarmé* 223) He further expanded on the subject in an undated letter to Camille Mauclair: "At bottom, about etchings: I believe any sentence or thought, if it has a rhythm, should take it from the object it aims at and reproduce, laid bare, instantaneous,

involved putting into play both the body of typographic characters and the body of the reader – any reader (turning pages, going back and forth, "hearing" differential series of voices in mixed speech), but also and more particularly the oral reader Mallarmé himself was during the famous staged evenings evoked by Valéry, and which he had called for in his introductory "observation" to *Un Coup de dés*.[3] In his wake, though of course quite differently, the Futurist avant-garde (Italian as well as Russian) took the book on paths more and more fraught with *movement*, instituting new relations between reader, written text, and images.

To reuse a word that originally belonged to mechanics and physiology before winning over the territories of aesthetics and art (with Canudo, Moussinac, L'Herbier, Eisenstein …), these books may be defined as *cinematic*[4]. Such instances of the book "set in motion", of a "cinematicization" of the written word point to two directions, as early as Mallarmé. The first is a labile and ductile "oralization" which gives the reader a decisive role and opens onto an almost exponential series of *variations*. Simultaneously (and sometimes with the same authors), this new space for *reading* confronts itself to the ideogrammatic model and to "total" writing, in which the sole juxtaposition of primary elements produces a global image, conceptual in nature. In such configuration, the writer and "emitter" does not program the totality of reception but leaves a structural and aleatory place for it (function and effectuation, respectively). Ezra Pound ("Image") and Eisenstein ("*Obraz*") represent examples of this.[5]

as though springing in the mind, some of that object's attitude regarding everything. Literature thus *proves itself*: no other reason to write on paper." ["Au fond, des estampes : je crois que toute phrase ou pensée, si elle a un rythme, doit le modeler sur l'objet qu'elle vise et reproduire, jeté à nu, immédiatement, comme jaillie en l'esprit, un peu de l'attitude de cet objet quant à tout. La littérature fait ainsi *sa preuve* : pas d'autre raison d'écrire sur du papier." In Camille Mauclair, *Mallarmé chez lui*, Paris, Bernard Grasset, 1935, 117]. The reference to "etchings" in the sense of a "print", of a trace, of what is left by a stamp – and not of a "representation" – manifestly pertains to a photographic paradigm in this instance. Finally, it should be mentioned that in 1977 Jean-Marie Straub and Danièle Huillet proposed a translation in voices and space of the poem on film with *Toute révolution est un coup de dés* ("Every Revolution Is a Throw of the Dice", 35mm, color, 10').

3   "Observation relative au poème *Un Coup de Dés jamais n'abolira le Hasard*", in *Cosmopolis* [1897], reprinted in *Œuvres complètes*, vol. 1, Paris, Gallimard, "la Pléiade", 1998, 391–392). Paul Valéry reported the experience of such "ideogrammatic spectacle" uttered by the poet behind a curtain in "Dernière visite à Mallarmé" ["Last visit to Mallarmé"]. Commenting on his first visual contact with the pages on which Mallarmé had composed his *Coup de dés*, he also referred to a "set-up" ["dispositif"], giving this word the abstract meaning of "brand new machine" ["machine toute nouvelle"]. Paul Valéry, "Le coup de dés", in *Variétés* II (Paris: Gallimard, 1930). Mallarmé also wrote in *Cosmopolis* that "for whoever wishes to read aloud, a score […] ensues". ["Pour qui veut lire à haute voix, résulte (…) une partition."] What is more, the "notes en vue du 'Livre' " ["Notes towards the 'Book' "] abound in scripts for collective reading "performances" in which the number of pages, volumes and interpretations raise the issue, with regard to "the crowd" of the cost and profitability of the operation (see *Œuvres complètes*, vol. 1, notably pages 580–622 and 965–1049, where Mallarmé also deals with the question of "voices").

4   In French the term « cinematic » is different to « cinematographic »: it exists before the cinema as a part of the physiology – study of movement – whose Marey was a specialist. But after the cinema emerged, the term is used by theoreticians and critics for including the movies in a bigger field.

5   Valéry well grasped these two options and proposed to articulate them, suggesting that oral reading was inseparable from an in-depth vision-reading of the poem. Mallarmé himself wrote in his "notes en vue du 'Livre' ": "…in short, there is a second reading for the initiated" (*Oeuvres complètes*, vol. 1, 1023).

The present examination of a few remarkable books "on cinema" proceeds from the context just outlined. Indeed, these works take both tendencies to the limit while confronting the paradox of either "representing" or putting into play the moving image, precisely (there lies a significant part of the problem) – through its main inception, the filmic image, in a medium devoted to still images yet offering a number of literal and figurative possibilities with respect to "setting into motion".

Argument

The notion that movement *belongs in* the film image, that the film-image is a *movement-image*, a "moving picture" leads to the preordained conclusion of an impossibility: the film image then cannot be part of a book except as a trace, a remain, an allusion, a referral – as scrap. If, on the other hand, the idea of an image set in motion – *motioned*, as some would have it – is endorsed, things look quite different. In other words, if the image and the movement applied to it are to be distinguished, as Bergson proposed from the beginning with his insistence on the *projection system* (and regardless of the objective he set to such dissociation), the question of the implementation of the film image in a print medium can be contemplated. It falls to the designer of the book to locate such effect *somewhere* – all in all, to find in the "writing-book-reading" setup, not the translation or the equivalent of the projection-of-intermittent-images-producing-the-illusion-of-continuity, but another mode of "setting into motion".

The few examples of "film books" dealt with in this contribution belong to the trend that takes as its starting point the idea that movement is *alien* to the image and that at issue is the possibility to mobilize the latter and *set it in motion* with the book as the medium, looking for substitutes to the movement generated by the projector. In short, such approach treats the book as a device in the production of movement, as a "machine", to paraphrase Valéry and Apollinaire, who used the term about Cubist collages.[6]

This led a first group – Soviets El Lissitzky on the one hand, Rodchenko and Stepanova on the other – to inscribe the film image in the lineage of *optical toys*, whose manipulation to set the image into motion, to produce a movement-effect was explicit, on display, and even flaunted. To them the reader-spectator-manipulator assumed it with his/her look as well as his/her body (his/her hands). The other group – Germans Hans Richter and Werner Gräff, and Swiss Hermann Eidenbenz – interiorized such material operation of setting into motion in a sense, through the page layout, the act of relating various images on a surface, and the creation of an "over-image" consisting in a simultaneous actualization of successive images of the film. Movement, relying on the look of the reader-

---

6   At the moment when Cubism invented the collage of letters, words, and images, Apollinaire described its intentions as the will "to mechanize poetry as the world has been mechanized." *Selected Writings of Guillaume Apollinaire*, ed. Roger Shattuck (New York: New Directions, 1971) 237.

spectator alone, should thus result in the formation of an overall image in his/her mind upon completion of the "reading".

At stake here is no less than the status granted to the individual film frame and the notion of "global" image, both invisible during the screening since the film frame dissolves in the succession of images and the global image is mental in nature. Eisenstein still linked them together, talking about film as successive immobilities jostling, overlapping, producing a mental movement in the spectator – a movement which he called concept (*Bewegung-Begriff*).[7] In the 1920s his reference to Chinese ideograms, in which assembled figurative elements (the equivalents of film frames) produce the concept (the global image), allowed him to give montage a decisive *constructive* role and to locate its intervention at the primary material level – that of film frames, from which it was usually excluded.[8]

Barthes, it should be recalled, devoted much – lonely – thinking to the issue of the film frame, starting precisely from some Eisenstein films. His brilliant essay was shelved immediately in the very periodical where it had appeared, was later ignored by all of Barthes's glossators and has since been covered over by Deleuze's own approach.[9] Barthes, who for years had worked within the *Institut de Filmologie* on isolating the "relevant elements" of the filmic, saw in the film frame the freeing up of a space for analysis. Indeed, "the constraint of movement" was "removed", as was that of "filmic time", thereby opening the space of "reading" – by opposition to "spectating", which would always remain caught up in the phenomenon attended to (phenomenological and neo-Bergsonian approaches have seized upon and emphasized this aspect). One of the only instances of response to Barthes's text came with Godard and Gorin in their film *Letter to Jane* (1972), in which they put forth a critical semiology of the filmic image "in actuality", founded on the "freeze frame" and its breaking down in signifying

7   Serguei Eisenstein, "The Dramaturgy of Film Form (The Dialectical Approach to Film Form)" [1929], trans. Richard Taylor, in *The Eisenstein Reader*, ed. Richard Taylor (London: BFI, 1998) 93–110 (the original German version of this text with autograph corrections is in the Library of the MoMA and reprinted in François Albera, *Eisenstein et le constructivisme russe*, Lausanne, L'Age d'Homme, 1989). The primary level [*Ur-Phänomen*] of the filmic is that between one frame and the next and produces an impression of movement – a mental effect since no movement occurs on the screen, only a rapid succession (superimposition). The generalization of this elementary phenomenon takes place again on the largest scale, that of the entire film and of its "global image" (the subject).

8   Save for some experimental filmmakers, among whom Werner Nekes stands out. He theorized for himself this phenomenon with his "kineme", the basic unit in the relation of one frame to another and experimented with it in many a film (*Jüm Jüm, Uliisses*, etc.). See W. Nekes, « Whatever Happens between the Pictures », *Afterimage* 5 (November 1977).

9   Roland Barthes, "The Third Meaning. Research Notes on Some Eisenstein Stills", *A Barthes Reader*, ed. Susan Sontag (New York: Hill and Wang, 1983) 317–333. Translator's note: despite the original English translation of Barthes's unit of analysis as "still", I have chosen to maintain "film frame" throughout the translation for two reasons. First, materiality is an important aspect of the argument and, without the reference to film, it seems to me, that would be partly lost. Second, in cinema "still" already refers to a photograph taken on the set, to the end of documenting the shooting and/or of later promoting and advertising the film. While such photographs may be made from a frame from the film, they do not have to. To clarify and summarize the distinction, I would say that Barthes's primary object of study and theoretization was the film frame; these film frames were reproduced in his text as still photographs.

units. Godard and Miéville later resorted to such analytics in *Six fois deux/Sur et sous la communication* ("Six Times Two/Over and Under Communication"), in which a single image was broken down, examined thorougly – in a word, opened out.

If the movement comes from the outside and sets the image into motion, as Bergson put it (movement is *inside the apparatus* and *mobilizes* still figures, snapshots such as those of the regiment marching[10]), how about a book? Where is the driving force behind movement in it?

El Lissitzky in his *Yaponskoie kino* ("Japanese Cinema", Moscow, 1928) and Rodchenko and Stepanova in their *Le Cinéma en* URSS/*Soviet Cinema* (Editor in chief A. Arossev, design and photomontage by V. Stepanova and A. Rodchenko, Moscow, VOKS, 1935) answered that the book should be considered as a machine, an apparatus – a *setup* operated by the spectator. Hans Richter and Werner Gräff, in *Filmgegner von heute – Filmfreunde von morgen* ("Enemy of film today – friend of film tomorrow", Berlin, 1929), followed by Hermann Eidenbenz in the book by Georg Schmidt, Werner Schmalenbach and Peter Bächlin, *Der Film wirtschaflich gesellschaftlich künstlerisch* (Basel, 1947, *The Film: Its Economic, Social and Artistic Problems*, Basel, 1948), considered by contrast that movement was in part implied in the image as potentiality and virtuality – in view of the construction of the image – and that it lay in the relation of images to one another (editing, cutting and pasting). They attempted to set it loose from the immobility of the medium (still reproduction) to open it out. The assembling of various images and the graphic montage on the page then prevailed, as well as the layout of film frames, the extent of the gaps and the blank intervals separating them.

Of course, Russians also played with page layout and montage. In Rodchenko and Stepanova's case, several constructive *patterns* were used, including a cruciform one (a possible reference to Malevich). Yet their originality and their importance lie elsewhere – in approaching the book as an apparatus, not as a receptacle whose materiality and technicity, among other things, would be neglected.

The term *setup* [*dispositif*], no matter the irritation its inflationist use may give rise to nowadays (as we saw, it appeared in Valéry's writing in relation to *Un Coup de Dés*), makes it possible to summon up the elements involved in a *situation* (film, apparatus, screen, spectator) and to think about their respective places and functions in the *organization* that brings and binds them together.

The Cinematic Book

A good example is Lissitzky's *Japanese Cinema* (*Yaponskoie kino*), a brochure-catalogue for a 1928 Moscow retrospective and exhibition (long format, 15 x 21 cm, or 5.91 x 8.27 in.) (Fig. 1). What immediately stands out is the insistence on the

---

10 Henri Bergson, *Creative Evolution* [1907], trans. Arthur Mitchell (New York: Barnes and Noble, 2005) 251–252.

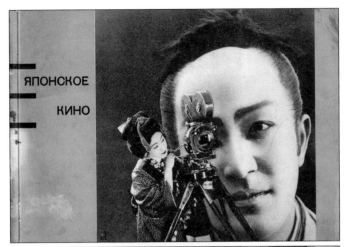

Fig. 1. El Lissitzky,
Yaponskoie kino
(Japanese Cinema),
1928: cover.

Fig. 2. E. Lissitzky,
Yaponskoie kino
(Japanese Cinema),
1928: 9.

shooting equipment, which appears on the cover, and on the strip of film, the perforated medium, the film frames, which all recur throughout the pages. In typical Constructivist fashion, the camera and the film medium are thus inscribed as such in the representation, in the manner of a collage. A vertical strip of film regularly appears side by side with individual photographs, a reminder of their material reality (Fig. 2).

However, the medium as *image in movement* is put into play elsewhere and rests on the reading practice freely initiated by whoever opens the book. Indeed, the reader turning the pages faces a transformative iconography thanks to their variable format. Some are narrower and let parts of the next page show, thus creating one image out of two by juxtaposition before transforming it when the page is turned, or reconstructing it thanks to the reversibility of movement.

For instance, on page 5, the crouching samourai on the defense, his saber raised

Fig. 3. E. Lissitzky,
Yaponskoie kino
(Japanese Cinema),
1928: 5 and 7.

Fig. 4. E. Lissitzky,
Yaponskoie kino
(Japanese Cinema),
1928: 7.

to the right, "faces" a fellow samourai, who stands with his saber up above his head, as though he were poised to attack to the left. The latter figure is on page 7, but the format of the previous page "already" makes it possible to see it. Quickly flipping page 5 back and forth as with a *flick-book*, one gets the impression of seeing two soldiers fighting it off (Figs. 3, 4).

Let us turn to Rodchenko and Stepanova with *Soviet Cinema* (312 pages, including 150 with photographs, in a format of 20 x 26 cm, or 7.87 x 10.27 in.). There again, from the cover on, the film strip is presented in its raw material reality: the repetition of a similar snapshot. On the flyleaf, however, the strip is horizontal (Fig. 5), which corresponds to its position on the flatbed viewer or the editing table. By contrast, Lissitzky presented it in a vertical position, as in the projector or when the film is examined manually (see the section on filmmakers at work below).

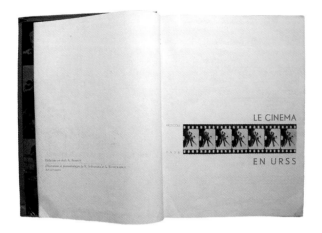

Fig. 5. Alexandre Rodtchenko and Varvara Stepanova, Le Cinéma en URSS *(Soviet Cinema), 1936: flyleaf.*

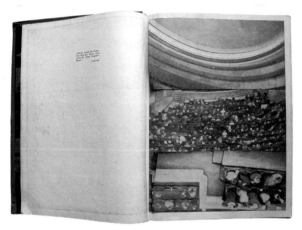

Fig. 6. A. Rodtchenko and V. Stepanova, Le Cinéma en URSS *(Soviet Cinema), 1936: 10–11.*

Fig. 7. A. Rodtchenko and V. Stepanova, Le Cinéma en URSS *(Soviet Cinema), 1936: 12–13.*

Fig. 8. Alexandre Rodtchenko and Varvara Stepanova, Le Cinéma en URSS *(Soviet Cinema), 1936: 10–11.*

Fig. 9. A. Rodtchenko and V. Stepanova, Le Cinéma en URSS *(Soviet Cinema), 1936: 12–13.*

As one goes farther into the book, the "machine" becomes more complex: turning the pages, the reader gets to unfold them, to make choices, to go back, to establish relationships, to compare, etc. Pages 10 to 13 (unpaginated) at the beginning of the book are a case in point.

Page 10 is almost entirely blank and features a quotation printed in red over four lines in a small typographic rectangle: "For us cine/ma is of all the/arts the most import/tant"/Lenin[11] (Fig. 6). Its counterpart, page 11, is quite particular, involv-

---

11   Let us not go back over the apocryphal nature of this quotation, launched by Lunacharski and repeated ad nauseam ever since. It became a "prerequisite" in the USSR of the time.

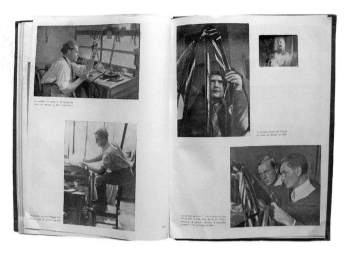

ing as it does the photograph of a theater that could be described as "turned upside down". It comprises three strips, which represent, from top to bottom: (a) the curves of a ceiling that could be described as convex; (b) rows of seats with spectators, their backs turned; (c) a closer high angle shot of a few more rows of spectators, their heads directed towards the bottom of the page. On the back, page 12 features the same film theatre but with a left-right inversion, as though it were seen through a transparent sheet (or on a strip of film) (Fig. 7). In this instance, the connection between inversion and verso appears quite obvious. Besides, a 1.77 x 2.17 inch screen cut out from the page opens onto a series of curves – a non-figurative whole, "without object" (as the Russian terminology of the time would have called it), which is in fact a detail of the ceiling already shown on page 11. On the following page (13), a photograph of Lenin takes up a third of the space which has otherwise been left blank and empty. The orator is framed at shoulder level, and a background of listeners turned in a direction similar to his form a kind of human pyramid. The image was probably made from a film frame in a newsreel.

Still, these pages may be browsed in other ways. Let us go back to pages 10–11 (Fig. 8): the top and the bottom strips aforementioned are flaps and may be opened. The theatre then unfolds beyond the limits of the book's format, the curves of the ceiling appear upside down (they become concave) and the auditorium expands by a few more rows of spectators on the mezzanine (these are the same as the ones described in c), but upside down). The theatre turns out to be a film theater; a screen appears in front of the audience. Cut out in the page, it opens onto a portrait of Lenin wearing a Russian fur hat, head up, a portrait which is itself but the "framing" of a portion of the larger photograph seen previously (p. 13).

On the verso (Fig. 9), the same film theater is shown in reverse (left-right) and

Fig. 11. A. Rodtchenko
and V. Stepanova, Le
Cinéma en URSS
(Soviet Cinema), 1936:
274–275.

the screen cut out in the page opens onto the Lenin quotation already seen on page 10.

Evidently, a third sequence combining these two would be possible: starting from page 11 with the flaps unfolded, the screen with Lenin's portrait would appear immediately. Regardless, viewers have four pages and six images at their disposal to effect the transformations by turning the pages and opening the flaps.

If we now take into account the relation between opposite pages as well as the double page as a whole (a unit Mallarmé much valued), these four pages offer *ten* reading possibilities: the Lenin quotation on the left and the upside down theater; the theater with abstract shapes on the screen on the left and the Lenin photograph on the right, or the Lenin quotation on the left and his portrait on the screen on the right, or the quotation by Lenin on the screen on the left and his photograph on the right. These readings involve different significations: moving from chaos, from the "upside down" to the screen showing Lenin; or, on the verso, shifting from the curves of the ceiling (non-figurative) to the printed slogan (meaning); or from the portrait to the entire image of which it constitutes a detail, and so on …

This opening of the book thus stages the film theater, the place of spectators, that of the screen, the reversible nature of the film image (transparency and inversion), and plays on these components through a screen cut out in the very page. Moreover, all the states that have been considered refer to the material aspects of a whole called "cinema": the theatre and its projecting setup, framing as a dimension of shooting, editing, the transparency of the film strip. Finally, the fact that each manipulation amounts to framing and montage is emphasized. Framing, for many Soviet filmmakers of the time (Kuleshov, Vertov, Eisenstein, Pudovkin, and others), involved wrenching from a whole through a cut-out. This does not constitute masking – in Bazin's sense of the frame as masking – but fragmenting, cutting out a piece. The image resulting from this operation is the "kadr" and individual film frames are called "kadriki" (small frames), where the French language privileges spatial distance (the shot and its scale) or the trace (the photogram, in its etymological sense).

None of these operations are *given* to see or represented: the reader-manipulator alone can effect them.

The same system of screen(s) cut out in the page and the production of differential relations between two consecutive pages are repeated further on in the book (pp. 272–275), but without any unfolding or transparence effect: only the view, through a page, of a part of the page that follows or precedes; a point of view on these other pages; the discovery of the image as a whole as the page is turned; or the discovery of what appears of a whole image when it is framed.

Pages 272 and 273 are devoted to filmmakers in the process of editing their films (Fig. 10): Eisenstein sitting with scissors, examining a strip of film in front of the Moviola; Vertov sitting on the back of his chair, also in front of the Moviola; Shub shown in a head-and-shoulder photograph, looking at some film she holds in her hands at eye level; Pudovkin and an actor, also examining some film. All of them look at images: not images in movement, projected on a screen or on the frosted glass of the flatbed viewer, but still images aligned on the film strip – film frames, or *kadriki*. For some, as already appeared in the graphists' choices, the film strip runs horizontally while for some others it runs vertically.

In the upper right corner of page 273 a small frame (3.5 x 4.5 cm, or 1.38 x 1.77 in.), cut out in the page, reveals the portrait of a general in uniform with his decorations, surrounded by smoke, and singing or shouting. In the upper left corner of page 274 (Fig. 11), the frame cut out in the page reveals Eisenstein's portrait, "torn" from the photograph where he was shown editing *October*, with two photographs taken on the shooting of *The General Line* (later *The Old and the New*) appearing underneath it: Eisenstein at the camera and Eisenstein among hogs.

On the right, page 275 features a photograph taken on the set of *October* that takes up about a third of a page and represents Eisenstein by the side of an actor playing a czarist general shouting hurrahs or singing with propmen crouched at his feet, blowing smoke around the military figure, who is supposed to be in a church in the midst of censers.

The frame on page 273 isolated the general's face and extracted him from the profilmic situation to make him filmic through a cutout. The frame stood next to the image of Shub looking at film strips. The situation of the shooting is here reunited with the elements which the frame excluded: the "scaffolding" of the image and its making, and even the trick involved in it. A – real – scaffolding appears below that image, on the photograph taken on the set of *The General Line*.

Each reframing involves a different relation between profilmic and filmic. In Eisenstein's case, as previously with Lenin, the meaning of the original photograph is neither altered nor transformed and a portion of it is preserved (the portrait). In the other case there is, in a sense, a trick. Besides, the double page shows the portrait of Eisenstein "looking at" the "engineered" shooting of the scene from *October*, where he himself stands outside the frame. All images on this double page involve the filmmaker as a "reigning" figure, including against the sunlight: an analogy may legitimately be drawn between the pages devoted to Stalin and their cult of personality (see below). The treatment given to Vertov, to whom Rodchenko was much closer than he was to Eisenstein, offers a sharp contrast (only one image) and calls to mind the reserve attached to the figure of Lenin.

Those four pages, irrespective of their explicit discourse, thus emphasize film-makers and crew, the conditions or even the artifices of shooting, while the first four pages opened the book with an introduction to the place of the spectator. Between that initial moment and the later one a shift can be observed in the activity of the reader-spectator elicited by the book, as well as between the cutout of the screen (45 x 55 mm) and that of the film frame, whose format is 24 x 36 mm, or a ratio of 2 to 3. These respective moments and their modalities manifestly refer to Vertov's concerns in *The Man with a Movie Camera*: film theater, screen, film frame, framing, "acted" cinema and its tricks. Besides, the book echoes Vertov's credo throughout and concludes with the work of newsreel cameramen, the "men with the shooting equipment" (*kino apparatom*), as the original Russian title of Vertov's film translates.

Let us go back for a moment. After the "Lenin" sequence of the album, the reader comes across a play with another constituent element of the filmic image approached in its material sense, its *transparency* – this time not as the inversion of a photographic image seen on both sides, but literally through a translucent page. Indeed, one of the contradictions in the "transfer" of the filmic image onto the printed page is, not only its stasis (the book, as we have seen, has moved "beyond" such aspect), but also an opacity due to printing (ink and paper). The notion of transparency is introduced in this instance with a translucent sheet that makes it possible to combine Stalin's medallion portrait with the Russian text of the Soviet leader's hail to the film industry, translated in French on the left page. Where the Russian text bears the title "[To the] Soviet film industry, to Shumyat-sky", the title of the French text reads, "Comrade Stalin Hails the Film Industry" (Fig. 12).

With the transparent page turned (Fig. 13), the Russian text appears backwards and the silhouette looks to the right, where a small, full-face portrait of Stalin and his signature appear in the upper right quarter of the page on a white background.

Neither irony nor an unsubtle overstatement can be ruled out in bringing these elements into play. The very different nature of the treatment granted to Stalin by comparison to that given to Lenin can hardly be ignored: in this instance,

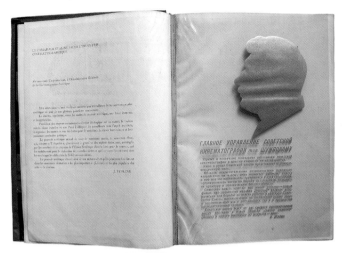

*Fig. 12. Alexandre
Rodtchenko and Varvara
Stepanova,* Le Cinéma
en URSS *(Soviet
Cinema), 1936: 14–15.*

*Fig. 13. A. Rodtchenko
and V. Stepanova,* Le
Cinéma en URSS
*(Soviet Cinema), 1936:
16–17.*

redundancy prevails since Stalin's profile first masks his own photograph before appearing superimposed on the French text once the page is turned. Seemingly looking at his own photograph on the page thus revealed, he also looks as if he is smiling to himself. Moreover, the medallion profile and the silhouette belong to other iconographic series than film. If one recalls the violent debates instituted by Constructivists against an imagery revolving around Lenin (candy wrappers, postage stamps, etc.) and their slogan ("Don't trade in Lenin!", an echo of which can be found in the bureaucrats sequence in Eisenstein's *The General Line*), Stalin's inscription in such a series manifestly bears certain connotations.

Such a suspicion of irony is reasonable in this case only because the album as a whole is something of a mystery. Indeed, two starkly different discourses are developed in it: that of the iconographic part, in which graphic designers clearly

Fig. 14. Alexandre Rodtchenko and Varvara Stepanova, Le Cinéma en URSS *(Soviet Cinema), 1936: 22–23.*

had a free hand and chose images and assemblages of images; and that of official texts, which express the dominant political and ideological point of view of the moment – Stalin's hail to Shumyatsky (the head of Soyuzkino, a quasi minister in terms of status), texts by Shumyatsky himself, by VOKS president Aroseff (who as such oversaw the publication of the book), by Dinamov, Pletniov, Katsigras, etc. These discourses contradict each other to the point of antagonism, and this album of "celebration" thus becomes the expression of a battle "between two lines": the avant-garde filmmakers who started Soviet cinema in the early 1920s (Kuleshov, Vertov, Eisenstein, Shub, Kozintzev and Trauberg, Pudovkin) and their successors (Barnet, Yutkevich, Dovzhenko, Ermler, Medvedkin, Zhemchuzhni), most of them marginalized in 1935 during the Congress of the 15th anniversary of Soviet cinema or even banned from shooting by Shumyatsky, who promoted another, more narrative cinema closer to the Hollywood model (an explicit reference), and represented by Raizman, Matcheret, Alexandrov ...

The Vassiliev brothers' epic-revolutionary film *Chapaev*, the first of its kind in the sound era (and the last as well, though it offered a template for later films), occupies the center of the book and immediately follows the "Stalin sequence", with the Bolshevik machine gunner taking the place of the Soviet leader in the page layout (Fig. 14).

The book is split almost equally between the two discourses, since there are 150 pages of illustrations out of a total of 312 (18 may be taken out of these 150, as they are portraits of filmmakers or cameramen). Iconography is therefore not marginal and structures the whole volume, its distribution even throughout the book rather than concentrated in one place or organized by sets.

The type of cinema advocated by the various political and ideological leaders came to dominate the 1930s after the fundamental reorganization of 1928. The apolitical cinema aiming at entertainment was condemned, but so was avant-garde cinema, from then on labelled as formalist. This aspect, while not central to my argument, should still be kept in mind if one is to understand what is at play in the book between these two incompatible discursive modes. Indeed, Rodchenko and Stepanova, besides their choices of graphic construction, gave precedence to the cinema of their close relations, all of whom had been criticized and were in a tight corner in the industry. The pair highlighted films on which these relations had collaborated, and which had been condemned and shelved (*Moscow in October*, *By the Law*, *The General Line*, *Man with a Movie Camera*, *Happiness*, etc.), while some titles advanced by officials were barely illustrated, save for *Chapaev*. The graphic designers' choices reflect the permanence of their commitment to Constructivism and their history of involvement in some of these films: Vertov's *Kino Pravda* (intertitles by Rodchenko), Kuleshov's *Your Acquaintance* (sets by Rodchenko), Zhemchuzhni's adaptations of Mayakovsky (sets by Rodchenko and Stepanova), and the posters they designed (*Battleship Potemkin*, *One Sixth of the World*, etc.).

May the fact that VOKS published the book for a foreign audience[12] help account for the scope of the evocation of a type of filmmaking more or less rejected by authorities – in the past, at any rate? The VOKS was the pan-Soviet society for cultural exchanges with foreign countries. This autonomous "social" organization had in fact close ties with the People's Commissariat for Foreign Affairs created in 1925 to "develop knowledge about Soviet culture abroad and inform about the main cultural events abroad within the USSR". Such cultural propaganda aimed to spread a positive image of the USSR and also included writers' and artists' trips.[13] This argument may be questioned, however, as promotion and propaganda literature devised for foreign countries had never differed from domestic literature, at least during the period. The problems Eisenstein ran into with Shumyatsky during the shooting of *Bezhin Meadow* in 1937 thus resulted in the publication of Rotokov's violent condemnation in *International Literature* (n°7, 1937) and the filmmaker's humiliating "self-criticism". The incoherence of the book likely owes more to varying levels of attention: a close watch for written materials, a certain indifference towards images.

At any rate, and until the "mystery" is solved,[14] graphic and iconographic propositions should be considered for what they are and as they are.

Lissitzky and the Rodchenko-Stepanova tandem continued the "line" of the Futurist and later of the Constructivist book.[15] They created object-books (Rod-

---

12   Besides the Russian edition, there were French, English and German editions.

13   Olga Kameneva (Trotsky's sister) presided over the VOKS from 1925 to 1929. In 1936 it was headed by Alexander Aroseff, a writer, publisher, and diplomat who had served in France. He had been appointed in 1933.

14   The VOKS collection at the GARF archives in Moscow (F.5283) includes some 13.351 files (my thanks to Jean-François Fayet, Université de Genève, who gave me this information).

15   This line survived until the end of the USSR in children literature, particularly with animated books and hand-drawn foldout books.

chenko with Tretyakov, for instance, with poems and photographs of paper cut-outs in shapes of animals – *Samozveri* [*Self animals*]) and in the 1930s put together similar albums devoted to the Red Army as well as special issues for magazines. That on parachuting for *SSSR Na Stroïka* [USSR in construction] (n° 12, 1935) particularly stands out: its pages can be folded in triangles and open like a parachute. Rodchenko and Stepanova had studied in detail how such an object could be folded by spreading an actual parachute on the floor of their studio.

Indeed, one principle of Constructivism is to draw from the object under examination the law of construction of its figuration or operation in the space of representation. These film books do follow this principle. In this instance, the acknowledgment of the reality of the film frame, framing, editing, intertitles, and a movement external to the image situates them in the lineage of moving images and their various devices, sometimes hastily grouped together under the heading "optical toys". In the type of images they produce, the immobility of the components is a given (a strip of paper to place in the drum, a still disk, a mirror arranged *ad hoc*, etc.) and it is up to the spectator to set them into motion by spinning the drum or the disk. In any case, movement is patent – not concealed "in the image" as "movement-image". The distinctive features of this type of image in motion are circularity, repetitiveness, and reversibility, but it would be too restrictive to assign it to a "pre-cinema". Lumière screenings often began with the projection of a still film frame – a "photographic print" (the cultural series to which early cinema belongs) that was demonstratively animated by a turn of the crank.[16] Similarly, the same view could be shown twice, once forward, another backwards ("demolition of a wall"). These features and these practices may be found with some variations in Vertov's cinema (in *Kino Pravda* the slaughtered ox recovers its integrity, is stitched back together and returns to its pasture), as well as with most experimental filmmakers.

Furthermore, the book is an object, not a surface of representation. As it happens, the debate on the distinction between composition and construction that had taken place at the Inkhuk in the early 1920s had led Rodchenko to state that construction (the goal) had supplanted composition (which was a matter of taste and choice). As to Babichev, he defined such a construction as follows: "to bring to date all the possibilities of the material and to find the form that corresponds to the work on the material".[17] During discussion Rodchenko ruled out any possible distinction between artistic construction and technical construction: "there is but one type of construction, the bare construction whose goal is in the organization of elements and materials of a given work". Then to the question, "Can painting offer a construction proper, since it is in representation?" (6th

---

16   René Clair's *Paris qui dort* (*Paris Asleep*) demonstratively made such process explicit by turning it into an element driving the development of fiction.

17   Alexandre Rodchenko, "Débats du groupe de travail d'analyse objective de l'Inkhouk" ["Debates of the Inkhuk objective analysis working group"] (1921), *in Écrits complets* (Paris: Philippe Sers, 1988) 183. See also *Vhoutemas. Moscou 1920–1930*, ed. Khan Magomedov (Paris: Editions du Regard, 1990), 2 vols.

session of the debate), the answer was negative and three-dimensionality was deemed a requisite, construction taking place only in reality ("in real things occupying a real space"), not in representation. If one considers the characteristics of photography (which disposes of the hand) and the material assemblage of components, such real space is manifold, since collage and photomontage also develop it. Cinema is undoubtedly part of the same issue.

The book as film

Hans Richter and Werner Gräff's graphic propositions characterize another successful approach to cinema books, one starkly different from the realizations considered so far. These propositions were to dominate the best subsequent examples of "cinema books", as evidenced by Hermann Eidenbenz's work for *Der Film* [*The Film*] or the iconographic composition of *La Revue du cinéma* in France in the immediate postwar years (the latter proceeded from another lineage, that of Malraux's *Musée imaginaire* [*Museum without walls*]).

An evolution may be traced between these three "moments".

Hans Richter and Werner Gräff's book, *Filmgegner von heute – Filmfreunde von morgen* ("Enemy of film today – friend of film tomorrow", Fig. 15) was related to the 1929 Stuttgart exhibition "Film und Foto".[18] For the first time, photography and film were exhibited together in an artistic setting. Much has already been said about the presentation of works at the event, particularly in the Soviet section where Lissitzky and Sophie Küppers were in charge of it.[19]

Richter was responsible for the "cinema" half of the event, and in a way his book came as an accompanying piece to the program of screenings and conferences organized during the exhibition. It should be noted that his collaborator Werner Gräff authored *Es Kommt der Neue Fotograf!* ("Here Comes the New Photographer!") that same year and with the same publisher (Berlin, Hermann Reckendorf, 1929). Gräff's book was also related to "Film und Foto" and offered a typology of the "new vision" induced by the photo camera. Likewise, the demonstrative axis of the book on cinema means to bring to light the "new vision" effected by cinema. However, despite its relation to the Stuttgart exhibition, Richter and Gräff's book cannot be considered as a form of restitution of the physical space of the event: on the contrary, the space of the book itself is, with the formats of both single and double pages, explored from multiple angles.

Like the Soviet artists with whom he had ties (he had moved from Dada to Lissitzky and Ehrenburg's Constructivist International), Richter insists on the

18   Berlin, Hermann Reckendorf, 1929, 125 p., 26 x 19 cm. A fac simile of the book was published in 1968. An Italian edition also exists, which I have not been able to consult: *Nemici del cinema oggi, amici del cinema domani* (Udine, 1991).

19   See François Albera, "Les passages entre les arts : cinéma, architecture, peinture, sculpture" ["Passages between the Arts: Cinema, Architecture, Painting, Sculpture"] in *Qu'est-ce que l'art au 20e siècle ?* ["What Is Art in the Twentieth Century?"], ed. Jean-Christophe Royoux (Paris: Fondation Cartier/Ecole nationale supérieure des Beaux-Arts, 1992).

Fig. 15. Hans Richter, Filmgegner von heute - Filmfreunde von morgen *(Enemy of film today – friend of film tomorrow), 1929: dust cover.*

Fig. 16. Hans Richter, Filmgegner von heute - Filmfreunde von morgen *(Enemy of film today – friend of film tomorrow), 1929: 7.*

camera, the film strip, film frames, and the mechanism producing movement through the animation of snapshots. In the opening of the book, a piece of film strip from Pudovkin's *Mother* is shown folded and in its actual size on the page (Fig. 16), a collage of sorts.[20] From the beginning, the nature of the medium thus reveals the repetitiveness of snapshots succeeding one another as well as the transparency of the print (the fold shows part of the strip in reverse). Subsequently, several fragments of avant-garde films are laid out as such on the page (pp. 38, 71, Fig. 17). Yet film frames are also dissociated from one another (pp. 34–35, Fig. 18) to emphasize such successiveness of immobilities, whose logic may be transgressed to ends of alternation, contrast, and rhythm (montage). Some original compositions of film frames are even structured in staggered rows, separated by gaps, or assembled on the surface of the page and spatially organized, with *kadriki* out of line with one another for instance. Besides, images not given as film frames – the medium is not shown, the gaps between film frames make it impossible to imagine them in succession – are "edited" together so as to correlate them to one another and, all in all, turn them into "shots", leaving aside the repetitiveness of series of film frames (Fig. 19).

Film stills are also laid out "like" film frames, but without their materiality (sprocket holes, gaps between images). Finally, single images can be blown up or

---

20   In the typescript of his intervention as part of the exhibition (which he was not able to deliver), Eisenstein glued a fragment of film strip and the photograph of a camera. See my *Eisenstein et le constructivisme russe* (Lausanne: L'Âge d'homme, 1989) 43.

images from different films placed side by side to emphasize compositional choices. This is the case page 70 with an – erroneously captioned – image from *October* (a Bolshevik with his gun in a pronounced diagonal) and another from Dreyer's *The Passion of Joan of Arc* (Falconetti's Joan with her cross in a similar position): the equivalence between gun and cross is clearly emphasized, and through it the pictorialness of the filmic image (Fig. 17).

Spectators do not have to set images into motion or manipulate the medium to obtain differential effects: rather, they are shown a movement *signified* by the relation of a number of images on the page. Such graphic montage differs from cinematic montage in its reliance on the co-presence of elements, which it does not place in succession or in superimposition, but in a *composition* within the visual economy of the single or the double page. Such proposition consists in pointing to a movement of the filmic image in the simultaneity of elements, as the time of visual "reading" is to be subsumed under the production of an overall image resulting from the various singular images.

In the course of the book, Richter tellingly *puts together* – literally – the experiment attributed to Kuleshov by Pudovkin at several conferences in Amsterdam and London that same year (1929) and later published in book form.[21]

Such realization (p. 29, Fig. 20) testifies to his belief in a graphic equivalent to cinematic language, which the book can relate *in the order of representation*. Yet how could the "K effect" operate in the context of a simultaneity of elements when, according to the description of its very procedure, these elements have to appear in succession and create associations of ideas a posteriori? This example, and many others in the book, clearly show the dilemma faced by Richter and Gräff. On the one hand, they favored a graphic approach to cinema that revived visual experiments such Richter's painted scrolls, and in which overall composition organizes the page quite suggestively. On the other hand, they also aimed for a rendition of operations involved in film. Such a contradiction led to the prevalence of a non-figurative form, a play of abstract forms running through figurative images.[22]

---

21 On the myth of the "Kuleshov effect", see *Iris* 4:1 (1986), "L'effet-Koulechov/The Kuleshov Effect", which first called it into question. Since the publication in French of Kuleshov's writings (*L'Art du cinéma et autres écrits*, Lausanne, L'Age d'Homme, 1990, published in English earlier as Lev Kuleshov, *Selected Works. Fifty Years in Films*, ed. Ekaterina Khokhlova, Moscou: Raduga, 1987), evidence has grown substantially larger and I have given the latest synthesis of it in "Koulechov en effet…" ["Kuleshov in effect"], *Brûler les planches. Crever l'écran. La présence de l'acteur* ["Consuming performances, incandescent screens: the actor's presence"], eds. Gérard-Denis Farcy and René Prédal (Saint-Jean-de-Védas: L'Entretemps, 2001) 97–113.

22 Such "graphic" conception went through developments in USSR in the 1930s with Eisenstein after the "break" noted by David Bordwell in the filmmaker's theoretical thought ("Eisenstein's Epistemological Shift", *Screen* 15:4 (1974) 29–46). Eisenstein's collaborator Vladimir Nilsen synthesized the new direction, which pervades the major unfinished projects of the filmmaker (*Montage, Non-Indifferent Nature*, etc.), in his *The Cinema as a Graphic Art* (the title of the original Russian edition published in Moscow in 1936 read as "The Construction of representation in cinema"). See François Albera, "Le retour à la peinture de Vladimir Nilsen: le cinéma comme art graphique" ["Vladimir Nilsen's return to painting: the cinema as graphic art"] in *Cinéma et peinture. Approches*, eds. R. Bellour and L. Marin (Paris: PUF, 1990).

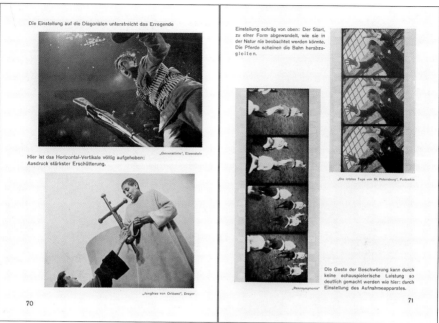

Fig. 17. H. Richter, Filmgegner von heute - Filmfreunde von morgen
(Enemy of film today - friend of film tomorrow), 1929: 70–71.

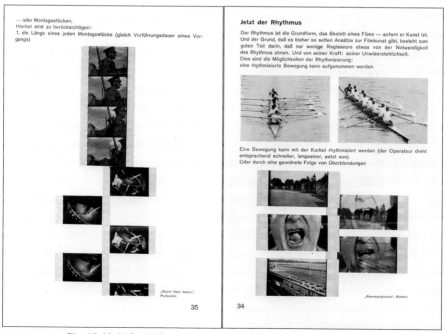

Fig. 18. H. Richter, Filmgegner von heute - Filmfreunde von morgen
(Enemy of film today - friend of film tomorrow), 1929: 34–35.

man suche das Gewohnte durch ungewöhnliche Erfassung wieder lebendig zu machen.

Schließlich können auch die Objekte künstlich zu natürlichem Eindruck erschaffen werden. In Sensationsstücken beispielsweise werden gefährliche Sprünge usw. meist nicht vom Hauptdarsteller, sondern von geeigneten Artisten ausgeführt: durch geschickte Montage von Bildern, die mit verschiedenen Darstellern gekurbelt wurden, erhält der Zuschauer den Eindruck, es handle sich um eine Person. Durch die Montage lassen sich selbst Gefühlsausdrücke künstlich zu natürlichem Ausdruck zusammensetzen.
Hier zum Beispiel zeigen wir Ihnen die Wiederholung eines Experiments, das K u l e s c h o w im Jahre 1921 machte. Sie sehen das g l e i c h e Bild, mit v e r - s c h i e d e n e n Folgebildern montiert

Fig. 19. Hans Richter, Filmgegner von heute - Filmfreunde von morgen *(Enemy of film today – friend of film tomorrow), 1929: 52.*

Fig. 20. Hans Richter, Filmgegner von heute - Filmfreunde von morgen *(Enemy of film today – friend of film tomorrow), 1929: 29.*

The book is remarkable for the importance it gives to images and their montage, to the production of a visual rhythm through the repetition of a motif, assonances, or the inversion of various parameters (masses and voids, light and darkness, geometric structure, etc.), and for the minimalism of its texts – most often, captions that "let images speak". Yet its approach also results in a loss: the material reality of the film as well as the place of the spectator as a site, not only of contemplation, but also of reception *and* formulation.

The book Peter Bächlin, Werner Schmalenbach, and Georg Schmidt published in 1947, *Der Film wirtschaflich gesellschaftlich künstlerisch* (Basel, Holbein-Verlag), with graphic designer Hermann Eidenbenz as the art editor, took this trend even further (Fig. 21).

This 124-page outstanding book has opposite pages numbered in duplicate in Arabic numerals (thus amounting to 62), with 14 pages numbered in Roman numerals in between the table of contents and the list of illustrations (the format is 30 x 21 cm, or 11.81 x 8.27 in.). A short-lived French edition appeared in 1951, as for financial reasons the publisher was not able to have it bound. I was not able to consult the English edition (*The Film: Its Economic, Social and Artistic Problems* in 1948).

This book is also tied to an exhibition: it is even the direct outcome of "Der Film gestern und heute" ["Film yesterday and today"] organized in 1943 by the Basel Museum of Decorative Arts on the occasion of the city's first Film Week, curated

*Fig. 21. Peter Bächlin,
Werner Schmalenbach
and Georg Schmidt,
Der Film
wirtschaftlich
gesellschaftlich
künstlerisch (The
Film: Its Economic,
Social and Artistic
Problems), 1947: cover.*

by Georg Schmidt and taken up by Bern in 1944, Zurich in 1945, and Brussels in 1947. The choice of didacticism, examplified by explanatory panels in the show, should be understood as a background to the book which, according to the preface, responded to requests by many visitors to find a visual discourse akin to that of the exhibition in print.

Georg Schmidt was then a curator at the Basel Museum of Fine Arts. His political commitment went to the extreme left; his brother, architect Hans Schmidt, worked for several years in the USSR before leaving for the GDR. An art historian, he had taken part in the Congress for Independent Cinema in La Sarraz in 1929 and had met Balázs, Richter, Ruttmann, and Eisenstein there. Georg Schmidt had also accommodated Vertov during the filmmaker's trip to Switzerland. Werner Schmalenbach was also an art historian (he had written on Kurt Schwitters) and a museum curator. He was an organizer and a speaker at the Basel Congress for International Cinema in September 1945. The event also led to a

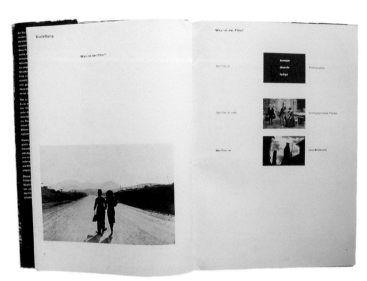

Fig. 22. Peter Bächlin, Werner Schmalenbach and Georg Schmidt, Der Film wirtschaftlich gesellschaftlich künstlerisch *(The Film: Its Economic, Social and Artistic Problems), 1947: 1.*

publication[23] in which he wrote on "film dialog and sound affects" to reaffirm the preeminence of image over sound ... Peter Bächlin was an economist and had published the first book on the economy of cinema from a Marxist perspective. He was the president of the organization committee of the Basel Congress. The three men created the Archives suisses du film (ACS) in Basel in 1943, to which the Cinémathèque suisse in Lausanne succeeded in 1948 after authorities in Basel cut off ACS funding for political reasons.

Hermann Eidenbenz was in charge of the section on experimental photography at the Lucerne World Exhibition of Photography. In 1952 and 1953 this monumental event had a great impact throughout Europe and in the United States, arousing Otto Steinert's interest.

In Eidenbenz's work the reference to the film frame comes through the layout and size of film stills. The film is not epitomized in an emblematic single image, as is often the case with cinema books, particularly albums. Its fragmentary and successive character is underlined and both qualities contribute to the understanding of the "laws" of composition of the images as well as of the construction of their relations (contrast, link, assonance). On the other hand, any allusion to the film strip, to the sprocket holes, and to celluloid disappears. Rather, the succession of "small frames" aims to create a new, specifically graphic compositional and rhythmic arrangement (Fig. 22).

Quite obviously, Eidenbenz had in mind (and possibly even before his eyes) Richter and Gräff's book when he designed his own. Some pages borrow some

---

23   Serge Lang, ed., *Cinéma d'aujourd'hui, Cahiers de Traits* 10 (Geneva, Paris: Les Trois Collines, 1945).

Fig. 23. H. Richter, Filmgegner von heute - Filmfreunde von morgen *(Enemy of film today - friend of film tomorrow), 1929: 25.*

parallels or some montages, thereby naturalizing them. *Entr'acte* offers an example, with four film frames juxtaposed in a column: arms in a ring above a head, feet touching ground as seen from below, legs, and again the view from below as the body rises (Figs. 23, 24).

The catalogue of the exhibition *Der Film* at the Zurich Kunstgewerbemuseum in 1960 may be considered as an ultimate avatar of Richter and Gräff's approach. The cover, which was also the poster for the exhibition, plays on the notions of transparency and superimposition. A famous Swiss graphic designer, Josef Müller-Brockmann, created it; he was a close friend of Max Bill's and had as a consequence inherited a Bauhaus influence (Fig. 25).

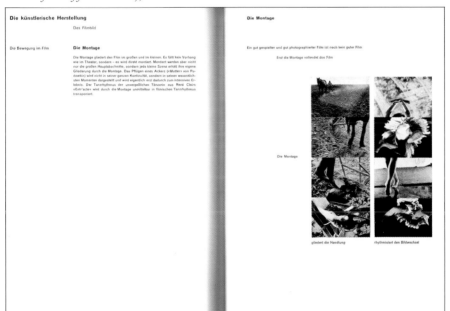

Fig. 24. H. Richter, Filmgegner von heute - Filmfreunde von morgen *(Enemy of film today - friend of film tomorrow), 1929: 42.*

Fig. 25. Der Film *(The Film), 1960: cover.*

The catalogue as a whole does not take up, however, this type of thinking on the medium. The page layout by Jörg Hamburger and Serge Stauffer, with its great qualities of clarity and sobriety, has little to do with the questions at hand except in its insistent emphasis on the successiveness of images whose small, 24 x 36 format remains the last reference to the film frame. The book tells the story of films in a few photographs: narrative logic has overridden any other considerations. The narration of Chaplin's *The Circus* shows it quite strongly (Fig. 26), with the choice of images from the beginning and the end of the film serving as clear bounds for the narrative – and reviving the Pathéorama still-image viewer, in some way…

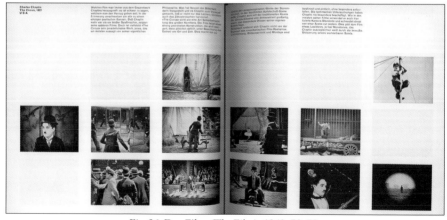

Fig. 26. Der Film *(The Film), 1960: 78–79.*

Section IV
Freeze Frames

Introduction:
Between Deadly Trace and Memorial Scansion: The Frozen Image in Film

Laurent Guido

S tarting with the first theories of film, examined in the opening section, the frequent equation of photography to the "dark" side of cinema has owed not only to its fixity – an aberration in the eyes of advocates of the cinematographic art, who had identified the essence of the medium with absolute mobility – but also to its *indexical* nature. Many critics and theorists did indeed approach the unshakeable relation between the reality recorded by the camera and the "objective" image proceeding from it as a mere point of departure, a raw material offered to the imagination of creators. At stake was not so much the celebration of a life revealed by the mechanical techniques of visual capture and reproduction as the emphasis on the poetic potential of these machines for artists, who from then on were able to perform within conditions perceived as the continuation of the psyche or the unconscious. By contrast, the second half of the twentieth century was deeply marked by a more intense reflection on the realistic potential of visual techniques produced by scientific modernity. André Bazin's thought in the postwar period[1] and its fertile translation into a Peircean termi-nology from the late 1970s on[2] posit as an evidence that the mechanical recording taking place with photography and cinema produces a genuine trace of reality, a trace that may not be considered separately from its visual source. Starting in the 1920s, experimentations that set dominant narrative forms in crisis certainly continued actively in the realm of cinema, but in accordance with a general consideration of the share of the real conveyed in images. While Man Ray viewed the discontinuous, non-narrative structure of *Le Retour à la raison* (1923) as "a

---

1   In "The Ontology of the Photographic Image" (1945), but also in the less often cited "Theater and Cinema" (1951, beginning of the second volume). Both texts appear in *What Is Cinema?* [1967], vol. 1, ed. Hugh Gray (Berkeley, Los Angeles: University of California Press, 2005).

2   Katia Schneller, "Sur les traces de Rosalind Krauss. La réception française de la notion d'index. 1977–1990", *Etudes photographiques* 21 (December 2007): 123–143. See more particularly Philippe Dubois, *L'Acte photographique et autres essais* (Paris: Nathan, 1990) 40–53.

series of fragments", for his part Bazin saw the "fragment of raw reality" as the basic unit of a neorealist film such as Roberto Rossellini's *Paisa* (1948).

In the opening contribution to this new section David Forgacs examines this neorealist strand to identify the moments of "denarrativization" situated outside the dominant logic of the plot. These "decisive episode[s]" aim to elicit a contemplative attitude by stretching time, which translates into longer shots, minimal visual information, and an elementary isochrony of filmed movements. According to Forgacs, these specific segments, immobilizing narration in the form of stases, "return cinema to some of the conditions of the still photograph, or the series of photographs". This reduction of filming to a strictly "photographic" dimension became one of the important figures of cinematographic creation in the postwar period. Raymond Bellour has notably defined it: "This means that almost every shot is a still, often very long take in which some movement occurs, probably, but of an aleatory, open-ended, documentary kind, comparable to the development of what a snapshot captures".[3]

Forgacs supports the hypothesis through a thorough study of post-WWII discourses, since a substantial share of the semantic productivity of images characteristic of neorealist culture came out of spectatorial activity. These images were thus approached as frozen, enigmatic "surfaces" whose figurative evidence did not necessarily entail univocal meaning. Insisting on the dynamism of the point of view of spectators faced with the fundamental "stillness" of denarrativized sequences, Forgacs writes within a tradition of thought that underlines the omnipresence of the temporal process, including in plastic arts apparently devoid of mobility. Indeed, the idea constitutes a central arguments in the various rebuttals – by Paul Klee[4] or Ernst Gombrich,[5] among others – of the traditional dichotomy between arts of time and arts of space.

The comparison of films with the wide spectrum of media and visual culture of the 1930s and 1940s (illustrated newspapers, film stories and photo romances, photographic essays, exhibitions …) points to a coherent iconography that deeply pervaded the postwar Italian film production. The influence of the American documentary style was more particularly perceptible in the new, anti-formalist tendencies triumphant at the time, and which found their emblematic formulation in the defense of location shooting. The aesthetic concerns of many film

3   Raymond Bellour, "Six films en passant" ["Six Films in Passing"] (1989), reprinted in *L'entre-images: photo, cinéma, video* (Paris: La Différence, 1990) 139.

4   Paul Klee, *Schriften, Rezensionen und Aufsätze* (Köln: DuMont, 1976) 119. In 1920, Klee notably stated that "the activity of the spectator is a temporal one. [...] Pictorial art springs from movement, is itself fixed movement and is perceived through movement (eye muscles)." Paul Klee, "Schöpferische Konfession", *Tribüne der Kunst und Zeit*, Berlin (1920): 34–35, translated as "Opinions on Creation" in Paul Klee, *Three Exhibitions* [1945] (New York: Museum of Modern Art, 1968) 12.

5   "If the perception of the visible world and images were not a process in time, and a rather slow and complex process at that, static images could not arouse in us the memories and anticipations of movement." Ernst Hans Gombrich, "Moment and Movement in Art", in *The Image of the Eye. Further Studies in the Psychology of Pictorial Representation* [1982] (London: Phaidon, 1999) 61.

theorists, the most prominent being André Bazin and Cesare Zavattini, involved advocating an increased realism in which the inscription of individuals in their social context was primarily grounded in the rejection of the hyperbolic and reflexive visuality that had defined the interwar period (see section 1). David Campany is one of several authors relating this "change of pace" characteristic of the postwar era, a moment when the rhetoric founded on the frenzy of montage exhausted itself: "The accelerated image world began to feel dehumanizing, repetitive and monotonous. In this context *slowness*, the deliberate refusal of speed, became central in vanguard art and culture and we can see this change of pace both in photography and film."[6]

This historical shift refers in several ways to the one leading from Gilles Deleuze's "movement-image" to the "time-image". While the terminology is explicitly taken up and qualified by David Forgacs, he opts for a conception of neorealism in which denarrativized segments exist in relations of dynamic integration or tension with narrative elements. In a series of important articles, Raymond Bellour repeatedly outlines "this cinema of time which was born after the war and out of the war, with neorealism and the New Wave".[7] Discussing this new cinematographic "modernity", he draws not only on Deleuze's theses, but also on Roland Barthes's ideas on the lack of pensiveness affecting cinema and severely limiting it with respect to the contemplative temporality still photographs can give rise to. For Barthes, these photographs involve a host of emotional and intellectual, openly subjective engagements which he identifies at various theoretical moments as the "obtuse meaning" of film frames repressed by the film[8] or the *punctum* caused by snapshots.[9] In a groundbreaking piece, Peter Wollen argues in favour of a cinema that would break free from "an imposed reading time" resulting from cinematographic movement to instead privilege "a free re-writing time" guaranteed by photographic stillness.[10] Wollen posits the same recurrent opposition as Barthes between two major modes of perception, an opposition that Christian Metz (among others) reformulates when he reckons that cinema's "additional perceptive registers [...] contributed to putting in check the *power of silence and immobility* [...] that belongs to photography and defines it".[11] On this confrontation between the two media, Bellour concludes for

6   David Campany, *Photography and Cinema* (London: Reaktion Books, 2008) 36.

7   Bellour, *L'Entre-Images* 113.

8   Roland Barthes, "Le troisième sens. Notes de recherches sur quelques photogrammes de S.M. Eisenstein", *Cahiers du cinéma* 222 (July 1970), translated in English as "The Third Meaning. Research Notes on Some Eisenstein Stills", in *A Barthes Reader*, ed. Susan Sontag (New York: Hill and Wang, 1983) 317–333. See also Bellour, *L'Entre-Images* 71, 109–133. Translator's note: on the translation of "photogrammes" as "film frames", and not as "stills" as in the English translation of Barthes's text, see note 8 in François Albera's contribution to this volume.

9   Roland Barthes, *Camera Lucida: Reflections on Photography* (New York: Farrar, Strauss and Giroux, 1981) 40–60.

10   Peter Wollen, "Fire and Ice", *The Photography Reader*, ed. Liz Wells (Oxon: Routledge, 2003) 76–81, 76.

11   Christian Metz, "Cinéma, photo, fétiche", *CinémAction* 50, special issue "Cinéma et psychanalyse" (Paris: Corlet, 1989): 168–175.

his part that the presence of photography in cinema – which amounts to invoking stillness in the form of the freeze frame, the allusion to the film frame, or the presentation on the screen of photographs – could not fail to produce "effects of suspension, freezing, reflexivity".[12]

The identification of this aesthetic hybridity proves very productive in understanding the complex forms developing out of the articulation between stillness and movement in postwar "new cinemas", beyond the neorealist example proper. *Cleo from 5 to 7* (1962), directed by photographer and filmmaker Agnès Varda during the New Wave, exemplifies the successive representation of the two temporal modes exposed above. The structure of a sequence, early in the film, largely overlaps with the shift from avant-garde "series of fragments" already mentioned to neorealist de-narrativized stases (Fig. 1). When the main character leaves the consulting room of a Parisian clairvoyant to walk out onto the rue de

12   Raymond Bellour, "The Pensive Spectator", *Wide Angle* 9:1 (1987): 6–10, 10.

Fig. 1. Cleo from 5 to 7 *(Cléo de 5 à 7, Agnès Varda, 1962).*

Rivoli, everything places the two stages of a progressive transition from inside to outside in opposition. Intensive cutting first characterizes the moment when Cléo walks down the stairs. Effects of symmetry are emphasized (the detailed capture of the body from every angle, frontally (Fig. 1b, e), from the back (a, d), and a point-of-view shot (c, i), repeated in an absolutely similar order), while the metrical scansion of the whole is stressed out. Indeed, the echoes of the protagonist's metronomic steps are synchronized exactly on the martelé notes of a repeated musical bass: *mickeymousing*, rhythmic editing and automatic gestures ceaselessly point to the mechanical isochrony that supports the illusion of movement produced by cinema out of single film frames.

The passage of *Cléo* involves several aspects examined in the first section of this book. First, it evidently manifests a conception of movement based on arbitrary, regular sections – of the kind envisioned by scientific rationality and condemned by Henri Bergson as "cinematographic method". Yet Cléo's fragmented progression also seems to actualize a famous text by Jean Epstein, quoted in the introduction to the first section, in which he describes his own walking down a staircase decorated with a number of mirrors reflecting him. The filmmaker expresses the agitation created by the frenzied multiplication and the increasingly alienating variability of secondary images generated by the cinematographic recording of corporeal movement. The start given to one of the close-ups of Cléo's face makes even more explicit the reference to the decisive presence of stillness within the flow of mobility: on the three successive beats of the same musical bar, the same, extremely brief image is repeated, that of a neutral facial expression suddenly appearing from the background to stop in sharp focus (f, g, h).

Once outside, Cléo paces the sidewalk in the midst of the Parisian crowd. This time she is shown in a single panning shot, an extended, high-angle long shot seemingly captured unawares from a window (k). For this parade of the main character, a deeply moving melody played on a cello has been added to the musical repeat. The representation of a stretched time, in which the female protagonist now develops in the prolonged continuity of a single image, finds its justification within the filmic narrative. Indeed, this regained self-assurance on the part of the character takes place after a "static" passage situated exactly in the interval between the two moments just described. In fact, at the bottom of the staircase, in the hall of the building, Cléo has stopped for a moment to admire herself in the mirror (j). This narcissistic look at her own, flawless beauty[13] helps her relativize a terrible prediction by the clairvoyant, who has just announced to her that she would soon contract an incurable disease. By contrast to the burst of short shots used in the scene where she walks down the stairs, the awareness is conveyed in a single shot focused on the mirror. A zoom-in summarily eliminates the multiple reflections of Cléo's face to concentrate on her still, smiling composure at the moment when her inner speech can be heard in voice over ("minute, beau papillon …!", or "hold on, beautiful butterfly …!", an address to herself that insists on freezing time).

The temporal suspension is thus initiated by a gradual reduction of cinematographic parameters, leaving aside little by little the hysterical production of movement (the product of an animation of stillness, which forces the individual into a mechanical behaviour) to result in a pared-down immobility (time flows in the continuous fullness of an inner duration where the mobile thought of the subject may thrive). The start given to one of the frames as she walks down the stairs may then be interpreted, not only as the visible display of the saturation of the film apparatus, of the operative limits to its so-called fluidity, but also as the manifestation of a necessary emancipation of the photographic element within film, a dimension usually overshadowed and which becomes bit by bit a model of stillness and reflexivity within representation.

---

13   On the relation between the myth of Narcissus and the photographic trace, see Dubois, *L'Acte photographique et autres essais* 134–150.

Traumatic Fixations, from the Universal to the Autobiographical

Once more, this example attests to the equation between the issue of stillness and movement and various psychic states, more often than not traumatic. In the wake of reflections on the "optical unconscious" dealt with at the beginning of the book, the reference to traumatology constitutes one of the essential lines of this new section. In fact, all authors refer to it in approaching the question of multiple intersections between stillness and movement in cultural representations. After being referred to the psychological disorders caused by the new conditions of modern life (see section 1), this recurrent relation is here situated in a specific historical context, that of the collective experience of the Second World War. This major upheaval is for instance seen by David Forgacs as a "catalyst that precipitated cinema as a whole towards the condition of documentary, and hence towards an ethically-grounded realism". The cases of post-traumatic stress disorder noted in the aftermath of the war affected photographic culture: reportage as well as specialized books then focused on urban ruins and the lifeless beings haunting them. The most famous photography film in the history of cinema, Chris Marker's 1962 *La Jetée*, develops a similar post-apocalyptic point of view, as its succession of still images evokes the consequences of a hypothetical Third World War. This essential monument and the important studies it generated (Philippe Dubois's and Roger Odin's, in particular) serve as references as Diane Arnaud reflects on the implications for identity and memory of works in which the still image is approached as the "foundation" in "the death to come and a 'beyond' of the disaster". The de-narrativized fragments of neorealism, modeled on photography books, are in this instance reshaped into "film segments akin to photo albums of accidental, individual, worldwide, or universal disasters". The Freudian psychoanalysis of neuroses makes it possible to zero in on the nexus between the individual and the collective, the personal and the universal within various figurations of this trauma produced by war. Arnaud thus distinguishes between the strategies of *remembrance* and *avoidance* at work in a number of films from the 1970s referring to the imagination of the nuclear disaster, from a Japanese production touching on Hiroshima to a work of science-fiction. The editing of still images together – sometimes associated with freeze frames, in accordance to an obsessional logic at work in Japanese cinema in the 1960s and the 1970s[14] – whether in the credits or punctuating the film narrative itself, refer in various ways to the strategies of rebuilding or repression mentioned above. The images of yakuza in the films analysed by Arnaud cannot fail to bring up violence and death, thereby reinscribing "the fact that the action is getting increasingly unsettled and that the postwar situation is an impasse".

---

14 The topic of the freeze frame alone would require a specific development for its central place in the Japanese culture of the 1960s and 1970s. Among dozens of salient examples: *Story of a Prostitute* (Suzuki Seijun, 1965); *The Face of Another* (Hiroshi Teshigahara, 1966); *Assassination* (Masahiro Shinoda, 1964); *Blackmail is My Life* (Kinji Fukasaku, 1968); *A Woman Called Sada Abe* (Noboru Tanaka, 1975). The importance of illustrated books and mangas may be one possible explanation for the lasting appearance of these frozen moments, which can take on extremely varied meanings.

In her analysis of some passages Arnaud emphasizes multiple ways in which photos are linked up in the films (zoom, reframing, superimpositions of images, acceleration in the display of views, split-screen, etc.). The frantic rhythm goes together with a proliferation of different angles that creates a geometric world difficult to grasp for the individual spectator in all its successive developments (still images look "as though they were infinite, and hence interchangeable: enlargement, reduction, organization in three- or four-part tabulations"). At first sight, these techniques seem to re-activate the kaleidoscopic model that marked the historical avant-gardes (see section 1). Yet these sequential figures, which also played out in many slide shows and screening shows in the 1960s and the 1970s (see section 5), are primarily dealt with according to another logic that proceeds from a common, widely shared experience of arranging still images in a series: leafing through a photographic album.

In this form of "cine-photo album", the film then appears as the orchestration of a mode of subjective "commentary", animation, and appropriation that register a constant tension between the dimensions of universality and intimacy. In that respect, Arnaud's text is precious in the transition it effects between the corpus of the 1970s and contemporary autobiographical trends by way of a characteristic work: Jonathan Caouette's 2003 *Tarnation*. In the film the canonical figures of anxiety and alienation tied to modernity redevelop following a personal trauma. A former fashion magazine model, the mother of the main protagonist suffers a cerebral accident that results in a coma and sends him in search of his identity. Memorial work and editing work (structured by family pictures in some parts of the film) then merge. As in the example from *Cleo from 5 to 7* and several contemporary autobiographical films,[15] the news of the disease appears to spark off a process that will prove central to the narrative. The act of remembrance thus triggered is more often than not founded on the reactivation of the fragmentary traces of a memory that will not be captured but in still, enigmatic images – those represented by photographs. In *Tarnation*, the resort to freeze frames and to the visual distortion of photographs (through lighting, colour saturation, or flickering) vividly crystallizes the film's practices of manipulating still images.

The search of an identity that characterizes the autobiographical film also often amounts to confronting memory and its inevitably fragmented nature with places from the past – whether traveled in youth, or marked more or less deeply by some actions. In her short film *Embracing* (1992), Naomi Kawase sets out on the track

---

15 *The Long Holiday* (Johan van der Keuken, 2000) probably constitutes one of the most developed and accomplished forms of this idea. The relation between stillness and movement runs through the beginning of the film, with still forms (including a series of photographs increasingly moved, reframed, commented) gradually re-inhabited by the energetic movement of the author fighting his own passing away. Similarly, the narrative of Sophie Calle's 1992 *No Sex Last Night* begins with Hervé Guibert's death. This question has been notably examined by Liu Yung Hao, *L'Écriture du Je au cinéma: pathos et thanatos dans l'autobiographie filmique* ["Writing the I in Cinema: Pathos and Thanatos in the Filmed Autobiography"], doctoral dissertation under the supervision of Marie-Claire Ropars-Wuilleumier, Université de Paris-VIII – Saint-Denis, 2002.

of a father who once abandoned her, describing her path during a sequence devoted to the return to places of her childhood. This exploration progresses through different series in which aspects of stillness and movement are used with much singularity. The filmmaker, who throughout the film appears almost exclusively in the form of an uncertain and elusive image-body (shadows, reflections, superimpositions on a television screen, fast motion...), represents herself as a traveler in black-and-white photographs that emphasize the discontinuity of her memorial path. One of these photographs is prolonged in a succession of images in which the very close phases of the same movement of the protagonist's eyes are broken down in repeated fits and starts.[16] Most of these images alternate with colour images, introduced in a very peculiar manner: each and every time the photographic trace of the past (a print on paper where Kawase as a child may be identified) is flaunted in front of the lens before being withdrawn from the frame in the continuity of the take, unveiling the space as it appears on the day of the film shooting. The method produces the sense of a still image shifting to another form of stillness (a setting without much movement, except for leaves trembling or curtains moving with the wind, or even the camera itself slightly shaking). Still, between two moments in the same shot, we have moved from the irreversible past of the photograph to the permanent present of cinema (Fig. 2).

In her text Patricia Kruth also deals with the issue of the insertion of still images in the autobiographical film, and more particularly the home movie. Indeed, her study – devoted to a few of Martin Scorsese's films – takes as its starting point a documentary the filmmaker made on his parents, *Italianamerican* (1974). Like Diane Arnaud with the contrasted strategies involved by the "fallout of stillness" in films, Kruth chooses to highlight the multiple functions and meanings that may be assigned to the paradoxical instances of stillness within a given work. The gradual modification of a shot of Scorsese's mother, which literally turns into a photographic image through a series of operations (fixation in freeze frame, de-saturation, reframing), thus does not only indicate the still dimension of cinema. It also refers to the more or less pronounced conflicts in Scorsese's relation to maternal authority.

After considering Scorsese's first works, Kruth focuses on *Raging Bull* (1980), *GoodFellas* (1990) and *Casino* (1995) so as to examine how the figure of the freeze

---

16 In a sequence of the swedish thriller *Millennium* (Niels Arden Oplev, 2009), the look of a young woman is similarly reconstructed from old photographs gathered, digitized, and enlarged. The movement of the eyes takes on life again with the regular clicks of the investigator on his computer, a gesture that in a sense meets the click of the camera that recorded these same images, years earlier. More broadly, the question of the relation between photography and cinema runs through the film, adapted to the circulation and systematic analysis of images in the computer age. The look described above suddenly freezes as a threat appears off the frame (an invisible zone later revealed through a new search in the album of a tourist trip); the gait of a man looks decomposed when a series of images is gradually downloaded to the heroine's computer; the same heroine is explicitly shown to have a visual, or "photographic" memory caused by a childhood trauma; the killer collects photographs of his victims' expressions at the very moment of their killing; the investigation demonstrates the importance of the systematic digitization of photographic archives; and so on...

Fig. 2. Embracing *(Ni tsutsumarete), Naomi Kawase, 1992.*

frame interacts with other techniques based upon the relation between stillness and movement: presence of photographs in the profilmic domain, slow motion, repetition of similar images ... More specifically, she attempts to account for the various modes of transformation that may characterize the freeze frame. At which points does the shot freeze or (re)turn to movement? Is it possible to identify variations in terms of rhythm and speed? Do the photographs appearing on the screen already imply a representation of mobility, for instance through the use of the blur? Kruth reminds her readers of the importance of the freeze frame in the context – already established above – of a certain cinematographic "modernity" defined by semantic ambiguity and narrative deconstruction. In an impressive book, Garrett Stewart discusses this question to reformulate it out of the "post-modern", and even "post-human" foundations characteristic of contemporary cinema. Beyond the inscription of films in genres or currents, an interpretive community emerges from the various detailed analyses and singular interpretations of emblematic works. Among these are the narrative stasis of Frank Capra's *It's a Wonderful Life* (1946); the temporal fits and starts punctuating Jean-Luc Godard's *Sauve qui peut la vie* (1980); or the suspended conclusions of François Truffaut's *Four Hundred Blows* (1959), George Roy Hill's *Butch Cassidy and the Sundance Kid* (1969), or Ridley Scott's *Thelma and Louise* (1991). Indeed, the main writings on the freeze frame do interpret these re-developments of stillness within the cinematographic flow not only as the mark of an enunciative agency trying to exteriorize a photographic truth typically repressed, hidden in the invisible infrastructure of film, but also as the irreducible trace of a vanished time, and for that reason associated with death.

This perception of a deadly dimension of the photographic instant in film constitutes a leitmotiv of historiography. In his analysis of *The Machine That Kills Bad People* (Roberto Rossellini, 1952) or *Persona* (Ingmar Bergman, 1966), Raymond Bellour thus puts forth the idea that "photography carries the power of death through the film", "an inscription of death" ceaselessly confirmed, in his view, by the expressions of the photographic within "a cinema-apparatus haunted by death and its own death".[17] Garrett Stewart follows suit as he sees the photographic trace as pointing at once to the origin and to the negation of cinema: "whereas photography engraves the death it resembles, cinema defers the death whose escape it simulates".[18] Whether relying on photographs or emphasizing the single film frame, these cinematographic interventions of still images refer, in Stewart's view, to the "the still work of death".[19] This recurring discourse has its main theoretical references in "The Ontology of the Photographic Image" brought out by André Bazin, but above all in the ideas developed by Roland Barthes in *Camera Lucida*.[20] Both texts underscore the particular role played by photography in the preservation of a trace of the dead, an act all the more perceptible as the indexical value that characterizes mechanical recording comes to reinforce it. To the Bazinian insistence on the religious, or even transcendental value of the funerary ritual played out again in the modern period with photographic embalming, Barthes responds with the paradox according to which a snapshot produces the feeling of a co-presence with the moment captured on a photographic image as much as it testifies to the irreparable death of the subject photographed in the past. To describe this dizzying temporal gap, Barthes writes of a dazzling light, like a flash suddenly coming up from the unconscious.[21] The meaning of this new reference to trauma, which several contributors to this book point to, is notably explained by Laura Mulvey as she establishes a comparison between the print left by light on the film and "the memory left in the unconscious by an incident lost to consciousness". In her view, cinema has as a primary objective to decipher this information retrospectively through the "delayed time" characterizing the many variations of the stillness/movement dialectic in film.[22]

As the several allusions to family mourning in Bazin's and Barthes's writings demonstrate – their common reference to the ambiguous charm of photographic albums being an example – the problem of the memorial trace evidently finds a

17   Bellour, *L'Entre-Images* 117–119, 123.

18   Stewart, *Between Film and Screen* xi.

19   Stewart, *Between Film and Screen* xi.

20   For a contemporary rereading, see Laura Mulvey, *Death 24 x A Second* (London: Reaktion Books, 2005), in particular "The Index and the Uncanny: Life and Death in the Photograph", 54–66.

21   Roland Barthes, *Camera Lucida* 30–32, 49–51, 80–82 et passim. For his part, Christian Metz defined the Barthesian punctum as a "traumatic point located in the frame". See Metz, "Cinéma, photo, fétiche" 174.

22   Mulvey, *Death 24 x A Second* 9.

wide echo within autobiographical cinema. Diane Arnaud's analysis of *Tarnation* provides an excellent illustration, since Jonathan Caouette's film similarly relates the overexposure in the media experienced by the filmmaker's mother to the pain that overwhelms her before being passed on to her son. The morbidity of the mechanical click of the camera is explicitly cited in one of the series of snapshots edited together that punctuate the film: the flash associated with it is symbolized by a "lightning" fade to white that belongs in the iconography of the deadly capture associated with the photographic act. With Scorsese, freeze frames also reveal a "state of mental confusion" which in many ways refers to the traumatic shocks associated with the alienation produced by mass culture. In keeping with a tradition dating back to *King Kong* (Ernest Schoedsack & Merian C. Cooper, 1933),[23] the blinding flashes of photographers relay – in *Casino* (1995) as well as in *Aviator* (2004) – the aggressive dimension of the cultural industry.

Christa Blümlinger also deals with the traumatic relation between traces of memory and feeling of individual loss, as her article approaches Agnès Varda's work from the standpoint of another visual production originating in mass culture, the postcard. Indeed, between standardized means of communication and individualized use, the object "entails the ersatz and the psychic obliteration of memory-images". To support her argument on fragmented montage in Varda's work and her original way of emphasizing the photographic index toward an irreparably lost past, Blümlinger refers not so much to Bazin and Barthes as to Siegfried Kracauer's reflections on the "ghostlike reality" and the "disintegrated unity" of the photographic portrait, which the German writer compares to the feelings experienced upon reading forgotten letters or new performances of older music.

In *Opéra Mouffe* (1958), opposing portraits of real people, a photographic enumeration supposed to evoke the departed, to a few shots as brief as snapshots showing the expressions of passers-by, the filmmaker instituted a type of confrontation (between still photographs from the past and photographs apprehended in an immediate continuity within the living world) which later assumed an almost conventional value in contemporary cinema. An example is Mathieu Lis's 2006 short film *Les Veilleurs* ["The Wakers"],[24] in which a young assistant gravedigger writes page after page in notebooks to document the personal stories of deceased people. Their appearance on the screen is limited to the basic presentation of black-and-white photographs. In the uninterrupted flow of polychromic moving images, the sudden absence of colours reinforces the impression

---

23 It is the famous sequence in which the great ape, reduced to a fairground attraction with reporters feasting on the spectacle, breaks his ties and wreaks havoc in New York after the "aggression" of the flashguns going off.

24 Lis's work deals more generally with the exploration of relations between photography and cinema. In his 2003 *Vernissages* ["Exhibition previews"], the filmmaker thus recounts – as in an autofiction by Vincent Dieutre – the confessions of a male prostitute, punctuating the film with verbal descriptions of different photographs acquired by the protagonist with his earnings.

of a found object, unmoored from the filmic chain and which comes to re-present the past in the form of a print both accurate and fragmentary. Lis's film combines the representation of a passionate, dynamic memorial work, bound to fail due to its overweening ambition, and photographic portraits bearing the stamp of authenticity, but attesting as much to the identity of a person as to his/her death. Autobiographical cinema always crystallizes this type of contradiction. In *Ce répondeur ne prend pas de messages* (1979), for instance, Alain Cavalier juxtaposes the attitude of gradual hiding and dimming adopted by his own character[25] and a few photographs of the loved ones whose death he must now come to terms with. The idea is used again in Cavalier's *Irène* (2009), a film entirely devoted to a reflection on the memory-images of a spouse who met with a tragic ending. The strategy of delaying the moment when her face would be shown in the film is encapsulated in a sequence where a black-and-white portrait of the young woman, initially denied and rejected off the frame, is gradually revealed in its totality, from details selected along successive reframing movements. Various temporal processes (camera movement, editing, verbal commentary) thus define, explain, emphasize the instant frozen in the photographic image.[26] Among the few photographs of Irène then following one another is the brutal revelation of her wrecked car, an image which both functions as a blunt break in the nostalgic flow of remembrance and advances the work of understanding and mourning, like a necessary shock.

The autobiographical reference involves a constant circulation between private and public, personal and universal dimensions. In cinema the reduction of autobiography (which tells the story of one's existence, or that of one's relatives) to the self-portrait (in which the self-reflexive gesture attempts to appear in the very moment of its expression)[27] is certainly reinforced, or even privileged by the presence of the photographic element and its more strongly indexical nature. Indeed, the notion of self-portrait implies that the artist primarily captures the very moment of creation.[28] According to Christa Blümlinger, Agnès Varda's work shares more similarities with the "fragments of a self-portrait" which "do not necessarily appear as an effigy of herself" but "obey subjective modes of perception". The case of Varda's *Ulysse* (1954) Blümlinger sees as epitomizing the characteristic trend of the use of photography in cinema. Little by little, the exploration of a single photographic image moves away from the certainties of

---

25 Wrapped like a mummy or James Whale's invisible man, he lives in an apartment he increasingly seals off from light.

26 Since *La Rencontre* (1996) and *Le Filmeur* (2004), Alain Cavalier's cinema has focused on the juxtaposition of minimalist shots in digital video, images commented off-frame by the filmmaker in synchronous sound. The trace of the voice, captured at the same time as the image, is thus included in the recording done by the camera. This constraint is not incompatible with the production of complex effects of semantic overlay (reported stories, association of ideas...).

27 On the subject, see Muriel Tinel, *L'autoportrait cinématographique*, doctoral dissertation under the supervision of Jacques Aumont, Ecole des Hautes Etudes en Sciences Sociales, Paris, 2004.

28 See Bellour, *L'Entre-images* 271–337 ["Autoportraits", 1988].

knowledge to privilege associations of ideas tinged with subjectivity. To use Barthes's categories once again, the film – shifting from the *studium* to the *punctum* – gradually reinforces the enigmatic dimension of the photographic surface. David Forgacs already pointed out this aspect with respect to the neorealist context: the same photograph may entail a variety of relations and interpretations. Its semantic fecundity (freeze frame, insertion of a photograph, or even long take tending towards immobility) makes such a surface available for a wide range of uses, in particular through the spoken word.

Voices, Bodies, Rhythms: Intermedia Appropriations

The presence of a verbal commentary over a still image does in effect inscribe the film in temporality by reaffirming, in the face of visual immobility, the discursive movement of the cinematographic work. Roger Odin greatly contributed to thinking through such a question, not only with his seminal essay on *La Jetée*,[29] but also with his decisive work on the functions of the voice in the autobiographical film. The dialectic between personal and universal preoccupations, which Odin terms "Lyrical-I" and "Historical-I", respectively, seems to him indissociable from the images with which the voice interacts.[30] These visual elements generally tend towards minimal movement, and even immobility; this does not so much resonate directly with the meaning of speech as it serves as a neutral, impassive background to it (a car driving across desert landscapes, anonymous urban crowds ...). Many autobiographical films experiment with the idea, in particular those taking as their object urban American landscapes, from *News from Home* (Chantal Akerman, 1977) to *Entering Indifference. Lettre de Chicago* (Vincent Dieutre, 2000).

As to music, another sound parameter that may dialogue with stillness, it does not simply carry certain cultural connotations, but also forces its own modes of structuring movement on still images (from beats in a meter to lyrical expression). Accordingly, music can accompany or contrast with the particular rhythms produced by certain effects of montage between still images (juxtapositions, serial arrangements, dynamic relations ...), as actualized in the credits of *Soylent Green* and the frantic sequences of *Tarnation* analysed by Diane Arnaud. In *Salut les Cubains* (1963), Agnès Varda artificially re-animates the dance steps of a local musician out of a few photographic portraits. Perfectly suited to the swaying tempo of the music, the animation of these salient attitudes results in a stirring cinematographic scansion whose syncopated rhythms come from the uneven shifts from one photograph to the next. Still, as Christa Blümlinger stresses out,

---

29   Roger Odin, "Le film de fiction saisi par la photographie et sauvé par la bande-son. A propos de *La Jetée* de Chris Marker" ["The Fiction Film Seized by Photography and Saved by the Soundtrack"], in *Cinémas de la modernité, films, théories* (Paris: Klincksieck, 1981).

30   Roger Odin, "Lecture autobiographique et travail du JE" ["Autobiographical Reading and Work of the I"], in Roger Odin, *De la fiction* (Brussels: De Boeck Université, 2000) 141–152.

the exaggerated dynamism of this passage soon gives way to a new series of photographs of the same Cuban musician, this time as an accompaniment to a verbal tribute by Varda to the man who has died since the shots were made. The filmmaker thus reintroduces the canonical use of photographic images, in charge of conveying memory while explicitly asserting their quasi-funerary function. Still, the Frankensteinian overtones of the *montuno* – which literally re-animates a dead – appears retrospectively less as a macabre dance than as the self-reflexive celebration of the demiurgic powers of filmic movement, which can freely master time out of iconic fragments snatched from the material world.

Approached from different angles in some of the texts in this collection (such as those on early cinema or the Surrealist aesthetic), the choreographic model – like the musical model – appears to fulfill a decisive function in the rhythmic arrangements of images in cinema. The importance given to dance originates in the foundational period for the articulation of stillness and movement, that is, the time when the chronophotographic camera was developed. Among the decompositions of movement produced during the period, the most systematically encouraged and celebrated ones were undeniably those focusing on human gestures. Consequently, a privileged relationship developed in the vast domain of music and movement. At the core of many points shared by both dance and chronophotography, which stand at the intersection of a wide spectrum of determinations, are the works of a pioneer in the rational study of gesture, George Demenÿ. In 1894 he attempted to verify, through the analysis of filmed reconstructions, the validity of essential positions in gestures inscribed since Antiquity in the still form of bas reliefs. In this case, the intermedia chain of the experiment is impressive: statue-like poses carved in stone were performed by dancers; these dancers were then filmed so as to produce photographic plates; some of these were used in the scientific and aesthetic analysis of the choreographic gesture; others were transformed in subjects for moving projections with the phonoscope, thereby assuming an even stronger spectacular value (Fig. 3). The primacy of the association between the tool of chronophotography and the rational study of the elementary principles of gestures – whether it puts to the test some privileged instants from the past or, by contrast, aims to uncover some laws in human movement still unknown at the time – explains the symbiotic relation between dance and the filmic exploration of the ties between stillness and movement, which became customary in the course of the twentieth century. The same fascination ceaselessly resurfaced, from experimental cinema (Norman McLaren's 1967 *Pas de deux*, in which the optical printer produces effects of superimposition, reinterpreting a ballet in the form of streaks evoking Marey's successive chronophotographs) to music videos (*My Drive Thru*, made in 2009, imparts a two-dimensional effect to its human figures, which look like paper cutouts): the playful or aesthetic examination of the countless fits and starts of gestures hidden between the essential phases of movement (Fig. 4).

Whether in montage effects bringing a rhythmic linearity to visual succession or

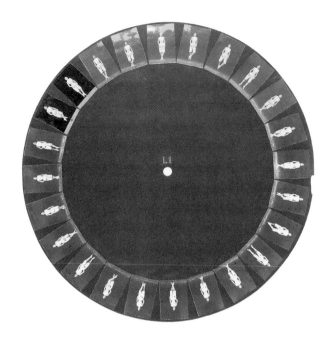

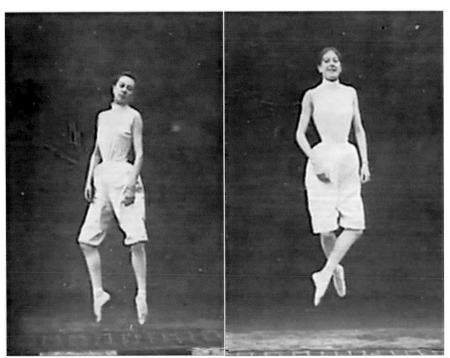

Fig. 3. George Demenÿ, Phonoscope disk, c. 1894.

Fig. 4. Pas de deux,
Norman McLaren, 1968;

*Santogold, Julian
Casablancas et Pharrell
Williams,* My Drive
Thru, *Marco Spier and
Marie Hyon, 2009.*

in the production of a relation between image and sound (spoken word and/or music), cinema – in the many ways it integrates photographs – brings new configurations to the various modes of observation, interpretation, or relation characterizing the always mobile perception of the still image. The specific techniques enrolled by film refer to general principles of organization, succession, and orientation which impart form not only to some visual techniques like the slide show, but also and more generally to apparatuses found in art exhibitions. If the protean activity of professionals of the image at the turn of the twentieth century often grew within the space of the fairground,[31] the contemporary, pluri-media approach does for its part essentially take place in the more legitimate context of the art gallery. In fact, the practice of exhibition does not involve the photographic image alone: it also extends to film itself, exhibited from the interwar period on as part of avant-garde events (see introduction to section 2). The shift of film from movie theater to museum even became one of

---

31   A pioneer of cinema like Max Skladanowsky, for instance, worked at the crossroads between light show, circus act, decor done in trompe-l'oeil, with mobile figures and sets, chronophotographic engineering, and flip books.

the main facets of artistic production in the late 20th century with video installations. It echoes more specifically common aesthetics based on citation, reuse, or distortion, as all these approaches are correlated to the fact that digital technologies have become the rule in visual recording and reproduction.

Christa Blümlinger deals with this extension of the relation between cinema and photography as she considers Agnès Varda's exhibition of the still image in film as well as in the more concrete setting of a 2006 art installation by the filmmaker, *L'Île et elle* ["The Island and Her"], in which video overlays help film and postcards trade their usual apparatuses. André Habib and Viva Paci examine the space of the museum more specifically as they consider the emblematic work of Chris Marker. Pointing out the intermedia connections established by the filmmaker between film, book, installation, or CD-ROM, the two authors set out to describe operations of *serialization* (understood here as an arrangement in series) and *exhibition* where what may be experienced – as in other media before – is the idea that looking at an image also involves discovering it through a gesture, browsing or clicking on a file, for instance. Their study concentrates on *Staring Back*, in which Marker confronts images captured all over the world from 1952 and 2006. In the exhibition, according to Paci and Habib, the artist gives visibility to one of the major principles of his artistic itinerary (and one of the main perspectives open by exchanges between photography and cinema): the production of a complex discourse on memory, which "lies less in the moment of captation than in the moment when what has been captured is reconsidered, when the person who took the picture enters a dialogue with the person looking at it, a few months or a few decades later".

In *Staring Back* the images excerpted from films (photographs or film frames) may also be reprocessed thanks to the computer. Indeed, the computer has now become the unavoidable third term between photo and cinema, as digitization increases the circulation between images, undeniably fostering phenomena of adjustment and reformulation. Insofar as digital technique, contrary to a received idea, preserves an essential part of the indexical value attached to mechanical recording,[32] it provides artists such as Marker or Varda with the possibility of proceeding with their experimentations on the reflexive, and even melancholic rearrangement of the multiple temporal strata involved in photographic images.

Artistic work on sampling archive films is not limited to such evocations of memories; it also opens the possibility of questioning the scansion of film frames at the centre of the film. This principle did for instance inspire Douglas Gordon as he famously stretched feature films through slow motion, image after image (*24 Hour Psycho*, 1993; *5 Year Drive By*, 1995). With his 2000 *Temps/Travail* ["Time/Work"], designed for an installation at the Centre Georges Pompidou, Johan van der Keuken reorganized a series of shots taken from his documentary

---

32   Tom Gunning, "What's the Point of an Index ? Or, Faking Photographs", in *StillMoving. Between Cinema and Photography*, eds. Karen Beckman and Jean Ma (Durham, London: Duke University Press, 2008) 23–40.

work. Shot on several continents, these images are all devoted to the gestures of work, artisanal as well as industrial. As a consequence, a parallel appears between the archaic, fundamental, and universal rhythm and the Taylorized "meter" imposed by machines. The confrontation assumes an emblematic value, since it emphasizes the paradox at work in the creations of the mechanical age: the very manipulation of still units imbedded within the technical reproduction of movement – of images as well as sounds – produces a new mobile reality. In *Temps/ Travail*, as in most works relying on sampling, the looping of a sequence thus produces an actual form of bewitchment while explicitly resorting to perfectly regular mechanisms of repetition in which the material illusion of movement originates.

The same fascination plays out in the poetic and artistic fantasies spawned by speeded-up motion. In the wake of interwar theoreticians, who saw "new rhythms, new gestures" in it, something akin to the revelation of the "eternal repetitions of nature" (Philippe Soupault),[33] the technique made it possible to materialize for the eye, in a stylized, almost abstract form, the mechanical and luminous swarms animating urban space, from the final sequence of *Le Joli mai* (Chris Marker, 1963) to Godfrey Reggio's "symphonies of the world" of the 1980s. Nowadays, this use of speeded-up motion inspires many artists working on the Internet like photographer Noah Kalinah, whose film *Noah K. Everyday*, a work in progress began in 2000 and broadcast on YouTube, consists in the juxtaposition of shots of himself always framed in the same way, made at regular intervals, day in, day out. The frame-by-frame animation of these daily photographs produces the effect of fast aging on the face represented. The impression, both hypnotic and harrowing, owes to the convergence between the indexical value of each photograph (each shot appears as the expression of a precise moment in a human existence) and the perfectly logical, visual, and mobile continuity revealed to the eyes of spectators as if by magic.[34]

---

33 Philippe Soupault, "Un film décevant : *Erotikon* – A propos d'un documentaire" ["A Disappointing Film: *Erotikon* – About A Documentary"], *L'Europe Nouvelle* 609 (October 12, 1929), reprinted in *Ecrits de cinéma 1918–1931* (Paris: Plon, 1979) 65; see also Germaine Dulac, "Les esthétiques. Les entraves. La cinégraphie intégrale" ["Aesthetics. Shackles. Integral Cinegraphy"], in *L'Art cinématographique*, vol. II (1927), reprinted in *Ecrits sur le cinéma (1919–1937)* (Paris: Paris Expérimental, 1994) 104.

34 An advertisement for the *Fondation Estime de soi/Dove* (*Evolution*, Tim Piper and Yael Staav, 2006), which had a mass circulation on YouTube (and was just as massively parodied) relied on the same principle to emphasize the alterations gradually transforming the face of a plain-looking young woman into a beauty icon fitting the standards of commercials. As in Godfrey Reggio's films (with the music of Philip Glass), all these short films using both speeded-up motion and frame-by-frame animation resort to the same minimalist and repetitive tones on the piano. These double the regular rhythm and the implacable repetitiveness involved in the visual setup, while also providing it with the various sentimental connotations conveyed by the musical harmony. I want to thank Laurent Dauvister for this reference.

1

Photography and the Denarrativization of Cinematic Practice in Italy, 1935–55

David Forgacs

In 1951 Roberto Rossellini told the film critic Mario Verdone in an interview that when he made a film, he was always interested in just one scene or episode in particular, a "fact" ("fatto") from which the idea for the film had originated and around which it was in effect constructed. He said that in directing the other parts of the film, which he called "cronachistici" ("merely narrative"), he felt "distracted", "tired", "annoyed", "impotent." He gave three examples of what he meant by the "fact", or the "decisive episode":

> *Germany Year Zero*, to tell the truth, was conceived specifically for the scene with the boy wandering on his own through the ruins. The whole of the preceding part had no interest for me. 'The Miracle', too stemmed from the episode of the tin bowls. And when I filmed the last episode of *Paisà* I had an image in my head of those dead bodies floating by on the water, being carried slowly down the Po, with placards bearing the word 'Partisan'. The river carried those corpses for months. You were likely to come across several on a single day.[1]

It is a striking statement. Rossellini is claiming that his films centre on moments of "denarrativization", that is to say on episodes or scenes when the "merely narrative" function is abandoned. "I hate the logical nexus of a story", he said later in the same interview.[2] In the denarrativized sequence the same movement is repeated over several shots, dialogue is stripped to a bare minimum, the sequence is accompanied by music, few new story events take place so that a single narrative situation is stretched out in time. Rossellini seems to be saying that his films exist for these moments, those in which their main narrative work is over,

---

1 "A discussion of neo-realism: Rossellini interviewed by Mario Verdone," translated by Judith White, in David Forgacs, Sarah Lutton and Geoffrey Nowell-Smith, eds, *Roberto Rossellini, Magician of the Real* (London: BFI Publishing, 2000) 152.

2 Ibid., 153.

or has not yet properly commenced. But if a film can centre on the moments when the narrative is pared right down this would appear to call into question the commonly-held notion that the fiction film is essentially a narrative medium. It obliges us to consider that a film may, at least in certain cases, be something else.

Rossellini's statement should not be taken, perhaps, as a wholly reliable account of how his films were actually made. We know, for instance, that the script of *Germany, Year Zero*, which was filmed in 1947 and released in 1948, had a complicated gestation and that Rossellini was quite closely involved in developing it through its different phases. He seems to have been projecting back onto his films here, as he would do in many other interviews, ideas about them that he had formed, or clarified, after he had finished them. He was also probably influenced in this case by the critical opinions of others. His answer echoes not only the description of his films that Verdone had put to him in his immediately preceding question (a highly leading question beginning with "Do you agree that ...?"), but also André Bazin's claim, made in January 1948, that the unit of narrative in Paisan was not the shot but the "fact", the "fragment of raw reality".[3] Yet, in a way, his statement is even more significant because of this work of retrospective adjustment, since it communicates how he wanted his films to be seen by the early 1950s.

Let us consider more closely the three examples he gives. In *Germany, Year Zero* the long final sequence of Edmund walking through war-damaged Berlin, interrupted by the key scene of his visit to his former teacher, Henning (Erich Gühne), and ending with his suicide by jumping from an upper storey of a deserted building, lasts thirteen minutes and is punctuated by very small amounts of dialogue. In *The Miracle* (1948), the unmarried goatherd Nannina (Anna Magnani), carrying a bundle of clothing and mess tins, is mocked by her fellow villagers because she has got pregnant, that the baby's father is Saint Joseph and that she is in a state of grace. She runs away from the jeering crowd uphill. Again the dialogue is very sparse. There are other scenes of Nannina running or walking, including the long final sequence which starts just after this scene of her humiliation and continues to the end of the film. She leaves the village and ascends a hill, with great effort, in the heat to reach the deserted church where she will give birth. This sequence as a whole lasts eleven minutes. In the sixth and final episode of *Paisan* (1946) the body of a dead resistance fighter floats downstream in a lifebelt bearing a placard on a stake placed by the Germans as a warning to others (Fig. 1). The first six minutes of the episode centre on this dead

3   Verdone had asked: "Is it true to say that in your films there is a break between a particularly good episode, like for example the boy walking through the city in *Germany Year Zero*, and other parts which are inexplicably left incomplete or at least much more hastily sketched in?" See Forgacs, Lutton and Nowell-Smith, *Roberto Rossellini*, 152. Bazin had written: "The unit of cinematic narrative in *Paisà* is not the 'shot,' an abstract view of reality which is being analysed, but the 'fact.' A fragment of concrete reality in itself multiple and full of ambiguity, whose meaning emerges only after the fact, thanks to other imposed facts between which the mind establishes certain relationships." "Cinematic Realism and the Italian School of the Liberation" in André Bazin, *What Is Cinema?* trans. Hugh Gray, vol. II (Los Angeles: University of California Press, 2004) 37.

Fig. 1. Paisà, *Roberto Rossellini, 1946.*   Fig. 2. Paisà, *Roberto Rossellini, 1946.*

body – over a quarter of the length of the whole episode. Other actions develop around it, but there is hardly any speech.

Moments of denarrativization in a film by Rossellini are not moments 'without' narrative. They are moments that are not driven by the narrative function, when this function is depleted. The opening shot of the body drifting downstream initiates a sequence of events that in themselves constitute the narrative of the first part of that episode of *Paisan*, but this narrative is limited. A group of civilians watch the floating body from the riverbank. A partisan, who will subsequently be named as Cigolani, pulls it out of the water onto his boat while the American intelligence officer, Dale, distracts the German soldiers in a sentry tower by exploding a charge and then firing at them with a rifle. Cigolani rows the boat ashore and the body is buried by him and other partisans, who fix the placard 'Partigiano' with its wooden stake in the earth to mark the grave, inverting its function by changing it from a Nazi deterrent to a burial cross and a Resistance plaque of honour (Fig. 2). The story information given here is certainly important but the real narrative centre of this episode of the film lies elsewhere: in the subsequent chain of events that go from the family of peasants offering Cigolani and Dale a meal, the botched parachute drop, the discovery by Cigolani and Dale of the same family massacred by German soldiers just hours later (the massacre itself is not shown), evidently as a reprisal for their act of hospitality, then the capture and finally the killing by the Germans of the partisans and Allied soldiers.

One could add other examples of such denarrativized sequences in Rossellini's films which he himself does not cite in his statement to Verdone, most notably the long walk of the pregnant Karin (Ingrid Bergman) to the top of the volcano, where she is exhausted and overcome by fumes, and finally sleeps, at the end of *Stromboli, Land of God* (1949). This replicates Nannina's long walk up the hill at the end of *The Miracle*. In both cases the walk is loaded with religious symbolism of the ascent, just as the scene of Nannina's humiliation, including her crowning with an upturned tin bowl, alludes to the mocking of Christ on Calvary and the crucifixion. *Europa '51* (1952) ends with a sequence where Irene (Ingrid Bergman again) looks out of her room in the psychiatric hospital, where she has been committed by her husband: shots of her face at the window are intercut with reverse shots of what she sees: the poor people she has helped, who have come to visit her. There will be other instances of the same kind of temporally stretched, denarrativized shots in Rossellini's later films. In *Voyage to Italy* (1954), Ingrid Bergman, playing Katherine Joyce, repeatedly walks or drives around Naples and its environs, looking around her with curiosity and anxiety. What she sees are pregnant women and mothers, the plaster cast of a married couple who died in Pompei embracing one another, statues of athletic men. Her own marriage is childless and her husband Alex (George Sanders) seems emotionally detached until the end of the film.

It is tempting to describe these denarrativized sequences as like those in a silent film. There is indeed some truth in the claim that Rossellini's films, at least from the last episode of *Paisan* onwards, revert to some of the conditions of silent cinema. This is perhaps most true of *The Miracle*, where the 'Saint Joseph' character (played by Federico Fellini, who also wrote the treatment for the film) never speaks, where Nannina in the latter part of the film speaks few words, and these are mainly muttered to herself, to God or to the Saint, and where much of the acting is gestural and facial. But the claim is also inaccurate, since silent cinema developed its own elaborate narrative codes and conventions over more than thirty years, and these codes and conventions are unlike anything in these films by Rossellini. It would be more accurate to say of the denarrativized sequences in Rossellini's films that they return cinema to some of the conditions of the still photograph, or the series of photographs. Indeed the phrase he uses, "decisive episode", is similar to the expression "decisive instant" or "decisive moment" that would be used by Henri-Cartier Bresson to characterise the moment when a particular visual configuration 'acquires meaning' and is captured by the photographer.[4]

In moments of denarrativization, the spectator's attention tends to be concentrated on a repeated image – usually a single human figure (a corpse, in the example from *Paisan*) – and on its physical surroundings. Some audiences experience these moments as longueurs; others see them as meditative, or as points of intense visual concentration. The denarrativized sequence may be remembered or summed up by one or more of its component shots. Georges Sadoul, reviewing *Paisan* when it was first shown in a preview screening to critics in Paris in November 1946, said he would give the whole of Cocteau's *Beauty and*

---

4   Cartier-Bresson borrowed and "repurposed" the phrase from Cardinal de Retz, who in his *Mémoires* (1717) had applied it to ethical conduct: "There is nothing in the world that does not have its decisive moment, and the epitome of proper conduct is to know and seize that moment." The expression was popularized by the American edition of Cartier-Bresson's *Images à la sauvette* (1952), which was given the title *The Decisive Moment* by its publisher, Simon and Schuster.

Fig. 3. Germany Year Zero
(Germania anno zero, Roberto Rossellini,
1947).

the Beast, released at the same time, for the single opening shot in the last episode of the partisan's body floating towards the camera until it fills the lower half of the screen.[5] Rossellini explicitly says in his statement to Verdone that what he had in his mind when he filmed this episode of *Paisan* was the *image* of the dead body in the river. In other words, the 'decisive episode' is condensed or concentrated into one image and this image is then reproduced across a series of shots. When there are few story events, where interactions between characters are limited and the dialogue is sparse, the photographic image is given particular prominence. In watching a denarrativized sequence one searches for visual clues on the screen: one scans and rescans the image for information from the face, movements of the body, gestures, as well as from the landscape or built space around the character.

In the case of *Germany Year Zero*, this search is impeded by the fact that the clues from the face and body are not clear, or are ambiguous. Rossellini cast, for the central role, a twelve-year-old boy, Edmund Koehler, who was found working in a circus and was therefore used to performing in public but who had no professional acting training or film experience. In the sequences where Edmund walks through the city his face remains inexpressive (Fig. 3), and even his walk seems mechanical, with his arms hanging by his side. Consider, by contrast, the highly expressive performances that Vittorio De Sica was able to draw from the equally untrained and inexperienced boys Franco Interlenghi (Pasquale) and Rinaldo Smordoni (Giuseppe) in *Shoeshine* (1946) or from Enzo Staiola (Bruno) in *The Bicycle Thief* (1948), or even the relatively emotional performances that Rossellini himself had previously elicited from the boys Vito Annicchiarico (Marcello) in *Open City* or Alfonsino Bovino (Pasquale) in the Naples episode of *Paisan.*

Contemporary critics noted the peculiar lack of expressiveness in Edmund. Jules Gritti, who saw *Germany Year Zero* at a film club near the Trocadéro in Paris in October 1949, recalled that he had stood up after the screening and defended the film, which had not been well received by the audience, maintaining that it was

5   Georges Sadoul, "Cinéma italien, cinéma couleur des temps" (review of Open City and Paisan), *Les Lettres Françaises* 15 November 1946: 8.

"a failure for three quarters of it, but brilliant in its last sequence." Edmund, he said, "is here before us as a whole, his acting neither good nor bad, his figure neither nice nor unpleasant, close to toys and prematurely aged, intensely present, carrying a mysterious weight".[6] André Bazin maintained that this lack of expression was the result of a deliberate choice by Rossellini not to attribute or project an adult's interpretation or explanation onto the actions of the child: "Rossellini could have given us an interpretation of the murder only through a piece of trickery, by projecting his own explanation onto the boy and having him reflect it for us".[7] The viewer's investigative gaze does have any of its inquiries returned. The photographic image yields up no information other than what can be seen on its surface.

It would seem that Rossellini deliberately chose to direct Edmund Koehler's acting, or chose to neglect to direct it, so that it did communicate any obvious emotional depth. He stated in an interview in November 1948, shortly before the film went on general release in Italy and when it had already received adverse reviews in the press after the screening at Locarno, that "it's a film that is cold like a sheet of glass. [...] It is certainly not a piece of entertainment, and one does not have fun watching it".[8] Events in his own life may have contributed to this. His nine year-old son, Romano, the elder of the two children he had with his wife Marcella De Marchis, had died in August 1946 while staying with Rossellini's sister and father in Madrid, after what one of Rossellini's biographers describes as "a common disease poorly treated".[9] It was soon after this that Rossellini began his relationship with Anna Magnani, whose son, Luca, born in 1942, had contracted polio when he was two. De Marchis later attributed the onset of her husband's affair with Magnani to a shared sense of grief: "Roberto and Anna met in Paris and fell into each other's arms with this huge pain they felt after the loss of their respective sons. Pain brought them together, this is how it started".[10] A few weeks later Rossellini went to start work on *Germany Year Zero* in a devastated city pervaded by the smell of death.[11]

Rossellini noted the indifference of the inhabitants of Berlin to the presence of the camera crew in the street, so unlike the curiosity it would arouse in Rome, London, Paris or New York. "In Berlin it seemed to me that people were interested in only one thing: eating and surviving. This, I believe, is the result

---

6   Jules Gritti, "Avant-propos", in Amédée Ayfre, *Le Cinéma et sa vérité* (Paris: Éditions du Cerf, 1969) 11.

7   André Bazin, "Germany Year Zero", in *Bazin at Work: Major Essays and Reviews from the Forties and Fifties*, Bert Cardullo, ed. (New York: Routledge, 1997) 123.

8   Fernaldo Di Giammatteo, "Rossellini si difende", *Il Progresso d'Italia* (Bologna), 9 December 1948 (interview of November 1948); reproduced in Rossellini, *My Method*.

9   Gianni Rondolino, *Roberto Rossellini* (Turin: UTET, 1989) 98.

10   De Marchis's testimony is in Rondolino, *Roberto Rossellini* 99.

11   Carlo Lizzani, assistant director on the film, recalled: "In Berlin there was only rubble, and there was still a smell of dead bodies everywhere." The recollection appears in Barbara Palombelli, *Registi d'Italia* (Milan: Rizzoli, 2006) 95.

of a defeat without precedent in history, which has annihilated the conscience of an entire people."[12] This was no doubt the same apathy, and with the same cause, as that which Alfred Döblin had observed in southwest Germany when he returned from America in 1945. People walked "down the street and past the dreadful ruins as if nothing had happened, and [...] the town had always looked like that".[13] Among the diagnostic criteria of what some psychiatrists now categorise as Post Traumatic Stress Disorder (PTSD) are diminished interest in significant activities, a feeling of detachment or estrangement from others and "constricted affect".[14] The repression or removal from public memory of the destruction of German cities was deep and lasting. W.G. Sebald noted, over half a century after the end of the Second World War, that the destruction "seems to have left scarcely a trace of pain behind in the collective consciousness, it has been largely obliterated from the collective understanding of those affected".[15]

If the nature and scale of the destruction of German cities was not publicly written or spoken about in Germany, some of its effects were photographed and recorded on film in the years just after the war. Among those who photographed these cities were foreign photojournalists such as Margaret Bourke-White and Lee Miller (American), Robert Capa (Hungarian, naturalized American in 1946) and Werner Bischof (Swiss), but also Germans like Richard Peter and Hermann Claasen, who photographed, respectively, the ruins of Dresden and Cologne in 1945.[16] Humphrey Jennings's 18-minute film *A Defeated People* (1946) showed filmed images both of devastated cities and of the same kind of listlessness or apparent apathy in people's faces and gait as that described by Döblin. In Britain in 1947 Victor Gollancz published *In Darkest Germany* with 119 pages of text (written by Gollancz) and 144 photographic plates, each of which occupies a page, so that the pictures (all taken by German photographers) outnumber the pages of text. Most of these photographs were published with captions, but at the same time they also 'stand in' for narrative descriptions. They are frozen moments of time captured for public circulation.

Children had featured in many photographs and reports on postwar Germany and on other European countries that had been involved in the war. In 1945

---

12 Rossellini, "Su *Germania anno zero*" (statement by Rossellini in the press book of the US distributor, Distributing Releasing Corporation, 1949), reprinted in Rossellini, *My Method*.

13 Quoted in W.G. Sebald, *On the Natural History of Destruction* (London: Hamish Hamilton, 2003), translated by Anthea Bell from *Luftkrieg und Literatur* (Munich: Hanser, 1999) 5.

14 Quoted and paraphrased from the entry on PTSD in the American Psychiatric Association's *Manual* by James Garbarino and Kathleen Kostelny, "Children's Responses to War: What do we Know?" in Lewis A. Leavitt and Nathan A. Fox, eds., *The Psychological Effects of War and Violence on Children* (Hillsdale, N.J.: Lawrence Erlbaum Associates, 1993) 26.

15 Sebald, *On the Natural History of Destruction* 3-4. On the scale and nature of the destruction see Hans Rumpf, *The Bombing of Germany*, trans. Edward Fitzgerald, (London: White Lion, 1963); and Jörg Friedrich, *Der Brand: Deutschland im Bombenkrieg 1940-1945* (Berlin: Propylaen, 2002).

16 See Klaus Honnef, Rolf Sachsse and Karin Thomas, eds., *German Photography 1870-1970: Power of a Medium* (Cologne: DuMont Buchverlag, 1997), plates 74–76. Richard Peter's Dresden photographs were collected and published in *Dresden – eine Kamera klagt an* (1949).

Gollancz had published, and written a preface to, a sixteen-page pamphlet of photographs of naked starving German children in a hospital called *Is It Nothing To You?*, published by his company in 1945 and designed to goad the conscience of British readers with enough to eat and stir them to act. At around the same time that Rossellini was directing in Berlin the exterior scenes of *Germany Year Zero*, Fred Zinnemann was shooting in Nuremberg and Munich some of those for *The Search* (1948) – also a story about a boy, in this case Karel (Ivan Landl), a nine-year-old traumatised by his experience of war, imprisonment and separation from his mother, with whom he is reunited at the end. Zinnemann later claimed that the original stimulus for the film had come from Thérèse Bonney's photo-book *Europe's Children, 1939–1943*, which included pictures of children evacuated or in Displaced Persons camps.[17] In the same year that Rossellini's and Zinnemann's films were released there appeared the photoreportage *Children of Post-War Europe*, commissioned by UNESCO and UNICEF and carried out in Austria, Italy and Poland by Magnum photographer Chim who was of Polish Jewish origin (he was born David Szimin, changed to David Seymour when he took US citizenship in 1942). Jennings's *A Defeated People* also includes several shots of children.

The denarrativized parts of *Germany Year Zero* may be seen in this context as constituting a photographic essay on a destroyed city and a damaged child. Contemporary reviewers remarked on how powerfully the film's photography, directed by Robert Juillard (who was responsible also for the photography of *The Miracle*, along with Aldo Tonti) communicated the sense of what postwar Berlin was like. Bosley Crowther, despite finding the film as a whole "oddly passive", with "a strange emptiness of genuine feeling", remarked on its "pictorial brilliance." "No irony of the desolation of Hitler's 'empire' escapes his [Rossellini's] camera. The endless background of ruined buildings frames a foreground of scarred and ruined lives."[18] Amédée Ayfre also found its shots of ruins remarkable and compared them with the "the plastic poverty" of the ruins in *The Search*.[19]

Germany Year Zero does of course, as Rossellini acknowledged, have a story and this revolves around Edmund, the youngest child in the family, having to work to help them make ends meet. Their precarious economic situation, as tenants in arrears with their rent and fuel bills, is carefully spelt out. Edmund's elder sister Eva (Ingetraud Hinze) also brings in money, some of it from sex work, but there is no mother, the father (Ernst Pittschau) is ill and bedridden (he says he has considered committing suicide but lacks the courage) and the elder brother

17 Thérèse Bonney, *Europe's Children, 1939-1943* (New York: Rhode, 1943). Bonney's photographs were taken in France, Spain, England, Sweden and Finland. See Fred Zinnemann, "The Story of *The Search*", *Screen Writer* 4.2 (August 1948): 12; and *An Autobiography* (London: Bloomsbury 1992) 57. Apart from the location work in these two German cities most of the film was shot in Switzerland.

18 Bosley Crowther, " 'Germany Year Zero,' Post-War Picture by Rossellini, Opens at the Ambassador", *New York Times* 20 September 1949.

19 Ayfre, *Le Cinéma et sa vérité* 139–140.

Fig. 4. Robert Capa, Berlin, August, 1945. The Kurfürstendamm, with the Kaiser-Wilhelm-Gedächtniskirche, damaged in the air raid of 23 November 1943.

Karlheinz (Franz Krüger) is unemployed, hiding at home in fear of arrest and retribution because he is a former Nazi who had fought to the last. Edmund, influenced by the speech made to him by Henning, another ex-Nazi, about his father being one of the weak who has to die so that others can survive, deliberately poisons his own father. When Edmund later tells Henning what he has done the latter reacts with horror, Edmund runs away, and his walk culminates in his suicide. Yet, alongside this narrative, the film also works as a series of images of postwar Berlin: the panoramic shots of the city's skyline, including the bombed Reichstag and Brandenburg Gate, behind the opening titles; the digging of graves; a dead horse being cut up for meat; the food queues; the bombed and gutted church in which the pastor plays the organ; children stealing food or playing in the rubble and, above all, the repeated backgrounds of ruined buildings; fragments of walls jutting up like stalagmites from the ground behind pavements with neatly piled up stones. Many of these images were familiar from single photographs and from photoreportages of Europe's cities after the war (Fig. 4).

The use of real locations and of untrained actors are often cited as defining features of neorealism in cinema. There had been long location sequences in some early Italian sound films, such as *Gli uomini, che mascalzoni ...* (What Scoundrels Men Are, Mario Camerini, 1932) and *1860* (Alessandro Blasetti, 1934), but the dominant trend during the 1930s was towards studio-shot dramas with occasional location shots. It is true that some neorealist films, for example *Shoeshine* (Vittorio De Sica, 1946), were also shot largely in studios and only *La terra trema* (Luchino Visconti, 1948) was filmed wholly on location, but typically there was a mix. The exteriors of *Germany Year Zero* were shot in Berlin and the interiors in a Rome studio. The move towards location shooting has sometimes been attributed mainly to the constraints imposed by wartime disruption of studio

Fig. 5. Cineromanzo version of Johnny Guitar *(Nicholas Ray, USA, 1954, director of photography Harry Stradling) in* Bolero Film, *21 November 1954.*

production but in reality it was part of a convergence between documentary film, photography and fiction film that predated the war. This convergence was influenced by a number of changes in the media system and in visual culture since the mid-1930s.

In the first place, there was the increased capability of taking pictures in natural light, even at low levels, and of taking several shots in quick succession. These changes were the result of the development in the 1920s of small cameras with wider lens apertures and shorter exposure times and of film stocks with increased speeds – in other words, greater degrees of sensitivity to light. Compared to the Ermanox, the other small German camera, which still used plates that had to be changed after each exposure, the Leica – designed by Oscar Barnack, who had made the prototype in 1914 – had the advantage of being loaded with a continuous strip of 35mm film that could be rapidly advanced (the same as movie film, but wound horizontally rather than vertically behind the lens). Small cameras were increasingly used to record breaking news, such as the Hindenburg airship disaster of 1937, and to report wars and attacks on civilian targets, including night-time air raids (the 1930s were a decade of wars and invasions: Abyssinia, Spain, China, Poland, Czechoslovakia, Albania). They were also used to capture athletes in movement, notably at the Olympic Games in Los Angeles (1932) and Berlin (1936).

Second, alongside this acceleration of photography came the expansion of roto-

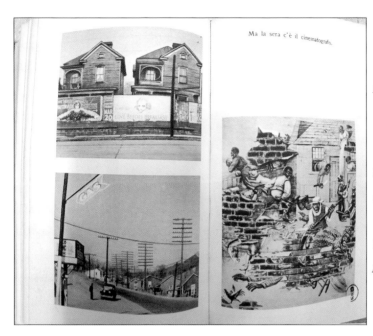

Fig. 6.
Photographic pages
in Americana.
Raccolta di
narratori dalle
origini ai nostri
giorni, *edited by*
Elio Vittorini,
Milan: Bompiani,
1942, including
uncredited pictures
by Walker Evans
taken from
American
Photographs, New
York, Museum of
Modern Art, 1938.

gravure printing, originally developed in the 1910s, which made possible high-quality reproductions of photographs and led to a proliferation of photographic newspaper supplements and illustrated magazines. These developed novel picture layouts such as photo-spreads over several pages and narrative sequences of photographs. In April 1937 the Milan publisher Rizzoli launched *Omnibus*, Italy's first modern-style weekly, with a layout modelled on the photo-weeklies in Germany established in the late 1920s (*Berliner Illustrierte Zeitung* and *Die Dame*), France (*Vu*) and the USA (notably *Life* magazine, an established title that had been relaunched in 1936 as a photo-weekly, the same year as *Look*). In Britain *Picture Post* was launched in 1938. *Omnibus* was forced to close because of censorship in January 1939 but by then it had attained a weekly circulation of 70,000 and would give rise to two similar magazines launched a few months later: *Oggi* (also published by Rizzoli) and *Tempo* (published by Mondadori). The latter was short-lived but it would provide the design template for Mondadori's successful postwar weekly *Epoca*, launched in 1950. There was also, from the 1930s, a proliferation of illustrated film magazines, as well as collectible cards with photographs of film stars and, after the war, a new kind of weekly magazine, exemplified by *Grand Hôtel* (launched in 1946) and *Bolero Film* (1947), dedicated largely to the stories known as *cineromanzi* and *fotoromanzi*. These were photo-strips, modelled on the comic strip, with the characters' speech written in bubbles. The former were 'reductions' of actual films into a sequence of stills with speech bubbles (Fig. 5); the latter were original photo-stories posed by actors. There was, in other words, an extensive 'remediation' of film into other media and a continual exchange between the film and the still photograph. The original nucleus of *Shoeshine* was a photo-story, with text by De Sica and photographs by Piero Portalupi, about the shoeshine boys of Rome, published in June 1945.[20]

Third, in part through the channel of the illustrated news magazines, foreign documentary photography, in particular American photography, started to become known in Italy. The photographs taken by Arthur Rothstein, Dorothea Lange, Ben Shahn and others of the Dust Bowl and the labour migrations of the Depression years were syndicated to European magazines. Walker Evans's *American Photographs*, the catalogue of his 1938 show at the Museum of Modern Art in New York, was appreciatively reviewed by Giulia Veronesi in the journal *Corrente* in October 1939:

> There are no particular technical aids, special cropping or framing, romantic soft focus or any decorative elements that bring the photographs into relief: they are simply documents. To be sure this book lacks humour, but it is full of deep and conscious human interest. Perhaps only photography – and naturally cinema is included in that category – allows one to document life with such measure.[21]

In 1942 twenty-seven pictures from *American Photographs* were reproduced, uncredited, in *Americana*, the anthology of American literature edited by Elio Vittorini, mixed with photos from other sources and reproductions of paintings and engravings and with captions added (Fig. 6).[22] American documentary photography began to exercise a strong attraction on a number of Italian photographers and helped them turn away from 'formalist' tendencies such as the photograms and superimpositions of photographers such as Gege Bottinelli, Tato (Guglielmo Sansoni) and Luigi Veronesi. Alberto Lattuada's *Occhio quadrato*, published in 1941, consisted of twenty-six photographs taken in Milan between 1937 and 1940, depicting street cleaners, empty streets, flea markets and people living down and out in makeshift dwellings. Lattuada said in a 1980 interview that the inspiration had come from "one of those publications whose title I can't remember but which were widely available in the USA and enjoyed great prestige" and that

> It shocked me and made me realize that the photograph had to be extracted

20   "Il film della strada. Sciuscià, Giò? Regia di Vittorio di Sica", *Film d'oggi* I.3 (23 June 1945): 4-5. The text, photographs and captions are reproduced, together with a facsimile of the original article, in *Sciuscià di Vittorio De Sica. Letture documenti testimonianze*, Lino Miccichè, ed. (Turin: Associazione Philip Morris Progetto Cinema, Lindau, 1994) 237-40. On the concept of remediation, see David Bolter and Richard Grusin, *Remediation: Understanding New Media* (Cambridge, Mass.: MIT Press, 1999).

21   Giulia Veronesi, review of *American Photographs, Corrente* II.19 (31 October 1939): 2. The review is cited and quoted in Ennery Taramelli's book *Viaggio nell'Italia del neorealismo. La fotografia tra letteratura e cinema* (Turin: SEI, 1995) 75-76.

22   *Americana. Raccolta di narratori dalle origini ai nostri giorni*, Elio Vittorini, ed. (Milan: Bompiani, 1942). The inclusion of illustrations was part of the format of the series, called Pantheon, to which the anthology belonged and which included similar anthologies of Spanish (1940) and German (1942) literature. However, *Americana* was the only book in the series to use photographs. The Minister of Popular Culture, Alessandro Pavolini, had blocked publication of *Americana* because Vittorini, who by then had an antifascist reputation, had written unacceptable introductions to the various sections. The publisher, Bompiani, compromised by withdrawing these and replacing them with a more 'balanced' preface by Emilio Cecchi.

Fig. 7. Frame enlargement from opening sequence of The Grapes of Wrath *(John Ford, USA, 1940, director of photography Gregg Toland).*

from purely formal research, from calculated spaces and abstract things, which, even when they were very beautiful, did not impinge on the viewer emotionally but only abstractly, for aesthetic pleasure, whereas I was always looking for contact with man.[23]

Fourth, from the end of the 1930s there was increased advocacy in Italian film criticism, notably by critics writing for the journal *Cinema*, of the idea that Italian films should become also photographic records of real places in which the characters were socially and physically located. The key articles here were those by Mario Alicata and Giuseppe De Santis, both of whom would work on the screenplay of *Ossessione*, directed by Visconti, filmed in 1942 and released in 1943.

> We want to take our movie camera into the fields, ports and factories of Italy: we too are convinced that one day we will create our best film by following the slow and weary steps of a worker returning home.[24]

Ossessione was the first film to put into practice the call for a photographing of place and a rooting of characters in Italian locations. Visconti worked with two cinematographers, Domenico Scala, who had shot *Gli uomini, che mascalzoni ...,* and Aldo Tonti, whose postwar work would include, as well as *The Miracle*, *Il bandito* (The Bandit, Alberto Lattuada, 1946) and *Il sole sorge ancora* (Outcry, Aldo Vergano, 1946). Given the lack of indigenous models he drew on French cinema, in particular Carné and Renoir, and on the various American films about the Depression such as *Our Daily Bread* (King Vidor, 1934), *The Grapes of Wrath* (John Ford, 1940) and *Tobacco Road* (John Ford, 1941), as well as the photographs of Rothstein, Lang, Evans and Shahn (Fig. 7). These visual sources were married with the film's American narrative source, James M. Cain's *The Postman Always Rings Twice* (1934), which Visconti and his co-screenwriters had read in a French translation. The evocation of these films and photographs may be seen from the opening of *Ossessione* in its landscape shots (the roadside filmed through the truck

---

23   "Alberto Lattuada – regista", article and interview by Piero Berengo Gardin, in "Dal privato al pubblico", *Progresso Fotografico* 87.7-8 (July–August 1980): 35-85, 52. This article is also cited by Taramelli, *Viaggio nell'Italia del neorealismo* 76.

24   Mario Alicata, Giuseppe De Santis, "Ancora di Verga e del cinema italiano", *Cinema* VI.130 (25 November 1941): 217.

windscreen in the credits sequence; the dusty road by the petrol station), the costumes (Gino's threadbare clothes, Bragana's baggy trousers and braces, Giovanna's apron) and the interior sets (the furniture and utensils in the kitchen, the interior of the shed where Bragana keeps his car). This concern with communicating a whole social world by the choice of what is photographed was applied again after the war in *La terra trema* on which the director of photography was G.R. Aldo (pseudonym of Aldo Graziati), but in fact it would be equally characteristic of Visconti's later films depicting the world of the rich, from *Senso* (1954) to *The Leopard* (1963), *The Damned* (1969), *Ludwig* (1972) and *L'innocente* (1976). In a key article of 1950 on the origins of neorealism, Franco Venturini stressed the importance of the "discovery of an original Italian landscape" in *Ossessione*:

> The flatlands and the sandbanks of the river Po, the narrow streets of Ferrara dappled with sunlight, the festival of Saint Cyriac of Ancona, the third-class railway carriages: all of these offer us the image of an extremely live and real Italy, one that is not only lifelike but also true, artistically valid, a complete expression of a distinctively Italian atmosphere.[25]

Fifth, there was the Second World War. The importance of the collective experience of the war as a catalyst that precipitated cinema as a whole towards the condition of documentary, and hence towards an ethically-grounded realism, was memorably expressed by Bazin in his essay of 1946 on the American *Why We Fight* propaganda films:

> the cruelty and violence of war have taught us to respect – almost to make a cult of – actual facts, in comparison with which any reconstitution, even made in good faith, seems dubious, indecent, and sacrilegious.[26]

A similar idea of the war as a watershed in the evolution of cinema was expressed by the principal Italian theorist of neorealism, Cesare Zavattini. Taking stock in 1949 of the first half-century of the cinema, from 1895 to the end of the Second World War, he wrote:

> We realized amidst the rubble that we had spent two few images on opening people's eyes and helping them face, if not prevent, those monstrous events. To put it simply, cinema had failed by choosing the path of Méliès and not that of Lumière where the thorns of reality lay scattered. [...] One day we emerged from the dark of the cinema auditorium and the newspaper vendors were shouting that war had broken out, in other words a woman's arm being ripped from her body and hurled onto the telegraph wires and the head of one Paolo Gai ending up a flower vase in front of a house with the number 3. [...] The report on the first half century of cinema's existence concluded with the judgment: "pointless." But something has appeared on the horizon. We have started to write the history of cinema, which was formerly just technical or aesthetic, as a means of examining man and contemporary society.[27]

25   Franco Venturini, "Origini del neorealismo", *Bianco e nero* XI.2 (February 1950) 38.

26   André Bazin, "On *Why We Fight*: History, Documentation, and Newsreels", *Bazin at Work* 188.

Fig. 8. Production shot by Paul Ronald of La terra trema *(Luchino Visconti, Italy, 1948) showing tarpaulins and additional lighting used in a daytime outdoor shoot. Visconti (in dark glasses and cap) is seated on the far side of the light. Behind it are the director of photography, G.R. Aldo (Aldo Graziati) (seated on ground) and the assistant directors Francesco Rosi (on stool with continuity book) and Franco Zeffirelli (standing). Under the microphone pole are the actors playing Antonio (Antonio Arcidiacono) and Alfio (Salvatore Vicari).*

This revaluation of cinema involved also a revaluation of photography in the cinema. The Hungarian-born Hollywood cinematographer John Alton (Jacob Altman) wrote in a book first published in 1949:

> In interiors as well as exteriors, Hollywood was addicted to the candied (not candid) type of chocolate-coated sweet unreal photography. Then came the war. The enemy was real and could not be present at production meetings. There were no rehearsals on battlefields or during naval or air battles. There was only *one take* of each scene. There were no boosters, no sun reflectors, no butterflies, and no diffusers. The pictures were starkly real. Explosions rocked the cameras, but they also rocked the world, and with it rocked Hollywood out of its old-fashioned ideas about photography. The year 1947 brought a new photographic technique. *Boomerang* and *T-Men*, photographed in original locations, prove that realistic photography is popular, and is accepted by the great majority. Let us have more realism.[28]

As Alton had explained earlier in the same chapter, however, even when filming outdoors cinematographers often used additional light and tarpaulins, not least to give control when the sun was behind clouds or daylight started to fade.[29] Aldo, who had worked as a studio photographer before moving into film photography, shot some of the outdoor scenes of *La terra trema* under white tarpaulins to diffuse the sunlight and then lit the actors with boosters: a large arc next to the camera and cross lights to the side (see Fig. 8).

Zavattini writes of cinema as a "means of examining" people and society, Bazin of "the cult of... actual facts", Alton of the reaction against "unreal photography." All these accounts attribute a decisive importance to the war as a watershed. Once a more consciously humanistic cinema develops, in the shadow of the war, attention gets redirected towards the way in which landscapes, interiors and faces are shown and photographed. It becomes possible to stall or even temporarily

---

27   Cesare Zavattini, "Inutile" (1949), in Diario cinematografico (Milan: Bompiani, 1979), reproduced in *Opere. Cinema*, eds. Valentina Fortichiari and Mino Argentieri (Milan: Bompiani, 2002) 107.

28   John Alton, *Painting with Light*, second edition, (Berkeley, Los Angeles: University of California Press, 1995) 134-5. The book, originally published by Macmillan in 1949, started as a series of articles for *International Photographer*, of which the first had appeared in 1945. A butterfly is a gauze used to soften harsh sunlight.

29   Alton, *Painting with Light* 129.

Fig. 9. Umberto D, *Vittorio De Sica, 1952.*

arrest the forward movement of the story and invite the audience to look at other things within the frame. This is partly what Gilles Deleuze was describing when he argued that neorealism effected a shift from the movement-image to the time-image by the creation of new kinds of signs that allowed the image to be seen "beyond movement".[30] The examples Deleuze gave are of moments within a film when the character stops to look, to contemplate something, and purposive action is rendered impossible: the maid Maria (Maria Pia Casilio) in *Umberto D* (Vittorio De Sica, 1952) mechanically carrying out household tasks and contemplating her pregnant body (Fig. 9); the displaced Karin in *Stromboli* who "cannot react in a way that softens or compensates the violence of what she sees" (the tuna fishing and the volcanic eruption); Katherine's discovery in *Voyage to Italy* of "something unbearable" in the world around her. "A cinema of seeing replaces action", wrote Deleuze, and he found it already present in *Ossessione*, where "objects and settings take on an autonomous, material reality which gives them an importance in themselves".[31]

Deleuze's remarks were brilliantly perceptive but also, I feel, overstated. This is still a cinema of narration, but one that has elements and moments of denarrativization embedded within it, so that there are two opposing tendencies. It is the tension between the onward flow of the narrative and moments of emptying of narrative that is the peculiarity of these films. This tension is most strongly exemplified in the late 1940s and early 1950s in the films of Rossellini, but it will be found again, in intensified form, in the films of Antonioni, particularly those from *Il grido* (1957) onwards, where each film could be said to be actually constructed around the opposition between the forward movement of the story and the denarrativizing attentions of the camera, which at certain moments simply wanders away from the characters to photograph the built or natural environment.

---

30 Gilles Deleuze, *Cinema 2: The Time-Image* [1989] (Minneapolis: The University of Minnesota Press, 2001) 1.

31 Deleuze, *Cinema 2: The Time-Image* 2, 9, 4.

2

After *La Jetée*. Cine-Photo Albums of the Disaster

Diane Arnaud

The present study on an "after" of *La Jetée* does not mean to establish what lies beyond the film. Chris Marker's work probably constitutes an impassable limit on many accounts. For more than forty-five years, any resort to sequences of still images (taking into account both freeze frames and photographs), whether at the beginning, at the end, or in the midst of a film, has been directly thought of after *La Jetée*. The overall narrative situation of the photo-novel involved a journey across time, at once theoretical and fictional, which contemplated the aftermath of the catastrophic event (the Third World War) through the circuits of memory and *via* the real return to the scene where the vivid childhood memory had originated. It is the path, represented in still images, of a man who as a child witnessed the troubling scene of his own murder and becomes aware of it only at the end – an end that establishes, with an interval, a diegetic return to the beginning. Marker's "film photograph of consciousness" has previously been characterized: the past running in the present, images begetting memory, the consciousness of time. The advent of thought as still images appear might be a consciousness of images more than a consciousness of the subject, "a consciousness of the image as pure substance of time".[1] From *La Jetée* on, the death to come and a "beyond" of the disaster became the foundations for a better understanding of the stakes of prolonging and reusing a cinematic sequence of still images.

Questions may accordingly be raised as to the aesthetic, historical, and even ideological dimension of film segments akin to photo albums of accidental, individual, worldwide, or universal disasters. From Virilio to Agamben, contemporary thinkers have underlined the danger inherent in the acceleration of exchanges and technological advances for a society undergoing a process of de-subjectification. The catastrophe thus ranges in scope from nuclear devasta-

---

1   Philippe Dubois, "*La Jetée* de Chris Marker ou le cinématogramme de la conscience" ["Chris Marker's *La Jetée*, or the Film Photograph of Consciousness"] in *Théorème, Recherches sur Chris Marker* 6, Philippe Dubois, ed. (Paris: Presses de la Sorbonne Nouvelle, 2006): 40.

tion to family dysfunction, and will be glimpsed through as many moving snapshots prefiguring the future of humankind in a hostile environment. Not incidentally, all three films examined most closely here have to do with the 1970s: *War without a Code* (*Jingi naki takakai*, Kinji Fukasaku, 1973), *Soylent Green* (Richard Fleischer, 1973), and *Tarnation* (2003), directed by Jonathan Caouette (born in 1973). The connection makes sense in the context of a period in which still and moving images were very present beyond cinema, be it in world fairs (New York, 1964; Montreal, 1967; Osaka, 1970) or in contemporary art slideshows (Dan Graham's and Robert Smithson's photo-installations). The cinematic montage of still images with serial disasters as a background mainly comprises sequences close to the make-up of photo albums, themselves in relative decline from the 1960s on.[2]

Apparatuses of Post-trauma Subjectification: Aesthetics of the Cine-Photo Album

The cinema of trauma takes over from a mode of preservation and a destination for photographic images. The photo album, a personal means of archiving, is put together to be seen, read, commented upon. The principles of the series and the layout come into play time and time again as finds and travels gradually transform the blank book into a photo album. Composition consists in emphasizing the specificity of each image within each page; pages are themselves more or less organized by chapters in a life, stages in a collection. Leafing through usually implies a commentary on family pictures or archival documents already captioned. The album is thus designed to accommodate several points of view, at once or separately, to be always handled back and forth with the permanent temptations of going back and leaping forward. Gestures, looks, and voices jointly constitute a new order in the transmission of images. The play of randomness and the desire for (re-)vision then lead to the (re-)discovery of memories through images.

In cinema this use has translated into different poetic and aesthetic modes, since the object can be conceived and perceived in one direction only, that of the film strip unwinding. Such film segments, which share in the fashion of projected photographs of the period, are thus akin to a new type of photo album. A cine-photo album – to be distinguished from a filmed photo album – may be defined by the montage and reframing of the photographs succeeding one another in the frame.[3] Indeed, its visualization across shots associates this suc-

---

2   Michel Frizot, *A New History of Photography* (New York: Konemann, 1998). The author gives the introduction of colour and the Polaroid as well as the generalization of personal photographs as reasons for this decline.

3   The surface of film screening and film exhibition accordingly becomes an album page subject to a double "off" space: on the one hand, the contiguous extension of film, on the other hand the discontinuous leafing-through, resulting in a double uncertainty as to the limits of each photograph and the volume of "pages-shots" thus turned.

cession with a critical thought of reflexivity. The film's viewers end up confronting several dimensions: the representation of photographs, the film's animation of still images, the contrast between *film as strip* and *film as screening*,[4] the introduction of a written, spoken, or musical commentary. Who designs the album? To whom is it shown? This *who*, multiplying in as many subjects, is as a consequence intimately related to the *how*, and cannot be thought separately from it.[5]

Catastrophe is our topic here, as we pay attention to the ways in which the subject who forgot the traumatic memory is approached, called up, denied by photo albums in cinema. Freudian thought on traumatic neuroses developed (after he abandoned his neurotica in 1897) in direct relation to the devastation of the First World War, notably in *Beyond the Pleasure Principle* (1920). Even though Freud shed light on the mechanism starting from an internal economy, he never renounced finding a real external traumatic foundation, be it at an individual or phylogenetic level. His conception of the transmission of original fantasies, intimately tied to the après-coup, rests on a fantasy of disaster. In his correspondence with Ferenczi, between 1915 and 1917, he thus refers to a generalized psychic trauma which humankind would have gone through with the advent of the ice age, a catastrophe on a large scale that resulted in the traumatic inhibition of sexuality in order to survive.[6] Likewise, current English-language studies such as Janet Walker's, focusing at once on documentary films on the Holocaust and on incest, cross histories large and small to try and understand the stakes of *trauma cinema*.[7] Freud's final insight on the question opens methodological perspectives that can connect the individual and the collective. In 1939 he returned to traumatic experiences situated in the past, and more specifically in the period of infantile amnesia, and which later play out in a number of cultural manifestations. He then put forward a capital distinction between two paths for the trauma: *positive* effects linked to *remembrance* and *negative* effects linked to avoidance, or *forgetting*. More precisely, Freud associated positive effects with a dynamic "to revive the trauma, to remember the forgotten experience, or, better still, to make it real – to live through once more a repetition of it".[8] In his text

---

4   The distinction between *film as strip* (each film frame, but also the overall articulation of film frames) and *film as screening* (the projected work) was introduced by Thierry Kuntzel in "Le défilement" ["The Run of the Film"], *Revue d'Esthétique. Cinéma, théories, lectures* 2–4 (1973).

5   The construction, preservation, and recollection of a memory through still images may evoke the subjective relation to desire. See Barbara Le Maître, *Entre film et photographie. Essai sur l'empreinte* ["Between Film and Photography. An Essay on the Imprint"] (Paris: Presses Universitaires de Vincennes, 2004) 20. According to the author, the subject of desire in cinema, *which cannot be reduced to the individual any more than its object can reduced to a real object*, may be grasped in its dimension of "in between" through the plastic forms given to the visual sets that articulate photo and film.

6   Thierry Bokanovski, "Entre Freud et Ferenczi: le traumatisme", *Revue Française de Psychanalyse, Traumatismes*, vol. LII (Nov.-Dec. 1988): 1288.

7   Janet Walker, *Trauma Cinema. Documenting Incest and The Holocaust* (Berkeley: University of California Press, 2005).

8   Sigmund Freud, *Moses and Monotheism* [1939], trans. Katherine Jones (New York: Vintage, 1967) 95.

these efforts are explained in terms of *fixations* on the trauma thus repeated. On the other hand, according to Freud, negative effects sanction strategies of non-remembrance through avoidance and phobia. The trauma then becomes as "a state within the state"[9] capable of forcing its law on the psychic reality of life.

The various adventures of the *subject* in cinema, from traumatic avoidance to traumatic remembrance, could then be unveiled starting from poetic rhythm, and accordingly in relation to the appearance of stillness and the returns of movement. From the standpoint of the spectator, the subject of film aesthetics corresponds to a construction *via* processes such as an identification to the progression of characters or an increased sensitivity to the formal marks of mise en scène. The Freudian distinction may be relevant in the aesthetics of cine-photo albums of the disaster when it comes to differentiating two fictional strategies of de-subjectification and subjectification actualized by the montage and the reframing of still images. Like negative (avoidance) and positive (remembrance) psychic processes, some of these strategies would be able to re-impose the law of the trauma in the unfolding perception, as though to erase it, while some others could represent what was previously unable to reach a level of figuration in order to try and remember it. How may we become subjects again, without any psychology whatsoever, yet with a consciousness of this future past history, of this disastrous future perfect which connects us to the issues of modernity? The question of processes of subjectification is crucial, complex, and multiple. The echoes between the thought on trauma in psychoanalysis and the thought on the apparatus in philosophy should be further examined, for cine-photo albums are artistic conceptions which mobilize knowledge and power in the capture of reality. In a recent work Agamben writes that an apparatus defines an "activity of governance devoid of any foundation in being". Apparatuses must accordingly "imply a process of subjectification, that is to say, they must produce their subject" for the living.[10] However, according to the essayist, "the current phase of capitalism" shares the same direction as a society which is undergoing "massive processes of desubjectification"[11] and is rushing headlong into disaster.

Our hypothesis thus posits a distinction between negative (desubjectification apparatus) and positive (subjectification apparatus) effects for cine-photo albums as identifiable sets of images and sounds. The desubjectification apparatus corresponds to a liminal position. Following an imposed law, the montage of still images mobilizes the passage between fiction and film, in a generative mode that can in turns be matricial, inaugural, or retrospective. The visualization of the catastrophe then unfolds in images-sounds in the narrative, against the active forces of the narrative progression which it re-impacts and on which it imposes

---

9   Freud, *Moses and Monotheism* 96.

10   Giorgio Agamben, *What Is an Apparatus?* [2006], trans. David Kishik and Stefan Pedatella (Stanford: Stanford University Press, 2009) 11. Agamben's thought obviously constitutes a continuation of Foucault's.

11   Agamben, *What Is an Apparatus?* 21.

the traumatic law of a "state within the state". There are many examples of photographic montages at the beginning (a family album in the form of a slideshow in Gaspar Noé's *I Stand Alone*, made in 1998), but also at the end of films (the vertical succession and framing of WWII reportages in Clint Eastwood's *Flags of Our Fathers*, 2006;[12] the projection of reportage photographs of society's rejects from the Great Depression to the present in Lars von Trier's *Dogville*, 2003, accompanied by David Bowie's 1975 song "Young Americans"). I will here focus on the film credits that fall within the cultural turn of the 1970s. As to the subjectification apparatus, it corresponds to the repetition of the cine-photo album in the course of the film. The photo album unfolds as part of the process of narration in the form of a looped sequence in order to describe and to avail oneself of a new subjective reality. A work of elaboration of the non-represented trauma is put into action through successive après-coups: "Then only, because it 'represents' itself – in all the senses of the term – in the relation to an other, the past trauma will be able to find a place in the time of a history".[13] More contemporary autofictions – by the following generation – will accordingly be examined in this instance.

Film matrices for photographs: "the fallout of stillness"

Both films examined deal with the ideological dimension of society's ills, starting from the cine-photo album of the disaster (past or to come). This fictional matrix uses photographic images to expose the effects of capitalism and imperialism, behind the legend. Let us start with *War without a Code* (Kinji Fukasaku, 1973). The opening gesture of this *yakuza eiga*, which is reminiscent of the "take off" on a still image at the beginning of *La Jetée*, is but a bottom-to-top tracking shot on a photograph of the nuclear explosion. The movement of the shot thus puts forth

Fig. 1. War without a Code *(Jingi naki takakai), Kinji Fukasaku, 1973.*

---

12 The succession of photographs framed on the left side of the screen, even as the credits roll on a black background on the right side, frees a kind of retrospective look on the conception of the fiction according to a principle of analogy with Joe Rosenthal's famous photograph in Iwo Jima. Let us recall that the photograph was not touched up: the deception comes from the caption, as the soldiers represented were not the ones who had put up the flag during the battle.

13 Catherine Couvreur, "Le trauma: les trois temps d'une valse" ["The Trauma: the Triple Time of a Waltz"], *Revue Française de Psychanalyse* 53 (1988): 1433.

a swift, uneven exploration, from the smoke at ground level to the white swelling of the mushroom cloud. This movement then comes to a halt, with the thundering music and the title in red letters soon hitting the reframed image (Fig. 1). For a few seconds, a slight trembling maintains the threat of this suspension. Animation by sound[14] and filmic reframing make the impact of the represented scene, the photographic "that has been", pregnant on the media visible on the screen. The explosion takes place again in the shot, unless it is already its dire fallout. Could it be a *pika* effect? The *pika* is the term by which the *Hibakusha*, the survivors of the nuclear bomb, refer to the *flash* of the explosion. According to Jun Fujita, a nuclear bomb precisely constitutes "a delayed-action bomb, insofar as the full effect of its impact is always delayed, deferred, to come."[15] The fallout in this instance finds its expression in the trembling of a photograph made possible by the run of the cine album, the time machine that makes the photographic past present or cancels out the diegetic present. The other meaning imparted by this first filmic exploration is none other than the relation between historical and artistic contexts: off-frame inscriptions, from then on, will appear, then disappear like blood stains on each document, both of which are framed as a whole. Ten photographs succeed one another in straight cuts, following a progression that goes from the explosion to the reconstruction, from the disaster to the new order in the streets of Tokyo, from the rubble to the resumption of a commercial activity in Hiroshima.

The cine album then closes so as to beget fiction. What might appear as the eleventh photograph looks oddly gray and sharp. The crowd already seen, the overhanging point of view, the eventual inscription of the director's name, serve both to prolong and to closure. The pictures shown in still shots (eight out of ten) give way to a shot disguised as a photograph and re-animated as part of the movement of the narrative in images-sounds. This occurs in successive stages: the music of the credits stops; an inscription, "Kure, south of Hiroshima, 1946", appears in white type; a gradual passage to colour, or rather, a shift from the photographic tint to the original colour of the film shooting, may be observed; information on the context is provided in voice-over; the zoom is much more pronounced than on the second photograph; and a camera movement accompanies the crowd. Echoing the commentary on "the law of every man for himself" and "the violence of chaos", the film issues from a *negative effect* of the trauma at that point.

The catastrophic memory of Hiroshima leafed through at the very beginning, just for our eyes, does not operate for the characters, who seem to avoid it. The avoidance is signaled by the "fallout of stillness". Immediately after the credits, shots of the protagonists in the heat of action are suddenly frozen at the end of

---

14   It should be noted that a sound effect (the sound of an explosion) is heard at the beginning of the shot showing the still image, the re-filmed historical document.

15   See Jun Fujita, "La double temporalité du *pika* dans le cinéma japonais", *Drôle d'époque* 16, "Penser Hiroshima et Nagasaki 40 ans après" (Spring 2005): 89.

the first three sequences. Hirono's run as the military police chase him and an arm flying off after Wakasugi slashed it in retaliation are abruptly interrupted. While the run of the film is frozen only apparently, the represented movement freezes for good, potentially affecting the sequence and narratively foreshadowing the commentary. White letters inscribe the diegesis to come on the image suddenly frozen: "Hirono. Future clan: Yamamori". The film frame returns *via* the captioned cine-photo album . In the narrative progression, the frozen movement is systematically actualized as a death warrant with executions between yakuzas, as epitomized in the high-angle shot of Hirono's blood-brother, his chest stained with a pictorial red-orange blood that is all the more reminiscent of the credits as his identification sheet at the morgue then appears in white type. Iconographic data,[16] graphic inscriptions,[17] the characteristics of the overhanging or high-angle composition of the matricial photographic images are also more and more frequently reused to convey the fact that the action is getting increasingly unsettled and that the postwar situation is an impasse. A shot of the Gembaku Dom, which was already featured in the second photograph of the initial album, reappears in a colour, film version (voice-over, zoom in), as Hirono seeks the protection of the Kaito family in Hiroshima. Issuing from a still image, the shot works to re-establish and reaffirm the catastrophe within the situation while avoiding it.

Hiroshima indirectly affects the behaviour of the gangsters, blind to the point of committing serial killings without looking at the larger picture of widespread corruption. On a smaller scale – that of the fiction – this inability to picture the disaster for oneself but through the resort to archival documents also threatens the said fiction with the devastating power of temporarily still shots. Another device also comes to prolong the deadly signature of the freeze frame. During the inaugural cocktail of a necessarily corrupt society, bargaining between yakuzas may be heard in voice-off while the narrator's commentary runs in voice-over, with shots frozen into clichés. The fiction, which imposed the law of "the state within the state" upon itself, has become a "photo-detective novel" by way of the matricial cine album. This apparatus reintroduces the stillness of photography to freeze the movement of the film. From that point on, the narrative may be thought of as a kind of macabre agitation of shots orchestrated by the precision of a voice-over, a spoken caption which goes from assessment to disappointment.

Soylent Green's credits, composed by Chuck Braverman out of daguerreotypes and Magnum photographs on an original music by Fred Myrow, may be understood

---

16 Indeed, some figurative, sartorial, or monumental elements of the album (a man with a cap, an agent of the military police of the American occupation forces seen in Ginza next to the Wako department store, a bare back in the public baths surrounded by rubble, a building with its ruined circular roof) reappear in the narrative.

17 The graphic interplay between the inscription of the credits in red and the black-and-white linguistic mentions for the photographs occurs on two occasions, with newspaper clippings parodying the Emperor's capitulation message, and a demonstration in Tokyo with slogans expressing discontent on the flags.

Fig. 2. Soylent Green, *Richard Fleischer, 1973.*

through the same strategy of avoidance. The consciousness of the disaster is made impossible by collective blindness. As at the beginning of Fukasaku's film, the historical context is reintroduced.[18] In this case, however, a fast-paced story tells the frenzy and the madness of industrialization, starting from the framed photograph of a family posing in a field circa 1900 and ending with the shot of a smogged out New York City in 2022 (Fig. 2).

Three phases may be noted in the overall sequence. The first phase – motorization and urbanization – is shown through black-and-white photographs, snapshots of an old world, which look as though they were "leafed through", like the pages of a photo album. A number of techniques set stillness into motion: an oblique zoom in followed by an oblique zoom out, creating an impression of flight within the "photo-shots;" and a superimposition that reinforces the notion of photographs sliding under one another. The second phase sanctions the proliferation of images through the use of colour and split screens, which connects them to the multiplication of screens at the world fairs of the late 1960s.[19] It begins with a zenithal high-angle shot of automobile traffic, doubled and coloured, so as to underline the development of means of transportation and communication. The

18 Let us note the cinematographic influence of the credits of Cornel Wilde's 1970 *No Blade of Grass*, which resort to multiple frames within the frame and full-frame insertions of photographs (from the black and white of older photographs to contemporary colour prints). A nuclear explosion concludes the prologue.

19 For more specific information on the *congorama* (a set of systems of automated lighting, slideshow, or film screenings, with visual and sound effects) as well as on the *diapolyécran* (a wall mosaic of 112 square sections on which still images are projected, making up a single, coherent theme or a fragmented one thanks to two projectors per section) presented at the New York (1964), Montreal (1967), and Osaka (1970) World Fairs, see Valérie Peseux, *La Projection grand spectacle. Du cinérama à l'omnimax* (Paris: Editions Dujarric, 2004) 178.

photomontage relies on straight cuts at this point. The frenzied musical rhythm goes hand in hand with an acceleration of vertical or lateral reframing movements, with the multiplication of full-frame photographs, or of photographs within multiple screens. Still images are from then on handled as though they were infinite, and hence interchangeable: enlargement, reduction, organization in three- or four-part tabulations. In their new production framework – an archival collection appearing over a black background – they are presented one after the other, as if pushed aside by way of wipes. Finally, a phase of deceleration, which includes another sequence of superimposed photographs, accompanies a slower music. The damage caused by pollution, increased poverty, and draught may be seen full-frame on aerial views, details on the ground, and masked faces. The return to black and white can be understood, from a formal standpoint, as the result of a process of smearing muted colours and, from an ideological perspective, as the fallout of new capitalism.

The end of music marks the entry into fiction. Data on urban overpopulation ("40 million people") can be read in the first, high-angle shot. While *Soylent Green* announces an ecological disaster, global warming, and the predictable end of the human species, the conduct of the action itself is not as influenced by the threats spelled out in the opening credits as it was in the Japanese gangster film, made with the blind memory of the postwar reconstruction period. Still, the final freeze frame should be mentioned: as the ultimate lines of the dialogue are heard ("we've got to stop them, somehow"), a pious hope gradually covered by the extradiegetic music, a zoom in centers the composition on the main character's bloody hand. The very limits of the still image are given a new dimension through a gradual framing in black akin to the sliding effects in *The Boston Strangler* (1968), another film directed by Fleischer. The shot, once one of its frames has been frozen, becomes a photograph, adjustable in its format, ready to be placed, moved, filmed again as part of a cine album of the disaster. In this instance, avoidance as a strategy obviously consists in not giving away the crucial piece of information (i.e., *soylent green* is not exactly a vegetal product). To be sure, the film puts forth an "image machine" to mitigate the *negative effects* of the trauma, which impose the law of stillness. Yet the regenerator of moving images only gives rise to a clichéd image of the past for dead spectators promised to recycling, since older citizens are in fact anesthetized on the occasion of a "high-tech ritual"[20] that involves viewing – from a coffin-bed – the moving images of a lost nature with symphonic music playing. The matricial cine album has managed to mobilize but a movement of "folding back over" the catastrophe.

Looped Albums: "A Dynamics of *Fixations*"

A sequence of still images with music, whether freeze frames or photographs, is

---

20   Fredric Jameson, *The Cultural Turn. Selected Writings on the Postmodern 1983–1998* (London, New York: Verso, 1998) 126.

an audiovisual event that occasionally has to be repeated as a means to move beyond the trauma. These looped albums, these generations of still images re-play out a malaise in documentary autofictions such as Asia Argento's 2000 *Scarlet Diva*. Our present study will focus solely on Jonathan Caouette's 2003 *Tarnation*. According to Jacques Aumont, in this *apparatus*-film, the variations on the split screen "move past cinema as an apparatus".[21] It could certainly be compared to slideshows such as Jonas Mekas's *Rillettes* (2002)[22] and Michael Snow's *Sidelength* (1969–1971),[23] which were both made out of material from works of the late 1960s. The play on reuse between film sequences and slideshows, filmed life and projected life, is common to all these artistic practices. However, a genetic relation with contemporary art should not overshadow the cinematographic value of *Tarnation*, which lies in the alternation between sections of photo albums accompanied with music, and scenes shot throughout the life of the born film-maker.

The first succession of still images takes place, not at the beginning of the narrative in images-sounds (situated in New York in 2002), but at a key moment of the family history as it is told, re-edited, and replayed. Jonathan Caouette has just learned that his mother has gone into a coma following a lithium overdose. He takes the bus to Texas. The point-of-view shots make other, noticeably more grainy views resurface: houses in the country, or what are clearly super-8 images of Jonathan as a child, speaking about his chances of being on Johnny Carson's show some day. This journey through memory rests on the mode of reuse made possible by the practice of an archivist of intimacy and a budding filmmaker. The conversation continues over a black image out of which the first pages of the photo album emerge, as though leafed through. A – literally – fabulous narration of family history has substituted for the expected caption, an explanatory commentary on the context. On the dark background, the white letters stand out sharply: "Once upon a time in a small Texas town". Reading to themselves, spectators assume the position of the narrator in *La Jetée*, keeping in mind the (auto)biographical dimension of the photo edit. The third-person fairytale on the birth of Renee Leblanc (Jonathan's mother), a perfect little girl who will end up in electric shock treatment in life and on the screen, is from the start at odds with the autofictional dimension. The passage of commented photographs may be divided in three sections, each of which corresponds to a different song – rock and folk melodies, in a progression towards listlessness. These are music videos

21   Jacques Aumont, *Moderne ? Comment le cinéma est devenu le plus singulier des arts* ["Modern? How the Cinema Became the Most Singular of Arts"] (Paris: Cahiers du cinéma, 2007) 106.

22   Jean-Michel Ribettes, *Le Diaphane et l'obscur. Une histoire de la diapositive dans l'art contemporain* ["The Diaphanous and the Obscure: A History of the Slide in Contemporary Art"] (Paris: Maison Européenne de la photographie, 2002) 50. This projection-installation is made of 100 photographic slides reproducing film frames from the trims of Jonas Mekas's film diaries. It prolongs his exhibitions of prints (*Frozen Film Frames*, 2003).

23   This slideshow featuring 24 slides projected in loops at the pace of a slide every fifteen seconds was generated out of his film *Wavelength* (1967).

in reverse, since family pictures constitute the primary material of the audiovisual whole, yet the musical quality of the editing creates a sense of solid unity. If the family narrative is taken as the main thread, the three sections of the album do follow a chronological order.

Renee's birth and fall. The alternation between facts of life and family pictures is steady. Renee's story is one of dramatic change from the wonderful to the tragic. A model for magazines and television commercials by the age of 11, she fell off from the roof the following year and was left paralysed as a result. Her parents, Adolph and Rosemary (which would have made her "Rosemary's Baby"), then decided to have her sent to the hospital, where for two years she underwent a first series of electric shocks. In the first, glorious pages of the album, black-and-white photographs appear full-frame, their succession set in motion and paced by "flashed" fades to white. The impression of "flashed succession" produces the illusion that a photograph is being taken at the moment it appears. This temporal dazzle, close to a slideshow effect, is short-lived. Indeed, what follows is characterized by a number of aspects: the multiplication of Renee's image, related to her overexposure as a model (a four-part screen repeats the same photograph as in a serial photo ID or a kaleidoscopic contact sheet); the fluctuations of jerky camera movements to reframe photographs and the instability in the wake of electric shocks; the threat of evaporation, expressed through a visual effect of disappearance spreading in stain-like shapes. According to the caption in one of the intertitles, upon her release from the hospital Renee felt as though the sun was going to cause her to evaporate. The constitution of the album twists and short-circuits the family chronology written out on the screen, for instance by featuring a picture of Jonathan, who was not yet born at the time.

Jonathan's birth and the deterioration of his mother's health. Some photographs are reused in this section and anachronistic sound recordings are added, which run counter to the progression of a narrative of increasingly frequent stays in psychiatric hospitals for Renee – an intertitle mentions more than 100 since 1965. The final loop of images – full-frame, superimposed portraits – gives a haunting quality to some photographs, particularly that of Renee with the wind blowing in her hair and her head inclined (Fig. 3).

Misfortunes and hardships. This part lists events: the fire in Adolph's small business, Rosemary's hysterectomy, Renee and Jonathan's departure for Chicago, the rape in front of the child, the mother's psychiatric ordeal, the abuse of the son in foster homes. At that point, the first "shot" of the album appears – out of place, since it is a recording of Joshua, Jonathan's son in life, an element not documented in the film. This attempt to have the traumatic scenes reenacted by his own child – via editing – without explicitly stating the fact, is dizzying. The running commentary at the end of this first "leafing through" self-destroys in indicating that Jonathan's (that is, the filmmaker's) memories of his own mother have almost completely faded. The autobiographical narrative thereby exposes its falsification. The third section of the album thus relies on the alternation

Fig. 3. Tarnation,
Jonathan Caouette,
2003.

between frozen shots and visually distorted photographs (lower lighting, a "pop" saturation of colours, a flicker reminiscent of horror genres).[24] The jolting animation of images partakes of another documentary history, in a close relation to the cultural and artistic heritage of the 1970s.

These passages of images, in turn frozen, remobilized, distorted, multiplied, outline the path of a family trauma, of an amnesia passed on from mother to son.

---

24 At the end of the film, the horror of the family narrative – a new series of electric shocks – constitute a terrible reverse shot to Renee and Jonathan's photo booth picture. At that point, the shot of a woman cornered in a shower marks the return of 1970s genre cinema (the horror film). Indeed, a visually deteriorated image – the freeze frame of a reflection of Jonathan's yelling at the mirror like a zombie – concludes another section.

The origin assigned to the paralysis and the depersonalization by discourse corresponds to an unseen image both moving and frozen: that of Renee's fall to the ground on her two stiff legs. All movements involving the reuse of still images proceed from the impossible figuration of that event, not from any consequences of the past disaster. A "dynamic of fixations" is staged in order to move beyond a repetition of the same: reenacting the fall in horror films, going into a coma, flaunting oneself onstage, fainting under the influence of drugs …

Step by step, in the six other sections of the cine album, the same shock treatment is applied to the selected photographs and the shots already made: multiplication on the screen, use of framing, plastic distortion of the portraits, faster editing pace. In recycling and reassembling images already chosen and sequenced, these audiovisual groupings perform a specific type of work. What is given to see is a circuit, more than a healing narrative. The last series of photographs appearing in the film takes place after a very harsh conversation between Jonathan and his grandfather, who does not want to answer the question on sexual abuse, the seduction of a child by an adult, the traumatic childhood memory par excellence. The run of the film appears to be jammed until it comes to a complete stop. The same fast-paced editing of superimposed images – full-frame portraits of Renee[25] – reappears between two shots representing a (fake) burn in the film strip.

The cine-photo album features short circuits of images between stillness and movement, reuse and reenactment. With the risk of depersonalization tied to an individual or collective disaster, loops of photographs edited together to the point of dissolution, may also hold a possibility for subjectification through the powers of fake memories. The intimate collages of *Tarnation*, which re-process photographic portraits, thus lead to question the capacity of film apparatuses to connect heterogeneous elements together in a perceptible manner, to be sure, but most of all to create memory objects and subjects, modern memory "machines".

---

25   This fast-paced recapitulative editing of photographs already appears at the end of the second section. The effect itself may be found in Asia Argento's *The Heart Is Deceitful Above All Things* (2004), with various frozen frames of the film swiftly "leafed through".

3

Postcards in Agnès Varda's cinema

Christa Blümlinger

If we are to follow Jacques Derrida's reflections, the postcard (always already a reproduction, a cliché, or a decalcomania) means the ruin of the letter, which it parcels out and anonymizes.[1] Open, devoid of secret, stemming from print technology and the military wire, the postcard lacks privacy. As Bernhard Siegert notes in his in-depth investigation,[2] it partakes of a ghostlike form of communication manufactured industrially. Indeed, in the "postal" universe, individuality has to be expressed in standard formats.[3] Siegert's précis on the medium owes to the ambivalent uses of photography as much as it does to postal culture: with its photographic view, the postcard entails the ersatz and the psychic obliteration of memory-images. Agnès Varda's early commissioned films take into account this ambiguity of model images through the thought it weaves between words and images. Beyond ghost communication, model images then open the possibility of visual and mental points of view.

The figure of the postcard assumes two forms in Agnès Varda's films: as a direct or indirect citation, and as a diegetic or makeshift apparatus. The relation of filmic writing to photographic clichés parallels that of the personal letter to the standardized postcard. In such a context, there is more to the film than a mere

1 See Jacques Derrida, *The Postcard. From Socrates to Freud and Beyond*, trans. Alan Bass (Chicago: University of Chicago Press, 1987).

2 In his history of the fortunes ("Geschicke") of literature in the age of the modern postal service, Bernhard Siegert describes the end of the classical and romantic exchange of letters after the mass introduction around 1870 of the postcard as a medium to send messages. See Bernhard Siegert, *Relays: Literature as an Epoch of the Postal System*, trans. Kevin Repp (Stanford: Stanford University Press, 1999) 146–164.

3 The photographic postcard, which was launched shortly after the military postcard, borrowed the same principles of mass reproduction, format standardization, and a dressed-up signifying practice. Still, approaching the history of the postcard, not from its military origins or from the standpoint of the fortunes of literature (as Siegert does), but rather from the multitude of its forms and motifs, leads to a relativization of these borrowings – on a historiographic level, precisely, with the manufacture of postcards within the craft industry for instance. The development of photographic paper in postcard format by Eastman Kodak from 1902 on, accessible even to amateur photographers, should also lead to a reassessment of the status of personal, everyday postal views, which remained very popular until the 1930s. See Robert Delpire, ed., *L'Amérique au fil des jours. Cartes postales photographiques, 1900–1920* ["America Day after Day. Photographic Postcards, 1900–1920"] (Paris: Delpire, 1983); and Clément Chéroux and Ute Eskildsen, eds., *The Stamp of Fantasy. The Visual Inventiveness of Photographic Postcards* (Paris, Göttingen: Steidl, 2008).

iconographic consciousness. Those of Varda's early film essays that take as a point of departure hackneyed views or linguistic meanings display an ambivalent culture of memory, in which a kind of positive forgetfulness has a place.

Four types of interrelations between film and photography may be distinguished in the figure of the postcard in Varda's work: the iconographic reuse of a view (an indirect citation or a diegetization of the photographic view); the film as an exhibition site for images, in a sort of competition with the gallery and the museum (we are here in the sphere of influence of Malraux's *Musée imaginaire*[4]); the film in between fixity and movement (in the films consisting of photographs); finally, the film/the video within photography, as part of an installation.

Iconographic Reuses of a View

This first type of overlap between film and photography, whose aim is to initiate reflection on iconography, may be found in Varda's essays as well as in her fiction films. This dimension probably has roots in her work with still images. As other filmmakers before and after her – Lászlo Moholy-Nagy, Helen Levitt, William Klein, Robert Frank, or her fellow traveler Chris Marker – Varda comes from photography. Before she caught the attention of critics with her first feature film, *La Pointe Courte* (1954), she was already the renowned photographer of the *Théâtre National Populaire*. In the early 1950s Roland Barthes already acknowledged avant-garde qualities in Varda's portraits of actors. In his essay on the face, later reprinted in his *Mythologies*, Barthes noted about Varda's photographs that "… they always bequeath the actor his fleshy face and enclose it frankly, with an exemplary humility, in its social function, which is to "represent" and not to lie".[5]

The idea of a social function may be found even in the series of photographic portraits of the inhabitants of an island made for a recent multimedia exhibition, *L'Île et elle* ["The Island and Her"].[6] A little wood cabin stood at the beginning of the exhibition: in *La Cabane aux portraits* two series of photographs of faces grouped by gender faced each other. Each image shows the islanders outdoors in front of a painted background, an initial frame itself framed by the larger landscape of the fishermen's village. It is thus an unusual combination of studio pose and on-location shooting, conscious posture and unconscious expression. While Varda transposed this type of hybridation in her shift from photography to cinema, its ambiguity also derives from the modulation of movement.

Her short film *Du côté de la côte* (1958) was commissioned by the Office National

4   On this influence, see Christa Blümlinger, "Marker, Varda, l'art des correspondances", in *Le Court métrage documentaire français de 1945 à 1968: créations et créateurs* ["The Documentary Short Film in France from 1945 to 1968: Creations and Creators"], Dominique Bluher and Philippe Pilard, eds. (Rennes: Presses Universitaires de Rennes, 2008).

5   Barthes (Roland), *The Eiffel Tower and Other Mythologies*, trans. Richard Howard (Berkeley, Los Angeles : University of California Press, 1997) 22.

6   The exhibition was presented at the Fondation Cartier (Paris) in 2006.

du Tourisme. In that respect, the essay not only represents a stylistic renewal of the genre of the tourist film, it also functions as a metafilm on the genre, a *détournement* of sorts. As the opening credits appear on a background of postcard views, a historical and cultural relation implicitly becomes the object of examination: the industrialization of postcards prevailed at the end of the 19th century and developed – like cinema – in the context of other emerging industries such as transportation, tourism, or leisure. This explains why the first cinematographic views had already taken the postcards as an iconographic model.[7] They added movement to the *panoramas* of these still views.

Fig. 1. Postcard from Menton.

Du côté de la côte puts into play visual configurations and commentary to throw light on the Riviera and its *mythologies* (in Barthes's sense). Varda

Fig. 2. Du côté de la côte, Agnès Varda, 1958.

7   See Pelle Snickars, "Vues instantanées. Stereographs, Lantern Slides, Postcards and Nonfiction Film", in Leonardo Quaresima and Laura Vichi, eds., *Le decima musa / il cinema e le altre arti / the tenth muse / cinema and other arts* (Udine: Forum, 2001) 55–61.

also works on *clichés*, understood in two ways – as photographic products and decals (the word "cliché" also means "photographic negative" in French), but also as the sedimentations of a myth. With its form coming out of a complex relation between movement and stillness, the film thus gives visibility to the different levels of signification comprising a mythology. The opening credits of *Du côté de la côte* show this emblematically. After a series of postcards and prints of Nice, Cannes, and Menton accompanied with a song, a number of tableaux vivants in turn open up serial meanings. The play with polysemies goes on through less stylized, more mobile shots. Still, these are never given as "natural" views, and the function of the commentary is poetic as much as it is pensive. In the book adapted from the film by Varda,[8] an equivalent transposition of montages emerges between text and image, as the views of the Riviera never illustrate a discourse, partaking instead of a complex circulation between reading and vision.[9] In the film as in the book on the Riviera, the reference to postcards is thus not limited to an iconographic dimension: it also affects an enunciative system.

At first sight, the visual apparatuses of cinema and postcards could not be more different: the small card may be manipulated while projection produces the larger, immaterial image; and unlike a film, the card has a reverse side. However, the parallel between photographic views and film may be extended to another level, particularly the emotion of the viewer or spectator. Serge Daney, a great postcard lover, spoke of a "politics of authors" based on his examination of different types of photographs and framing styles among the main postcard publishers. His favourite views did not feature any inscriptions, signatures, prints, or postal marks, representing instead – in a purely Bazinian logic – "the imaginary sampling of a piece of landscape, which becomes an image in the process".[10] For Daney, postcards – like cinema – are situated between the public and the private: "These normal, informal images, mysteriously issued from reality itself, had to be the very place of a *private* communication. This involves both the respect for reality through the most visible of its images and opacification for all."[11] According to Daney, despite the standardized, universally accessible form of these images, each of them may be integrated by as many individual viewers it in their personal hieroglyphs. A card without a caption would lose its destination, resembling an undecipherable dream image.

Postcards with captions, however, may be part of a cartography, a system of traveled paths. In *One Sings, the Other Doesn't* (1976), the figure of the postcard operates exactly in this cartographic sense, punctuating narration and condens-

8   For Varda, the Riviera is "both a locality and a sociological phenomenon". See Agnès Varda, *La Côte d'Azur, d'azur, d'azur* (Nantes: Les Editions du Temps, 1961) 6.

9   Around the metaphor and myth of "paradise", for instance. For more detail, see Christa Blümlinger, "Marker, Varda, l'art des correspondances".

10   Serge Daney, *Persévérance. Entretien avec Serge Toubiana* (Paris: P.O.L.,1994) 73.

11   Daney, *Persévérance* 75.

ing narrative elements within photographic signs. After the reunion of the two main female characters, Suzanne and Pomme, following a long separation, they start sending each other postcards on the places where they are staying as well as their moods, be it through the images of figured landscapes or the words they write to each other. Towards the end of the film, Pomme's concert tour across southern France unfolds through a series of postcards that concludes with a view of the Riviera. While historically the advent of the postcard signaled the end of the Romantic exchange of letters, it serves in this instance to publish openly the private testimonies of a generation of women who committed themselves to fighting for their rights and made the body an explicit political issue. Postcards, as the signs of a writing made public, match the portraits of anonymous women exhibited in the photographer's studio.[12] Indeed, both types of images turn out to be imaginary openings in the narrative. The principle of the studio pose changes at the end of the film: female workers pose for a documentary film and their look is addressed to Suzanne.

If the photographic views and portraits in Varda's film cannot be reduced to their narrative function (be it of signification, condensation, or interruption), neither do the photography films (in a literal sense) come down to the idea of a photo romance or to a photomontage. Rather, these interrelations between film and photography often involve temporality, affects, and thought because of the nature of the media in question. By expanding photography through film, and film through installations, Varda's work produces specific forms of memory often linked to a notion of exhibition that could be likened to the imaginary museum (in Malraux's sense) or to an art of memory (in Frances Yates's sense).

The Film as Exhibition Site

The second type of articulation between film and photography in Varda's works has the film transformed into an exhibition site. Wandering through sites of memory, delving into portraits and personal collections, Varda has been fashioning, since her beginnings as a filmmaker, fragments of a self-portrait. These do not necessarily appear as an effigy of herself; they obey subjective perceptive modes and function according to specific constellations. The permanent hybridization of mise en scène and documentary, thanks to an iconic montage following objects and motifs as well as a steady rhythm produced by stillness and movement, gives rise to a topological form, in an attempt to link perception and memory.

L'Opéra Mouffe (1958) thus is, according to Varda, a "subjective documentary".[13] This film essay presents the fantasies of a pregnant stroller, who connects the

---

12   Claudine Delvaux analysed the particular status of photography and the figure of the (male) photographer in this "women's film", referring to Roland Barthes, but her study barely takes postcards into account. See Claudine Delvaux, "Agnès Varda, Cinéphotographie", in *Revue belge du cinéma* 20 (summer 1987) 25–31.

13   Agnès Varda, *Varda par Agnès* (Paris: Cahiers du Cinéma, 1994) 230.

Fig. 3.
L'Opéra-Mouffe,
A. Varda, 1958.

expressions of passers-by and the forms of objects to her own organic state. *L'Opéra Mouffe* features very short, relatively still takes to which editing gives a fictional inflection.[14] The film also includes genuine photographs, exhibited, edited, and ordered to refer to another temporality: the past of the "departed", the dead of Mouffetard street, as opposed to the organic "becoming" of the body of the pregnant stroller.

Daguerréotypes (1974–1975), like *L'Opéra Mouffe*, may be characterized as a documentary essay on the life of a street. Varda herself made a paradoxical comment on her portrait of a street, concerning *Daguerréotypes*: "The permanence of this little neighbourhood took the form of filmed photographs (...), portraits frozen in time".[15] Conversely, those of Varda's films that could literally be referred to as "photography films" (made up in part or in totality of photographs) often consist in a temporalization of photography by cinema.

Ulysse (1982), for example, is based on the filmmaker's collection of images, and more particularly on a photograph made in 1954 that provides the occasion to contemplate the power(lessness) of memory. The image represents a pebble beach, with a dead goat in the foreground on the right, a little boy watching the goat farther on the left, and a naked man standing by the child, his back turned on the observer. The filmmaker experiments with a *studium* (in Barthes's sense), which takes as a point of departure the gap between the present of the investigation and the past of the shooting. The primary question seems to bear on the performative act that lies at the foundation of a photograph: how was the camera

---

14 By contrast, a scene of *Cleo from 5 to 7*, made three years later, features portraits of similar passers-by which, repeated within that particular fiction film, figure flashes of memory and express an involuntary memory on the part of the stroller. In *L'Opéra Mouffe*, these "photographic" portraits take on movement through editing whereas in *Cléo* they have a function of interruption, of mental retrospection, to mark the instantaneous suspension of a movement and thus call into question the idea of an "objective" or mechanical time.

15 Varda, *Varda par Agnès* 143.

Figs. 4, 5, 6. Ulysse,
A. Varda, 1982.

positioned? Which posture did the models take in front of the camera? What is the relationship between the human bodies and the dead goat? Varda provides no univocal answers in *Ulysse*. Towards the end of a series of readings, the commentary goes as follows: "The image is there, that's all. You can see what you want in an image. An image is that, and everything else." The form of this reading, repeated several times, does not only take Varda from the *studium* to the enigmatic *punctum* of photography (again, in Barthes's sense), as Jacques Kermabon noted.[16] It also takes her back to her real models, 28 years later, to mark – from their bodies and their speech (or their silence) – the difference with respect to the past, the immemorial dimension of photography. This observation of a photograph does not seek to bring the reading to a close or produce autobiographical certainties: first and foremost, it introduces doubt in an attempt to reconstruct the founding photographic act. While Varda underscores the year in which the photograph in question was taken and its contemporaneity with the shooting of her first film *La Pointe Courte* (1954), the indication does not so much situate the construction of a context of creation as it calls into question the degree of significance of a chronology. Thanks to a fragmented form and an associative commentary that privileges analogies and metaphors over the order of facts and certainties, the resulting narrative is anything but closed. Through a system of associations and correspondences, a gesture related to the self-portrait rather than the autobiography develops.[17]

In *Ulysse*, all chronological processes are stretched to the limit, including research on the historical context relevant to the selected photograph. The insertion of newsreels of the time does not serve a synchronic reconstruction, but instead becomes the pretext for an excursion and its association of ideas. In that respect, Molotov's and Zhou Enlai's visit to Geneva on the day the photograph was made constitutes a kind of parallel action: Varda edited archival images from May 1954 with postcards representing the walk alongside Lake Geneva. Handwriting appears over the last view, which features a man on the shore, walking towards gulls flying away over the water. This is the occasion for a poetic digression and a Lamartine poem, cited by Varda in her commentary: "O time! Suspend your flight …!"[18]

16 See Jacques Kermabon, "*Ulysse*. Un film d'Agnès Varda", Dossiers Lycéens au cinéma series (Paris: CNC 2000) 4–7, page 7 for this specific comment. Barthes describes the *punctum* of photography as "what pricks me", a detail for instance. This cannot be shown through an analysis or an act of naming, but only through "a certain latency", "a kind of subtle *beyond*". Roland Barthes, *Camera Lucida. Reflections on Photography*, trans. Richard Howard (New York: Hill and Wang, 1982) 27, 42, 51, 53, 59.

17 Philippe Dubois analysed this film as part of a corpus of photography films he labeled as autobiography, yet without further elaborating on the genre. The central doubt highlighted in *Ulysse*, namely, the very possibility of the reconstruction of memory through photography, is not considered in this reading. See Philippe Dubois, "Le documentaire autobiographique moderne (entre cinéma et photographie)", in *Admiranda. Cahiers d'Analyse du Film et de l'Image* 10, special issue on "The Genius of Documentary" (Aix-en-Provence: Université de Provence, 1995) 96–105.

18 Alphonse de Lamartine, "Le lac" (1849), in *Méditations poétiques*, *Oeuvres poétiques complètes*, Bibliothèque de la Pléiade (Paris: Gallimard, 1963) 39.

Besides the parallels between the motifs of the postcard written over and Varda's 1954 photograph (water, a man with his back turned, animals), an allegory of the insertion of photographs in the film also surfaces. Indeed, the film adds an excess of connotations and associations to the photograph to raise the issue of its temporal status, while the postcard shows an inscription that eludes the meanings related to the visual motifs proper. In the context of moving images, the photograph of Ulysses, just like the postcard with its frozen flock of birds, seems to respond to a utopia of interruption evoked by the quotation of the famous line from Lamartine's poem.

In this 20-minute film essay, Varda first shows a photograph in its entirety before analysing it in detail, accompanying it with internal and voice-over commentary, combining it with other takes, and presenting it again as a whole at the end. The film thus exemplifies a reading process, as the photograph, read and edited over and over again throughout a film, no longer seems the same at the end as it was at the beginning.

Through its structure, *Ulysse* shows that the temporalization of photography occurs not only through editing, but through a reiteration of the disappearance of the still image within the moving image itself. This perpetual disappearance triggers a specific process of memory and imagination in the audience. The function of commentary is essential, for it seeks an imaginary expansion of photography through film, rather than settling reading through words. The distance of the commentary marks the position of the observer *in front of* the image, not *within* it, and is emphasized by the system of the exhibition, which appears several times in *Ulysse* – down to the very combinations of photographs and objects organized within certain shots.

The photographic act is therefore not given by Varda as an intentional key to reading the meanings of an image: it is also embodied by the film itself, as a gesture towards a self-portrait. That is also and again the case with *The Gleaners* (Les Glaneurs et la glaneuse, 2000), her film essay on the cultural history of gleaning and recycling. Varda inscribes her own tactile relation to objects and to the camera, filming herself as she looks at potatoes with strange shapes or makes a frame with her hands. The image takes on a haptic dimension not only because of her motifs, but also because it retains the trace of its manual production. The close-ups of Varda's own wrinkled hands, which always have an immobile, photographic dimension, are part of a series of vanitas and express the passing of time in a melancholic way.

Looking at artistic postcards, Varda notes, out of frame: "That's what my project is about: holding my camera with one hand to film my other hand. (...) There's Rembrandt's self-portrait – it's the same thing, in fact." Varda records her aging hands as a temporal sign. The close-up of Jacques Demy's hand, as he was gravely ill, assumed a similar function in the portrait film *Jacquot* (1990), in which the sand slipping through the fingers metaphorized the finitude of life. Such a

Figs. 7–11. Salut les Cubains, A. Varda, 1963.

close-up, inserted in a series of mobile shots, has suspension as an effect – but, like the photographic, it also crystallizes affects.[19]

Stillness and movement: the photography films

The third type of overlap between film and photography resides in what could be termed the "photography film". The relation between movement and stillness proves paradoxical when it comes to assessing the function of photography in this type of film. In *Salut les Cubains* (1963),[20] the moments of animation of still images may precisely be read in the light of melancholy, as soon as temporal

---

19   Regarding the notion of the "photographic" as a moment of interruption or as a pregnant moment within a film, see Raymond Bellour, "L'interruption, l'instant" [1987], in Raymond Bellour, "The film stilled", *Camera Obscura* N° 24/ 1990, 99–123.

20   The title *Salut les Cubains* is a play on the title of a popular magazine of the time, *Salut les copains*, published by Daniel Filipacchi and devoted to stars such as Johnny Hallyday. Varda's film obviously has to do with *another* culture of music and stars.

sections succeed one another within a movement, when photographs come the closest to moving images.

Rapid changes characterize the editing. For this half-hour photography film, Varda used 1500 photographs she had taken during a trip to Cuba with a Rolleiflex and a Leica without automatic release. Varda stresses instantaneity and fragmentation through the mechanicalness[21] of the editing. The film thus underscores the function of photography as a second nature. Indeed, photography does not appear in the form of a postcard, a "window on the world", or an ideal image, but rather as a sample of framing choices, motifs, and compositions. In that sense, *Salut les Cubains* looks to the reverse of the production of postcards showing "views" of foreign countries; as a travelogue confronted with the heritage of this iconography, the film appears, in part because of its "dislocated" aspect, as a comment on the genre.

Successive temporal sections, some of them organized as series, produce a contrary effect to that of postcards, which present themselves as "natural", or even "ideal" representations of the world, or as "the imaginary sampling of a piece of landscape" (Serge Daney).[22] These series create brief temporal ellipses (four such animations appear in the film) and differ from other accelerated series of shots, in which intervals between filmed photographs are characterized by jumps in spaces or motifs.[23] The fragmentary editing showcases the temporal dimension of photography in the sense of some theoreticians of the photographic image, whether they refer to it as "the spatial configuration of a moment" or as a "ghostlike reality" (Kracauer), as a mummy, an impression, or a print (Bazin), bearing as its *noema* "the living image of a dead thing" (Barthes).[24]

At the very moment when still images become more "lively" thanks to successive photographs outlining a movement, *Salut les Cubains* thus paradoxically presents a memento mori. In a wide, bright hall, a man dances according to this serial principle: Cuban singer Beny Moré, the "king of rhythm". Varda photographed his spontaneous choreography to a *montuno* in rapid series. With the rostrum camera, she made the dancer vibrate again. Moré's body then moves as an effect of stroboscopic movements, in sync with the song. From time to time, the rostrum camera dwells a little longer on one of the poses to intensify the syncopation with a forward movement. A fade to black ends the performance and opens on a complement to the sequence, a series of portraits accompanied by

---

21 Frieda Grafe reads a sensitivity to natural rhythm into the "non-natural" rhythm of the film. On the paradoxical nature of the film, see Frieda Grafe, "Les Créatures" (1967), in *Film für Film, Schriften*, vol. 9 (Berlin: Brinkmann & Bose, 2006) 57.

22 Daney, *Persévérance* 73.

23 Agnès Varda explains the musical rhythm of these shots by the manual release of her Leica. See Varda, *Varda par Agnès* 133.

24 Siegfried Kracauer, "Photography" [1927], trans. Thomas Levin, *Critical Inquiry* 19.3 (Spring 1993): 431; André Bazin, "The Ontology of the Photographic Image" (1945), in *What Is Cinema?*, trans. Hugh Gray, vol. 1 (Berkeley: University of California Press, 2004) 9–16; Barthes, *Camera Lucida* 79.

Varda's commentary: "Hail to Beni Moré, who unfortunately passed away between the moment these images were made and the film's completion. Hail to
the dead king." This coda to the dance sequence does not rely on the form of the
series as previously, but on another, even more unsettling mobile form: a play of
dissolves which does not suggest the movement of a body, but its intermittent
appearance, and even its disappearance.[25]

In this instance, the commentary names the temporal function of photography,
pointing out its sudden "ageing". To quote Kracauer, "The recent past that
claims to be alive is more outdated than that which existed long ago and whose
meaning has changed".[26] Photography, once current, now represents "what is
utterly past"; it has become a ruin, a ghost, like letters from a distant past – and
old melodies, which play the same role, according to Kracauer.[27]

Only the filmic form can actualize this embodiment of disappearance and the
second nature of photography – for through photography, it is "the first time the
inert world presents itself in its independence from human beings".[28] Kracauer
also stresses the disintegration of natural elements in the reality of photography,
which is comparable to that of an archive: "This warehousing of nature promotes
the confrontation of consciousness with nature".[29] If the memento mori of *Salut
les Cubains*, conveyed by the commentary, may thus serve as a kind of allegory
for photography, Kracauer also outlines in this passage the historical function of
storing photography assumed by the moving image – through its deliberate form
of exhibition, serialization, and fragmentation.

Salut les Cubains opens with moving images showing the preview of an exhibition
on Cuba in Paris. A group of photographers and cameramen appears at the center
of these images in the opening credits. The film's title appears superimposed on
a freeze frame that features Alain Resnais shooting, which may be interpreted not
only as Varda's nod to her former editor and filmmaker-friend (during the
opening credits, she can be seen in the company of Joris Ivens, Jacques Demy,
and later, Chris Marker), but also as a foretoken for a form that suspends and
fragments at once.

In the end, the film assumes the status of a *photography archive* fully in line with
Kracauer's utopia of the deliberately fragmented organization of a "general
inventory" of photography, through the associative juxtaposition of sections in
"unusual combinations".[30] Kracauer thus refers to the spatiotemporal disconti-

---

25   The legendary science-fiction photography film *La Jetée*, directed by Chris Marker and released the same
      year (1963), relies on similar effects.

26   Kracauer, "Photography" 430.

27   Kracauer, "Photography" 430. Further on Kracauer also writes: "Like the photographic image, the playing
      of an old hit song or the reading of letters written long ago also conjures up anew a disintegrated unity.
      This ghostlike reality is *unredeemed*." Kracauer, "Photography" 431.

28   Kracauer, "Photography" 435.

29   Kracauer, "Photography" 435.

nuity of images characteristic of film, which is also the principle best suited to describe the fragmentation of photography: "The disorder of the detritus reflected in photography cannot be elucidated more clearly than through the suspension of every habitual relationship between the elements of nature".[31] According to Kracauer, one of the central functions of cinema may be the adequate exhibition of photography by means of editing.

Photo – Film – Installation

The last type of relationship between photography and film in Varda's work is also the most current. Recent installations, including as part of the exhibition *L'Île et elle*, are but an extension of photography through other means. Photography, but also cinema, are now exhibited in an expanded form. Since the 1950s, Varda's films have certainly evinced a predilection for the apparatus of the exhibition and the art of contemplation. Running through her work are many citations from painting (partly owing to her training at the École du Louvre) and references to photography (punctuated by rhythms oscillating between stillness and movement), but also the artistic expression of a figurative semiology of everyday culture based on the study of a collection of objects or images. Just as she was able, for her commissioned short film *Du côté de la côte*, to cast light on the mythologies of the Riviera through gorgeous colours and citations-compositions, Varda presented the visitor of her installation *La grande carte postale*,[32] a giant interactive postcard, with visual clichés attached to Noirmoutier island as they are materialized in this type of mass-production of memory images.

In her book *L'Île et elle*, Varda devotes several pages to a montage of texts and images on postcard culture, obviously an object of her passion as a collector. Looking at postcards from World War I, she notes – like Serge Daney – a particular mixture of individual expression and cliché: "Reading these private correspondences seemed less inquisitive when they traveled in the open; but since those that traveled in envelopes may be found in attics or secondhand markets, they are read with more affection than curiosity".[33] *La grande carte postale* thus pays homage to the ambivalence generated by this type of object.

The foreground of the giant postcard features a blond beauty, colourised in the style of the 1950s, turning her naked body towards the sea and her face towards the beach (and accordingly towards the onlooker). In the background, the insertion of a beacon indicates that we are looking at an island that can be accessed by foot at low tide. In the installation, the respective apparatuses of cinema and photography are finally turned upside down by the scale of images. On the one

30   Kracauer, "Photography" 435.

31   Kracauer, "Photography" 436.

32   The installation was designed in 2006 as part of the exhibition *L'Île et elle* at the Fondation Cartier.

33   Agnès Varda, *L'Île et elle* (Arles: Actes Sud, 2006) 12.

Fig. 12. La Grande
Carte postale ou
Souvenir de
Noirmoutier,
A. Varda, 2006.
[©Agnès Varda.]

hand the miniature, which usually invites to manipulation and writing, has turned into a giant surface. To be sure, this surface may be manipulated, but only at a distance, through a console with push buttons that looks like a viewpoint indicator placed before a coastal and bodily landscape – with the large nude of a woman voluptuously lying in the sand in the foreground. On the other hand, the cinema screen has been transformed into a series of hidden miniatures: indeed, small openings are carved out within the painting of *La Grande carte postale*. These films do not appear spontaneously – they have to be opened, like letters, by the visitors manipulating the buttons. However, their intervention is not necessary for a black-and-white water sprite to be projected on the body as soon as the miniatures close again.

In different areas of the maritime view, five windows are inserted to present other images, like fields of association. Behind the typical Noirmoutier motif (the

Fig. 13. La Grande
Carte postale ou
Souvenir de
Noirmoutier
A. Varda, 2006,
view of an installation
(Fondation Cartier).
[©Agnès Varda.]

beacons of the passage du Gois), a series of postcards unfold, featuring other views of the island; behind the flight of a gull, the video image of a bird covered in oil suddenly appears; between the buttocks of the naked lady, Varda inserted a sketch that tells a naughty story of little boys in the manner of Jacques Demy's childhood portrait in *Jacquot*. A window also opens in the shimmering surface of the sea to reveal bodies floating under water. In creating this system of oppositions, Varda said she was inspired by Jacques Prévert: "When I see a swimmer, I paint a drowned man".[34]

Finally, a fifth window provides a direct citation from *Jacquot*: the close up of Jacques Demy's hands as he lets the sand run through his fingers is the hidden memento mori of the installation. It is Varda's signature on *La Grande carte postale*, the image of an island she discovered and loved thanks to her husband, who is now dead.[35] The "large postcard" thus turns out to be the paradigm of a whole work where death and life, kitsch and art, photography and cinema, stillness and movement do not conflict. In Agnès Varda's figurative worlds, they are always thought in their mutual relations.

---

34 Varda quotes the line from the character of the painter in Marcel Carné's *Le Quai des Brumes* (1938) in her book on the exhibition. Varda, *L'Île et elle* 30.

35 Varda, *Varda par Agnès* 26.

4

Freeze frame, Photograph, and Re-animation in Martin Scorsese's Films

Patricia Kruth

F reezing a frame, turning it into a black-and-white photograph lined with a white strip the size of the screen's edges, re-animating the subject: these are the three successive acts with which Martin Scorsese ends *Italianameri-can* (1974). The final segment of a film akin to a family album, and which the filmmaker structured around his mother, will serve as a main thread for this study. An essential work in the director's oeuvre,[1] *Italianamerican* will indeed function as a matrix of sorts in our examination of the relations between stillness and movement in Scorsese's cinema.

The freeze frame involves freezing an image, by contrast to stop motion, which consists in stopping the camera, then resuming filming, as Georges Méliès did to produce his visual tricks. In his dictionary, Frank Beaver defines it as "a motion-picture effect that stops (freezes) the motion of the film on a single frame and allows the chosen image to continue as if it were a still photograph".[2] Our thinking on the issue will center around four major films, *Italianamerican*, *Raging Bull* (1980), *GoodFellas* (1990), and *Casino* (1995), punctuating a time period over which the freeze frame was prominent in Scorsese's films (see filmography in the appendix). The figure, through a constant interaction with similar devices, allowed Scorsese to vary the movement of images: profilmic presence of photographs in the films, slow motions, double framing[3] (some shots in *The Age of Innocence*, 1993), as well as what I will refer to as "still images". In these shots, movement is frozen throughout, which makes the *process* resulting in the freezing

---

1 This strange film, which is also very funny, broaches themes central to the filmmaker: New York, Italian-Americans, family, and cooking – all expressed with unprecedented artistic freedom and humour. Quite a few years later, Scorsese did in fact tell his biographer, "*Italianamerican* [...] is, I think, the best film I ever made. It really *freed* me in style." Mary Pat Kelly, *Martin Scorsese: A Journey* (New York: Thunder's Mouth Press, 1991) 17.

2 Frank Beaver, *Dictionary of Film Terms* (New York: Twayne Publishers, 1994) 164.

3 "The process of duplicating and repeating every frame in an image sequence. The result is a new image sequence that appears to be moving at half the original speed." See http://www.highend3d.com/dictionary/d/double_framing.

of movement imperceptible. After *Casino* freeze frames disappeared almost completely, with the exception of two or three, barely perceptible, towards the end of *The Departed* (2006), in an altercation scene between gangsters and the police. As to variations in image speed, *Bringing Out the Dead* (1999) privileges fast motion, yet is exempt of freeze frames. Scorsese, it seems, has almost given up this figure as his cinema has become less "experimental" and more "classical".

Scorsese and the Freeze Frame

Scorsese is the only filmmaker in contemporary American cinema to have used the freeze frame with such consistency and regularity. Relations between stillness and movement appear inextricable from his very early films on, and are literally a matter of life and death in his first short, *What's a Girl Like You Doing in a Place Like This* (1963). The film playfully tells the story of a writer obsessing over the photograph of a man boating on a river (played by Scorsese himself). Neither his wedding to a painter nor psychoanalysis will help the writer overcome his obsession for the picture hanging on the wall, which turns into a photograph of the sea, then into moving images of the ocean where he will eventually drown. A filmic metalepsis has him jump from the diegesis into the apparatus represented by the animated photograph – thus become a film within the film. The experimental exploration of the relations between stillness and movement went on in the other short films and climaxed with Scorsese's thesis film *Who's That Knocking at My Door* (1969), a medley of filmic figures which features three freeze frames, some slow motions, still images, as well as single frames and posters of Hollywood films over the course of a plot proceeding through flashbacks.

The film was strongly inspired by New Wave filmmakers, who had dazzled Scorsese and were objects of unbounded admiration on his part. The origins of the figure of the freeze frame in the work of the American director could be traced back to François Truffaut. Coming after several avant-garde filmmakers such as Dziga Vertov and his *Man with a Movie Camera* (1929), Truffaut pioneered the extensive use of the freeze frame. While classical Hollywood cinema did involve a few examples such as Fritz Lang's *Liliom* (1934) and *Fury* (1936), or Joseph Mankiewicz's *All about Eve* (1950), the freeze frame has remained "virtually unfamiliar to 'classical' cinema", as Raymond Bellour noted.[4]

The figure, instead, seems inseparable from modernity, in the sense given to the notion in a certain tradition of film historiography. Kristin Thompson and David Bordwell thus write that "the famous ending to *400 Blows* (Truffaut, 1959) [in which Antoine Doinel faces the sea, then turns to the spectator, with the image freezing] turned the freeze frame into a privileged device to express an unresolved situation".[5] In fact, the technique has contributed to further reinforcing one of

---

4   Raymond Bellour, "L'interruption, l'instant" [1987], *L'Entre-Images. Photo. Cinéma. Vidéo* ["In Between Images. Photo. Cinema. Video"] (1990; Paris: La Différence, 2002) 112. See also p. 112–113 for a few commented examples.

the conventions of art cinema (the New Wave, Antonioni, Fellini), the open-ended narrative. The last shot of *It's Not Just You Murray!* (1964) falls into this category, as the crew of the film within the film, after dancing a Felliniesque farandole, pose for a camera using a flash. The family picture *concluding* Scorsese's short film *opens* it anew: the freeze frame, the arrested movement also constitute a new departure, as the thundering strains of a musical piece (Elgar's *Pomp and Circumstance March n°1*) can then be heard on the soundtrack and continues into the closing credits.

The use of the freeze frame as a closing figure bringing the development of the plot to a stop largely exceeds the boundaries of art cinema. To mention well-known examples, *Butch Cassidy and the Sundance Kid* (George Roy Hill, 1969) already featured a "frozen" final shot; so did *Thelma and Louise* (Ridley Scott, 1991) more recently. In the latter case, the suspension of narration was literally figured by the two female protagonists in their car, suspended in the air above the Grand Canyon and captured between life and death in a moment turning into eternity. The freeze frame has even become commonplace in contemporary cinema: in Woody Allen's *Melinda and Melinda* (2004), a photographic still marks (only once, not systematically) a provisional end to the fiction set within the fiction in the form of fragments, and the return to the primary fiction.

Other instances of the freeze frame in Truffaut's work seem to have made an impression upon Scorsese. In *Jules and Jim* the two friends reunite after a long separation and embrace: a brief freeze frame immortalizes the moment of happiness within the flow of time. Similarly, in *New York, New York* (1977), Jimmy Doyle puts his hand on Francine Evans's knee during a cab ride; she does not turn him away, and a barely noticeable freeze frame seals the beginning of their love affair. In *Jules and Jim* successive freeze frames of Catherine expressing a range of emotions also play out as snapshots; they pave the way for the still images resulting from the rapid-fire photo shoot of *Life Lessons* (1989). A last instance of influence could be the freeze frames in *L'argent de poche* (1976), which Truffaut used as transitions. Scorsese remembered it for *GoodFellas*, adapting and personalizing the figure. This is precisely what we propose to show: Scorsese eventually appropriated the freeze frame to integrate it into his own figurative system and reinvent it.

Italianamerican: To Show the Photographs That Make Up a Film

Italianamerican is a 16-mm, 45-minute documentary. Shot in two sessions of three hours each, the film is an interview by Scorsese of his parents Catherine and Charles in their New York apartment over the preparations for a meal, then around the table. The work, an example of direct cinema, features elements of

5   Kristin Thompson and David Bordwell, *Film History: An Introduction* (New York: McGraw-Hill, 1994) 523–524.

Fig. 1. Italianamerican,
Martin Scorsese, 1974.

the home movie and amateur cinema (or even of the cooking show) without quite turning into either one. It is also an experimental film for Scorsese, who never did anything like it before or afterwards.

Towards the end of the film Catherine, whose witty eloquence is inexhaustible, says that following her death, the fig tree her mother hated never blossomed again. The image of Mrs Scorsese then changes into a photograph thanks to a freeze frame. For analytical purposes, three steps may be distinguished in the transformation: first the smile freezes in the frame, which then turns black and white through a gradual desaturation of colours, before the camera zooms out, revealing a white edge around the portrait and suggesting a paper print [44'34] (Fig. 1). The single frame has taken on the materiality of a photograph – or at least, its equivalent in the film. Indeed, the run of film in the projector (and in this case, the length of the freeze frame) commands the length of the look, as "reading" time is one of the elements that distinguish photography from cinema.[6] The white-edge, black-and-white photograph is the outcome of a process that begins with a colour freeze frame and goes through a black-and-white freeze frame. It could be described as a series of degrees in the photographic freeze, as part of a dynamic of the photographic freeze, or even as a rather well-suited oxymoron for Scorsese's universe: "a moving photographic freeze frame".

The mise-en-scène on the screen of various stages, from shooting to printing – in other terms, what Philippe Dubois calls the "photographic act" – is in this instance *suggested* and condensed in a few seconds. Besides, the indexical status of photography, what Barthes calls "deictic language",[7] its value as an enunciative trace, is "squared" in a sense: by zooming out the film points to the photograph, which itself figures its referent (the filmmaker's mother) through a metonymical process consisting in showing only her face. The joint shift to black and white and gradual loss of movement emphasize immobility and death.

6   See Peter Wollen, "Fire and Ice", [1984] in *The Photography Reader*, ed. Liz Wells (London, New York: Routledge, 2003) 76–80; commented on by Christian Metz, "Cinéma, photo, fétiche", in "Cinéma et psychanalyse," ed. Alain Dhote, *CinémAction* 50 (Condé-sur-Noireau: Corlet, 1989): 168–175.

7   Roland Barthes, *Camera Lucida. Reflections on Photography*, trans. Richard Howard (1980; New York: Farrar, Straus and Giroux, 1981) 5.

The freeze frame is also an essentially photographic act, resulting as it does in an "image that produces Death while trying to preserve life",[8] as Roland Barthes defined photography. The macabre play with the body of the mother illustrates Serge Daney's fine writing on the freeze frame: "a way to refer the film to its skeleton of still images, like one would a corpse to the ashes it always is".[9] What Régis Debray calls the "funerary genealogy of the image"[10] also comes to mind, as he writes: "*Simulacrum?* The specter. *Imago?* The wax cast of the faces of the dead."[11] The face, becoming *Spectrum*, refers both to the return of the dead and spectacle, and takes us back to the common origins of photography and film. It also suggests, in the wake of André Bazin or Gilles Deleuze, that photography be defined as "a kind of 'moulding.'"[12]

Still, Scorsese refuses photography, or the "flat Death",[13] and re-animates his mother – resuscitates her, as it were. The temptation of photography lasted but one moment and the photograph, which had temporarily reduced his mother to a two-dimensional image, eventually brings her out thanks to cinema – a medium which, by contrast, appears capable of sculpting in time.

Furthermore, the context of the family album should be underlined. As a theme, the family holds much importance for Scorsese, as is well-known. In *The Age of Innocence* (1993), he played himself the part of the wedding photographer. Besides *Italianamerican,* family photographs are also featured in *Who's That Knocking at My Door, New York, New York, Raging Bull, GoodFellas,* and *Casino,* while home movies appear in *Mean Streets* and *Raging Bull. Italianamerican,* a portrait of the filmmaker's parents telling their memories, is often shot as a home movie and includes all the figures of the "poorly made", to paraphrase Roger Odin: shaky camera, sudden and unjustified zooms, etc. As an album, it is largely invisible though. The real film, narrated through stories by Catherine and Charles in a succession of oral flashbacks recounting the past of the family, is the one never seen. Indeed, a few old family pictures have been magnified to the dimensions of the screen, and Catherine can be seen showing photos of the honeymoon the couple has just taken to Italy after forty years of marriage. Yet in the end Scorsese does not give much to see and spectators are invited to imagine the family memories and make their own movie.

8   Barthes, *Camera Lucida* 92.

9   "Façon de renvoyer le film à son squelette d'images fixes, comme un cadavre aux cendres qu'il est de toute façon." Serge Daney, *Photogénies* 5 (1984), quoted in Bellour, *L'Entre-Images* 113.

10   Régis Debray, *Vie et mort de l'image. Une histoire du regard en Occident* ["Life and Death of the Image: A History of the Look in the West"] (Paris: Gallimard, 1992) 28.

11   Debray, *Vie et mort de l'image* 19.

12   "One might consider photography [...] as a molding, the taking of an impression, by the manipulation of light." André Bazin, *What Is Cinema?*, "The Ontology of the Photographic Image", trans. Hugh Gray, *Film Quarterly* 13:4 (1960): 7. "Photography is a kind of 'moulding'." Gilles Deleuze, *Cinema 1. The Movement-Image* [1983] (Minneapolis: The University of Minnesota Press, 1986) 24.

13   Barthes, *Camera Lucida* 92.

Fig. 2. Raging Bull,
M. Scorsese, 1980.

Finally, the photographic freeze also reveals a major Scorsesian figure,[14] the association of opposites (life and death, in this case), which I have elsewhere referred to as the chaudfroid, a culinary term.[15] The freeze frame in *Raging Bull* illustrates it in a variety of ways.

Raging Bull: the Figured Figure

After his defeat against Sugar Ray Robinson, Jake La Motta (Robert de Niro) stands alone in the changing-room. A camera movement encircles him as he looks at himself in a full-length mirror, then draws near the reflecting surface. The atmosphere is one of complete silence. After a straight cut to the next shot, the camera moves from the bottom of the mirror to come to a standstill on a close up of a bucket filled with water and ice in which the boxer has put his hand. He moves it and clenches his fist. The watery noise of stirred ice cubes then gives way to the musical theme, the intermezzo in Pietro Mascagni's *Cavalleria Rusticana*, which slowly emerges and grows louder, as if it were coming out of the water at the same time as the fist, in the foreground and in the center of the frame, is shown stiff, "frozen" in the midst of ice cubes. A short forward tracking shot seems to make us closer to this ice sea, inviting us to penetrate inside the image. [39' 35"] (Fig. 2).

This constitutes a model figure, a rare moment when content and form, diegesis

14 Other reasons besides the family as subject matter make the freeze frame on Mrs Scorsese very... Scorsesian. The edge that serves as a frame, transforming the film image into a photograph, goes hand in hand with the disappearance of off-screen space: suddenly anemic and lifeless, Catherine cannot escape the framed picture in which she is captive. The image, with its frame within the frame, may be related to the motif of the cage and the theme of confinement, both recurrent from one film to the next. See "Cages scorsésiennes. Thème de l'enfermement" ["Scorsesian Cages. The Theme of Confinement"], which includes captures of single frames examplifying different types of "frame within the frame" in Scorsese's films. Patricia Kruth, *Figures filmiques: les mondes new-yorkais de Martin Scorsese et Woody Allen* (Villeneuve d'Ascq: Presses du Septentrion, 2002) 395–408.

15 See the nomenclature of Scorsesian figures in Kruth, *Figures filmiques* 519, as well as Patricia Kruth, "La cuisine et la peinture: aux origines du monde de Martin Scorsese" ["Cooking and Painting: the Origins of Martin Scorsese's World"], *CinémAction* 108 (2003): 141–50.

and apparatus become one through the literalization of the figure of the *freeze frame*, which is taken to the letter: an image that gets frozen. In this brief moment, "the form that space takes and that which language gives itself"[16] coincide in a figured figure. This shot, in which content appears as an aspect of form, also refers to Freud's "means of representation in dreams",[17] that is, to the form of the dream often used to represent its content. It instantly gives the biographical summary that it introduces an oneiric tonality and an imaginary dimension, along with the music already present from the beginning. The presence of the mirror further contributes to this, as though things had already shifted to the other side.

Insofar as the freeze takes place in several stages, as in *Italianamerican*, the expression "moving photographic freeze frame" seems appropriate. Indeed, once the freeze has been performed and the image is frozen, the forward tracking shot appears to impart a slight movement to the water, causing it to scintillate. Such *dynamic stasis* or *static dynamic* is part of *Raging Bull*'s overall theme, the deformation of the body. Already, in *Italianamerican*, Scorsese subjected the body of his mother to a visual play.

Indeed, in the sequence that follows, photographs of La Motta all point to a dynamic stasis: either the boxer's movement is suggested by its trace (the passing of time is figured by the blur), or the movement is captured through a "section", with the pugilist's posture representing one instant in a more ample gesture that it leaves to the imagination, as when Jake is shown raising his arms, for example. The opposition between stillness and movement also finds a resolution in the slow motions that break up movements. Scorsese thus explores different image speeds and different possibilities in the expression of movement: the photographic freeze frame of the ice bucket is one of these and may be considered as one step on a scale ranging from twenty four images per second (there is no speeded-up motion in the film) to a photograph or a freeze frame.

The shot of the bucket calls to mind both frost (the *freeze frame*, the fist that freezes, the presence of ice) and thaw (melting ice cubes, music metaphorically spreading). Finally, the photographic freeze frame which serves as a transition both concludes the changing-room sequence and opens the following one.

The following sequence is like a backward progression in a film which itself relies on a series of chronological flashbacks within a circular structure (*Raging Bull* begins and ends in La Motta's dressing room in 1964). The editing of the sequence marks the passing of time in an accelerated form (four years are condensed in 2'30" thanks to ellipses), drawing a parallel between Jake's private life through sepia home movies and his professional life through black and white footage.

16 This is the definition Gérard Genette gives of the figure in "La littérature et l'espace" (1969), *Figures II* (Paris: Le Seuil, 1979) 47.

17 Sigmund Freud, *The Interpretation of Dreams* [1900], trans. James Strachey (New York: Discus Books, 1965) chapter VI, section C.

The first paradox of this summary, arising as it does from a freeze frame, is that the figured time produces an impression of slowdown, of dilatation not unlike that of the musical air escaped from the ice bucket. The sense of suspended time, of a time between brackets, does indeed owe to the slow rhythm of the nostalgic music and the use of still images and slow motions for boxing fights. In fact, the way in which the editing sequence is introduced (the camera moves closer to the water and the sound grows louder) seems to announce a flashback. Just as paradoxical is the use of a series of mock old-fashioned home movies, with their washed-out colours and the scratches caused by too many runs in the projector – in short, of films functioning as memories – to represent a progression towards the future.[18]

GoodFellas: Freezing the Image to Hear the Film?

Difference and repetition operate again in *GoodFellas* (136'), which features twelve freeze frames, including six over the first fifteen minutes (see list in the appendix). These frequent, visible pauses are flaunted, concentrated as they are at the beginning of the film.

Eleven of these freezes appear over the voice of the male protagonist and main narrator, Henry Hill (Ray Liotta), and contribute to the expression of a subjective point of view. The last one, which appears in sixth position in the film (Henry being congratulated by the "goodfellas" as he exits the courthouse, Fig. 3) serves to fix a memorable moment in the manner of a family picture and functions as a shifter within fiction (Henry is an adult in the following sequence), not unlike the freeze in *It's a Wonderful Life* (Frank Capra, 1946).

The freeze frames in *GoodFellas* have as their primary, possibly paradoxical function, to allow to better hear. Indeed, in this visually rich and complex work – with the care given to the choice of sets and settings, colours, details, virtuoso camera movements, etc. – the overflowing voice-over can be dizzying. The freeze frame, inseparable from the visual and verbal frenzy, occasionally gives spectators time to catch their breath and fix their attention: it is in the service of the voice-over, so to speak. A visual figure, it also functions as an acoustic device. When Jimmy (Robert de Niro) appears for the first time, for instance (5), the photographic freeze frame makes it possible for the voice-over portraying him to add further information, and for the audience to process it. Similarly, as Jimmy and Henry walk in the street (9), a freeze helps bringing out an important piece of information (still conveyed in voice-over), namely, that the former is going to murder Morrie. Towards the end of the film, freezes 11 and 12 underline the changing relationship between Jimmy and Henry, with mutual mistrust creeping in and the gap between appearances and reality widening. Such gap is already

---

18   To put things differently, this freeze frame and the summary that follows it are examples of an elementary
        Scorsesian figure, the repetition or variation on a theme – in this case, the association of opposites.

Fig. 3. GoodFellas,
M. Scorsese, 1990.

Fig. 4. GoodFellas,
M. Scorsese, 1990.

hinted at earlier in the sequence through what might be called a "compensated tracking shot" (the camera simultaneously zooms in and tracks back so that the backdrop undergoes subtle changes even as characters sitting at the table in the foreground do not move) and a voice-over commentary ("on the surface of things, of course everything was supposed to be fine"). Together, the compensated tracking shot and the freeze frames concur to convey somewhat redundantly a death threat, the "beginning of the end" to the rule of the "goodfellas".

It would be inaccurate, however, to equate freeze frame with important information. Scorsese's use of the figure has nothing systematic to it. Before the sequence just mentioned, for example, the babysitter who is going to smuggle the drugs on the plane is shown in the kitchen. As she prepares to give a phone call, a freeze frame shows her hands, one holding a cigarette, the other a plane ticket, with her head partly out of the frame (10) (Fig. 4). This is a random instant and the freeze could have been performed on another image in the sequence, or could even have been skipped. Like previous freeze frames in the street or at the restaurant, there is nothing remarkable about its composition; it does not stress an emotion on a face, since the face is out of frame, precisely. By contrast to the freezes already examined, the intention to elicit an emotion from the audience cannot be put forward as a justification, either. Combined with the use of slow motion, ceaseless camera movements, and occasionally boisterous music (the helicopter sequence), the twelve freeze frames in *GoodFellas* constitute breaks in the rhythm of the film and partake of its fitful, halting movement – in the end, a form well-suited to the portrayal of a protagonist whose behaviour is often hit-and-miss and unpredictable. The freezes help express the state of mental confusion in which he lives, a world of interchangeable signs where the preparation of tomato sauce competes with that of the drugs (as in the parallel editing sequence at the end of the film), where delivering firearms and cooking ribs for dinner hold the same importance.

Seven of the freeze frames take place in the course of a sequence or a shot and set the action moving again, in the mode of the chaudfroid already noted in other films. Among these, the first of two freeze frames in the sequence of the burial of a gangster killed by a goodfella, at night in the forest, is a new instance of freeze frame (7). It consists in a low-angle shot of Jimmy and could be referred to as a "moving frame" insofar as it is a freeze frame that suddenly "unfreezes". This freeze, along with the following one (8, which repeats 1), also points to an important aspect of Scorsese's work, montage. Indeed, the episode has already appeared in the pre-credits sequence, with some of the same shots, but edited differently. Scorsese thus demonstrates how the "same" story may be told in a different form. What is more, this cutaway shot (7) and the slow motion shot of Tommy that follows belong in the sequence of the bar murder, which has already been shown. Still, their visual aspect perfectly fits in its new context, a forest at night, and the power of the voice-over is so central in the construction of a narrative continuity that the fact that these are indoor shots and have little to do with the context may be overlooked in watching the segment.

The five other freeze frames are used to close a sequence. Could they be exceptions to what seems to be the rule, a dynamic of contradictory forces in which the Scorsesian freeze frames take place in the context of new departures, of a freeze soon followed by "unfreezing"? In fact, the opposite is true.

Two of them get the action moving again or serve as a transition between sequences. One is freeze frame 6, which I have already mentioned, and the other is the first freeze frame of the film, which puts a stress on the last word uttered in Henry's sentence, "I always wanted to be a gangster". Following Henry's movement of slamming the car trunk, it launches the opening credits, with the music already beginning and bridging between the two.

The remaining three freeze frames quite clearly mark the end of sequences as well as their apex. These three "frozen" images are associated with heat and/or flames and/or colours red or orange. So it goes with the mailman, whom the gangsters have threatened to put in the pizza oven, frozen in an horizontal position and grimacing with pain, his open mouth showing broken teeth, the whole picture calling to mind a Francis Bacon painting (3) (Fig. 5). The second one features Henry, immobilized in his run as he flees the scene after setting cars on fire (4) (Fig. 6), while the third, a freeze frame of Henry, gradually turns to an orange tint while the sizzle of oil can be heard on the soundtrack – a sound that recurs

Fig. 5. GoodFellas,
M. Scorsese, 1990.

Fig. 6. GoodFellas,
M. Scorsese, 1990.

throughout the film any time some meat is cooked. (8) This all takes place in a context in which, from pizza places to diners to gangsters' names (Mr and Mrs. Roastbeef) to macabre gastronomic jokes (as the corpse/chicken is unburied), cooking plays an essential part, as in many other of Scorsese's films, *Italianameri-can* to begin with.

Casino: Freezes, Flashes, and Hysteria

Casino alone would deserve a whole chapter, as it marks a culmination in the number of freeze frames and the diversity of relations between stillness and movement it explores. I will simply point to a few avenues for analysis. Scorsese constantly plays with the boundaries between freeze frame, still image, and immobile framing with no diegetic movement (situations involving for instance a still or dead character). The film features 14 freeze frames, in addition to about 13 still images.[19] (see list in the appendix)

Casino also constitutes a climax because in it the staging of the photographic act

---

19 The approximation in the latter figure owes to the swift editing pace, which does not always allow to distinguish between different categories and, quite obviously in such a case, pausing the image oneself does not prove of any help at all.

Fig. 7. Casino,
M. Scorsese, 1995.

Fig. 8. Casino,
M. Scorsese, 1995.

suggested in *Italianamerican* is *actualized* on a large scale thanks to the presence throughout the film of public, posed photo shoots as well as snapshots, often taken with a flash. This could be described as a mise-en-abyme of the act of shooting, since it ushers in freeze frames and still images.

The noisy photo shoots make it possible both to contrast and draw parallels between the public domain of appearances (Sam/Ace Rothstein, played by Robert de Niro, is a Las Vegas celebrity) and the reality of privacy (his wife Ginger – Sharon Stone –, who has an affair with his best friend, is tailed by private detectives). The two protagonists are repeatedly photographed, once together and several times separately (Sam in his official duties, Ginger without her knowing) in rather similar ways: cameras equipped with flashguns whose activation causes a loud noise and gives out a blinding light. Boundaries between posed photographs and snapshots thus get blurred, and accordingly the distinction between privileged moments and random moments, sampled from temporal continuity, is erased.[20] For example, when the couple are photographed next to the swimming pool (a situation already found in *Raging Bull*) at an official party, they are bombarded, "caught" by photo reporters and their aggressive flashguns. The photograph does not feature a smiling couple in the immortalization of a privileged moment, but rather a moving image punctuated with the flashes of the shoots, which appear as interchangeable moments among other possibilities and underscore the artificiality of the situation.

20   On the different types of moments, and more particularly Bergson's opposition between privileged moment and any-moment whatever, see Maria Tortajada, "La vérité de l'instant. L'instant photographique dans les films de Rohmer" ["The Truth of the Moment. The Photographic Instant in Rohmer's Films"], *Cinémathèque* 10 (Fall 1996): 81.

In *Raging Bull*'s pool-side photo-shoot scene, La Motta asks his wife and children to pose, so that a photographer equipped with a huge camera and a bulb flashgun immortalizes his happiness, which he tells a reporter about. The episode is punctuated with his commands ("Smile!"). At that point the couple are already divided but the photographs have to provide the semblance of family felicity and social success. The photographic context is set up through quick shots on camera parts and on the photographer, yet without any freeze frame. The only freeze frame corresponds to the moment when La Motta's wife and one of their sons are photographed – again, with a flash. The features of the two smiling faces are visible on the overexposed image, in what could be referred to as a "forced" privileged moment.

The swimming pool scene in *Casino*, a variation on the *Raging Bull* scene, features six freeze frames resulting from the shoot: they do not immortalize the happiness of the couple, as superficial as it may be, but the context of the shoot itself. They are banal images, extremely brief shots corresponding to random moments, isolating a few anonymous faces and interchangeable objects of the photographic environment: photographers, cameras, electronic flashguns (Figs. 7, 8). *Casino*, a very violent film in the tradition of Michael Powell's 1960 *Peeping Tom*, is a work on the violence and danger, not of cinema, but of photography, often materialized in the brutality of flashlights.[21]

This violence is also foreshadowed – without freeze frames – in *Raging Bull*, with the photographs of the caged boxer, taken with a flash; and in *The Aviator* (2005), as the protagonist, blinded by the flashlights, appears in court like a hunted animal. A comparison is established between killing and photographing, and they become synonymous through the similarity of the noises that characterize them: the amplified and repeated rattle of guns echoes the sound of flashguns going off all around and the shutter releases that allow cameras to take photographs in rapid-fire succession.

Freeze frames, still images, and/or camera sounds, with or without flashes, are also associated with strong emotions, pathological states, exhibitionism – in short, with all types of excesses: Ace's love at first sight with Ginger (Fig. 9), conjugal jealousy, Ginger's hysterical behaviour, murders, and the death of the main female character. Most of the time, however, they do not single out a paroxysmal moment, but a random one, and/or do not bring a sequence to its conclusion. This is the case for the freeze on Ace, spattered with the blue glare of flashlights during an official ceremony (Fig. 10) or the two freezes on the fall of a man riddled with bullets during a bar shootout (5), which could have occurred somewhere else, or which, like the freeze on the babysitter in *GoodFellas*, could

---

21 On the flash as the cause for the fits of hysterical catalepsy triggered by Charcot in his female patients, and the photographs that bear witness to these experiments, see Tom Gunning, "Bodies in Motion", in *Arrêt sur image, fragmentation du temps: aux sources de la culture visuelle moderne/Stop Motion, Fragmentation of Time: exploring the Roots of Modern Visual Culture*, eds. François Albera, Marta Braun, and André Gaudreault (Lausanne: Payot, 2002) 26.

Fig. 9. Casino,
M. Scorsese, 1995.

Fig. 10. Casino,
M. Scorsese, 1995.

even have been dispensed with. Another example among several is the close shot of a sadistic killer using a baseball bat (14), which evokes the father belting his son in *GoodFellas*. His impetus seems to come to a halt for a moment, before the action resumes during the unbearable torture scene in the forest when Sam's best friend is buried alive with his brother. In *Casino*, the freeze frame is tied to the death of characters, increasingly so as the film progresses; in the context of gambling that defines Las Vegas, Scorsese himself "signs the death warrant".[22]

In "Cinéma, Photo, Fétiche", Christian Metz discerningly notes that "one thing is [...] striking: while we know that a film is made out of photographs, we do not see any of these".[23] Scorsese's freeze frames do have us *see* these invisible still images, constantly reminding the audience of the existence of the film as film, emphasizing its *materiality*. This is one of the reasons why freeze frames in Scorsese's cinema, which exist within a system of figures that gives *time* some elasticity, should also be examined in relation to *spatial* figures that underline the presence of a filmic object. I am thinking, for example, of the irises in the pictorial context of *Life Lessons* (1989), which serve as rubber bands ceaselessly stretching the canvass of the screen, materializing the surface of the shot and its plasticity; of the chromatic fades in *The Age of Innocence*, which constitute exits from the diegesis and refer to the very colour of the film stock, to its emulsion; or of the foreshadowed effects in *Cape Fear* (1991), in which colouring combines with the

22 "L'arrêt sur image (...) joue avec *l'arrêt de mort*." Bellour, *L'Entre-images* 11. Translator's note: the play on words is lost in translation here – in French, the same word, *arrêt*, refers to the freeze frame (*arrêt sur image*) and to the death warrant (*arrêt de mort*).

23 Metz, "Cinéma, Photo, Fétiche": 175.

use of negatives in a context of X-ray photographs. To put it differently, examining freeze frames in Scorsese's films leads to a study of the relations between photography, cinema, and painting.

Besides, whether associated with silence as in *Italianamerican*, with opera music (*Raging Bull*), the voiceover (*GoodFellas*), or the rapid-fire photograph shoot (*Casino*), freeze frames allow the filmmaker to stop the film to have us *hear* movement. While it does change the rhythm, it is not so much to show us New York or Las Vegas asleep or dead as to involve us in what may be called the "rattle" of Scorsese's cinema.

Appendix:

MARTIN SCORSESE FILMOGRAPHY

FICTION FILMS (FEATURE FILMS AND MID-LENGTH FILMS): FREEZE FRAMES and other figures relevant in their study

In the list and descriptions below, "still images" refer to shots in which movement is frozen throughout, and where, contrary to the "freeze frame" (also referred to as "freeze"), the *process* preceding the stilled movement is not seen.

1969 **Who's That Knocking at My Door? (3 freeze frames + single frames and posters from Hollywood films + still images)**

1972 *Boxcar Bertha*

1973 *Mean Streets*

1974 *Alice Doesn't Live Here Anymore* / ***Italianamerican* (1 freeze frame)**

1976 *Taxi Driver*

1977 **New York, New York (1 freeze frame + 1 still image)**

1980 **Raging Bull (1 freeze frame + a few still images)**

1983 **The King of Comedy (1 freeze frame)**

1985 *After Hours*

1986 *The Color of Money*

1988 *The Last Temptation of Christ*

1989 **Life Lessons (episode from New York Stories) (1 freeze frame + a few still images)**

1990 **GoodFellas (12 freeze frames + 1 still image)**

1991 *Cape Fear* (X-ray photographs, negatives, tints)

1993 *The Age of Innocence* (tints)

1995 *Casino* (14 freeze frames + 13 still images)

1997 *Kundun*

1999 *Bringing Out the Dead* (speeded-up motion on several occasions)

2002 *Gangs of New York*

2005 *The Aviator* (photographs with flash, no freeze frames)

2006 *The Departed* (2 freeze frames)

Finally, it should be mentioned that photographs as profilmic objects and slow motions recur throughout Scorsese's work.

FREEZE FRAMES in *GoodFellas*

The voice-over associated to the freeze frames is always that of protagonist Henry Hill. There is no voice-over in shot 6.

1. [2' 03] END of sequence. Voice-over: "As far back as I can remember, I always wanted to be a gangster." Henry is then seen shutting the car's trunk close as the camera tracks forward before a freeze occurs on a medium close up of Henry. The song begins over the opening credits.

2. [6' 06] MIDDLE of sequence. Freeze on a pronounced low-angle shot: Henry's father belts him. Voice-over: "But after a while, he was mostly pissed because I hung around the cabstand. He knew what went on at that cabstand. And every once in a while I'd have to take a beating. But by then, I didn't care. The way I saw it : everybody takes a beating sometime."

3. [7' 08] END of sequence. The mailman grimaces with pain as his head is about to be shoved into an oven. Voice-over: "That was it. No more letters from the truant officers. No more letters from school. In fact, no more letters from anybody. Finally, after a couple of weeks, my mother had to go to the police and complain."

4. [9' 25] END. Henry's figure is seen as he runs away from the arson. Voice-over: "One day, one day, some of the kids from the neighborhood carried my mother's groceries all the way home. You know why ? It was out of respect."

5. [11' 39] END. Medium close-up of Jimmy and Paulie. Voice-over: "You see, Jimmy was one of the most feared guys in the city. He was first locked up at eleven and he was doing hits for mob bosses at sixteen."

6. [14' 36] END. Slight high-angle shot: Henry is congratulated by the gang as he exits the courthouse. A song begins.

7. [58' 28] MIDDLE. As Billy Batts is buried in the forest, Jimmy is seen in a pronounced low-angle shot with his arms outspread. A cutaway shot from the scene of Batts's murder in a bar follows. Part of a sentence is heard in voice-over : "Batts was part of the Gambino crew" [and was considered untouchable.]

8. [58' 38] END. Burial (continued). Same shot of Henry as 1. The shot turns amber to the sizzling sound of meat being broiled.

9. [1h 38' 50] MIDDLE. Henry and Jimmy walk in the street. Voice-over: "That's when I knew Jimmy was gonna wack Morrie. That's how it happens. That's how fast it takes for a guy to get wacked."

10. [1h 55' 42] MIDDLE. The baby-sitter in the kitchen with her plane ticket. Voice-over (beginning of sentence): "After everything I told her, after all her yeah, yeah bullshit" [she picks up the phone and calls from the house.]

11. [2h 09' 00] MIDDLE. At the diner. Close-up of Jimmy. Voice-over: "Jimmy had never asked me to wack somebody before and now he's asking me to go to Florida and do a hit with Anthony."

12. [2h 09' 13] MIDDLE. Reverse shot: a close-up of Henry. Voice-over : "That's when I knew I would have never come back from Florida alive."

FREEZE FRAMES in *Casino*

1. [10' 31] END OF SEQUENCE. Freeze with a blue tint (a **photograph** of Ace Rothstein **taken with a flash** as reporters shoot him during an official ceremony. **A public figure caught on the spot.** Retrospectively, he turns out to be a hounded character. (Following shot: a vertical high-angle shot)

2. [22' 54] Freeze / medium close-up of Ginger throwing chips in the casino as Ace observes her. (The song "Baby... you're the one" starts with the next shot, before Ginger is shown walking in slow motion.) **Love at first sight.**

3. [53' 00] A set of 6 very brief freezes on the photographers, the cameras, flashes during a photo shoot of the Rothstein couple at a banquet at the casino. **Emphasis on the context of a photo shoot in a public place** (not characters caught unaware). This is a variation on the photo shoot in the art gallery mixing freeze frames and still images at the end of *Life Lessons*.

4. [54' 37] END OF SEQUENCE. Very brief freeze: a close-up of Ace with a forced smile addressed at Ginger. His comment on the young man who complimented him on the beauty of his wife was heard just before: "I fired him the next day." **The freeze functions as a pause allowing the voice-over to resonate**, highlighting the public/private opposition, and pointing to **how deceitful appearances may be.**

5. [1h 04' 30] 2 very brief freezes within a sequence in slow motion showing a killing in a bar. **An aesthetics of violence.**

6. [1h 23' 20] END OF SEQUENCE. Freeze / medium close-up of the jacket of a man pocketing money. The voice-over mentioned just before that the bosses had noticed how the suitcases were becoming a bit lighter. **The pause emphasizes the voice-over** (see 4), illustrating it and fixing it visually.

7. [1h 33' 56] Freeze tinted blue (photograph with a flash) of a dead character in a montage sequence evoking a series of particularly bloody crimes culminating in an arson. **An aesthetics of violence.** See 5 and 1.

8. 9. 10. [2h 16' 22] Two gangsters are seated at a table, talking. One is asking for the truth, the other swears to tell it and stops speaking. A freeze is then followed by two still images, the shot and reverse shot of the characters. The movement resumes (the character keeps speaking after the suspension) at the end of the third shot (in a start from a freeze frame). This makes possible the (unexpected) intrusion in voice-over of a secondary character explaining the lie he is about to tell. Here we have a **function related to sound** (freezing the image to provide sound information), the truth of the voice opposed to **the deceitful appearances of the image** (see 4), as well as two mentions of **death** in the commentary (see the diner scene in *GoodFellas*).

11. [2h 18' 16] Freeze followed by a blurred zoom on a sandwich wrapped in foil: two policemen shoot at a man and kill him, mistaking the sandwich for a gun. Dark humor. Parallel with the photo shoots using flashes, **between killing and photographing.**

12. [2h 30' 19] Freeze on Ginger's hand as she forces a drawer open to get the keys for the safe at the bank (keys opening and locking are a leitmotiv in the film, and more generally keys and confinement are a Scorsesian theme).

13. [2h 38' 50] END OF SEQUENCE. Ginger's **death.** She collapses on the carpet.

14. [2h 42' 00] Freeze / medium close-up on a killer with a baseball bat during the **murder** of the two brothers in the forest. A random moment in the midst of a context of extreme **violence** (see *GoodFellas*).

5

Photo Browse and Film Browse: Between Images that Move and Images that Remain (in Chris Marker's Work)

André Habib and Viva Paci

"Photography is hunting, it is the hunting instinct without the desire to kill. It is the hunting of angels... You track down, you aim, you shoot, and... click! In place of death, you have the eternal."
Chris Marker, *If I Had Four Dromedaries* (1966)

"First the look, then the cinema which is the printing press of the look."
Chris Marker, *Le train en marche* ["The Train Rolls On", 1971]

Examining contact sheets, commenting on the images of a photo album, browsing through the photographs of a documentary collection, enjoying the digitalized images of a book of travel photographs with the click of a mouse: as many actions whose list refers to common, everyday processes in handling photographs. The same processes all appear in the work present in many pages of this collection of essays: Chris Marker's.

To attend to the work of this filmmaker – and already, to the familiar mention opening his films, "Chris Marker is a filmmaker, photographer, traveler, writer..."[1] – is to attend to a permanent work on photography. Marker's landmark creation, a constant question addressed to any thinking on the relations between photography and cinema, is evidently *La Jetée* (1962). Yet the few operations of *serialization* and *exhibition* of photography we have just enumerated – examining, commenting, browsing, reorganizing a series of photos – do not refer to *La Jetée*.

---

1   Our emphasis. Those of Marker's films produced by Anatole Dauman's production company Argos Films between 1956 and 1997 began with these words on a black background, before the opening credits. They include *Sunday in Peking* (1956), *Letter from Siberia* (1958), *La Jetée* (1962), *Junkopia* (1981), *Sans Soleil* (1982), and *Level Five* (1996). See *Anatole Dauman, Argos Films : Souvenir/Écran*, ed. Jacques Gerber (Paris: Éditions du Centre Pompidou, 1989). Similar phrases ceaselessly appear: "Chris Marker travels, films, photographs, and likes cats" is for instance the biographical note sent by Marker to Philippe Dagen for his entry in the volume *De mémoires* (Tourcoing/Paris: Le Fresnoy/Hazan, 2003), the catalogue for the exhibition *De mémoires*, which brought together various contemporary works raising the issue of memory.

From 1959 to 2009, many pieces in his work have involved processes of manipulation of photography and, of course, cinema: films (*If I Had Four Dromedaries*, *Photo Browse*, *Casque bleu* ["Blue Helmet"], *Souvenir d'un avenir* (*Remembrance of Things to Come*)), books (*Les Coréennes*, *Commentaires 1*, *Commentaires 2*, *Le Dépays* ["The Un-Homeland"]), CD-ROM (*Immemory*), blogs (Guillaume-en-Egypte), video installation (*The Hollow Men*), poster (*Petite planète*), or photography exhibits (*Staring Back*).

As it emphasizes permeability and passages between photography and cinema, this text simultaneously proposes that a triangular relation be considered when it comes to cinema and photography, with the notion of exhibition as the third pole.

Indeed, its premise is twofold. First, a film is always a site of exhibition for photography – mainly through its material characteristics, since the strip of film orders and exhibits a succession of single frames. This becomes all the more obvious and measurable when a film comes close to photography, calls it into question, uses it, places it in a mise en abyme, displays it. Often, besides simply showing a photograph to spectators – thereby exhibiting it – film bears on its very strip a series of single frames identical to one another, thus transporting the *photograph* itself, still and wrenched from movement, in its very heart. In that regard, a relevant corpus of films would include *Salut les cubains* (Agnès Varda, 1963), *Broadway by Light* (William Klein, 1958), *One Second in Montreal* (Michael Snow, 1969), *Letter to Jane* (Godard and Gorin, 1972), *Les photos d'Alix* (Jean Eustache, 1980) *Nostalgia* (Hollis Frampton, 1971) or, precisely, Marker's *La Jetée* (1962) and *Souvenir d'un avenir* (*Remembrance of Things to Come*) (2001).

Second, when photography is exhibited in the space of the museum or the gallery, it imposes an experience of time not limited to that of the time frozen in the image shot: as spectators move in front of the images hung on the walls, photography assumes a new temporality. An exhibition of photographs may in that sense become a *remediation* of cinema, even more so when the photographs in question come from the realm of cinema.[2]

Accordingly, what follows is a number of thoughts on *Staring Back*, a recent work by Chris Marker, operating *between* photography and cinema – playing on their common ground – and thereby offering readings on the practice of the filmmaker.

Attending the photography exhibit *Staring Back*, presented in Ohio, New York City, Paris, and Zurich (more locations have since been added to the list), and flipping through the book of photographs accompanying it,[3] visitors become the

---

2   See David Jay Bolter and Richard Grusin, *Remediation. Understanding New Media* (Cambridge, Mass.: MIT Press, 2001).

3   *Staring Back* was featured at the Wexner Center for the Arts, Ohio, May 12 – August 12, 2007, and at the Peter Blum Gallery in New York City, September 8 – November 3, 2007. It has since been presented – among other places – in Paris and Zurich, where it was part of the exhibition *Abschied von Kino/A Farewell to Movies* in the spring of 2008. See Chris Marker, *Staring Back* (Columbus, Ohio/Cambridge, Mass.: Wexner Center for the Arts and The Ohio State University/MIT Press, 2007), as well as *Chris Marker. A Farewell*

spectators of Chris Marker's cinematographic work as a whole.[4] In a way, passing by the exhibited photos places spectators in the position of unwinding a reel in front of a projector: they set them in motion and serialize them. The pieces of this exhibition should be approached retrospectively, as indicated in its title, to underline the major principles of a practice and to shed light on a strategy that has always been at work in Marker's production: return and reuse.[5] For Marker, going back over sites, touchstones, instants, faces captured at one point in the past consists in a reversal of the look, a search in the remains of memory for the object once looked at.[6] For the spectators, a familiarity with Marker's film work affords to trace back the stages in a life of travels, enthusiasms, commitments, and deep-seated loyalties in these photographs, in a play of oscillations. These traces lived in the memory previously unwound by a film, and are now *caught* in a photograph hung on a wall, with a single frame bridging between the two. Such is the case of the close-up of the girl of the Praia market whom Marker had met, observed, filmed and *fixed* in *Sans soleil* (1982), and who may now be seen in one of the photographic prints included in *Staring Back*. Some photograph or other, taken in China, Siberia, or Korea immediately evokes the cinematographic corollary that once set it into motion, furthering through a virtual duration (that of the films seen) the time peculiar to traveling, but also the time of the chronology of a work more than a half-century long, some moments of which are traveled. On these fragments torn from the flow of a film, one of Raymond Bellour's insights on the video installation *The Hollow Men* seems to apply particularly well to *Staring Back* as well, supporting the idea of a strong continuity between Chris Marker's various experiments with media: [7]

> The time of this fiction is indeed the pure experience of time produced through a multiplication of spaces, as the unmemorizable memory of an excess of movement wrenched from states of stillness. Such would be the necessary conditions for a memory of the century.[8]

The decisive operation in Marker's work lies less in the moment of captation than in the moment when what has been captured is reconsidered, when the person

---

to Movies/*Abschied vom Kino* (Zurich: Museum für Gestaltung, 2008). On these two exhibitions, see also *Chris Marker et l'imprimerie du regard*, eds. André Habib and Viva Paci (Paris: L'Harmattan, 2008).

4   On the increasingly frequent relations between the practice of filmmakers and their photographic exhibitions, see André Habib and Viva Paci's chapter "Exposer, entre photographie et cinéma" ["Exhibiting, between Photography and Cinema"], in *Les Espaces de l'image*, ed. Gaëlle Morel (Montreal: Éditions "Le mois de la photo", 2009).

5   On the strategies of *reuse* in Marker's work, see Viva Paci: *"This is (not) the end*. Quelques notes sur l'œuvre de Chris Marker et sur des images et des mots qui restent, et reviennent, comme des souvenirs [*"This is not the end*. Some Notes on Chris Marker's Work and on Some Images and Words That Remain and Recur, Like Memories"], in *Fonction/Fiction*, (Montreal: Dazibao, 2008) 73–89.

6   Marker's work features Orphic motifs, which we cannot develop here. Let us simply mention that he authored an article on Cocteau's *Orphée* in 1950: "Orphée", *Esprit* 173 (November 1950): 694–701.

7   See Habib and Paci, *Chris Marker et l'imprimerie du regard*.

8   Raymond Bellour, "Trois gestes (Jonas Mekas, Rinko Kawauchi, Chris Marker)", *Trafic* 60 (Winter 2006): 27.

who took the picture enters a dialogue with the person looking at it, a few months or a few decades later. From *Le Dépays* (1982) to *Sans Soleil* (1982), from *The Koumiko Mystery* (1965) to *Le Fond de l'air est rouge* (*Grin without a Cat*, 1977) to *If I Had Four Dromedaries* (1966) and *Immemory* (1997), a similar reversal, a reminiscence fixing the past in memory while reactivating its promise, appear at different levels, reestablishing a link with the past through the look the other once cast with his camera. This tension runs throughout the work: the gallery of "portraits" in grisaille exhibited in *Staring Back* was already largely incorporated in *Immemory* (the "Photo" section of the CD-ROM, in particular), which itself partly included photography books *Le Dépays* and *Les Coréennes*. The latter is featured in *Si j'avais quatre dromadaires*, a certain number of images (and faces) of which may be identified in *Staring Back*. And so on... The section of *Staring Back* titled "I Stare 1" encompasses forty years of political demonstrations – each demonstration the face of its time – in a gesture calling forth that of *Grin without a Cat* (itself taken up again and rearranged in 1993, 1997, 2008), which *reused* and stitched together images from *The Sixth Face of the Pentagon*, *On vous parle du Chili* ["We're Telling You About Chile", or "Chile Talks to You"], *¡Cuba Sí!*, and others. This simultaneously allows viewers to mark the space traveled (and the connection) from *Le Joli Mai* (1961) to *Chats perchés* (*The Case of the Grinning Cat*, 2004). As it happens, the peculiarity of this treatment of the past in *Staring Back*, but also in the CD-ROM *Immemory* and in *The Hollow Men*, is its "dulling" of temporal markers that would make their ascription to a precise time possible. As Bill Horrigan notes about the photography portfolio published in *Artforum*, out of which came *Revenge of the Eye*, itself the matrix for *Staring Back*,

> The subsequent digital manipulation he has imposed, and the startlingly flattened depth of some of the compositions, results in images unlike any others he has ever exhibited; it's as though the faces of 2006 had become the faces of 1936 and 1236, the persistence of the Popular Front no less than the medieval among us.[9]

Equally, and perhaps even more, the various sections of *Staring Back* bring side by side images from 1952 to 2006, whether photographs or single frames excerpted from films shot in Cape Verde or in Paris, in Moscow or in Helsinki, refashioning them: shift to black and white, silky, shimmering texture, figures outlined in relation to a background made blurry – in short, a "technical" operation made on Photoshop which smoothes out discontinuities between periods, showing that images have in fact been reclaimed in the present of the viewer going over them again, where the montage of memory makes the most distant past close to the very recent. The gesture of reversal in *Staring Back* "petrifies" the past in the silver salts of memory while allowing a new redistribution, a new associative succession between periods and places. It thus liberates a potential arrangement and rehashing that points to the specific, and specifically melancholic dynamic at work in the Markerian "return". Several temporal layers

---

9 Bill Horrigan, "The Revenge of the Eye", *Artforum* 44.10 (June 2006): 313.

lie in each image of the past. The distribution on the gallery's wall makes it resurface, between the instant of the capture and the time to reread what was captured, to re-mark the same obsession, to make the past possible again or available through montage. In the end, the image of the past looks at us, enigmatically. The caesura between photography and cinema vanishes at that point.

Raymond Bellour, again, notes on the multimedia installation *Zapping Zone* – a work comprised of moving images – that spectators find themselves "wandering with precision on the edge of a present converted in memory on the spot".[10] This feature echoes *Staring Back*, a work made of still fragments: as viewers walk back and forth in the exhibition space, a place of memory, they cause the images to refract with those – the same – seen in a film, a photo album, the CD-ROM: single frames torn from the flow of a film (*¡Cuba Sí!*, *Description of a Struggle*, *Sans Soleil*, *The Last Bolshevik*, *The Case of the Grinning Cat*) or photographs (*Les Coréennes*, *Le Dépays*, *If I Had Four Dromedaries*) set back in motion in the space of the gallery thanks to the horizontal montage performed by visitors, as they pass by, their eyes sweeping over the walls.

Stop, Freeze; Reuse, Resumption

Stasis and dynamic montage are precisely two essential figures in Marker's thought. "This is the story of a man marked by an image from his childhood": in its turn, the incipit *marks* and opens the gallery of still images that is his science-fiction film *La Jetée*, a film on time as it goes off the rails and throws cinema in the arms of photography. Altering the time of single frames, it alters movement.

Still, endowed with movement or not, images remain images as long as they aim to connect to memory. This accounts for the poignancy of a moment in *Grin without a Cat*, when the following words are heard: "You never know what you are filming". What is seen of a reality that escapes our control, of a face or an event, we try to surround, to make still even as it flies by.

The montage (of an image and a text) makes it possible to connect to a temporal circuit, to explain it to oneself in the *future anterior*. Isn't this the fateful dynamic that already animated *La Jetée* and could be found in *Sans Soleil* with the recurrence of the face of the woman from the Praia market, solarized by Hayao Yamaneko's computer program?

According to Yamaneko, these images are not as deceptive as the ones seen on television. "At least they proclaim themselves to be what they are: images, not the portable and compact form of an already inaccessible reality", the voiceover commentary in the film goes.[11]

---

10 Raymond Bellour, "Éloge en si mineur", in *Passages de l'image* (Paris: Musée national d'art moderne/Éditions du Centre Pompidou, 1990) 169–171, reproduced in *L'entre-images 2* (Paris: P.O.L./Trafic, 1999) 43–46.

This idea, already unfolded in *Sans Soleil*, was also to become the core of the project *Souvenir d'un avenir* (*Remembrance of Things to Come*), and later of *Staring Back*: the permanence of a thought on the nature of images and their movement is always repeated and put back into play.

> "The first image he told me about was of three children on a road in Iceland, in 1965. He said that for him it was the image of happiness and also that he had tried several times to link it to other images, but it never worked. He wrote me: 'one day I'll have to put it all alone at the beginning of a film with a long piece of black leader; if they don't see happiness in the picture, at least they'll see the black'."[12]

At that point, the image track of *Sans Soleil* features a long black leader. In the sequence, Chris Marker attempts through contrapuntal montage (a shot of beautiful, blond, lively children on a country road, followed by shots of fighter jets) to emphasize what joy is, but he fails to obtain the desired effect and marks the "defeat" with the insertion of a black image. Happiness has not been seen, but at least black has. Images are only images: they do not contain remembrance or memories, but they may trigger them, bring about the mechanisms that lead to remembrance. There is the affinity with the Proustian idea arising from the madeleine: a woman, named Madeleine, the motif of the spiral somewhere in the image, the question of time everywhere in the story and, from *La Jetée* to *Sans Soleil*, from *Immemory* to *The Hollow Men*, as often in Marker's works, overlapping meanings allow spectators to tease them out,[13] provided they engage in the work designed by Marker and know *Vertigo* ... The effect of déjà vu allows a network of Markerian traces to emerge, a network already encapsulated in the incipit of *La Jetée* ("This is the story of a man marked by an image from his childhood"): a still or moving image remains an image, but may trigger the work of remembrance, of searching for memories that would otherwise be lost.

Acknowledgement: This text is part of Viva Paci's research, *Entre attractions et musée : cinéma, exposition et nouvelles technologies*, financed by the Quebec Research Fund on Society and Culture, or Fond québécois de la recherche sur la société et la culture (FQRSC, August 2008–August 2010) and affiliated with the Art History and Communication Studies Department, McGill University.

11 The English voiceover commentary of *Sans Soleil* is available online at http://www.markertext.com/ sans_soleil.htm.

12 See http://www.markertext.com/sans_soleil.htm.

13 Images of women and spirals migrate from *Immemory* to *The Hollow Men*, suggesting for instance a reuse of the motif of *Vertigo* (Alfred Hitchcock, 1958), of Saul Bass's opening credit sequence, of a few figures appearing here and there in the film (such as the famous image of the section of the sequoia tree, reused by Marker from *La Jetée* to *Sans soleil* to *Immemory*), and even the narrative, which functions as a spiral.

Section V
Contemporary Sequences

Introduction:
Sequencing, Looping

Olivier Lugon, Laurent Guido

The impact of Eadweard Muybridge's or Etienne-Jules Marey's chrono-photography on the first artistic avant-gardes in the early 20th century is well-known (see introduction to section 1). At the time, the invention seemed to represent the promise of new powers for images which, even in still form, could conquer a temporal and kinetic dimension, becoming a legitimate tool in the description of movement. Italian Futurists were enthused by it, and some works by the "Puteaux group" (from Frantisek Kupka's to Marcel Duchamp's) bear the mark of its influence. That interest, however, was short-lived: after the First World War, the presence of this iconography became much more sparse, even though the question of movement remained central for artistic and photographic avant-gardes. Did it seem already dated, made obsolete by the omnipresence of cinema? Did it contradict the dogma of media specificity with its uncertain position between photography and film? Whatever the reason, chronophotography did not appear in the 1929 exhibition *Film und Foto*, despite the fact that the event was by definition open to exchanges between photography and cinema (see section 3); nor was it featured in the wide range of parascientific forms celebrated by the New Vision. As the Modernist canon consolidated in the field of photography, it remained just as marginal, notably in its importation within the United States. While some Muybridge strips adorned the dust cover of *Photography 1839–1937*, the catalogue for the retrospective organized by Beaumont Newhall at New York's MoMA in 1937, they disappeared in augmented editions of the book published over the following decades under the title *The History of Photography*.

Even if chronophotography certainly enjoyed a revival of sorts in the 1940s and the 1950s with the wide diffusion of Arnold Edgerton's strobe photography, his sequential descriptions were nevertheless not as prominent as the single snap-shots that brought him fame, such as the "coronet" milk drop or the bullet piercing an apple. His disciple Gjon Mili, an accredited photographer for *Life*, also made a reputation thanks to sequences captured in a single frame like

Marey's, a specialty he then applied to the flashy worlds of show-business, dance, music, or sports. Still, while his production contributed to the reintroduction of this sequential form in popular culture, it did not reverberate much in the spheres of art photography, more and more dominated from the 1940s on by the primacy of the snapshot, the image made on the fly to capture unexpected events on the street, and the dogma of the irreducibly singular, isolated "decisive moment". The integrity of the single photograph almost became the rule in the 1960s with John Szarkowski, the powerful director of the department of photography at the MoMA, who made it a defining element of the aesthetics of photography. In his view, the power of the medium precisely rested on this radical suspension in the photographic capture as well as with semantic incompleteness, the open meaning it involved – a semantic vacillation which evokes to some degree the "obtuse meaning" Barthes was to look for in the single film frame. In the name of this photographic specificity, Szarkowski condemned anything that could reintroduce continuity, narration, or overall signification in these fragmentary images, whether a sequential organization or a text. It was also obvious – though Szarkowski never stated it explicitly – that only the primacy of the single image could bend the medium of photography to the criteria of the masterpiece, the object of exception, and the strong form that governed the value system of modern fine arts. Relatedly, this primacy conditioned the legitimacy of photography in an institution such as the MoMA.

The Return of Chronophotography

As it happens, the calling into question of this formalist and fetishistic definition of the art object, much more than a pointed interest for the analysis of movement, caused chronophotography to reemerge as a historical model in the art world at the turn of the 1970s – within the conceptual sphere, to be specific – more than a half-century after the Futurists. The plates of Muybridge's *Animal Locomotion*, in particular, suddenly found favour with art periodicals and caught the attention of artists such as Sol LeWitt, Dan Graham, or Hollis Frampton. Much in Muybridge's practice was liable to interest their generation: (1) a shift beyond the single image to the benefit of a serial procedure supposed to undermine the fetishization and the speculative value of the work of art; (2) a conception of photography as a means of knowledge rather than delight; (3) the performative nature of the production of the work, which is nothing but the recording of an action; (4) its resistance to any mythology of inspiration – it consists in carrying out strictly a gestural and technical protocol planned in advance; (5) finally, the visibility of the apparatus, exposed in the very recording of the results it makes possible. In his contribution on Muybridge's "comeback", which he focuses on the figure of Hollis Frampton, Guillaume Le Gall goes back over some of these aspects and points to others: the (then) new primacy of time in visual creation, the taste for archiving the most elementary gestures, or the interest in the iterative aspect of Muybridge's sequences. Indeed, if Muybridge had set out to break movement down so as to record differences between phases, Le Gall points out that conceptual artists were just as interested in the opposite, i.e., the uniform and repetitive nature of views placed side by side. In their accumulation, these seemed to call into question any idea of progression, narrative development, goal or resolution and, in the fundamental incompletion of the sequences, rather left "the impression that they could repeat themselves indefinitely". In this instance, Le Gall refers to a recurring implication in the exchanges between stillness and movement, one that could be observed from the optical toys of the 19th century to many film or video works in contemporary art: the omnipresence of the loop, of a paradoxical movement that keeps stalling, unfolding without going anywhere, developing without acme or any possible "composition" closed upon itself. In the art of the late 1960s, the emphasis of this iterative conception of time may be interpreted as an indirect criticism of the ideology of linear progress that founded the modernist conception of history. Hailed at the turn of the 20th century as quintessential to the modern historical momentum, chronophotography had become, some seventy years later, instrumental in questioning it.

Muybridge's sequences could be used all the better against the idea of linear progression as they were graphically organized, not in the form of strips, but as grids. In the end, these tabular networks identified chronophotography less with a primitive form of film than with a multidirectional comparative structure, a kind of application of the typological table to movement. In that respect, the model for the temporal *sequence* which Muybridge initiated does not appear so different from the model of the comparative *series* championed by Bernd and Hilla Becher during the same period. Some of their analytical tables, in which a building is looked at and captured from every angle, could even be construed as a subcategory of chronophotography involving a change in the point of view itself. In fact, Muybridge already combined the two options: multiplying camera positions as well as phases, he organized a double chronophotography crossing the movement of the model in the horizontal axis and the movement of the look within a vertical arrangement.

Around 1970 the critical potential of the Muybridgian model actually operated in the fields of both cinema and photography, as the intermediary position of Hollis Frampton shows. In photography, the principle of the sequence helped deconstruct the myth of the decisive moment and the autonomous image. Photographs were always taken in a form of montage and as part of an experimental and discursive protocol, thereby undermining any illusion of transparency. Conversely, the same illusion was also tested in cinema through a reminder of the presence of the constitutive element in the simulation of movement, the film frame. The exhumation of chronophotography was thus enrolled in the efforts of structural cinema – with which Frampton may be associated – where fits and starts, flickering, blunt cuts similarly tend to return the reality of the film machinery to the consciousness of the spectator. Reintroducing the sequence in photography, reintroducing the film frame in the film: in both cases, the chronophotographic model plays a part in a politics of structural analysis and in the deconstruction of ideological determinations shaping the illusion of transparency.

Slideshows

While conceptual artists celebrated it as anti-narrative, the chronophotographic sequence nevertheless largely contributed to re-inject the narrative potential of linked-up images into the field of photography. If captured actions became more complex or the pace let up, the chronophotographic sequence soon looked close to the photoromance. The phase then became an equivalent of the shot in film, the interval a form of the ellipsis. The growth of the sequence in the 1970s thus marked the development of an important strand of narrative photography whose most famous representative was without a doubt Duane Michals. Such works often assumed an autobiographical dimension, an aspect which more generally involved photography during the period, and specifically some documentary works devoted to marginality and counter-culture – from Larry Clark to Nan Goldin – where the sequence encompassed the length of an existence.

To tell the story of her life and her close relations', Nan Goldin – beginning in 1977 – turned to another sequential form halfway between photography and cinema, popular in the art world of the late 1960s and the 1970s: the slideshow. Since the postwar period the medium had proved enduring, thriving in two opposite directions. On the one hand, it was a privileged tool in didactic or commercial shows for several decades, as evidenced in its omnipresence at the World Fair: New York (1964), Montreal (1967), and Osaka (1970) (Fig. 1). Kodak had launched its Carousel projector in 1961, which proved decisive. Indeed, for the first time, the machine completely automated projection: long sequences could be looped for hours on end, at a preset speed, and synchronized with a soundtrack without any manual intervention. The magic lantern show was moving away from the domain of stage performance to become a full-fledged element in an exhibition, a phenomenon that was possible for moving images only with the advent of the videotape and the DVD.

The exhibition slideshow also revived the dream of a montage of simultaneous images and "polyvision" through countless multiple-screen projections, pursued since the 1920s (see the introduction to chapter 3). Charles and Ray Eames, for example, coordinated twenty-two screens for the IBM slideshow *Think* at the 1964 World Fair. In a montage both spatial and temporal, the rapid succession of images, producing effects of engulfment, of a movement proceeding in fits and starts, interacted with a multiplication of foci and a forced fluttering of the eyes. The experience of a fragmented time became interlinked with an unstable apprehension of space, and the combination of these two forms of discontinuity confronted the spectator with a sensation of ceaseless change, of *animation* stronger than the fluidity of the film. As a matter of fact, psychedelic culture was

*Fig. 1. Josef Svoboda,
Polyecran,
Czechoslovakian
Pavillon, World's Fair,
Montreal, 1967.*

soon to tap into the almost hypnotic rhythm of these discontinuous, polycentric projections. Many film or television credits of the period also benefited from the dynamic potential of these sequential mosaics (see Diane Arnaud's contribution in section 4).

On the other hand, a popular domestic practice of the slideshow also existed all these years, with quite different characteristics from the public and spectacular use just described. The single screen replaced the juxtaposition of images, speed gave way to the slow pace of scrutiny, automatism vanished as a lecturer-projectionist (generally a father) controlled the apparition of images, preventing them from turning into a destabilizing stream, and most of all provided the whole with narrative continuity through an oral commentary. As Wolfgang Brückle demonstrates, examining the implications of the practice of the slideshow for Nan Goldin, the presentations of the photographer did in some sense stand at the crossroads between these two uses, public and domestic, spectacular and intimate.

Before Goldin, however, it was the automated mode of projection that had drawn the art world to the media. From the late 1960s on, some had identified qualities in the slideshow that were already present in chronophotography. First, it allowed to move beyond a fetishistic conception of the image-as-commodity, to the benefit of an ephemeral work assumed to be more resistant to auctions or collections.[1] Secondly, the slideshow could produce a sequence without begin-

---

1   A neglected aspect at the time seems to have been that images, as a spectacle, may be but another form of commodity and that the fleetingness of luminous images, like the fetish object, finds a ready place in the capitalist logic of obsolescence and permanent turnover.

ning or end, and in a sense without structure, in which no moment would carry more weight than any other. Lastly, there was the metronomic regularity of succession, subjecting the projection of still images to the principle of a standardized speed at the root of both the industry and cinema. Where cinema maintained its invisibility, however, the slideshow made this scansion perceptible, a mechanical rhythmicity of projection further enhanced by the repetitive sound accompanying every slide change in the round slide tray. More than any other medium, then, the slideshow came as a reminder of the industrial foundation of the production and circulation of images in the 20th century. As Allan Sekula noted in 1972 about his work *Untitled Slide Sequence*, which deals with the industrial *and* cinematographic theme of workers leaving the plant: "it's a kind of primitive cinema, unable to synthesize movement. The slide projector is a quasi-industrial apparatus, similar to what one finds in many assembly lines [...]. The rhythm of the slide projector is the rhythm of the automated factory."[2]

As Brückle shows, Nan Goldin used the device very differently. At the end of the decade, at a time when the New York art world was reverting to images, owing in large part to the cinematographic model – from Robert Longo's bas-reliefs, cast after film frames, to Cindy Sherman's first "film stills" – Nan Goldin was developing "a sort of filmic home slideshow". From the cinematographic spectacle she borrowed the use of a musical score as well as a voice-over commentary, performed by the photographer herself, whose presence strengthened the credibility of images as authentic and their integration within a personal narrative that apparently reflects the continuous flow of life. Besides this narrative flow, the presence of individual photographs also contributed to the effect of authenticity characterizing a succession of "frozen moments in time", taken from life unscripted. Between film and photography, the slideshow ended up assuming a carnival-like quality, a metaphor Brückle borrows from Roland Barthes, who used it precisely to describe the "obtuse meaning" of film frames freed from the discursive continuity of the film. Similarly, the sequence comes close to cinema yet stops short of streamlining the fragments comprising it.

An explicitly anti-artistic form, whether "quasi-industrial" for Dan Graham or Allan Sekula or "carnival-like" for Nan Goldin, the slideshow still appealed to the upholders of a more traditional approach of auteurism in photography. The MoMa used it in the 1970s for presentations by Helen Levitt or Lee Friedlander; likewise, the Soirées des Rencontres internationales de la photographie d'Arles featured evening shows during the same period, returning to the scenic origins of the slideshow in a festive, and spectacular form of celebration of the masters. Indeed, a very large number of photographs could on these occasions be brought together into a quasi-cinematographic "work" thanks to a single event and author.

2   Allan Sekula, in "Allan Sekula, réalisme critique", interview by Pascal Beausse, *Art Press* 240 (November 1998): 23.

Fig. 2. Heinrich Freytag, Fotoserien Serienfotos *(Series of Photos, Serial Photos), 1935: cover and 7.*

Sequences and Contact Sheets

In a sense, chronophotography and slideshows stand as two possible poles of the photographic sequence, between an extreme temporal density and the scope of a lifetime, metronomic regularity and arrhythmic succession of captured episodes. In between, all modes of sequential organization, temporal condensation, and rhythm may be contemplated. Already, in 1935, Heinrich Freytag's amateur manual *Fotoserien Serienfotos* ["Series of Photos, Serial Photos"] featured examples of series ranging from the capture of an accident or the changing expressions of a child to the figuration of the cycle of seasons or everyday gestures (Fig. 2). The issue of sequential representation then became the central concern of professionals and amateurs alike with the widespread use of small-format cameras with flexible film – the Ermanox, the Leica, or the Rolleiflex, which made numerous consecutive shots possible for little money (see Michel Frizot's article above). If photographers had long since taken care to build narrative units out of the grouping of several existing shots, these cameras involved grouping images materially at the very moment of the shot. Their succession on the film already constituted the outline of a coherent totality and the photographer became its first spectator with the new tools of the trade, the contact sheet and the card with contact prints. With these, photographers no longer discovered their photographs one at a time, but always in the form of a chain from which a selection could be made – the strip or the sheet then being no more than the collection of attempts arranged in the chronological order of their production – or a coherent sequence directly finalized.

In the 1930s these new modes of creation founded on the management of

abundance were experienced as a major upheaval of the art of photography, as
Andreas Feininger wrote in his 1937 book *Fotografische Gestaltung* ["Photographic Creation"], a whole chapter of which was devoted to the sequence:

> The most important improvement accomplished in the domain of photog-
> raphy and its wealth of sensations since the invention of dry plates we
> undoubtedly owe to the appearance of the Leica and the Rolleiflex. [...]
> The possibility of shooting not just one, but three, four, or a dozen
> photographs of the same subject successively and quickly is a truly revolu-
> tionary breakthrough, which allows the capture in a large number of photos
> of a temporal succession, the description of the three dimensions of space
> from any direction, or the choice of a single photograph – the best – out of
> many. Representing movement instead of a "stopping point", the event
> rather than the "situation", and generally increasing the production average:
> such are the new possibilities introduced by serial photography![3]

For Feininger as for many others at the time, the sequence appeared as the logical
outcome of the conquest of instantaneity and a novel fragmentation of time,
which made it possible to capture life in its temporal depth and in the subtle
nuances of a permanent transformation of beings and things. From the 1950s on,
the imagination associated with the snapshot would be mainly linked to the ideal
of the decisive moment, the isolated masterpiece snatched from the flow of the
life through the talent of improvisation. By comparison, during the interwar
period, that imagination was also embodied in what would be more aptly described as a decisive sequence, i.e., the addition of moments not as strong
individually as taken together. Many theoreticians then thought that the new
conditions for photographic speed would not so much impose the search for an
illusory condensation of meaning in a single image as the opposite necessity of
moving beyond this image to move closer to film. Photography, as the art of
contingency, was deemed unsuitable for conveying an event, describing a place,
or suggesting the essence of an individual in a synthetic view, unlike painting.
Its temporal and spatial sections appeared so limited and fragmentary that only
their addition, it seemed, could provide a significant idea of an object. In 1931,
writer Sergei Tretyakov thus referred the single photograph as "an infinitely fine
scale that has been scratched from the surface of reality with the tip of the finger",
and in passing hailed the sequence as the only means to reach the "authentic
meaning" of things: "sequence and long-term photographic observation – that is
the method".[4] On the strength of this notion, many contemporary articles and
manuals advised photographers to take cinematographic creative techniques as
models: working out genuine scenarios before going out into the field, multiply-

---

3   Andreas Feininger, "Reihenaufnahmen" ["The Series"], in *Fotografische Gestaltung* (Harzburg: Walther
     Heering Verlag, 1937), English translation from François Mathieu's French translation in *La Photographie
     en Allemagne. Anthologie de textes, 1919–1939*, ed. Olivier Lugon (Nîmes: éditions Jacqueline Chambon, 1997)
     274, 275.

4   Quoted in Benjamin Buchloh, in "From Faktura to Factography", *October* 30 (Autumn 1984), reprinted in
     The Contest of Meaning. Critical Histories of Photography, ed. Richard Bolton (Cambridge, Mass.: The MIT
     Press, 1989) 68.

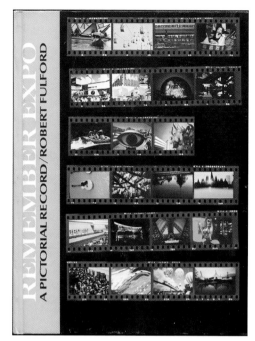

Fig. 3. Remember Expo.
A Pictorial Record, *1968: cover.*

ing shots during the assignment, and taking care over postproduction through montage, the creation of rhythmic effects, suspense, and dramatic progression between the photographs, before adding a "soundtrack" with captions. In doing so, photographers were not simply aping filmmakers: they were also supposed developing a new form of visual narration associating the dynamism and semantic mastery of cinema with the power of concentration of the still image.

This sequential conception of photography, as was said before, came back in force from the late 1960s on when the cult of the single image was called into question. At the time, the "contact sheet" – a standardized form of control print structured as a sequence – was becoming the norm among professionals.[5] The 35mm film was from that point on divided in sections of six frames aligned on the page as on a table to encourage a double reading of the photographs – chronological and comparative – as was possible with Muybridge's plates. The continuity of the film strip became a kind of photographic chart, allowing the comparison of what by definition couldn't coexist in chronological progression: time could accordingly be broken down in parallel samples as well as in consecutive moments. Far from being confined to the secret of studios, the contact sheet soon emerged in the public space, where – like the film frame in cinema – it was promoted to the rank of a possible graphic metaphor for photography (Fig. 3) or even of a work in and

---

5   In French, the term "planche-contact" appeared around the same time. On the history of the contact sheet, see Michel Wiedemann, "La planche-contact et sa préhistoire", *Les Cahiers de la photographie* 10 (1983): 77–82. Available online at http://symposium.over-blog.fr/article-31782664.html.

of itself in Ed van der Elsken's 1966 book *Sweet Life*, Ugo Mulas's 1970–1972 *Verifiche*, or in William Klein's and Yoshihiko Ito's more recent work.

In 1983, the contact sheet even became the object of a series of short films, *Contacts*. Launched by William Klein, the project – which totaled 30 episodes until its end in 2000 – involved filming the contact sheets of famous photographers in the continuity of shots, commented by their authors. On the one hand, the initiative could pass as a way to celebrate the decisive moment yet again, with the effect of epiphany produced by the sudden apparition of an emblematic image of contemporary photography in the midst of unfamiliar shots. On the other hand, the re-inscription of canonical images within the continuity of a sequence equally tends to relativize their exceptionality – are they truly superior to the shots surrounding them? – and most of all to redefine the photographic act as a temporal process akin to film, a form of continuous "shooting". Subjecting photographic film to surveying by the film camera, *Contacts* thus compares two related forms of sequential productions, each of which is questioned in its encounter with the other. Barbara Le Maître examines just this dialectic, focusing on Raymond Depardon's installment, which epitomized the series. The photographer-filmmaker reduced the exercise assigned by the series to long, uninterrupted tracking shots of the strips on the contact sheets. Far from the aesthetics of the decisive moment, these comprise photographs succeeding one another without much differentiation, as would the single frames of a film. As a consequence, Le Maître points out, the short film consists of two "correlated series of 'film frames'", that of the contact sheet and that of the film capturing it, with the former bringing visibility to the real film frames usually hidden from view due to the run of the film in the projector. At the same time as he unveils the processes of photographic production, Depardon thus questions cinematographic movement and manages to bring together the continuity of film and its decomposition, "formulating *in images* the dialectic of cinematographic movement by articulating the fulfillment of this movement and the photographic opening out or explanation of its principle".

Comics

The notion of sequence, between photography and cinema, also comes up with the various occurrences of stillness and movement in a third medium: comics. Pointing out "the danger of improperly equating any sequentialization of images with the cinematographic model", Alain Boillat examines rarely studied aspects of comics. His argument notably concentrates on the complexity of some representations of stillness – in the classic corpus of comics as well as in narrative and aesthetic experimentations that aim to expose "the fundamental discontinuity" inherent in this form of expression. Far from following univocal models, principles of contradiction between iconic and textual parameters often run through the succession of frames. While some elements do abide by the canonical concern to produce the impression of movement, others simultaneously attempt to refer to stillness – in particular the verbal parts, too often overlooked in visual studies because of an iconocentric bias.

As Alain Boillat looks at the insertion of photographic images in comics, some of which involve stills from famous films, he returns to the distinction inherited from Lessing and reformulated – among others – by Bergson, between the *any-moment-whatever* tied to the variations and multiple positions within a single movement, and the synthetic and essential value of *pregnant* moments. In an example cited by the author, the basic approach in comics is equated with the extraction of "pregnant instants out of photographs indiscriminately printed every 1/24 of a second". Despite its explicitly ironic stance, the proposition was in fact vindicated theoretically. American comics artists Will Eisner thus considered that the multiple body positions revealed by the analysis of gesture (and revisited by the specialists of animation films) could provide the material for the necessary selection of some strongly emblematic postures.[6]

This comparative approach between film and comics was rarely dealt with in as much detail as in *Moviemaking Illustrated. The Comicbook Filmbook* (1973). This "textbook of film grammar" ambitions to reveal the fundamental mechanisms in the making of a film, but exclusively through illustrations excerpted from comic books, most of them Marvel publications.[7] Save for a few exceptions and border-line cases (mostly related to formats),[8] the authors assume the "analogy between films and comics" to hold unquestionable validity. While light, perspective, composition, framing, or dissolves refer to questions shared with the plastic arts, many techniques characteristic of cinema are easily translatable in comics, from the still frame within which profilmic movements are recorded to the various spatio-temporal leaps effected through editing.[9] Succession of frames, all from existing comic books, thus illustrate the scenes as a shooting script may organize them: variations in angle, flashbacks, standard sequences (shot/reverse shot; point-of-view shot; mental inserts; parallel editing; types of cuts …), not to mention effects of discontinuity such as jump cuts and abrupt transitions. All these parameters may easily be identified in a medium like comics, which to a large extent rests on a certain type of narrative and aesthetic economy, including in forms that are not subject to the strict editorial constraints characterizing "regular" comics.

6   Will Eisner, *Comics and Sequential Art* (Tamarac: Poorhouse Press, 1985) 100–107.

7   James Morrow and Murray Suid, *Moviemaking Illustrated. The Comicbook Filmbook* (Rochelle Park, New Jersey: Hayden Book Company, 1973).

8   Even the question of relations between sound and image is examined through the status of the text: phylacteries thus refer to dialogue, texts to voice-overs, onomatopoeia to sound effects.

9   Still, some of these illustrated examples are reframed or re-edited so that they fit the method they exemplify. A sequence from *Conan* in which the same action of hanging is decomposed in a few frames is thus presented in more or less comprehensive versions to illustrate the notion of "timing" (an operation which does consist in withdrawing a few images in cinema, but at another level, i.e. in the succession of film frames). See Morrow and Suid, *Moviemaking Illustrated* 65–67.

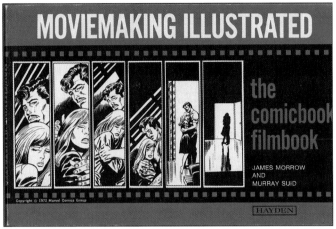

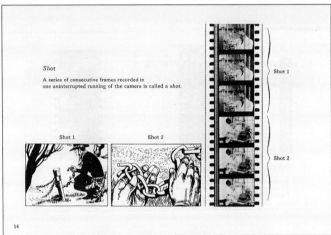

Fig. 4. James Morrow
and Murray Suid,
Moviemaking
Illustrated The
Comicbook
Filmbook, 1973.

The manual falls within the issue of interest to us even more directly when it defines the notion of shot as "a series of film frames recorded in a single, continuous shot"[10] (Fig. 4). The correspondence between shot and frame is notably justified by their common function: both are akin to building blocks with neatly delimited contours. Refusing to approach these in isolation, the authors of the *Comicbook Filmbook* insist on the notions of *sequence* and *scene*, through which spectators (and consequently readers) experience the arrangement of visual units. A key notion in the present chapter, the "sequence" is not considered in its usual meaning, as a synonym for "scene" – a segment autonomized by its temporal, spatial, or narrative coherence – but as a signifying succession of images, that is, "a series of shots connected to one another within a scene".[11] More than a logic of segmentation or closure, the term thus primarily refers to the succession of iconic segments and the multiple possible arrangements resulting from them.

As Alain Boillat stresses out, comics "can draw on the reading competences and the memorization of images acquired in the process of consuming other symbolic productions", whether these come from photography, cinema, or optical toys such as flip books. A historical approach that would take into account this constant circulation of methods and conventions between visual media is therefore in order. This notably holds for an aspect often brought up in the historiography of comics, but whose principles and countless actualizations remain little examined to this day[12]: the influence of the techniques of chronophotographic analysis that appeared in the last quarter of the 19th century on the representation of human motion.

Well before the series of Muybridge, Marey, or Anschütz appeared, tools for the decomposition of gesture had been used by many illustrators – most of the time in the form of a juxtaposition within the same image of various postures performed by a single mobile figure or even just a single part of the body (head, arms, legs).[13] Still, the impact of the mass-circulation of new, photographic images of movement unquestionably marked the history of comics. From the first years of the 20th century (Outcault, Winsor McCay)[14] to the interwar period (Hergé, Alain Saint-Ogan),[15] the recurring motif of a constellated movement of parts of the body

---

10   Morrow and Suid, *Moviemaking Illustrated* 14.

11   Morrow and Suid, *Moviemaking Illustrated* 17–18.

12   See for instance Harry Morgan, "Le mouvement: de Muybridge aux manga", in *Cinéma et bande dessinée*, special issue of *CinémAction*, ed. Gilles Ciment (Condé-sur-Noireau: Corlet/Télérama, 1990): 36–40; or Scott McCloud, *Understanding Comics. The Invisible Art* (New York: Kitchen Sink, 1993).

13   See for example Wilhelm Busch, *Der Virtuos* [*The Virtuoso*, 1865], *Bilderbogen* 465. For an overview, see David Kunzle, *The History of the Comic Strip 2. The Nineteenth Century* (Berkeley: University of California Press, 1990).

14   Outcault's *Buster Brown* was published in 1903–1904; Winsor McCay's *Little Nemo* first appeared on July 21, 1907.

15   *Tintin au pays des Soviets* appeared in 1929; *Tintin au Congo* in 1930; and Alain Saint-Ogan's *Zig et Puce ne veulent rien savoir* (from the *Zig and Flea* series) in 1934.

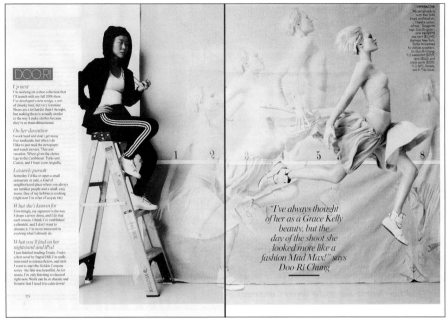

Fig. 5. Vogue US, *February 2008: 224–225.*

gradually innervated the details of sudden and violent actions such as fights. Often associated with lines of movement, the image of a decomposed gesture became a genuine distinguishing feature in some comics of the Golden Age with superheroes moving in an extraordinary spatiotemporal environment[16] as well as in Japanese mangas devoted to sports, dance, and martial arts.[17]

Most of these examples refer to the "foliated" presentation of the phases of a gesture within a single image – like the plates produced at Etienne-Jules Marey's Station Physiologique during the 1880s, before celluloid film was used. However, another iconic mode resulted from the chronophotographic techniques of gestural analysis: it consists in juxtaposing the stages of a given movement in the form of separate images, as did the plates published by Eadweard Muybridge. The figures inspired by the series of photographic snapshots could thus also appear in successive frames where the evolving positions of the same character, captured at different stages in the movement, spread over an entire plate. Besides systematic uses (Winsor McCay's *Little Sammy Sneeze*, 1904–1906), the method has mainly been used in sequences involving chases, leaps, or falls.

<hr />

16   *Superman* thus began in 1940–1941 (Jerry Siegel, Joe Shuster, and Jack Burnley), while Carmine Infantino's *The Flash* was first published in 1956. For a contemporary rereading, see Frank Miller's *Daredevil*, which started in the early 1980s.

17   On the permanent use of lines of movement and gestural breakdown, see Frederick L. Schodt, *Manga! Manga! The World of Japanese Comics* (Tokyo/New York: Kodansha, 1983) 81–87; and Hikaru Hayashi, *How to Draw Manga. Illustrating Battles* (Tokyo: Graphic-sha, 1998) 14–15.

Fig. 6. L'Equipe, *15 September 2009: 13.*

The use of photographic decompositions of human movement was frequent in sports periodicals in the early 20th century and aimed "to provide an exact idea of these various phases of movement that eluded even the keenest eye" and to help "all those who train improve".[18] It also abounds in today's newspapers and may be more systematically identified in fashion advertisements, a domain where repetition effects and variations on uniform and standardized figures can easily be justified (Fig. 5). Indeed, models are reduced to a succession of sheer graphic motifs, the latest manifestation of the logic of the assembly line that has cease-lessly given form to the representation of humankind within the massified culture of entertainment and spectacle since at least the interwar period – from Broadway stages to the spectacular sequences designed by Busby Berkeley.[19] The practice also appears in illustrations accompanying social, political, cultural, and

Fig. 7. Libération, *1 October 2007: 34–35.*

18 Lieutenant Rocher, "Le laboratoire de l'Ecole de Joinville", *La Vie au Grand Air* ["Outdoor Life"] 768 (June 7, 1913): 423; see in particular *La Vie au Grand Air* 757 (22 March 1913) and 791 (15 November 1913) (special issue on "style"). The method is often referred to as a "cinematography of gesture".

19 In return, this tradition of "standardized" representation of the female body influenced the field of contemporary photography. Some early works by Cindy Sherman, like *The Fairies* or *Mini* (both 1976), testify to this: their tight juxtaposition of cutout photographs of the artist wearing ridiculous outfits evidently imitates the effect of Marey's photographic plates.

Le conseiller national Yvan Perrin a testé volontairement les effets du Taser hier à Paris. A droite, le directeur français de la société. afp

Fig. 8. 20 Minutes *(Lausanne), 29 November 2007: 7.*

of course sports news (Fig. 6). In all occurrences, either mode handed down by chronophotographic analysis may be invoked. Both are used in the visual counterpoints in two recent articles on the Taser gun. The first image describes within a single frame the gradual fall of a victim in four moments deemed equally gripping (Fig. 7), while the other juxtaposes three frames to depict the essential steps in a similar collapse (Fig. 8). More than a century after the emergence of instantaneous photography and cinema, in particular *through* their articulation in the chronophotographic machine, the issues and the problems raised by these media with regard to stillness and movement inform, more than ever, the sequential modes of the representation of movement.

1

The Suspended Time of Movement: Muybridge, a Model for Conceptual Art

Guillaume Le Gall

In March 1973, artist Hollis Frampton devoted an essay to Eadweard Muybridge in American periodical *Artforum* (Fig. 1).[1] To elect an artist of the late 19th century in a magazine specializing in the most current art – at the time, conceptual art, essentially – amounted to making that artist a strong historical landmark. In fact, beginning in the late 1960s, Muybridge had become a model to artists such as Sol LeWitt, Dan Graham, and many others who found several of their concerns echoed in his work: activity, the sequence, the series, movement or time as related to space. As to Frampton's article, identifying all these characteristics in Muybridge, assigning a possible origin to them in a sense, it put forth a historicization of conceptual art or its practices through the photographic model of the plates of *Animal Locomotion*.[2]

Considering the 781 plates of *Animal Locomotion* (1887, Figs. 2, 3), this "unique monument", Frampton expresses his wonder at the "photographic sequences" showing men, women, old people, and children "engaged in hundreds of different activities".[3] If, as he makes it clear in his article, the main subject of Muybridge's work may have been time, artists of his generation seem to have been fascinated first and foremost by these hundreds of activities. Around the same time as the publication of Frampton's article in 1973, Lucy Lippard's famous reference work around conceptual art, *Six Years: The Dematerialization of the Art Object from 1966 to 1972*,[4] appeared in bookstores. The book emphasized how many artists had

---

1   Hollis Frampton, "Eadweard Muybridge: Fragments of a Tesseract", *Artforum* 11 (March 1973): 43–52, reproduced in *On the Camera Arts and Consecutive Matters: The Writings of Hollis Frampton*, ed. and intr. Bruce Jenkins (Cambridge: MIT, 2009) 22–32.

2   The images of *Animal Locomotion* have appeared in many successive publications. For the period of interest to us, let us mention Robert Taft, *The Human Figure in Motion* (Dover Publications: New York, 1955); S. Brown, *Animals in Motion* (Dover Publications: New York, 1957); Eadweard Muybridge, *Animal Locomotion* (Da Capo Press: New York, 1969); Anita Ventura and Robert Bartlett Haas, *Eadweard Muybridge: The Stanford Years, 1872–1882* (Stanford University: Stanford, 1972). Frampton seems to have written his article on the basis of this last reference, a catalogue.

3   Frampton, *On the Camera Arts* 23.

Fig. 1. Artforum 11 (March 1973).

called into question the art object as autonomous production to favour instead
artistic activity and the artistic process in general. Engaged in the dematerialization of art, these artists concentrated on elementary actions responding to simple
conceptual utterances while trying to discover through these gestures what could
be relevant to the ongoing artistic process. The actions commanded in these
simple utterances could resonate with those of *Animal Locomotion* such as walking, running, carrying a bucket of water, walking up or down a staircase, or sitting
down and standing up. In conceptual art, however, actions were mostly carried
out by the artists themselves, which distinguished them from Muybridge. Rather
than imposing actions on models, they questioned their own gestures. Indeed,

4   Lucy Lippard, *Six Years: The Dematerialization of the Art Object from 1966 to 1972* (Studi Vista: London, 1973).

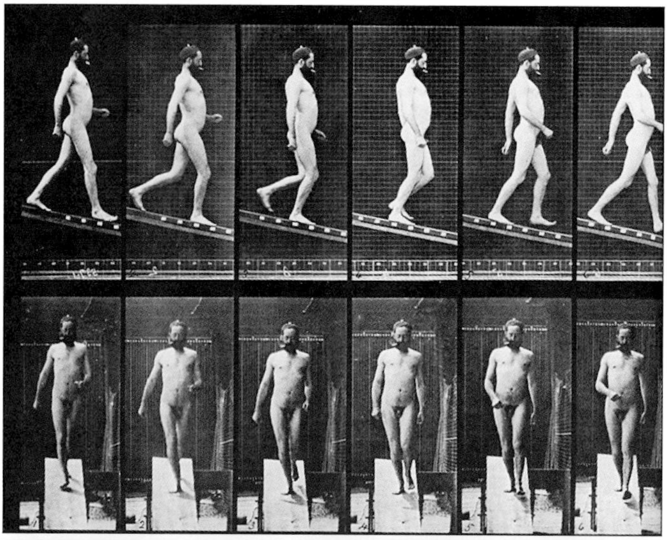

Fig. 2. Eadweard Muybridge, Animal Locomotion, *1887: plate 113 (detail).*

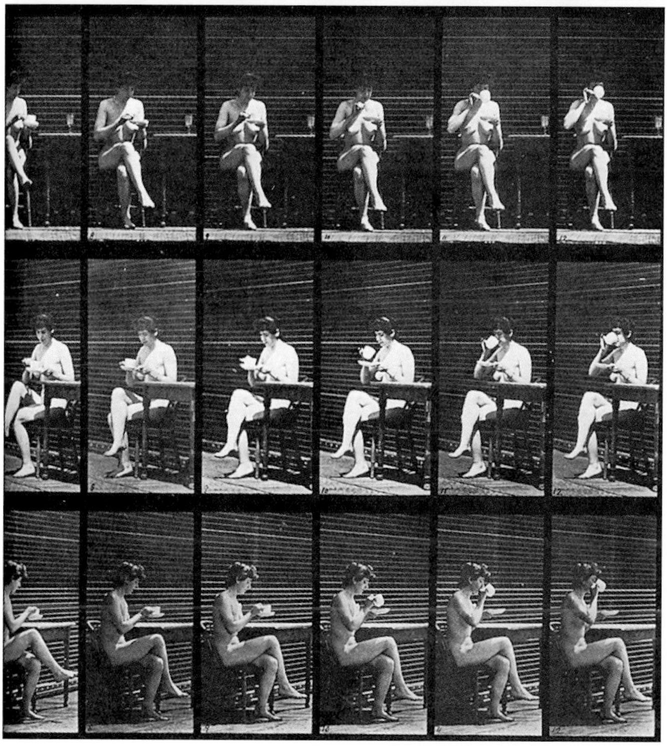

Fig. 3. E. Muybridge, Animal Locomotion, *1887: plate 238 (detail).*

the issue for them was not to create an inventory or a typology of all movements, but to understand the artistic activity and process in which they were the protagonists.

Fig. 4. Hollis Frampton, "Eadweard Muybridge: Fragments of a Tesseract", Artforum 11 (March 1973): 46–47.

Sequential representation constitutes one of the other essential points in Frampton's reading of Muybridge's work. The layout of the article published in *Artforum* makes it clear that Frampton was indeed putting forth a re-reading, or was even forcing it into a conceptual framework – merely on a formal level, initially. The organization of Muybridge's photographs of clouds on the page (Fig. 4), designed by Frampton himself, evokes the grid layout widely used by conceptual artists from Sol LeWitt to Eleanor Antin to Douglas Huebler or Jan Dibbets. Conversely, Muybridge's sequential representation largely inspired conceptual artists, for whom it represented an operating model. Muybridge perfected a photographic apparatus in order to produce the analytic view of the movement of an object. The successive shots of the same body moving in a defined spatiotemporal framework make it possible to follow the evolution of that object in space and time. On the one hand, the photographic apparatus breaks down movement in as many instants as there are shots; on the other hand, a succession or a sequence of images of the object frozen in its movement precisely allows to obtain an analytical view of the movement in question. This sequential dimension of the image affords the perception of difference within the same. The analysis of movement through a sequential presentation has influenced many artists, especially conceptual artists.[5]

As early as 1962, Sol LeWitt had made *Run I-IV* (Fig. 5). While *Run* stresses the

---

5   This study is limited to the field of conceptual or pre-conceptual art. However, an in-depth study remains to be done. For instance, Robert Morris's work in dance is worth noting – particularly his piece *Waterman Switch*, given at the Judson Memorial Church on March 25, 1965, and in which a naked man carrying a rock was followed by a performer engaged in the same action. See Robert Morris, "Notes on Dance", *The Tulane Drama Review* 10:2 (Winter 1965): 179–186.

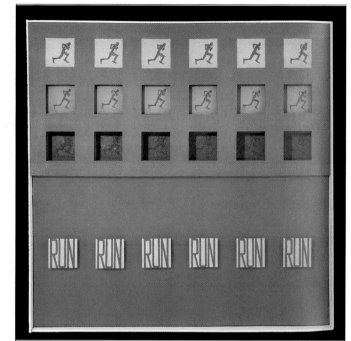

Fig. 5. Sol LeWitt,
Run I–IV, *1962.*

Fig. 6. S. LeWitt, Schematic Drawing for Muybridge II, *1964.*

sequential repetition of a simplified motif, itself very Muybridgian, the repetition remains analogical. The motif does not develop: the repetition of the same alone produces an idea of movement. Sol LeWitt integrated the Muybridgian model which, as reinterpreted in this particular work, seems to establish that any motif repeated serially becomes associated with movement or prompts an idea of movement. In other words, the repetition of the same motif would be enough to create the figurative illusion of movement. With *Schematic Drawing for Muybridge II* (Fig. 6), Sol LeWitt later worked out this kind of representation through the exposure of the same motif at different moments. Modeled after some of the plates from *Animal Locomotion, Schematic Drawing for Muybridge II* is a photographic sequence that represents a woman moving towards the lens of the photographer. The comparison of this sequence to similar ones by Muybridge brings out the fact that Sol LeWitt restricted it to this single visual angle. Moreover, where the chronophotographer put an end to the action, the conceptual artist let it continue, with the object getting so close to the objective as to block out the surrounding space. In *Duration Piece n°31* (1972) (Fig. 7), Douglas Huebler took up the same

Fig. 7. Douglas Huebler, Duration Piece 31, 1972 *(detail).*

principle as Sol LeWitt, further extending the action: "On December 31, 1972, ten photographs were made of the artist as he walked directly toward the camera, and then, right 'through' it while vanishing into the blackness on the other side".[6]

Sol LeWitt's piece was reproduced multiple times on the occasion its reedition in the famous catalogue-box for the renowned exhibition *Artists and Photographs*, organized by Lawrence Alloway in 1970, and which was one of the first to reveal the importance of photography as a medium in new artistic practices such as conceptual art, land art, and the happening. In his introduction, the critic advanced that "the artistic ideas and operations that need photographic documentation are especially those that are modified in time. Time, in fact, is central to photography."[7]

In a certain way, conceptual artists became interested in Muybridge in part because they themselves had been faced with the necessity of working with time or of "mapping time back upon space",[8] to borrow Frampton's expression in an

6   See *Douglas Huebler, "Variable", etc.*, ed. Frédéric Paul (F.R.A.C. Limousin: Limoges, 1993) [n. p.]

7   Lawrence Alloway, *Artists and Photographs* (Multiples Inc.: New York, 1970), reproduced in Douglas Fogle, *The Last Picture Show: Artists Using Photography 1960–1982* (Walker Art Center: Minneapolis, 2003) 21.

8   Frampton, *On the Camera Arts* 46.

Fig. 8. D. Huebler,
Location Piece 7,
1968 (detail).

article titled "Incisions in History/Segments in Eternity". When artists renounced to produce art objects, when they contented themselves with existing
objects in the world, they used photography as a means to record the variations
of objects in a given space.

American artist Douglas Huebler, who took part in one of the first exhibits of
conceptual art along with Robert Barry, Lawrence Weiner, and Joseph Kosuth,
organized by Seth Siegelaub in New York and usually referred to as *January 5–31
1969*, declared in the catalogue: "The world is full of objects, more or less
interesting; I do not wish to add any more. I prefer, simply, to state the existence
of things in terms of time and/or place."[9] While Huebler never considered
photography as superior to other media of representation such as cartography or
drawing, it still occupied a central place in his work and remained an ideal means
to document the existence of things in terms of time and/or place. For him, noting
the existence of things pertained to an experience and to the ongoing artistic
process. It was not called upon to "judge" or "to infer 'meaning' from particular
appearances", but simply involved the production of series of documents "that

9   Paul, *Douglas Huebler, "Variable", etc.* 173.

form the structure of an idea or system whose function is to create a conceptual 'frame' around a space/time content".[10] In other words, the use of photographic sequences within a predefined conceptual framework allowed him to establish a protocol for verifying and visualizing the behaviour of an object referred to in the statement of the work. On this account, *Location Piece #7 (Snow Sculpture Project) (1968)* (Fig. 8) constitutes an example of the protocols followed by Huebler: "On December 19, 1968, nine photographs were made at ten seconds intervals in time to document the changing physical appearance of a body of snow resting on the branch of a pine tree; the nine photographs join with this statement to constitute the form of this work". While Huebler, rarely respecting the chronological order of his photographic sequences, sought to avoid any form of narrativity in his work, he nevertheless tended to set the modes of an experience of perception of the ceaseless change of the world through the variations of an object, whatever it may be. On the same principle, but strictly following the order of the photographic sequence, Jan Dibbets made *The Shadows in My Studio as They Were at 27.07.1969 from 8.40–14.10 Photographed Every Ten Minutes* (1969) (Fig. 9). With this series, Dibbets broke down the movement of the shade created by the sun in his studio, thus making time legible, in a certain way.

Conceptual artists questioned the nature of time and the structure of the apparently endless flux in the movement of all things. There lies the paradox of this corpus of works which more or less integrate the Muybridgian model of the decomposition of movement. Since Muybridge had succeeded in synthesizing movement out of *still* images, it seemed logical to consider movement as a succession of brief and perfectly static instants. In their theoretical texts, some of these conceptual artists tellingly invoke Zeno's paradoxes to explain and give their own analysis of the structure of time and movement. Before Frampton, Dan Graham had already authored an article on Muybridge, published in *Arts Magazine* in 1967 and aptly titled "Muybridge Moments".[11] In his piece, Graham cited Zeno's thought which, together with Muybridge's works, allowed him to reconsider our representation of movement. For his part, Frampton stated in his article on Muybridge:

> It is remarkable that cinema depends from a philosophical fiction that we have from the paradoxes of Zeno, and that informs the infinitesimal calculus of Newton: namely, that it is possible to view the indivisible flow of time as if it were composed of an infinite succession of discrete and perfectly static instants.[12]

Two years earlier, in his article "For a Metahistory of Film", Frampton already noted that

> given that much, it was a short step to the assumption that motion consists

---

10   Paul, *Douglas Huebler, "Variable"*, etc., "Letter to Jack Burnham" (1969) 173.

11   Dan Graham, "Muybridge Moments", *Arts Magazine* (Feb. 1967) 23–24.

12   Frampton, *On the Camera Arts* 26.

of an endless succession of brief instants during which there is only stillness. Then motion could be factually defined as the set of differences among a series of static postures.[13]

In the same article, he turned round the principle of Muybridge's invention, which had made it possible to get to the moving image starting from instantaneous photography, postulating that "a still photograph is simply an isolated frame taken out of the infinite cinema".[14] This amounted to saying that any photographic image could in actuality be something like the image of a preexisting film frame.

In Frampton's thinking, the plates of *Animal Locomotion* are comprised of images already still, isolated, taken out of an infinite continuum analogous to an endless strip of film. He rather aptly notes that, taken in isolation from a more ample movement, the views of *Animal Locomotion* seem to be but "an archetypal fragment of living action".[15] In his view, this archetypal fragmentation of action is "potentially

Fig. 9. Jan Dibbets, The Shadows in My Studio as They Were at 27.07.1969 from 8.40-14.10 Photographed Every Ten Minute, *1969 (detail).*

subject to the incessant reiteration that is one of the most familiar and intolerable features of our dreams".[16] Indeed, many actions in Muybridge's work appear to be uncompleted and leave the impression that they could repeat themselves indefinitely. That is in fact the effect achieved when these images are set in motion by the zoopraxiscope invented by Muybridge, and based on the model of the phenakistiscope. Dan Graham also noted in his 1967 article that each series "might begin or end at any point".[17] Deprived of dramatic tension, actions do not mean anything outside the experimental framework of the decomposition of movement through a mechanical method of reproduction. This absence of narrative structure produces the sense that these actions could be repeated ad infinitum and that repetition alone could impart a given meaning to them.

13 Frampton, *On the Camera Arts* 132.

14 Frampton, *On the Camera Arts* 134.

15 Frampton, *On the Camera Arts* 29.

16 Frampton, *On the Camera Arts* 29.

17 Graham, "Muybridge Moments" 24.

Fig. 10. Hollis Frampton, Vegetable Locomotion, Apple Advancing, *1975.*

The study of the plates of *Animal Locomotion* involves the examination of thousands of images showing men or women walking, running, walking up an inclined plane, walking down the same plane, pouring water, carrying a jug, sitting down, standing up, jumping, falling, to mention but a few examples. Actions are repeated and follow one another: in fact, we could make an inventory of all the actions featured in the work, just as an artist could have done in a conceptual work in the 1960s. Confronted with these thousands of images, Frampton still raised the question of what could have been the cause and origin of what he called an obsession: "What need drove him beyond a reasonable limit of dozens or even hundreds of sequences to make them by thousands?"[18] To this question, Frampton answered with an intuition. Before he made *Animal Locomotion*, Muybridge had shot his wife's lover to death. That action, committing a murder, is also the moment of an "intense passion during which perception seems vividly arrested",[19] and Frampton sees it as the original impulse for Muybridge's studies of movement. He thus advances the idea that "that brief and banal action, outside time, was the theme upon which he was forced to devise variations in such numbers that he finally exhausted, for himself, its significance".[20] Frampton's intuition is interesting, but the key to understanding the question of Muybridge's obsession, it seems to me, lies at the very end of the article, when he cites a passage from Borges's *The Mirror of the Enigmas*: "The steps a man takes, from the day of his birth to the day of his death, trace an inconceivable figure in time. The Divine Intelligence perceives that figure at once, as man's intelligence

18   Frampton, *On the Camera Arts* 30.

19   Frampton, *On the Camera Arts* 30.

20   Frampton, *On the Camera Arts* 30.

Fig. 11. H. Frampton, Vegetable Locomotion, Tomatoes Descending a Ramp, *1975.*

perceives a triangle."[21] Muybridge may well have attempted, through these thousands of photographs, to break down all the gestures that outline and fill out the life of a man (or a woman) and that, assembling them in a photographic monument, he was looking for this unfathomable figure, the sum of all these gestures. The fantasy could be fulfilled only through work on movement and, out of technical necessity, on time.

Time, as we have seen, was at the centre of some works by conceptual artists who sought to attain a perception of variations in objects or phenomena. It is also a central question in Frampton's work and thought. When he wrote this article, he had just completed his film *Zorns Lemma*, which is more or less (to the exception of the incipit and the end), a succession of one-second still shots of words inscribed around the city. The work, which was initially photographic, allowed him to think of film "as a kind of ordering and control, a way of handling stills".[22] *Zorns Lemma*, with its definite structural framework – one second per shot – engaged him in thinking on time, which for him was "not a fiction [...] nor a phenomenon, but rather a condition of intelligibility, of the perception of all other phenomena".[23] For him, then, cinema was a way to master time and one of the prerequisites for the organization of his photographic activity. Significantly, after making the film and writing the article on Muybridge, he returned to a photographic work directly drawing on the model of *Animal Locomotion*. In 1975, he produced a rather curious photographic series of sixteen studies titled *Vegetable Locomotion* with the assistance of Marion Faller (Figs. 10, 11). Imbued with

21   Frampton, *On the Camera Arts* 31.

22   Peter Gidal, "Interview with Hollis Frampton", *October* 32 (Spring1985): 93.

23   Gidal, "Interview with Hollis Frampton" 100.

humour, it is obviously a tribute to Muybridge. Frampton reused the principles of the photographic series and the orthonormal background. In front of this backdrop, he prompted what may be called "vegetable actions" with the intention of breaking down their movement through photography. More seriously, he reused and summarized in some way the different works of conceptual artists who had appropriated the photographic model conveyed by *Animal Locomotion* in the 1960s and the early 1970s.[24] *Watermelon Falling* evokes Dibbets's series already mentioned, while *Apple Advancing* calls to mind Huebler's or Sol LeWitt's series. Yet the plates of *Vegetable Locomotion* also refer to Muybridge's plates, evidently, and it seems a little as though, two years after his text on the photographer, he wanted to reach a conclusion with a monument that obsessed him. On the images he can be seen repeating gestures which Muybridge's models could have performed, such as pouring vegetables on an inclined plank, and which also refer to other gestures in *Animal Locomotion*. All in all, Frampton was not done with Muybridge, and seems to have wanted to succeed in what he also called the failed marriage of photography and cinema. In a sense, it is as though the photographic parenthesis of *Vegetable Locomotion* in his film work indicated that the movement of things is never shown or signified as well as by the frozen images of photography.

24 In an article on Frampton and photography, Christopher Phillips confines himself to the sole influence of Muybridge on the artist, omitting to revisit the pieces of other conceptual artists issuing directly from *Animal Locomotion*. See Christopher Phillips, "Word Pictures: Frampton and Photography", *October* 32 (Summer 1985) 62–76.

2

Chronophotography of Another Order: Nan Goldin's Life Told in Her Slide Shows

Wolfgang Brückle

Some readers of this essay might still remember attending slide show evenings. We might have experienced them at domestic gatherings, where we would have watched, sometimes with ambivalent feelings, the follies of our own childhood embedded in family life. Some of us might also have attended public lectures that recounted the experiences of some traveller to the wilds of the world, listening to descriptions of adventurous journeys and insights into unexplored sites. Some may have even witnessed both at once. Whatever the nuances of our responses, fact is that the slide show as genre was, for a long time, a social institution that, in its traditional form, is presently fading away. The photographic industry settled its foretold death when Kodak stopped producing slide projectors in 2004. Observers frequently note that this event doomed the slide medium as a form of visual communication. There is life in the old dog yet, as is implied by recent works of Allan Sekula who has been interested in the slide show's cinematographic effects for a long time, and by the works of several other contemporary artists. I will, however, concentrate on an earlier aesthetic strategy of dealing with that medium, which was developed by the photographer Nan Goldin who aspired to high art but nonetheless profited from the ordinary practices that dominate our understanding of its documentary function in every-day life. In this context, I will focus on the paradigm of the motion picture because it nurtured the conceptualisation of the slide projector as a device in art. Slide projection had become a tool frequently used in art during the 1960s and 1970s for this and other reasons, and we will consider that tradition because theoretical writing from that period helps us to define the background against which my main example is silhouetted. Goldin's approach actually contrasts decisively with the preoccupations of the gatekeepers of the later avant-garde. She had her first success when bringing slide projection close to movie aesthetics in the 1980s, sneaking into art exhibitions her family slide shows, as it were. Since then, she has been profiting from the interpretational themes that at the time were

Fig. 1. Nan Goldin, Picnic On the Esplanade, Boston, *1973. [©Nan Goldin.]*

established around her photography, still oscillating between the private and the public uses of what Pierre Bourdieu, defining the medium's status without yet referring to projected images, once called a "middle-brow" art.

In the 1980s and 1990s, many photographers with a claim to art were concerned with attempts to evoke effects of speaking without artistic codes. Larry Clark had been a forerunner of this trend, while Nan Goldin and others gained more popularity in the gallery system when, though following the same path, they broke new ground in terms of artistic procedures and claims. Goldin has arguably become the most popular voice within this movement, and herself a point of reference in terms of tradition-making. She had started working seriously with photography in the early seventies, then became a student at the School of the Museum of Fine Arts in Boston, a step which allowed her to intensify her pursuit of photography. In 1978, she moved to New York, where she continued to photograph her friends and acquaintances just as she had done before. She is now famous for her radical illustrations of daily life in that period's subcultural New York milieu of junkies, homosexuals, transvestites, and drag queens (Figs. 1–3). These images show a world the public was not familiar with before. Not surprisingly, her work has gained attention mainly because of its thematic aspects.[1]

1   One gets an idea of the critical response to Goldin's work from Marie Bottin, "La critique en dépendance: La réception de l'œuvre de Nan Goldin en France (1987–2003)", in: *Études photographiques* no. 17 (2005), pp. 67–85, where on p. 79 the author complains that not enough attention is given to artistic contexts. Bottin's analysis strictly respects the boundaries of French criticism, but it is obvious that writing on Goldin in other countries does not differ much from the overall tendencies in France.

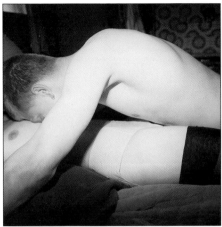

Fig. 2 (left). N. Goldin, Skinhead Having Sex, London, *1978. [©Nan Goldin.]*

Fig. 3 (above). N. Goldin, Suzanne in the Parents's Bed, Swampscott, Mass., *1985. [©Nan Goldin.]*

People felt shocked by and attracted to the bluntness of scenes exhibiting people who were stoned, drunk, and having sex or showing traces of physical violence, the photographer sometimes featuring herself in these themes. Such images claim, by their very iconography, to unveil a reality behind established conventions of public visual communication. Apparently, this effect contributed much to Goldin's success because it seemed to evoke an artistic search for truth. In 2002, Ursula Frohne suggested that repulsive images, which she sees at the core of the work of Goldin and other contemporary photographers, were an attempt to capture the veracity of a moment directly extracted from life itself.[2] While Frohne is not unaware that the artist makes formal choices regardless of the content of her subject, it must be stressed, in contrast to her overall argument, that repulsive subject matter is not exactly what invests the images with their aura of authenticity and life-capturing reliability. Explicit images of cruelty and of sexual activities have been known in the art world for centuries without provoking, on the exclusive basis of iconographic stimuli, any noteworthy authenticity effects of the kind Frohne perceives in Goldin's photographs. That said, it is certainly not far-fetched to introduce notions of authenticity when discussing Goldin's work. They are a helpful starting point especially when one intends to explain her strategies of claiming aesthetic credibility, which however are more complex than is apparent from the analysis of her topics and motifs alone.

Goldin has often admitted that, right from the beginning, her drive was to capture "life as it's being lived, and the flavour and the smell of it", or, to put it differently,

---

2   Cf. Ursula Frohne, "Berührung mit der Wirklichkeit: Körper und Kontingenz als Signaturen des Realen in der Gegenwartskunst", in: *Quel Corps? Eine Frage der Repräsentation*, eds Hans Belting a. o., Munich: Fink, 2002, pp. 401–426, p. 411. For a more comprehensive discussion of Frohne's argument, see Wolfgang Brückle, "Quests for Authenticity and the Problem of Artistic Style: The Case of Nan Goldin", in: *Art and Authenticity*, eds Jan Lloyd Jones and Julian Lamb, Melbourne: Australian Scholarly Publishing, 2010, pp. 189–196 and 232–233, p. 192. While that earlier essay is primarily concerned with the problems of iconography and style as related to the photographic picture, the present supplemental text concentrates on the format of slide shows and their aesthetic implications.

Fig. 4. N. Goldin, Edwige behind the Bar at Evelyne's, New York City, *1985. [©Nan Goldin.]*

the "evidence of life lived".[3] This seems to imply a strong belief in the aesthetic and ideological transparency of the medium. It is only fitting that Goldin should also have caused a stir due to the unconcealed casualness with which she dealt with questions of form-finding. Her calculations were those of reportage photography. The rule she applied to her project went as follows: the less involvement the artist makes felt in compositional questions, the more you get an impression of spontaneity and the more you will trust the artist's unadulterated contact to reality. Uncoordinated scenic arrangements, accidental framing, garish colour contrasts, unbalanced lighting, often achieved with flashlight, occasionally an insufficient monitoring of the sharpness of depth, those are the features that Goldin draws on to encode an unadulterated recording of truth (Fig. 4). This led Andy Grundberg to ascribe a "formlessness" to her pictures, and he was followed in this opinion by many other commentators.[4] In fact, Goldin herself pointed out that her closeness to her subjects is not obstructed by formal questions. That does not imply a renunciation of any structural activity, but when it came to arranging

---

3   Nan Goldin in "On Acceptance: a Conversation. Nan Goldin Talking with David Armstrong and Walter Keller", in: *Nan Goldin: I'll Be Your Mirror,* eds Nan Goldin a.o., New York: Whitney Museum of American Art, and Zürich: Scalo, 1996, pp. 447–454, p. 452. – The second quote is from Ingvild Goetz, "'I feel like I'm touching somebody': Interview With Nan Goldin", in: *Nobuyoshi Araki, Diane Arbus, Nan Goldin,* eds Ingvild Goetz and Christiane Meyer-Stoll, Munich: Kunstverlag Ingvild Goetz, 1997, pp. 116–126, p. 123.

4   Cf. Andy Grundberg, "Nan Goldin's Grim *Ballad*" [1986], in: id., *Crisis of the Real: Writings on Photography, 1974–1989,* New York: Aperture, 1990, pp. 96–99, p. 98.

her pictures in comprehensive sequences or, later on, in grids, she always evidently focused on storylines based on her own life, and on typologies that were based on her outlook on love as human bondage. Hence, her pictures do not seem to derive their impact primarily from their compositional properties. Goldin emphasised that she always had exclusively felt concerned with content.[5] But she probably would not rush to support such views with respect to her more recent work, which is becoming more sophisticated formally. Anyway, her earlier personal neglect of this issue evidently does not rule out that her photographs can be described in terms of style and of conceptual strategies. While we may take for granted here that a signature style can be perceived in the design of her pictures, it is one of the overall concepts in her production of artistic meaning that we are going to consider now.

It is crucial to the effect of Goldin's photographs, especially in the early years of her camera work, that the viewer understands her intimate personal involvement with the things and events seen. Goldin explicitly referred to *The Ballad of Sexual Dependency* as "an exploration of my own desires and problems", as if this declaration of her own suffering was additional proof as to the immediacy of the pictures.[6] Her interviews are full of more or less detailed accounts of precisely these passions, and it is clear that for a large proportion of her continuously-growing audience, which is not directly familiar with her cultural milieu, such metadata are a necessary complement to the pictures. It must be remembered, however, that the interviews and texts are only derivations of the spoken commentaries Goldin habitually offered alongside the pictures when she showed them to her first audiences. As a matter of fact, she first became famous in the 1980s for slide-shows that she compiled from her picture collection, accumulated through a virtually day-to-day practice of self-commissioned reportage. These shows, all developing from more or less private presentations in 1977–1978 and from a 1979 version, which was shown in New York City on Frank Zappa's birthday party in the Mudd Club, were not quickly fixed as a finished work. In contrast, identical pictures were to become part of different shows while the shows in turn could change in content without ever losing their integrity in the eyes of the artist. Goldin would present them in bars and clubs and, most noteworthy in the present context, in cinemas and also at film festivals before she gained access to the inner circle of the established art world, playing a soundtrack made of classical arias, songs from Brecht and Weill's *Threepenny Opera*, and rock music. First introduced in 1980, the background songs chosen by her would differ from one event to another up to 1987, and slide sequences in *The Ballad of Sexual Dependency*, which with its about 700 pictures was to become her most important work, varied well into the 1990s.[7] She would usually be present herself at the

---

5   Cf. Goldin's statement in: "'My Number One Medium All My Life'. Nan Goldin Talking With J. Hoberman", in: *Nan Goldin:* I'll Be Your Mirror (note 3), pp. 135–145, p. 137.

6   Nan Goldin, cited after id., "Nan Goldin's *Ballad of Sexual Dependency*: Interview With Mark Holborn", in: *Aperture* no. 103 (1986), pp. 38–47, p. 42.

shows, loading the slides one by one and commenting on the photographs first shown to an audience that was also the very subject of the documentation. Thus, she appropriated a domestic way of watching and talking about pictures for art when she switched over to the gallery system from a less institutionalised use of the medium. The reliability of Goldin's work, nourished in equal measure by her confessional mode and the unambitious installation scheme, evidently benefited much from the presentation arrangement.

Consequently, Goldin continued personally to introduce her slides even after professional success had allowed her to publish *The Ballad of Sexual Dependency* as a book. I remember witnessing one of these shows myself when she visited Hamburg in 1998, and I was bewildered by the event. I cannot say that what the artist told her public while showing the slides was very revealing or instructive. Rather, the contrary was the case, as she mainly concentrated on making bio-graphical remarks on the persons shown to us, and on the situations reported on the pictures. If I remember well, there was not much debate about her aesthetic aims and claims then, and people who had never liked family slide shows certainly risked feeling a little bored by hers, too. Having said this, the individual images gained an aura of authenticity by Goldin's presence in the Kunsthalle lounge. She augmented the that-has-been of the photograph, famously praised by Roland Barthes as its quintessential quality in his book on photography (just before his death), with its author's actual I-am-here.[8] The event was felt as an encounter with the reality of a person, and that effect turned out to be an important addendum to the experience of the slide show.[9] Unpretentious as the artists presiding over that evening were, it is best defined in terms of a perform-ance piece: if we consider the artist's 'I' to be the medium, then the medium was the message that night, as it had regularly been in her work. It was another way of confirming the author subject behind the camera. No wonder, therefore, that she maintained the habit of commentating on her pictures personally. That practice allowed her to give them a greater overall sense of reliability, not accessible by any means of visual style alone. The fact that Goldin frequently changed the arrangement of the shows, so they would reflect her mood swings and her shifting outlook on her life, presents a significant gesture as well, thwarting through blatant subjectivism the idea of an impartial documentation appropriate to a specific and defined subject matter. By her live commentaries

7   The underlying structure, though, had been settled in 1987, and only slightly altered thereafter. Cf. "Nan Goldin Talks to Tom Holert", in: *Artforum International* 41 (2003), no. 7, pp. 232–233, p. 232, where further information on the way the show developed can be found.

8   Cf. Roland Barthes, Camera Lucida: *Reflections on Photography*, New York: Hill and Wang, 1981, passim. It will turn out at the end of this essay that Barthes' conceptual contribution to what is at the core of Goldin's work exceeds mere commonplace. It is also worth recalling the idiosyncratic preoccupations that are at the roots of his approach, linking his phenomenological concept of looking at photographs to Goldin's diaristic and (neutrally speaking) sentimental use of the medium.

9   The event was organised on the occasion of the Kunsthalle exhibition "Emotions and Relations: Nan Goldin, David Armstrong, Mark Morrisroe, Philip-Lorca diCorcia und Jack Pierson", and as part of the series "Reden über Kunst".

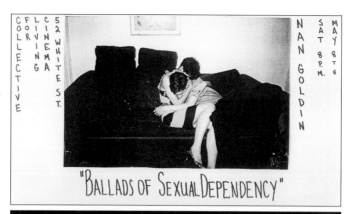

Fig. 5. A poster advertising Nan Goldin's Ballads of Sexual Dependency performance at the Collective for Living Cinema, New York, 1985. [©Anthology Film Archives, New York.]

Fig. 6. A view of the Collective for Living Cinema's projection room in the early 1980s. [©Anthology Film Archives, New York.]

and by her sound and image arrangements, she linked the parts of the picture sequence together: it is the ballad-monger's activity that, in her case, makes a more or less consistent, partly parabolic story out of the single events, and determines that the documents reporting those events cannot easily be understood as disconnected genre pictures.

At the same time, the slide projector and the soundtrack collaborate on yet another level, which has been frequently praised when it came to the particularities of Goldin's work. While the critical literature contains hardly any allusions to the obvious fact that Goldin's presentation mode is rooted in non-artistic visual communication, commentaries are constantly referring to its cinematographic features, thus acknowledging the high complexity and integrity of the shows, and a cross-media strategy that needs further clarification. One critic looks back on having first witnessed her picture sequences in a New York club, with slides changing every 10 to 15 seconds, as "a sort of filmic home slideshow consisting of image after image bombarding the viewer at the pace, more or less, of the average television shot".[10] Another writer asserts that it is "nearly cinema with its striking colours, music, themes, and characters, all in motion and telling a story that lasts 45 minutes". More or less identical testimonies can easily be found.[11] They all confirm an effect prefigured in Goldin's early choice of display contexts: it has already been mentioned in passing that in its early days, the *Ballad* would have been shown in movie theatres (Figs. 5, 6). As a matter of fact, Goldin's shows joined early punk film activities in New York, which were presented in the same kind of Lower East Side locations during these years, and hers shared their predilection for unsophisticatedly rough style phenomena.[12] Fittingly, the artist has repeatedly mentioned the influence that cinema experiences had on her own aesthetic approach. While certain films apparently had become important for Goldin due to their iconography and formal choices, she also makes clear, in a conversation with Jim Hoberman, that the very paradigm of the moving image is at the core of her work in structural terms. The "speed of images", and thus, despite frequent complaints of viewers who would prefer to contemplate certain single images at more length, the development of the "narrative thread" rather than the quality of the single photograph is what she was mainly interested in when she put her shows together.[13] While they basically intend to describe her own and her friends' lives, and the deaths of some of them, it cannot be dismissed that the notion of a particular narrative sometimes is at odds with the artist's engagement in bringing forward, by means of typologically-organised picture clusters, general opinions about the essentials of the relationship between the two sexes.[14] Yet, notwithstanding the difficulty of drawing

---

10 Henry M. Sayre, "Scars: Painting, Photography, Performance, Pornography, and the Disfigurement of Art", in: *Performance Art Journal* 16 (1994), no. 1, pp. 64–74, p. 64.

11 The cited passage is from Delphine Pineau, "La romance de Nan Goldin", in: *Cahiers du Cinéma* no. 501 (1996), p. 11. See also John Howell, "David Byrne and Nan Goldin", in: *Artforum International* 25 (1986), no. 2, pp. 8–10 (where, on p. 8, Goldin's printed *Ballad* is said to be based on a film work); Elisabeth Sussman, "In/Of her Time: Nan Goldin's Photographs", in: *Nan Goldin: I'll Be Your Mirror* (note 3), pp. 25–44, p. 26; Luc Sante, "All Yesterday's Parties", ibid., pp. 97–103, p. 101; Guido Costa, *Nan Goldin* [2001], London: Phaidon, 2005, n. p. [p. 11]; and other writers. Eric Mézil [untitled], in: *Nan Goldin: Love Streams*, Paris: Galerie Yvon Lambert, 1997, n. p. [pp. 62–72, p. 71], even goes as far as to suggest that each of Goldin's exhibitions, those of mounted prints obviously included, "is like watching a film".

12 Cf. Jim Hoberman, "A Context for Vivienne Dick", in: *October* no. 20 (1982), pp. 102–106, p. 104.

13 Cf. Goldin (note 5), p. 143. Fittingly, the caption of illustrations to one of the first critical essays dealing with Goldin's work made it perfectly clear that the *Ballad* claimed to guarantee a higher integrative quality to the isolated pictures, as it simply read: "Images from multimedia presentation of projected slides and taped soundtrack, 45 mins". Cf. Lisa Liebmann, "The Whitney Biennal: Almost Home", in: *Artforum International* 23 (1985), no. 10, pp. 57–61, p. 61. – See also Darsie Alexander, "Slide Show", in: id., *Slide Show: Projected Images in Contemporary Art*, London: Tate Publishing, 2005, pp. 3–32, p. 26 et seq., where short-lived projections are considered appropriate for Goldin's images of "people's fantasies and sorrows". Catherine David advocated a kindred opinion when she said that the ideal display of Goldin's pictures is the slide show (alongside the book) rather than the mounted print. She felt, however, that at the same time, slide shows put the intimacy of the works at risk. Cf. Chantal Pontbriand and Catherine David, "Entretien", in: *Désordres: Nan Goldin, Mike Kelley, Kiki Smith, Jana Sterbak, Tunga*, org. Catherine David, Paris: Éditions du Jeu de Paume, 1992, pp. 8–15, p. 9.

14 I share this opinion with Jonathan Weinberg, "Fantastic Tales: The Photography of Nan Goldin", in: *Fantastic Tales: The Photography of Nan Goldin*, Pennsylvania: Academy of the Fine Arts, 2005, pp. 1–30, p. 13. However, Weinberg states on p. 15 that the slide show format "heightens illusionism by effectively animating the events depicted", thus bringing them again close to a consistent narrative. On the increasing conceptualism in the *Ballad*, which at first had been a straightforward documentary of events past, see

conclusions about causal chains in the lives depicted, the picture sequences, with their continuous recurrence to certain characters and sites, stimulate thoughts on the passing of time and on the turning points in the particular lives we are becoming familiar with while watching Goldin's circle of friends. Audiences follow their paths beyond the chronology's frayed edges. Thus, a strong narrative remains present in any extensive presentation of her pictures, and most notably in her slide shows.

What is more, slide shows lend themselves to collective viewing, as their audiences do not have to walk along rows of mounted prints in order to consecutively take notice of the individual photographs. Absorption and the possibility of group experiences are thus both enhanced, just as they usually tend to be in the cinema. Now, what happens if we consider Goldin's slide show in terms of a motion picture as so many commentators have already done? The authority of the recording medium that is at the root of her documentary activities can arguably not be denied: we are obviously looking at still photographs when contemplating her work. However, the motion picture paradigm invites us to fill all the gaps between the individual pictures with the help of our imagination and, on a second level, with the help that our preconception adds to our imagination. Thus, we would treat Goldin's pictures as part of a never-ending series, telling the manifold epic of a New York-based community that has its protagonists as well as its minor characters. We would fill the missing links between individual images by connecting events from these people's lives, and, guided by some photographs obviously depicting crucial incidents, try to make sense and a story out of the historical fragments. But what is the consequence of this? Russian film director Andrey Tarkovsky once stated that filmmaking, according to his personal ideal, would involve picturing a real-existing personality from the time of her birth up to her death via millions of metres of film, which only afterwards would undergo a cutting in order to reduce the exceeding length of the report. It is noteworthy that this artist defines the "ideal piece" of filmmaking as a documentary process that encompasses a given entirety of events, and reshapes it by simply omitting the less instructive parts of the latter.[15] In a certain way Goldin's approach is close to that concept. She would not look at her own photographs primarily in terms of single works: they rather form a part of the very whole envisaged by Tarkovsky. They are reality bites, cut out from an unceasing stream of life, or fragments from that the integrity of that life (assum-

Goldin's remarks in Holert (note 7), p. 232. Lately, Goldin's slide show "Heartbeat" from 2001 has achieved narrative qualities that bring projected photographs closer to the motion picture's accepted way of story-telling. See, for a short notice on that work, Joanne Bernstein, "Playing With the Edge", in: *Seduced: Art and Sex From Antiquity to Now*, eds Marina Wallace a. o., London: Merrell, 2007, pp. 177–193, p. 188.

15   Cf. Andrey Tarkovsky, *Sculpting in Time. Reflections on the Cinema*, London: the Bodley Head, 1986, p. 65: "The point is to pick out and join together the bits of sequential fact, knowing, seeing and hearing precisely what lies between them and what kind of chain holds them together. That is cinema. Otherwise we can easily slip onto the accustomed path of theatrical playwriting, building a plot structure based on given characters."

ing that there is such). That said, doubts might arise about the integrity of the story that her pictures tell. Is it really obvious that they all belong to one meaningful complex of her own and her friends' lived lives? From this point of view, her resolution to present her images in the context of slide shows was again decisive, and it is significant that according to one witness the *Ballad*'s cinematographic effect was due to Goldin's intensive complementary story-telling.[16] The family slide shows that you might have watched at home when you were a child formed an integrative whole with the help of the family community's ability to recapitulate the past events shown, to share that knowledge, and to transform it into meaning. Slide shows would gain their own consistency by the ability of the audience to make, led by an accompanying discourse, a continuous story out of the visual fragments of history. Yet, there is a reciprocal effect between the formation of the show's narrative and the establishment of the audience's communal identity. The viewers would, on the one hand, create knowledge on the basis of the recall that the photographs offer to the viewers, describing to the audience those community members, facts, and events they have missed because they were not present at the moment the picture was taken, or were too young to remember, or have forgotten. On the other hand, the shows would confirm the consistency of the community by confronting the participants with things and events once shared by them.[17] If we keep all this in mind, it comes as no surprise that Goldin's actual presence was a regular feature of early shows of her work. Important as this presence was in terms of the authority it gave to a work that claims an author's subjectivity, it was even more important in this respect. In fact, the contribution of the artist's performative acts is crucial to the impact of the slide shows on the viewers, as it is also the case in comparable works of art.[18] Personal, live performance guarantees the narrative's integrity and reliability at the same time.

A short detour will help us to capture the reason for this. One of the rare attempts to theoretically justify the use of slides in art was written by Dan Graham who,

16 Käthe Kruse, "Die Slide Shows von Nan Goldin: Eine persönliche Betrachtung", in: *Dia / Slide / Transparency: Materialien zur Projektionskunst*, ed. Stéphane Bauer a. o., Berlin: Neue Gesellschaft für Bildende Kunst, 2000, pp. 76–79, p. 78.

17 Max Kozloff, "The Family of Nan", in: *Art in America* 75 (1987), no. 11, pp. 38–43, p. 41, pointed to a similar argument when mentioning the identificatory role that the soundtrack has on Goldin's slide show audience. See, for another confirmation of the music's relevance for collective identificatory processes, Kruse's account (note 16), p. 78. I wonder, though, why the author makes the point that the show did not have anything in common with homemade family slide projection. Her own statement that "all felt at home" while watching Goldin's show arguably points in the opposite direction.

18 Cf. Sydney-based William Yang's piece "From Sadness", which collected photographic evidence on the artist's friends suffering from AIDS and was frequently shown in public, thus becoming "part theatre, part group therapy and part public wake" according to a commentary written by Peter Blazey; cf. id., "Sadness: A Monologue with slides", in: *Outrage* 115 (1992), p. 42. His words make clear that social interaction and collective experience are crucial to the overall concept of this artist's work, and that he is drawing on the very same inherited qualities of the slide projection ritual that Goldin's work had previously been based on. Cf. also Ted Gott, "Agony Down Under: Australian Artists Addressing AIDS", in: *Don't Leave Me this Way: Art in the Age of AIDS*, ed. Ted Gott, Canberra: National Gallery of Australia, and London: Thames and Hudson, 1994, pp. 1–33, p. 28 et seq.

at that time, was a direct witness of minimalism's refusal of the author subject and of the self-sufficient material wholeness of autonomous artworks. Forming his own idea on the capacities of slide shows with respect to the nineteenth-century photographer Eadweard Muybridge's achievements in picturing movement with the help of a multitude of images, Graham pointed to the fact that "no single, fixed point of view" existed in this photographer's sequenced pictures, and admired serial photography of that kind for its deconstructing the conjunctive space of traditional narrative sequences. He argues that every image in Muybridge's series states an eternal presence, and that consecutive actions seem to lose their consequence. In Graham's eyes, Muybridge's photographs have no transcendent subject, as he cannot detect references to an artist's "I" behind the camera. All these observations and assumptions result in Graham's final qualification of the slide in terms of a flat serialised space, and as an art form in its own right.[19] One cannot help thinking that Graham was heavily driven by an agenda to enrol his work into the history of photography. It might thus be exaggerated to call this notion, as I have done above, a proper media theory. However, we can profit from his point of view when dealing with Goldin's epic. Whereas Graham underlines that projected series of photographs can enhance the decomposition of coherent space and time, she is reconstructing both using the very same medium. Goldin reported that at the time of her early shows, she was in a habit of replacing the slides with one hand while holding the projector in her other hand.[20] The artist might not always have been obliged to do without a projector pillar or, say, a table. Anyway, the practice can be seen as characteristic of the way Goldin used to handle her pictures, as it involves an antidote against the very properties of the medium that had caused Graham's admiration. From an allegorical perspective at least, this fusion of the artist and her tool reflects Goldin's relation to her subject matter. It is, in fact, identical with her self. Or should we rather say that her self is constructed by her subject matter? While Graham appreciated the possibility of overcoming the traditional darkroom of the cinema where the discursive functions of the medium would remain in disguise, Goldin rather tries to overcome the technical quality of her device, thus reinforcing Allan Sekula's point that the slide show, a "primitive cinema" as it were, allows us to individuate both the photographer and the subject.[21] Consequently, she never turned herself into a filmmaker with one exception, which in fact proves the rule in a particular way. In 1995, she was invited by the BBC to author a documentary on her own and her friends' lives with drugs and AIDS. The film, which was to be released as *I'll Be Your Mirror* in the following year, seems likely to reflect Goldin's will in aesthetic terms, though compromises were imposed on the artist

---

19   Cf. Dan Graham, "Photographs of Motion" [1969], in: *The Last Picture Show: Artists Using Photography, 1960–1982*, ed. Douglas Fogle, Minneapolis: Walker Art Center, 2003, pp. 97–98, p. 98.

20   Cf. Goldin's account in Holert (note 7), p. 232.

21   Cf. his remarks in Debra Risberg, "Imaginary Economies: An Interview with Allan Sekula", in: *Allan Sekula: Dismal science. Photo Works, 1972–1996*, Normal: University Galleries at Illinois State University, 1999, pp. 235–252, p. 241. Note that Sekula also refers to Muybridge's picture sequences.

during the production that left her unsatisfied with the result.[22] Thus, it is revealing that still photographs form a considerable part of it. Film footage from Goldin's early experiments with that medium interfere with pieces of newly added material. Overall, however, it appears that *I'll Be Your Mirror* does not give so much credit to moving pictures. Motion picture sequences merely swirl about the more substantial contribution that Goldin's still photography makes, and while the former have the advantage of allowing direct conversations, the latter arguably imposes itself more urgently on the viewer in visual terms.

Goldin's continuous predilection for her accepted medium arguably relies on that phenomenon of reception, whatever the pragmatic additional reasons for her fidelity to photography may have been. For her, the photograph apparently provides a pathos formula that motion pictures cannot achieve, or, to put it in Victor Burgin's terms, "a sort of representative autonomy".[23] The photograph claims, more effectively than any film, that life was precisely as it is shown by her representational activities. We might explain this with regard to the fact that still photography more easily implies the existence of an author subject. But this is only part of the cause. Photographs can satisfy the viewer's need or desire to find a reality, perhaps one that is linked to their own life, more adequately than films. Let us branch off once more in order to support this point from a phenomenological perspective. In 2002, Larry Clark, who had been an influential paragon of documentary photography and had become one of Goldin's own role models, released *Ken Park* (a motion picture much debated because of its very explicit sex and violence scenes). Part of the film is a scene in which a man shows the family's photo album to his daughter's boyfriend. Banal and meaningless as this scene seems in the course of the feature film's event, it can be regarded as a clue that helps us to decipher the significance of another element of the same film that in turn is important for its structure and aims, and that has an effect kindred to Goldin's pictures: the family album scene is about a virtually fetishistic contemplation of the frozen image as opposed to seeing a motion picture.[24] It thus teaches the audience how to deal with a series of still photographs that are spread over the first part of the film and present, one after another, the main characters of the film. These photographs want to be seen as "real" portraits of the personalities showing up in the film, accompanied by anecdotes on these very personalities

22 For an account of the production, see Hoberman (note 5), p. 143, and Heinz Herbert Jocks and Nan Goldin, "Der Glamour der Queer-Sicht oder, Warum ich mich wie ein schwuler Mann in einem weiblichen Körper fühle" [Conversation], in: *Kunstforum international* no. 154 (2001), pp. 294–313, esp. p. 300. Final editing was done by the BBC, and Goldin had to accept TV norms that she had misgivings about.

23 Cf. Victor Burgin, "Diderot, Barthes, Vertigo", in: id., *The End of Art Theory: Criticism and Postmodernity*, Basingstoke and London: MacMillan, 1986, pp. 112–139, S. 113. While Burgin refers to stills taken from films rather than to photographs taken directly from life, Goldin's life was, at least in the earlier of those years documented in the *Ballad*, modelled on cinema experiences, cf. her remarks in Hoberman (note 5), p. 135. Her slide show, then, suggests that her life has the narrative coherence of a film.

24 On the relevance of the fetish model in the comparative theory of moving and still images (and on related preconceptions on the side of the beholders), see Christian Metz, "Photography and Fetish", in: *October* no. 34 (1985), pp. 81–90, esp. p. 82, p. 84, p. 87 et seq.

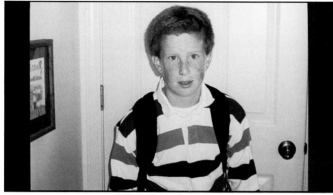

Fig. 7. Ken Park,
Larry Clark, 2002.
[©Pan Européenne
Edition.]

Fig. 8. Ken Park,
Larry Clark, 2002.
[©Pan Européenne
Edition.]

told in the voice-over (Figs. 7, 8). This alternative way of telling, adding information from beyond the film's narrative thread, supports the impression that all that follows is a reconstruction of real events rather than an invented story. Clark has always been engaged in giving authentic portraits of American youth. In an interview that was published on the occasion of his new film, he stated that he never stopped seeing himself as a documentary photographer.[25] The introduction of a private photo album into the film serves as a reference to this ambition. It represents the paradigm Clark's narrative follows: his film in effect, wants to compete with the authentifying testimonial value of snapshots. This is why the plot of his film falls into pieces as soon as one tries to recall it. It is restricted to a sequence of scenes that are not connected by a continuous thread. The redemption of physical reality through the cinematic medium, once famously proclaimed by Siegfried Kracauer, is thus guaranteed within the cinema by still photography.

However, a more important support for the argument that photographs are thus distinguished from film can be found in Barthes's attempt to deal with the very

---

25   Cf. Nikolaj Nikitin, "Alles zeigen: Larry Clark im Gespräch", in: *Schnitt* 4 (2004), no. 35, p. 59. A broader discussion of this feature film, and of the hybrid use of photography within its narrative, is given in Wolfgang Brückle, "Wiederkehr der Einzelbilder im Film: 'So ist es und nicht anders'", in: *Sehen Zeigen: Ute Eskildsen zum 60. Geburtstag*, eds Florian Ebner a. o., Göttingen: Steidl, 2007, pp. 94–97, esp. p. 96.

problem of comparing the impact of both media. He identified, besides an informational and a symbolic meaning of the photograph, a "third meaning" that establishes an erratic counter-narrative surplus, and a blunting of the meaning impossible to define in strict terms. In this respect, he is referring to accidental phenomena that, while perceivable on film stills, do not contribute explicitly to the context of the film plot, stating that "in this countenance, that grimace, that black veil, the heavy, ugly dullness of that skin you will have another temporality, another film". Being "a theme with neither variations nor development", as Barthes puts it in another paraphrase, the third meaning "can proceed only by appearing and disappearing" (whereby fetishism is actually evoked, albeit in disguise).[26] Obviously, this "third" or "obtuse" meaning anticipates what will become the photograph's punctum in Barthes' well-known book on photography, eventually evoked as a "camera lucida" by the author. In other words, it is what confirms the reality-claim of the photograph. No wonder he states that this third meaning can exclusively be detected in film stills. Actually he is turning them into individual photographs when dealing with the one unnameable feature of the images that comforts him, allowing for a notion of undefined reality in a system of referential codes. It comes as no surprise that he states in the opening paragraph of *Camera lucida* that he wrote the book "in opposition to the Cinema". Barthes found the complement to unresolvable reality in photography rather than in the over-structured movies, which are – to judge from her cine-matographic predilections, including Andy Warhol and John Cassavetes – disapproved of by Goldin as well.[27] With that in mind, it may be tempting also to associate Barthes's evocation of the "carnival" aspect in photography's resistance to encoded meaning with Goldin's own subcultural iconography. However, such an argument, rhetorical in the first instance, would not add much to the comparison between film and still photography, which is why it will not be pursued here. Yet, Goldin's slide show format is, on another level, carnival in Barthes' sense: coming as a series of fragments to the viewers, it cannot tame its recalcitrant individual parts. The parts profit from the symbolic value of frozen moments in time, suggesting that they share the complexity of reality's undisguised look. They are, thus, resistant to the pre-structured meaning that is implied in the author's sequential montage of the show and the latter's topical implications, and open to a life of their own, however short-lived it is within the shows.

26 Roland Barthes, "The Third Meaning: Research Notes on Several Eisenstein Stills" [1970], in: id., *The Responsibility of Forms: Critical Essays on Music, Art, and Representation*, Oxford: Basil Blackwell, 1986, pp. 41–62, p. 57. The "carnival" term, mentioned below in this essay, appears on his p. 44. On the significance of this essay in the context of Barthes' thinking, see Philippe Dubois, "Barthes et l'image", in: *French Review* 72 (1999), pp. 676–686, esp. p. 678 et seq.

27 Cf. Barthes (note 8), p. 3. On Goldin's idiosyncratic canon of directors, see the remarks in her conversation with Hoberman (note 5), p. 137 and p. 143. Warhol is primarily chosen by her as a model for the sake of his neglect of "the whole craft ethos", while she singles out Cassavetes with respect to his involving his own family and circle of friends in his work: "the same people over and over, basically playing themselves". In his catalogue essay on Goldin's "Love Streams", Mézil (note 11) surprisingly passes over the exhibition's evident reference to Cassavetes's feature film of the same title.

At first glance, Goldin's strategy looks familiar to all of us, and is not difficult to describe. Yet most critics focus on the content rather than on the medium when it comes to commenting on her tools and approach. This article's claim is that there is more to slide projection than the usual advocates of Goldin's shows reveal, and that the provocative iconography of her best-known imagery, though certainly not lost to importance in the overall structure of the work, does not necessarily need to be put at the centre of any attempt to explain Goldin's tremendous success in the art world. By means of the slide show, she appears as the speaking subject and underlines that there is an author to be found behind the camera eye and behind the story she is making of her pictures when introducing them into film-like integrative wholes. Thus, her credibility was not formed within the conventions of the art world but with respect to everyday visual commemorative culture and its customary media. Surprisingly, Pamela M. Lee did not concern herself with those qualities of the slide medium when she wrote a little obituary on the slide projector in 2004.[28] Yet we are probably facing a loss in this respect. While Kodak's abandonment of the projector does not mean that from now on slide shows become out of the question for artists, it nevertheless marks the ruin of the referential context that Goldin profited from when she performed her slide shows in the 1980s and 1990s. Her practice has to be seen as having direct dependency on the rituals of the home-made slide show, which was still a common genre when she started to make her art. Watching family picture-shows might have been boring sometimes, at least to some of us. But they helped to cultivate a way of watching and talking about pictures that is now at risk of losing some of its legitimacy in public. Looking at photographic prints is hardly as easy to turn into a performance event, and does not lend itself to story-telling such as is possible with slide shows that may partake in, yet also resist, the cinematographic experience.

---

[28] Cf. Pamela M. Lee, "Split Decision: On the Demise of the Slide Projector", in: *Artforum International* 43 (2004), no. 3, pp. 47–48.

3

Pensive Hybrids. On some of Raymond Depardon's filmo-photographic setups

Barbara Le Maître

This text originated in my recurrent puzzlement at the apparent (and perhaps deceptive) simplicity of a few objects articulating cinema and photography: *Contacts*, the series of short films produced by the Centre National de la Photographie since 1983. Before looking in more detail at one of these curious visual objects, it is worth recalling that the prototype for the series was directed by William Klein, who first had the idea of freely organizing and filming his contact sheets, adding a commentary that amounted to a statement of his conception of the photographic act.[1] The idea was deemed promising, since the C.N.P. asked other photographers to engage in a similar exercise after the five fellows initially chosen by Klein to launch the series.[2] Between 1983 and 2000, more than thirty films were thus devoted to works as different as those of Henri Cartier-Bresson, Don McCullin, Sophie Calle, Hiroshi Sugimoto, Bernd and Hilla Becher, or Jeff Wall, to mention but a few. As it is understandably difficult to broach such a heterogeneous series in its totality – from a thematic, but also from a formal standpoint, paradoxically – I will consider it through only one of its installments, conceived and directed in 1990 by Raymond Depardon.

I chose to concentrate on this episode for its obvious relevance with regard to exchanges between still and moving images that are the subject of this collective volume. At first sight, it might seem as though the encounter between stillness and movement is bound to be renewed and played out over and over again (and most of all, in a similar fashion), presenting only good objects to analysts as they make choices. After all, each installment of *Contacts* reiterates the minimal protocol presiding over the series, which consists in filming photographic images with a rostrum camera. On closer inspection, however, these objects are not equal

1 Raymond Bellour wrote on the prototype in "Six films (en passant)" in *L'Entre-Images. Photo. Cinéma. Vidéo* (Paris: La Différence, 1990) 135–137.

2 Robert Doisneau, Raymond Depardon, Sebastiao Salgado, Elliott Erwitt, and Marc Riboud. See Catherine Humblot, "Le roman-photo d'une photo" ["The Photo Romance of a Photograph"] *Le Monde*, 25–26 February 1990: 19.

when it comes to the problem of interest to us. Alain Fleischer, for instance (my choice of another filmmaker-photographer is deliberate here), does organize photographic elements and the cinematographic apparatus in a certain way. Yet he thinks of the dialectic of images less in strict terms of stillness and movement than according to a distinction between three overlapping systems of images (the reflection, the print, and the projection), which is known as a major preoccupation of his.[3] In short, despite a common protocol, the articulations between film and photography in *Contacts* may have rather different outcomes than simply questioning the relation between movement and stillness. By contrast, I will try and demonstrate that the visual object shaped by Raymond Depardon constitutes a project of detailed explanation of the cinematographic movement.

Another determining element in the choice of Depardon is that such thinking on the image and the conditions of possibility for representation, it seems to me, is not limited to his episode of *Contacts* and runs through much of his work, though according to different modes. Indeed, besides an often noted, quasi-permanent oscillation between fiction and documentary, a careful examination of the film work in its entirety reveals two sides: one concerned with representing, the other preoccupied with studying the terms of representation. More specifically, a first grouping would include the film works (in the usual sense of the term), and notably the many feature films exploring institutional systems, whether psychiatric (*Urgences*, 1987; *San Clemente*, 1980–82) or judiciary (*Délits Flagrants*, 1994), to mention the best known. The second group would comprise a number of films – like *Contacts* – variable in length and degree of hybridity, and which form the invisible part of the iceberg, so to speak. These, among which are titles such as *Amour* (1997) or *Montage* (1995), indicate the extent to which setups, more than images, are at the core of Depardon's investigations. In other words, the image is for him more than an instrument of representation, a single part or a cog operating within a mechanism rigorously assembled and capable, as such and proportionally to the rigour applied to its construction, of sustaining reflection on the terms of representation.[4] In Anne-Marie Duguet's words, concerning video installations: "what matters is not to produce one more image [...] but to manifest the process of its production, to reveal the terms of its perception through new propositions".[5]

As it happens, the setups which may be identified as integral to these films almost all involve a confrontation between film and photography. In that respect, they

3   All three image systems are implemented in an exemplary fashion in the following works: on reflection, see all *Objets capteurs d'images* (1982–1984); on projection, see the series of *Corps-écran ["Screen Bodies"]* (1971), in which slideshows projected on naked bodies are photographed; finally, with respect to the print (in French: empreinte), I refer the reader to *Autoportraits* (1993), which feature moldings of the artist's face made with a silver-emulsion paper.

4   It should be mentioned here that all these setups were devised in collaboration with editor Roger Ikhlef.

5   See *Déjouer l'Image. Créations électroniques et numériques ["Thwarting the Image. Electronic and Digital Creations"]* (Nîmes: Jacqueline Chambon, 2002) 21.

constitute as many ways to reexamine the relation between moving image and still image – as minor as they might seem at first sight, with durations sometimes not exceeding a few minutes. Accordingly, after examining the setup at work in his *Contacts*, I will broaden the scope of my argument to bring in another of Depardon's small films. But let us first consider what occurs in *Contacts*.

Like most episodes in the series, Depardon's work reproduces only one movement, that of the camera sliding horizontally over the photographic thumbnails – a movement *on* the image much more than a movement *in* or even *of* the image. Still, the shot is well and truly in movement and pertains to the "mobile section",[6] since photographic thumbnails succeed one another, appear and disappear, mercilessly rejected off the frame by the lateral movement of the camera. Consequently, it should be emphasized, I think, that in its prescription to combine camera movement(s) and static referents, *Contacts* as a series rests on the premise of a radical distinction between filmic movement and mobility of the referent – in other terms, between movement as pure power or pure faculty of the cinematographic mechanism, and movement as a phenomenon fundamentally independent of the image (if always liable to be recorded). Such a distinction is obvious; still, it is worth remembering insofar as, every time cinema is involved in the reproduction of the mobility of the world and its objects – even a few leaves stirred by the wind – the internal and external sides of movement tend to become confused, to overlap, with the mobility of the referent and the technical foundation for the movement of images mutually blending into each other and closely mingling, so to speak. On the basis of this initial observation – *movement in cinema is primarily the movement of the film, independently of the mobility of the referent* – Depardon's film engages into a more systematic analysis of filmic movement, which in my opinion sets it apart from other installments.

The singularity of this *Contacts* owes to the mode of its juxtaposition, in the form of series of three, five, six, and sometimes eight photographic thumbnails. Very minor differences may be distinguished between them: slight variations in framing, point of view, or light (Fig. 1). What is indeed striking when comparing several episodes of the series is that, where most photographers, and particularly William Klein or Henri Cartier-Bresson, privileged diversity in the photographed subjects as well as in strategies of photographic composition, Depardon opted for a type of organization founded on a principle of least differentiation between images. What is more, these images come from the same photographic

---

6   See Gilles Deleuze, *Cinema 1. The Mouvement Image*, trans. *Hugh Tomlinson and Barbara Habberjam* (Minneapolis: University of Minnesota Press, 1986), for instance on p. 24: "Epstein comes closest to the concept of the shot: it is a mobile section, that is, a *temporal perspective or a modulation*. The difference between the cinematographic image and the photographic image follows from this. Photography is a kind of 'moulding': the mould organizes the internal forces of the thing in such a way that they reach a state of equilibrium at a certain instant (immobile section). However, modulation [...] constantly modifies the mould, constitutes a variable, continuous, temporal mould." *Contacts* attests to the fact that the photographic dimension of the referent does not in any way preclude mobile (dis)sections in duration, as the freeze frame alone may result in an immobile section.

Fig. 1. Raymond Depardon, Contacts, *1990 (four juxtaposed screenshots)*

report devoted to Italian asylums. This pointed logic, which leads to linking snapshots barely different from one another to the point of producing series of photographic fragments seemingly interdependent, is unmistakable: it is the logic of the film frame, the primary condition for the impression of movement in cinema and a decisive element in the run of the film strip. To be sure, the films conducts its analysis of the ordinary movement of cinema through the same logic, made visible or reconstructed to that end, as well as – quite understandably – through the photographic snapshot,.

At this stage, it should probably be mentioned that the supposed "logic of the film frame" does not operate continuously in *Contacts*, since Depardon has series of almost similar snapshots alternate with other series involving more diverse images or, rather, series whose snapshots seem to regain their autonomy as photographic images rather than remain caught in an organization relying on the model of the film frame. Besides, the thumbnails of the contact sheet clearly derive from liberties taken with the pace characterizing cinematographic recording. Still, a parameter to take into account is the fact that the spatiotemporal interval between snapshots inherent to the recording in question is well and truly simulated and figured. As intermittent as it is incomplete, the logic that interests me here is nevertheless recurrent, and enough so that *Contacts* may be considered as playing, with a rather particular insistence and perversity, on a kind of exhibitionist and unconventional doubling of the fabric of film frames that makes it possible. So much so that we don't have one, but two, correlated "series of film frames" differing in status as well as effectiveness. On the one hand, actual film frames underlie this 35-mm short film yet remain invisible; on the other hand, curious articulations of photographic thumbnails, delivered more discontinuously and organized in horizontal rather than vertical series, *simultaneously imitate, forge, and expose the film frames upon which they establish themselves, making visible the mechanics of a movement that usually occurs in the utmost secrecy, next to the film strip*. I am writing "on the one hand" and "on the other hand", but both "film frame series" evidently unfold over the same media, the film strip – which in

itself makes the analytical process a bit dizzying. At this point, I would like to go into further detail to try and understand how this recapture of the filmic system takes place on a figurative level.

We are thus confronted with two series that overlap concretely without coinciding exactly, thus articulating the film frame as structural entity and the film frame as visual motif in a paradoxical fashion. Indeed, as I have underscored previously, the simulacra shown by Depardon contradict the ordinary invisibility of the real film frame, the standard unit of movement always annihilated by the projection:

> For the cinematograph had precisely been applied to vanquishing this immobile unit, *to outdoing it*. The quantity of successive images, calculated to arrive at a qualitative leap in the continuous unit of movement perceived by spectators had from the beginning forced the actual discontinuity of film back into invisibility: it had *occulted the film frame*.[7]

Something like a principle of anatomy may then lie at the basis of this setup, since with figuration we can now see the skeleton, the framework usually hidden under the effect of the run of the film through the projector. However, the way in which this mock skeleton appears proves ambiguous. In the first place, each film frame is figured as a still, juxtaposed unit here – which it is indeed, but only so long as the film print is approached outside the effects of projection and film outside the modes of its perception. Accordingly, what *Contacts* reveals is not so much the film frame itself as a type of film frame turned idle, deactivated, deprived of its usual role and effectiveness. To repeat the terms used before, Depardon converts an element defined by its *invisibility* and which primarily pertains to a *technical event* into a *visual motif* and a *figurative event* (even if the former makes the latter possible). Incidentally, the same goes for the run of the film strip, as the lateral movement of the camera, shifting from one photographic thumbnail to the next, substitutes a visible horizontal run for the vertical run that is a literal part of film – or, even more to the point, adds this horizontal run to the vertical one. All in

---

7   Sylvie Pierre, "Eléments pour une théorie du photogramme", in *Cahiers du cinéma* 226–227 (Jan.-Febr. 1971) 75.

all, this procedure of visual conversion allows a close look at the overall principle of filmic movement. Since this is where the paradox of this short film lies, I would like to insist on the fact that, at the same time as the principle of movement thus gets exhibited, the real film frames normally go on doing their work unnoticed so that, whether decomposed or analysed, the manufacture of movement keeps operating subterraneously.

In the end, the setup exemplified in this *Contacts* succeeds in formulating *in images* the dialectic of cinematographic movement by articulating the fulfillment of this movement and the examination or explanation of its principle. In granting the photographic snapshot a central place in his setup, Depardon acknowledges the conditions of possibility for the movement of film images, or better, its historical developments. Indeed, before it became a "logic of the film frame", the logic I have been ceaselessly referring to was Etienne-Jules Marey's logic of chronophotography on a mobile film strip.[8] In either case, the same analytical decomposition of movement is at work, expressed in the form of a juxtaposition of images barely different from one another, though separated by a temporal interval of varying length. Both the composition of the film in film frames and its chronophotographic origin thus surface in the organization of these simple contact sheets.

I would now like to expand on these thoughts on *Contacts* by evoking another of these setups involving photography and cinema that are Depardon's specialty, if not his secret. The object in question, a music video he directed in 1993 for the French band *Les Négresses vertes*, relies on the same protocol as *Contacts* (photographs filmed with a rostrum camera), but in a very different perspective. *Face à la mer* uses photographs taken by Depardon in Beyrouth in 1991 after years of bombings, all carefully placed side by side and over which the camera slides in a lateral movement. For all that, no logic of the film frame is at stake in this instance; neither is an explanation of the movement of images. Though this second setup shares the same photographic material[9] and technical equipment as *Contacts*, it turns out to be dealing with the history of photography more than with the history of cinema. Indeed, to put it succinctly, it seems to me that through this film Depardon revisits an old form of representation to which photography does not have an exclusive claim, but to which it still largely contributed: the panorama. In fact, the model of the panorama seems a logical choice insofar as *Face à la mer* has as its object the representation of a sprawling urban landscape.

In his article on panoramic views Philippe Dubois writes that

8   Or that of Muybridge who, in Philippe-Alain Michaud's words concerning the plates of *Animal in Motion*, effected a "fragmentation of the plate into distinct *photogrammatic units*". See *Le Mouvement des images/The Movement of Images* (Paris: Centre Pompidou, 2006) 21. [My emphasis]

9   With larger prints substituting for contact sheets, which implies the disappearance of 24 x 36 photographic film.

… two main types (as well as several subtypes) of photographic panoramas may be outlined: first, panoramas in the strict sense, that is, presenting a panoramic view *in a single image* (made in one shot); second, panoramas in a broad sense of the term (if I may say so), that is, produced by *assembling* several views (each of them more or less conventional), joined with precision […] so as to *reconstruct* the spatial continuity of a widespread field.

The same author also notes that

the subject matter [of panoramas] is always a little bit the same: landscapes (sea or mountains), sites of historical events (views of the siege of Sebastopol or of the theatre of operations during the Crimean war), large cities (especially Paris, seen from all its heights), monuments (always imposing, whether in length, as with the façade of the Louvre, or in a circle, with St Peter's square in Rome), large gatherings (military or corporative reviews).[10]

If this short film conjures up something of the panorama, it is perhaps more in the sense of the second type identified by Philippe Dubois – a piecing together of photographic fragments liable to offer a general, relatively complete vision of a widespread space – or in Muybridge's sense as he put together his *Panorama of San Francisco from California Street Hill* in 1878. However, where Muybridge's panorama did recreate the spatial continuity of the city of San Francisco, Depardon's seems to sculpt the broken physiognomy of a disfigured Beyrouth. The idea of a widespread field (the city as privileged subject of the tradition of panoramas) is present through small blocks of space precisely joined up while Depardon's filmo-photographic frieze unfolds a truly horrendous, perhaps inconceivable topography before our eyes.[11] Indeed, the "good form" of the photographic panorama, in order to reconstruct a given expanse, assembles *without any omission* pieces of space absolutely contiguous in reality. Yet *Face à la mer* places side by side non-contiguous spatial blocks and cobbles together a skewed, or forced contiguity – established over all that is missing, out of fragments which, while often finely connected, still attest to a lost continuity in reality. Depardon thus creates a genuine war panorama that makes it possible to assess the extent of the damage as well as the space itself. In the end, in this film as in *Contacts*, he invents a setup which does not stop at representation, but also constitutes a pronouncement on the modes and conditions of possibility for representation.

Ultimately, though it does not directly involve digital material, the work performed by Depardon with cinema and photography calls for a broadening of Anne-Marie Duguet's conclusion to her analysis of video installations, namely that all such work "…highlights, most of all, the fact that it is no longer possible to think of representation solely in terms of image. It should first be approached as a system, a process – technical, sensitive, and mental."[12]

---

10 For both quotations, see "Vue panoramique: l'affaire Marey-Lumière ou la question cinéma/photographie revisitée", in *Les Vingt premières années du cinéma français ["The First Twenty Years of French Cinema"]* (Paris: Presses de la Sorbonne Nouvelle, 1995) 424.

11 I proposed a more detailed description of this horrendous dimension in *Trafic* 39 (Fall 2001): 110–116.

If representation may no longer be thought "solely in terms of image", but rather in terms of "system", then something like the variable economy of movement and stillness within such systems remains to be mapped out, beyond the established categories of still and moving images.

Acknowledgments to Teresa Castro and Thierry Tissot.

12   Duguet, *Déjouer l'image* 42.

4

The paradoxical status of the referent of stillness in comics

Alain Boillat

Comics relies for its semiotic operations on a fundamental tension between still representations and the suggestion of diegetic movements. I therefore propose to shift the emphasis from exchanges between photography and cinema to this medium and examine what is at stake in comics, as far as the figuration of movement is concerned. Indeed, the sequentialization of drawn images stands between the pole of fixity, symbolized by the single photograph, and that of the moving image associated with cinema. With respect to such median position, movement generally constitutes the main guarantee of narrativity while remaining the inaccessible horizon of what can be represented. Accordingly, I would like to raise the issue of the expression of immobility or of the various speeds of action – more particularly in the cases where the absence of movement is signified through a reference to photography.

Of the necessity of the pregnant moment in comics: the theoretical interest of stillness as a signified

The case of illustrations whose referent is openly pointed out as still is paradoxical insofar as comics authors have traditionally used various formal devices to make their compositions more dynamic – and have the readers translate such impression of movement into mobility on the part of what is represented. A strip from the *Philémon* series (Fig. 1), in which Fred emphasizes the immobility of representation while ostensibly multiplying the ways in which a frame may be virtually animated,[1] showcases a few of these devices. Rather than presenting in succession the different phases in the progression of Anatole the donkey (the hero's sidekick), the author chooses to draw the animal several times in a strictly identical position. He markedly and gradually broadens the frame, however, so

---

1   Fred, *Philémon. Le Naufragé du "A"* (1972; Paris: Dargaud, 2003) 48. This strip, atypical in its format, does not follow other images. It stands as an isolated decorative insert on a page that serves as an interlude between two episodes.

Fig. 1. Fred, Philémon. Le Naufragé du « A » *"Philémon: The Shipwrecked of the 'A' ",*
Dargaud, 1987 (1972): 48.

that the animal as a whole eventually "fits" into one image. The play on the
dimension of the object of representation produces the impression of a movement, as the perceptive habitus of readers leads them to relate object size to the
distance from the source of the look. Besides, describing as he did a crescendo
through a series of steps that matches the direction of reading,[2] the artist
underlined the existence of a succession of stages. Characterized by the absence
of gutters between frames and a strong regularity (in terms of motif and extent
of enlargement), the strip brings to mind the seriality associated with the
decomposition of movement and one of its well-known historical inceptions,
Muybridge's work on the movement of quadrupeds. With their inanity exposed,
these devices designed to inject movement in the image appear in their rhetorical
artificiality.

Such an approach inevitably involves a self-reflexive dimension, as a page by Tori
Miki clearly illustrates (Fig. 2, read leftward).[3] This nine-frame, textless grid
takes as its object a flip book, a booklet that makes it possible to create the illusion
of an uninterrupted movement when its pages are flipped in quick succession
(each page features one phase of the same action in the form of a hand-drawn or
photographic image). In the first two tiers, the mangaka inserts a hand seemingly
flipping through the book on the edge of the frames, underlining the fact that
such non-mechanical, pre-cinematographic devices require spectators-users to
activate them. The movement of the character and objects represented in the flip
book is therefore suggested by the diegetic mise-en-scène of this specific reading
activity – on which the manga itself does not rely, even if the six frames in
question take advantage of the dynamization implied by the principle of animation of their referent. The mise en abyme effected by the last frame denaturalizes

2   The strip already appears on the previous page, but in the reverse order (the largest frame is on the left),
     suggesting an increasing distance. As it happens, the denial that anything has come to a *halt* is the subject
     of the meta-narrative text accompanying it: "L'histoire du naufragé du " A" ne s'arrête pas là…" ["the story
     of the shipwrecked of the "A" does not stop there…"].

3   Tori Miki, *Intermezzo,* vol. 2 (Paris: IMHO Editions, 2007) 92. The first volume appeared in English under
     the title *Anywhere But Here* (Seattle: Fantagraphics Books, 2005). I would like to thank Cuno Affolter,
     curator of the comic book collection at the Bibliothèque municipale de Lausanne, for pointing out this
     reference to me.

Fig. 2.
Tori Miki, Intermezzo,
vol. 2, IMHO Éditions, 2007:
92.

what had previously been considered on a diegetic level as an effective movement, not a reproduced one, i.e., the very act of manipulating the flip book, as though its underlying principle also held for reading mangas. The comparison between media tends in this instance to equate sequentialization in comics with the illusionist rendition of movement, while exposing the fundamental discontinuity of perception implicit in the characteristics of comics as a whole. Such is in fact the case every time cinema is brought up in comics in the form of film frames, as with the reference to *Battleship Potemkin* (S.M. Eisenstein, 1925) and the crib tumbling down the steps of monumental stairs on the cover of a film issue of *Pilote* drawn by Loro.[4] Significantly, this drawing intended for a specialized comics magazine opts for the pregnant moment of the comics frame, not the any-moment-whatever of the film frame.[5] In that respect, F'Murr puts forth a type of frame that taps into the potential humour of a hasty parallel between film and comics, ignoring the semiotic specificities of these two media of expression.[6]

---

4   *Spécial Cinéma!*, spec. issue of *Pilote* 599 (1971). I should also mention that in the lower part of the represented film strip, the logic of the comics page prevails again over film segmentation, as part of the crib's buckled wheel appears in the next "film frame".

5   I am using the dichotomy between *pregnant* instant as defined by Gotthold Ephraïm Lessing in his *Laocoön. An Essay on the Limits of Painting and Poetry*, trans. Edward Allen McCormick (1766; Baltimore, Johns Hopkins, 1984) and the *any-moment-whatever*, a Bergsonian notion that owes its notoriety in the field of film studies to Gilles Deleuze's reading of it.

6   F'Murr, *Le Génie des alpages* ["The Genius of the Mountain Pastures"], vol. 8, "Dans les nuages" ["In the Clouds"] (1987; Paris: Dargaud, 1996), central frame on page 35 (the frame does not belong in a sequence). On page 37, a medallion echoes this image: Copernicus, "jealous of Galileo, tries to create a comic book". However, as he does not rely on the cinematographic model, he proves unable to move beyond the still image.

Galileo is represented at his work table which, as it happens, is also an editing table. On the point of inventing the medium of comics out of a single film strip, he exclaims, "I cut the images needed for understanding from this film strip, I paste them on a white sheet of paper, adding dialogue in a chronological order…" Beyond the comic aspect resulting from the genealogical inversion of series of drawn images and cinema – in and of itself a telling element of the mutual influences between the two media – the mention of a choice of images "needed for understanding" is interesting, assuming as it does the extraction of pregnant instants out of photographs indiscriminately printed every 1/24 of a second.

When the stillness of the signifier in comics is displayed as it is in this type of references to devices that make the perceptive rendition of movement possible, the regime of enunciative transparency dominant in both comics and cinema is partly kept in check.[7] This represents an equivalent to the threat to narrative considered by Roger Odin in relation to Chris Marker's *La Jetée* (1962) and his examination of the "slideshow effect" resulting from the still nature of almost all the shots in the film.[8] In comics, however, the impact of the break introduced by stillness pertains to a different order, at least when comparing comics to the common conditions of the cinematographic projection. While both media deny the fundamental stillness of the single image to the benefit of the illusion or the suggestion of movement, the fact that the film runs through the projector bars the film spectator from any access to the film frame as a unit and makes it impossible to go back to a given shot. By contrast, comics readers have all latitude to observe each image in an autonomous manner, thereby gaining a more acute sensitivity to the individual existence of images.[9] The cinema, however, recaptures to some extent this particularity of comics reading through the various

7   The "transparency" in question is not as pronounced as in films characterized by "classical" editing practices, and clearly comics readers could hardly give themselves over to the content of frames or disregard the organization of the page. Still, it seems to me that comics may be approached in relation to the poles discourse/story theorized by linguist Emile Benveniste and adapted to cinema by Christian Metz. In fact, Thierry Groensteen admits to a degree of discursive transparency in comics as a medium when he writes that "every comics reader knows that, from the instant where he is projected into the fiction, […], he forgets, up to a certain point, the fragmented character and discontinuity of the enunciation". Thierry Groensteen, *The System of Comics* (Jackson: The University Press of Mississippi, 2007) [1999] 10. Trans. Bart Beaty and Nick Nguyen.

8   Roger Odin, "Le film de fiction menacé par la photographie et sauvé par la bande-son (à propos de *La Jetée* de Chris Marker)" ["The Fiction Film Threatened By Photography and Rescued by the Soundtrack (about Chris Marker's *La Jetée*)"] in Dominique Château, André Gardiès, and François Jost, eds., *Cinémas de la modernité : films, théories* (Paris: Klincksieck, 1981) 147–161.

9   Thierry Groensteen describes such difference between comics and cinema as follows: "For comics readers, each drawn image exists in its singularity. […] they may leave it behind, or they may go back to it as they like. […] What Deleuze aptly names the movement-image, and which is exactly the essence of the cinematograph, is nothing but the negation of the frozen image in which comics abounds. Thierry Groensteen, "Le support et le style" ["The Medium and the Style"], "Cinéma et BD" ["Cinema and Comics"] spec. issue of *Positif* 305–306 (July–August 1986) 54. Despite the questionable ontological conception of cinema as "movement-image", the difference Groensteen points out between the two means of expression matters in our context. Indeed, in the same issue of *Positif* Vincent Amiel uses the same theoretical framework when he proposes that an equivalent to Deleuze's time-image be identified in some comic books in which autonomous frames are let loose from the necessary reconstruction of an action. Amiel, "Ombres changeantes et papier glacé" ["Changing Shadows and Glossy Paper"] *Positif* 305–6, 47.

iconographies involved in the filmic paratext or even, when it comes to shots, in domestic viewing, with the freeze frame or rewinds made possible by the introduction of media such as VHS and DVD.

Approaching comics from the angle of the representation of stillness, it seems to me, presents the advantage of avoiding the danger of improperly equating any sequentialization of images with the cinematographic model. Moreover, I will resolutely argue from a position beyond dominant discourses in comics theory, which bear on the narrativity resulting from the organization of images in series or on the degree to which still images, whether unique or manifold, involve narrative content.[10] The examination of the narratological implications of the representation of stillness could take as its object the playful experiments with the medium such as those led by the members of the OUBAPO (an acronym for Ouvroir de Bande Dessinée Potentielle, or Workshop of Potential Comics), particularly in the form of what Groensteen terms "iconic iteration".[11] This type of exercise does not truly call into question the tension between stillness and movement, insofar as the image is systematically stripped of temporal referent (save for the temporality of the very activity of reading and the movement of the eye from one page to the next) to the benefit of a quasi-exclusive exploitation of the narrativizing potential of language.[12] The situation I propose to question here is the exact opposite, as I set out to examine less radical undertakings in which the succession of frames generally aims at suggesting movement, while a number of different techniques (and notably the use of verbal language) refer to the fundamental stillness of the medium itself.

Verbal neutralization of the suggestion of movement

It should first be noted that the action, and even the time it takes to unfold, may constitute the very referent of the text. In that respect, it is necessary to distinguish between the words ascribed to an extradiegetic agent (the caption) and those attributed to characters appearing in the frame and expressing themselves in the present of the figured actions (the speech balloon). Joann Sfar's *Le Petit monde du Golem* is a case in point in the latter instance: when a character points

---

10   On the subject, see Danièle Meaux, *La Photographie et le temps* (PUP: Aix-en-Provence, 1997).

11   In his inventory of constraints, whose creative potential he argues should be tapped into, Groensteen thus defines iconic iteration: "This constraint requires that sequences of varying lengths be built [...] around a single image or only a small number of recurring images. Not only are the framing and the point of view to be preserved [...], but also the image in all its components, to the exclusion of text." *Oubapo* 1 (Paris: L'Association, 1997) 20. Translator's note: a summary and translation of Groensteen's creative constraints by Matt Madden is available at http://www.tomhart.net/oubapo/constraints/groensteen/index.html on the OUBAPO America website. I want to thank Matt Madden, whose terminology I have partly used here.

12   In my opinion, such practices have still had a considerable influence on contemporary comics production. Indeed, after authors such as Lewis Trondheim, they have tended to be used from time to time in albums more traditional in their iconic narration. See my article, "Le récit suspendu: A propos du rythme singulier d'une certaine bande dessinée d'auteur" ["Suspended Narratives: On the Uncommon Rhythm of a Certain Auteur Comics"] in *Genève et la bande dessinée / Regards croisés* ["Geneva and Comics: Shared Perspectives"] (Geneva: Département des affaires culturelles de la Ville de Genève & AGPI, 2006) 12–19.

Fig. 3.
Joann Sfar, Le Petit monde
du Golem *"The Small World
of the Golem", Paris,
l'Association, 1998 (1995).*

a weapon at another, telling him "il faut que tu t'arrêtes" ("you've got to stop"), his line is taken literally. Indeed, everything freezes afterwards and the fired bullet remains in suspension in the air at a short distance from its target (Fig. 3).[13] In the following panel, framing effects a fragmentation of space that may suggest that the bullet has hit the victim "out of frame". Such an hypothesis implies that the first image shows Douffon right before he gets hit by the projectile. However, the larger, central panel, which encompasses the entirety of the space travelled by the bullet, reveals to the reader that the distance between the projectile and its target has not changed. The chasm that structures the composition of the page, whose last image constitutes a kind of reverse shot to the first while showing the same character, hints at the idea of stagnation. The text of the balloons makes it possible to convey to readers that they should deactivate the virtual animation they ordinarily rely on.

---

13   Joann Sfar, *Le Petit monde du Golem* ["The Small World of the Golem"] (1995; Paris: l'Association, 1998). In a line that reflects on the page that follows, Fernand says that the shot "broke the narrative continuum". Still, the plot keeps developing as this very stasis is taken into account by the two characters, who are still able to move their lips.

Fig. 4.
Daniel Clowes,
David Boring,
Cornélius, 2002
(2000): 10.

In the case of the extradiegetic caption, utterances are freed from any anchoring in the temporality hinted at on a visual level, as a frame from *David Boring* exemplifies with its narrator pointing out to the content of the image and referring to it as immobile (Fig. 4).[14] The page in question parodies representations of "love at first sight" that may be found in the slow-motion or freeze-frame shot of a film. The caption also mentions sound effects and music. With the meta-narrative perspective that dominates the album as a whole, Clowes thus refers to the moving image to allow himself the freedom to "oversignify" a stillness to which the medium he works in is essentially bound. Conversely, the parallel between media and the shift it causes activate the notion that the objects of representation in the ensuing panels are in movement.

Both these examples may lead to think that experiments with the exhibition of stillness are limited to underground comics or to comics published in the margins of the publishing industry. Still, the same goes for some productions subject to the constraints both graphic (an optimal legibility of the image) and narrative (an enunciation whose lack of inscription fosters "transparency") of what is usually called, in the French-Belgian comics tradition, the "ligne claire", or "clear line". While the implications are different, since no explicit reference to the medium appears in this type of production and stillness remains associated with

14   Daniel Clowes, *David Boring* (New York: Pantheon Books, 2000) 10.

Fig. 5.
Stan Lee and Jack
Kirby, Fantastic
Four, vol. 1, no 40,
July 1965 ("?The
Battle of the Baxter
Building?"): 12
(reprinted in
Fantastic Four.
L'Intégrale, Marvel
France, 2006: 137).

Fig. 5.
Stan Lee and Jack
Kirby, Fantastic
Four, vol. 1, no 40,
July 1965 ("?The
Battle of the Baxter
Building?"): 12
(reprinted in
Fantastic Four.
L'Intégrale, Marvel
France, 2006: 137).

the diegetic world, the dynamic of movement and stillness nevertheless exceeds the story world to encompass reading and interpreting. The frame that concludes page 23 in Edgar P. Jacobs's *La Marque jaune*[15] provides an example. The caption indicates that the mysterious character who has broken into the heroes' place "stopped short before the large Pharaonic mask", then specifies on a close up of the stone sculpture that "in the glimmer of the dying fire, the enigmatic face of the Egyptian ruler *suddenly seemed to come to life*!" To be sure, in the representation of the instant when mystical power temporarily reasserts itself on the being enslaved by the mad scientist's technology, diegetic temporality is not suspended. Yet movement is presented as the product of a character's imagination in a situation of "(ex)stasis", and identification with the character is encouraged in readers for the image of a still human simulacrum to come to life. Conversely, the awareness of an impaired motivity may partake of a nightmarish vision, with the character confronting a situation within the diegesis which concretely represents the paradox inherent in the activity of reading itself. The hero of Rossi and Giraud's *Nuit noire*,[16] who is prone to hallucinations, expresses this feeling of contradiction across two frames as follows: "Good Lord! I ... I'm moving forward ... and yet ... I am *at a standstill*!" Finally, the stillness of the medium was frequently referred to in the humoristic production of the 1970s spawned by magazine *Pilote*. F'Murr's *Le Génie des alpages* series epitomizes such a self-

15   *Blake et Mortimer*, Paris, Brussels: Dargaud-Lombard, 1987, 15.

16   *Jim Cutlass*, Tournai (Belgium): Casterman, 1999, 4.

reflexive approach, more particularly in an opus significantly titled *Bouge tranquille!* ("Move Still!").[17]

Durations internal to the frame: structuring in ph(r)ases

Two premises play an essential role within our framework: on the one hand, the text of phylacteries, or utterances assumed to belong to the diegetic world, institutes a duration; on the other hand, the virtual voice which supposedly comes out of the characters visible in the frame implies at least one movement, that of their lips.[18] The contribution of the linguistic component to what Harry Morgan calls the "internal duration" of the frame should thus not be neglected. When several characters are represented as speaking in the same image, several streams of speech coexist, which makes the temporal anchoring of drawn actions more complex – what is more, the speaker is often also a being that acts. As Morgan notes, "the words of interlocutors are obviously not in sync within the same image. The same goes for their actions, as each character lives at the time of its balloon."[19] Because of the possibility to institute a situation of "pluritemporality" in a frame, the suggestion of narrative tempo and movement as well as their management may involve many variations, since the different actions being represented do not necessarily occur at the same "speed".

By contrast to the vast majority of classical comic books, superhero comics paradoxically intensifies the phenomena linked to the virtual animation of characters, including through the suspension of their motivity. The extract of a page from a 1960s episode of *Fantastic Four* illustrates this aspect (Fig. 5).[20] The particularity of the panoramic frame that concludes the page lies in the fact that Jack Kirby represents a situation in which the gestures of most protagonists are frozen, even though they are assigned phylacteries. Quite evidently, this partial "freeze frame" is diegetically motivated since Fatalis, the group's eternal enemy, uses a weapon that can mortally freeze any opponent. This type of situation, in which heroes are threatened with reification or run the risk of being turned into

17   F'Murr, *Le Génie des alpages* 12, "Bouge tranquille!" (Paris: Dargaud, 1998). See for instance the last frame on page 19, in which one of the characters confronts the incredulity of others with his assertion that the mountain has moved, while a balloon attributed to the said mountain inscribes it in the unfolding of diegetic time. The gag remotely echoes that of the fourth book in the series, in which mountains, suddenly fitted with legs, decide to leave the pasture. See "Un grand silence frisé" ["A Big, Woolly Silence"] (Paris: Dargaud, 1978) 39.

18   Such virtual animation is also produced by the balloons grafted onto the still images of the singer in Agnès Varda's *Salut les Cubains* (1963). In her film, Varda used a process that evokes the invention of the "speaking cinema" patented by Charles F. Pidgin in 1917, and which consisted in introducing comics balloons in series of film images. See Rick Altman, *Silent Film Sound* (New York: Columbia University Press, 2004) 168. The process was also used in *Who Wants to Kill Jessie?* (Vaclav Vorlicek, 1966) as a direct reference to the world of comics superheroes.

19   Harry Morgan, *Principes des littératures dessinées* ["Principles of Graphic Literatures"] (Angoulême: Editions de l'An 2, 2003) 137.

20   Stan Lee and Jack Kirby, *Fantastic Four*, vol. 1, n°40, July 1965 ("The Battle of the Baxter Building") 12, reprinted in *Fantastic Four Omnibus*, vol. 2 (New York: Marvel Entertainment Group, 2005).

marionettes manipulated by a baleful figure, is recurrent in the series. In the case at hand, Dr Richards's elasticity (a justification for the most unlikely movements in *Fantastic Four*) defies the assailant's paralysing weapon. With this narrative motivation, movement and stillness meet within the same frame: while Fatalis can move freely and unhindered, the four protagonists are completely frozen. As to Richards, he is only partially immobilized. His arm is not paralysed and allows him to reach one of the switches of the machine.

The proximity of opposite elements of representation in terms of animation is frequent in action comics. Laurent Guido notes for example that the velocity of some comics heroes does not only owe to the simultaneous figuration of several phases in a gesture. It is also conveyed by the contrast between the swiftness of the main characters and the immobility that characterizes their environment in the amount of time corresponding to their actions:

> All these images put forth the fixed representation of an extremely short time, often juxtaposed with still elements in the same frame, whether potential spectators of the ultradynamic action or body parts that remain motionless, thereby contrasting with the represented gesture in its multiple figures.[21]

It should be mentioned that Carmine Infantino's *Flash*, the series Guido examines the most thoroughly, symbolizes the use of a decomposition of movement inspired by chronophotography[22] hardly shared by the majority of comics production and typically confined to comical works or works whose action is "choreographed".[23] The two types of *contrast* he identifies in the series (between parts of the same moving body and between distinct bodies, respectively) apply to many other types of representation of movement. Often, such differenciation in terms of motility is underscored by verbal indications.

The frame in *Fantastic Four* is certainly not devoid of visual elements connoting stillness: it does not feature any conventional figuration of movement, and the

---

21   Laurent Guido, "De l'instant prégnant aux gestes démultipliés: scansions filmiques du mouvement dans la bande dessinée" ["From the Pregnant Moment to the Multiple Figures of the Same Gestures. The Translation of Rhythmic Patterns from Film to Comics"], in Philippe Kaenel and Gilles Lugrin, eds., *Bédé, pub et art, d'un média l'autre* ["Comics, Advertising, and Art: Media to Media"] (Geneva: Infolio, 2007) 107.

22   In his famous illustrated manual of comics analysis Scott McCloud refers to the examples of Krigstein and Infantino in a note on what he calls "multiple images". See *Understanding Comics. The Invisible Art* (New York, Kitchen Sink, 1993) 112.

23   In a pedagogical book on the tricks of the trade in comics writing, Duc calls the device "stroboscopic effect", a term he significantly borrows from photography, and notably Harold E. Edgerton's strobe photography, pointing out that it is required to represent both acceleration and slow motion. Duc associates the former with a comical output and the latter with realistic comics. See *L'Art de la BD*, vol. 1 (Paris: Glénat, 1982) 85. In and of itself, the figure thus does not represent the speed of what is represented: it only indicates that speed should be paid attention by marking it off. The definition of speed also depends on the narrative context as a whole and on the postures of the character in movement. From my point of view, the paradox of a multiplication of phases of a same subject within a single frame lies in the fact that the rapidity signified at the syntagmatic level (the action unfolds before the gutter, and is completed by the next frame) finds itself thwarted by the longer time devoted to reading the frame. Given the stillness of the image, comics must to some extent spatialize temporality by guiding the eye on the page. The work of readers alone makes it possible to inject "from the outside" a duration liable to be correlated to what is represented.

position of a character in the lower right edge of the frame, rather than pointing to an out-of-frame space, simply marks the boundary of both the entire panoramic frame and the page. Besides, in the three previous frames, the consecution applied to the phases of one of Jane's movements helps convey the notion that the character still occupies the same position as previously. However, the presence of words is capital for the reader to grasp the still quality of most of the image. First, the dialogue between Fatalis and Richards implies a given diegetic duration which does not match in the least the density of action within the frame. Furthermore, access to the characters' thoughts makes it possible to allude to the partial paralysis of the Four's leader and to provide temporal indications (the time remaining to perform an action). Finally, the suspension points that punctuate some exclamatory phrases correspond to the phases of an action. The punctuation mark, which appears both in the balloon that contains the thoughts attributed to Richards and in Fatalis's address, seems particularly important to me insofar as "suspension", precisely, scans movement and segments the continuum brought about by the gradual extension of the arm. The page illustrates the role taken on by writing (with its connotations of orality) in guiding the reading of a frame along the lines of stillness or movement, as well as in assigning different speeds to some of the actions represented.

At the crossroads of media

It is worth remembering that it falls to readers to infer a movement from the frame and that such mental activity partly relies on a reading practice associated with the film image – at least when the reference is explicit. In his study of *Pif le Chien* published in the mid-1950s, film critic Barthélémy Amengual already suggested that the impression of movement be considered as "a factor that any eye cinematographically educated – and which eyes wouldn't be, nowadays? – spontaneously brings to reading comics, provided these works elicit it. Accordingly, any comic book may tap into such disposition." Amengual concluded with the assertion that "the objection opposing the stillness of comics to the movement of film may be dismissed as insignificant".[24] Despite differences on a perceptive level, with movement rendered and perceived in its continuity in cinema, due in part to the characteristics of human vision,[25] comics can draw on the reading competences and the memorization of images acquired in the process of consuming other symbolic productions. For instance, in reproducing images from Méliès's *Voyage dans la lune* (*A Trip to the Moon*, 1902) and Buñuel's *Un Chien andalou* (*An Andalusian Dog*, 1929) in his *La Dernière des salles obscures* ["The Last Movie Theater"], Paul Gillon refers to film heritage in a way that encourages

---

24   Barthélémy Amengual, *Le Monde de Pif le chien : Essai sur un comic français* ["The World of Pif the Dog: Essay on a French Comic Strip"] (Algiers: Travail et culture d'Algérie, 1955) 104.

25   Two phenomena come into play: the critical flicker fusion and the phi effect. See David Bordwell and Kristin Thompson, *Film Art: An Introduction*, 6th ed. (1979; New York: McGraw Hill, 2001) 2.

readers-spectators to inscribe the single frame in a continuum borrowed from a medium other than comics.[26]

Such modelling reference to another medium also involves photography, whose popularization of "speed streaks" from the 1910s on led a number of comics authors to a widespread use of the figure in their drawings. The codification rests on an analogical principle founded, not on a relation between representation in comics and the "real", but between such representation and a figurative mode assumed to mimic visual perception and strongly associated with photographic practice. Indeed, it consists in imitating the result obtained in photography when shooting is performed with a low shutter speed. Comics readers have internalized this convention partly on the basis of an *arché*[27] bearing on photographic technique. Drawing inspiration from cinema or (chrono)photography as early as the 1890s,[28] comics participated more generally in a "history of the eye" common to these various means of expression.

Explicit contacts in the form of citations thus represent a privileged site for the study of such cross-fertilizations. Given the object of this study, the second part of this article will be devoted to the discussion of the presence of photography in comic books. For the sake of space, drawn representations of photographs – often associated with the monstration of the act of taking photographs, as Hergé's work showed early on[29] – will not be treated. I will concentrate instead on the "collage" of actual photographs in the pages. Film citations thus presented should be taken into account, as they can blur the distinction between the photographic and the cinematographic.

Frankenstein: from the film to the photographic series

Images excerpted from a film[30] may be found, for example, in the third volume

26   Paul Gillon and Denis Lapierre, *La Dernière des salles obscures*, vol. 1 (Paris: Dupuis, 1996). On this work, and more generally on the question of the citation of film images, see my article "Mettre un film en cases, figer le mouvement: les enjeux de la citation filmique dans la bande dessinée" ["Putting a Film into Frames, Freezing Movement: The Stakes of Film Citations in Comics"], in *Cinema and Comics. Affinities, Differences and New Forms of Interference*, proceedings of the XVth International Film Studies Conference, Udine (Udine: Forum, 2009), 57–75. Despite the virtual dynamization implied by the reference to moving images, I note in the study that cinema is frequently instrumentalized by comics as a supplier of eternal icons and is thus paradoxically associated with still images.

27   The "savoir de l'arché", in Jean-Marie Schaeffer's words in *L'Image précaire* (Paris: Seuil, 1987) 41.

28   See for instance Thierry Smolderen's comments on the influence of Muybridge's work on illustrator and graphic artist A. B. Frost in "Ce qui se passe entre deux images ... L'héritage d'A. B. Frost dans l'œuvre de Winsor McCay" ["What Takes Place Between Two Images ... A. B. Frost's Legacy in Winsor McCay's Work"], in Thierry Smolderen and Jean-Philippe Bramanti, *McCay*, vol. 4 (Paris: Delcourt, 2006). Along with McCay or Frost, Frenchman Emile Cohl's diverse production should also be considered, as he moved from illustration to "comics" to animation, covering the whole spectrum from the still image to the moving image. See Donald Crafton, *Emile Cohl, Caricature, and Film* (Princeton: Princeton University Press, 1990) as well as my own text, which focuses more specifically on Cohl and comics, "Emile Cohl et les "histoires en images": le corps au pied de la lettre" ["Emile Cohl and "stories through images": The Body, to the Letter"], in *1895* 53 (December 2007) 111–127.

29   See *Le Sceptre d'Ottokar* (Brussels: Casterman, 1938) 3.

Figs. 6 and 7.
Jordi Bernet and Sanchez Abuli, Torpedo 1936, *vol. 3 (« Ni fleurs ni couronnes »*
[No Flowers or Wreaths]): 31–32.

of Bernet and Abuli's *Torpedo 1936*,[31] one of whose episodes begins with seven frames – each of them featuring an image of James Whale's *Frankenstein* (1931) full frame (Figs. 6, 7). In the book the film thus amounts to these seven images, two of which come from the opening and closing credits. These mark the boundaries of the citation and suggest that the film has been seen in its totality by the diegetic spectators, whose existence readers find out about shortly afterwards, and retrospectively. The presence of verbal language in written form in the titles creates a link with comics, itself most often characterized by the copresence of iconic and linguistic signs. In the first frame, the indications "Torpedo 1936" and Abuli and Bernet's signature appear superimposed with the title card from the film, itself inscribed over a blurred image of the monster. The position of the insert at the outset of the comic book heightens the importance of the cinematographic referent, as the world of the film substitutes for the world

30 From that perspective, a corpus worth studying would be the specialized comics magazines which, like *Pilote*, regularly devoted columns to theatrical film releases. Indeed, this particular context was an incentive for graphic artists to create page layouts involving film images while abiding by the composition model of a comics page. See for instance the four frames synthesizing the narrative of John Cassavetes's *Gloria* in *Pilote* 82 (March 1981, 21), a composition halfway between film poster and photo romance.

31 Jordi Bernet and Sanchez Abuli, *Torpedo 1936*, vol. 3, "Ni fleurs ni couronnes" ["No Flowers or Wreaths"] 31–32. This untitled episode is referred to as "Frankenstein" in the table of contents of the recent anthology of the *Torpedo* series, *Torpedo Intégrale* (Issy-les-Moulineaux: Vents d'Ouest, 2006) 117–118.

of comics expected by the readers of the series: the page has to be turned for the drawn characters to appear.

Reducing the 70-minute film to seven images, Abuli and Bernet could have sampled film frames every ten minutes, adopting a selective approach reminiscent of the conception of some Pathéorama films presented as summaries of film scenes.[32] From the second frame of this *Torpedo* episode, however, it appears that all images come from the same sequence, with some elements such as the threshhold of the door and the fire of the torch represented more than once. Such autonomy is only apparent though, as a precise comparison with the film reveals: frame 3 corresponds to the 29th minute of the film, frames 4 and 5 to the 35th minute, while the shot of the dying monster in the windmill's fire, also cited, only appears at the 64th minute of the film. The thin interval between images 4 and 5 makes it possible to reconstruct the defensive gesture of Dr. Frankenstein (Colin Clive) as he brandishes a torch. Despite the change in framing, which could be attributed to camera movement, these two moments could legitimately pass as consecutive in the film, with the comic book intertextually referring to continuity beyond the stillness of the two postures. The comparison of this series of images with the film invalidates such an hypothesis, since the movement by Frankenstein suggested in the fourth image does not appear in Whale's work. It is in fact a still – a photograph taken during the shooting – that was used as part of the film's promotional material. Besides, the image in the second frame also came from the filmic paratext; and the image in the third frame, while related to Boris Karloff's first appearance, differs in its framing from the corresponding shot in the version of the film I examined.[33] As to the fourth image, it was reframed in order to exclude the character of Dr Waldman who, shortly thereafter in the film, rushes towards the monster to stick a syringe of morphine in his back. Focusing on the creator and his creature, the authors of the comic book reinforced the impression of a narrative continuity between images 4 and 5. The transition from one image to the next, which represents a crucial moment in the economy of the page, significantly occurs where the insertion of a film frame follows that of a photograph, as though citation aimed to redirect the pregnant moment of horrific attraction towards the any-moment-whatever of a narration represented through acts. What is more, the use of stills initially meant for the promotion of *Frankenstein* provides insight into the constraints faced by Bernet and Abuli in trying to avoid devoting the integrality of the episode's pages to the film. Indeed, they had to select pregnant moments just as Universal had chosen striking, emblematic images for the film's posters. The intertext of the single still image, once circulated as part of the filmic paratext, thus finds its place between the still yet sequentialized images of comics and the moving images of film.

The exchanges between stillness and movement involved in such citational

---

32   See Valérie Vignaux's essay in this volume.

33   *Frankenstein*, DVD (zone 2), Universal, 2002.

practice highlight some implications of the difference between cinema and comics with respect to the figuration of movement. What lies between images is generally not perceptible in cinema. As to the frame in comics, Groensteen writes that "with regard to the length of time that it "represents" and condenses, its loose status is intermediate between that of the shot and that of the photogram".[34] The frame comes closer to one or the other depending on the circumstances, and this median position accounts for the constant tension between stillness and animation. Accordingly, comics authors rarely show much preoccupation with the reproduction of movement in its continuity. Rather, they favour the linearity of the *narrative*, singling out but a few phases useful to the general intelligibility of the action. Correlatively, readers come to rely on a competence which, as Paul Ricoeur explains in a broader context, consists in "[utilizing] in a significant manner the conceptual network that structurally distinguishes the domain of action from that of physical movement".[35] Ricoeur argues that the operation of mental reconstruction of the action does not require taking into account all the characteristics of movement.

The insertion of photography in comics

Whenever photographs are inserted in comic books, like transplants of foreign bodies, their function is twofold. On the one hand, they create a reality effect insofar as photographic images are considered from the standpoint of their indexical or documentary value, as traces also possessing a heightened degree of iconicity.[36] On the other hand, they entail a reflexive approach, as the change in medium denotes the materiality of the image or the modal heterogeneity of the diegetic world. These two aspects frequently combine, as with Mathieu[37] or Schuiten and Peeters.[38] Both functions can also be identified in a full page of *Fantastic Four* in which the characters, drawn in colours, stand out on the background of a setting photographed in black and white.[39] The accompanying comment humorously states that the reproduction of a photograph was preferred to what seemed the easy way – inserting a Surrealist drawing. The personal pronoun "we" used in the comment refers to the agency responsible for the production of the image, whose presence is often underlined in this popular

---

34   Groensteen, *The System of Comics* 26.

35   Paul Ricoeur, *Time and Narrative*, vol. 1 (Chicago: The University of Chicago Press, 1984) 54–55.

36   See for instance Art Spiegelman, *Maus*, vol. 2 (New York: Pantheon Books, 1991) 134; or, for a humorous use playing on the degree of figurativity, Gotlib, *Gai-Luron* 8, "Gai-Luron drague comme une bête" ["Gai-Luron Picks Up Girls Like Crazy"] (Paris: Audie, 1980) 27.

37   Marc-Antoine Mathieu, *Julius Corentin Acquefacques, prisonnier des rêves* ["Julius Corentin Acquefacques, Prisoner of Dreams"], vol. 2, "La Q..." ["The Qu..."] (Paris: Delcourt, 1991) 5.

38   François Schuiten and Benoît Peeters, *L'Enfant penchée* ["The Leaning Child"] (Tournai: Casterman, 1996) 139,142.

39   Stan Lee and Jack Kirby, *Fantastic Four Annual*, vol. 3, 1965 ("Bedlam at the Baxter Building") 20. Reprinted in *Fantastic Four Omnibus*, vol. 2 (New York: Marvel Comics, 2007).

comics intended for fans. The text in question takes a course opposite to a common one in the field of comics, which views photography as a cheap expedient suited to authors unwilling (or unable) to draw what they need to represent.[40] Such conception has to do with a quest for legitimacy, which leads to consider the insertion of photography as "unnatural". This resistance to the integration of photography *proper*[41] may be explained in part by the way in which the implacable stillness of photographs short-circuits the efforts of virtual animation characterizing creation in comics – as opposed to the practice of illustration, for instance, and steering clear of the highly discredited "genre" of the photo romance.[42] Danielle Chaperon reaches a similar conclusion in relation to the citation of pictorial works by comics authors:

> We are touching on a quality specific to images in comics: they are still images carried along by the movement of the represented action, thanks to the eye of the reader which hurries from one frame to the next, one tier to the next, from the top to the bottom of pages. [...] Compelling the eye to retroactively cancel this energy of animation is, when all is said and done, a gesture of great violence.[43]

If, in the case of inserted photographs, an increased heterogeneity of the signifier singles out citations, emphasizing their status as graft, the violence perpetrated against the activity of reading is just as significant. By way of conclusion, a succinct analysis of *Le Photographe* ["The Photographer"] will show how this question is dealt with in a successful attempt to combine drawn strips and photography.

The photographer and the drawer

An account of a 1986 Doctors Without Borders mission in Afghanistan, *Le Photographe*[44] associates text (phylacteries and captions), frames drawn in colours,

---

40   This excludes photography confined to the margins of albums (prefaces of postfaces), as is often the case with *Lucky Luke*.

41   Besides its use during the creation of the drawing, that is, since no traces of this early stage are supposed to remain in the final work, except with some authors such as Bilal.

42   Besides the exhibition of stillness, the nature of the referencing process constitutes another factor of resistance. The intrusion of photography produces a tension between its status as a trace, a print obtained mechanically and the complete reconstruction of a world done by drawing from a blank sheet of paper.

43   Danielle Chaperon, "De la toile à la bande: la représentation de l'œuvre picturale dans la BD" ["From the Canvass to the Strip: The Representation of the Pictorial Work in Comics"], in Kaenel and Lugrin, *Bédé, pub et art, d'un média l'autre* 38–39.

44   Emmanuel Guibert, Didier Lefèvre and Frédéric Lemercier, *Le Photographe* (Paris: Dupuis, 2003–2006). The account of this journey also exists across two other media, which further develop the exchanges between means of expression initiated with the comic book. Besides his contribution to the albums, photographer Didier Lefèvre published a long-format book on the model of the art book, with large-format images, *Voyages en Afghanistan: le pays des citrons doux et des oranges amères* ["Journeys in Afghanistan. The Land of Sweet Lemons and Sour Oranges"] (Rennes: Editions Ouest-France, 2003). Emmanuel Guibert authored the comics which serves as a preface to the book, while Juliette Fournot, who oversaw the expedition for Doctors Without Borders, made a mid-length documentary film. Significantly, the film is distributed on DVD along with the third volume of *Le Photographe*. The album drawn by Guibert remains the central work in a whole that also includes the two other productions.

Figs. 8.
Emmanuel Guibert,
Didier Lefèvre and
Frédéric Lemercier, Le
Photographe *(The*
Photographer)*, vol. 1,*
Dupuis, 2003: 38.

and black-and-white photographs in a whole that generally follows the conventions of comics, as far as images and page layout go. Field photographer Didier Lefèvre and comic-book artist Emmanuel Guibert collaborated on an original work which does not reduce the snapshots made during the expedition to a traditional function of documentary material preceding the period of creation. They are instead perfectly integrated to a narrative approaching autobiography (centering on the character of the photographer, as the title indicates) and to pages in which they periodically relay drawn frames. The exploitation of their status as traces involves exhibiting the stillness of what is represented, whereas most of Guibert's frames assume a virtual, traditional animation. Such relative autonomization of photographic frames, which partly disrupts the linear reading of sequentialized images, is in fact reinforced by the display of their materiality, the silver-based emulsion. Indeed, these images – laid out with less regularity than drawn frames, yet aligned with these and with blocks of text – look as though

Figs. 9. E. Guibert, D. Lefevre and F. Lemercier, Le Photographe (The Photographer), vol. 1, Dupuis, 2003: 33.

they came from a contact sheet. The presence of perforations or printed information ("Ilford HP5", the numbers of the photographs) as well as parts of adjacent
images occasionally suggest this (Fig. 8). These layout choices point to incompleteness, to a work in progress contrasting with the finish of drawn frames.[45]
Some photographs are thus circled or crossed out in red pencil as if they had been
selected for or rejected from a future publication. Their very insertion partakes
of biographical reconstruction, since the work of the main character is not limited
to shooting.

The respective amounts of space devoted to drawing and photography fluctuate
considerably from one page to the next, as some pages sometimes feature only
one type of images. Still, the dominant mode is mixity, which raises the issue of
"joints" between the two media as well as the question of a potential continuity
in the figuration of movement, with respect to the objects of representation. As
it happens, such continuity does not constitute a decisive parameter in the book:
drawing does not aim to pick up an action where photography left it off, and most
of the time the juxtaposition of photographs does not have as its purpose to instill
animation in the representation. In fact, drawing comes to fill in what was not

45 Though such characteristic applies to photographs and not to drawings, it seems to me that the very
    possibility of this type of work in the current publishing context of comics probably owes a lot to recent
    developments in what has been called the "Nouvelle bande dessinée" ["New Comics"], which privileges
    an autobiographic dimension and the sketch as such (personal diaries, travel notebooks, etc.).

Figs. 10.
E. Guibert, D.
Lefèvre and F.
Lemercier, Le
Photographe "The
Photographer", vol. 2,
Dupuis, 2004: 19.

photographed through the addition of elements useful to narration or of characters in a situation where they speak. As to the series of photographs depicting the same action, they do not so much exacerbate the phases of that action as they refer to the very act of taking pictures and to the rhythm of the various releases of the shutter on the camera, frequently mentioned in the first-person text focusing on the photographer's activity. The pages of the album also convey the impression that Lefèvre rarely shoots in rapid-fire mode, as he generally does not photograph fast-moving objects and does not take photographs from moving vehicles.[46] The authors, and notably Frédéric Lemercier, who was in charge of the page layout, nevertheless took a certain care in suggesting movement through sequentialization in the case of a specific type of represented element: draft animals. Horses boarding a trailer – a Muybridgean motif that attests to the enduring association between serialized images and animal physiology – (Fig. 9)[47] and cattle thrashing wheat in a circular movement (Fig. 10)[48] provide obvious examples.

46   By contrast, this type of images made blurry by movement may be found in Lefèvre, *Voyages en Afghanistan*.

Fig. 11.
E. Guibert, D.
Lefèvre and F.
Lemercier, Le
Photographe *(The*
Photographer), vol. 1,
Dupuis, 2003: 6.

What is more, a horse appears on the very first page of the first volume (Fig. 11).[49] Cropping up in the part of the book that shapes the "reading contract", the question of setting the photographic image in motion is put on the table so as to announce the mode that will dominate the trilogy as a whole. Indeed, the organization of photographs as a series does not aim at the analysis of movement since, like Fred's donkey, the animal keeps the same posture. The only change affects the quality of the image, which constantly improves, as it would in a developer. This logic of succession points to our attention that the authors share as their main concern the figuration of the birth of the image – not the temporality of what is represented, but that involved in the very making of representation. Finally, the parallel between the written mentions on this opening page and the credits of a film should be noted. *Le Photographe* constitutes one of these crossroads between media whose study, from a comparatist standpoint, proves productive in understanding the different ways to figure movement. For comics, these range from "oversignifying" stillness to suggesting the coexistence of different speeds within the same image.

47   Guibert, Lefèvre and Lemercier, *Le Photographe*, vol. 1 (2003) 33. It is one of the rare passages of the album that in a sense finds itself "animated" in a sequence of Juliette Fournot's film.

48   Guibert, Lefèvre and Lemercier, *Le Photographe*, vol. 2 (2004) 19.

49   Guibert, Lefèvre and Lemercier, *Le Photographe*, vol. 1, 6.

Biographical Notes on the Contributors

Laurent Guido is Professor and Chair at the University of Lausanne (Film Studies department). He was a Visiting Professor at the University of Montreal and the University of Paris Ouest Nanterre-La Défense. His work addresses the relations between cinema, music and dance, as well as film historiography. Most recent books and edited volumes include *L'Age du Rythme* (Payot, 2007); *Aux sources du burlesque* (AFRHC/Giornate del Cinema muto, 2010, with L. Le Forestier); *Rythmer/Rhythmize (Intermédialités* 18, Fall 2010, with M. Cowan). He is currently completing a book about dance in early cinema.

Olivier Lugon is art historian, Professor at the University of Lausanne (Film Studies department). His research has focused on German and American photography of the inter-wars years, documentary photography, exhibition design, the relationships of photography and architecture, and automotive vision. His publications include *La Photographie en Allemagne: Anthologie de textes, 1919-1939* (Chambon, 1997), *August Sander Landschaften* (Schirmer/Mosel, 1999), *Le Style documentaire: D'August Sander à Walker Evans, 1920-1945* (Macula, 2002, 3rd printing 2011), *Le Pont transbordeur de Marseille* (with Philippe Simay and François Bon, INHA/Ophrys, 2012) and *Exposition et médias: photographie, cinéma, télévision* (L'Age d'Homme, 2012). He was Ailsa Mellon Bruce Visiting Fellow at the Center for Advanced Study in the Visual Arts, National Gallery of Art, Washington, and Getty Scholar at the Getty Research Institute, Los Angeles. He currently directs the Swiss National Science Foundation research project "The modern exhibition of photography, 1920-1970".

★★★★

François Albera is Professor in Film Studies at the University of Lausanne, member of the Executive Committee of AFRHC and of the Editorial Board of *1895: revue d'histoire du cinéma*. He edited in French essays of Eisenstein, Kuleshov, the Russian Formalists, and is the author of *Eisenstein et le constructivisme russe* (Eisenstein and the Russian Constructivism) (1990), *Albatros, des Russes à Paris 1919-1929* (Albatros, Russians in Paris 1919-1929) (1995), *L'Avant-Garde au cinéma* (Avantgarde Cinema) (2006). Recent publications include (as co-editor) a special issue of *Cinemas: Journal of Film Studies* on Filmology (2009) and *Cinema Beyond Film: Media Epistemology in the Modern Era* (2010), *Ciné-dispositifs: Spectacles, cinéma, télévision, littérature* (2011).

Diane Arnaud is Senior Lecturer in Film Aesthetics at the University of Paris Diderot. She has authored *Figures d'enfermement. Le cinéma de Sokourov* (2005) and *Kiyoshi Kurosawa: Mémoire de la disparition* (2007). She is to complete a new essay on *Changements de têtes, de Georges Méliès à David Lynch* (2012).

Mireille Berton teaches Film History at the University of Lausanne. She is the author of articles on the relationships between cinema and sciences of mind/medecine/psychiatry. She is currently working on the publication of her doctoral research: *For a Crossed History of Audiovisual Dispositifs and Sciences of Mind around 1900. The construction of cinematographic spectatorship* (L'Age d'Homme, 2012). She also co-edited with Anne-Katrin Weber *Du Téléphonoscope à YouTube. Pour une archéologie de l'audiovision* (Antipodes, 2009).

Christa Blümlinger is Professor in Film Studies at the University Vincennes-Saint-Denis (Paris 8). Among her former teaching activities, she was Assistant Professor at the University Sorbonne

Nouvelle and Guest Professor at the Free University Berlin. Numerous curatorial and critical activities in Vienna, Berlin and Paris. Her publications include the edition of writings of Harun Farocki (in French) and of Serge Daney (in German) and books about essay film, media art, film aesthetics and Austrian cinema. Her most recent publication in German is: *Kino aus Zweiter Hand. Zur Ästhetik materieller Aneignung im Film und in der Medienkunst*, Berlin (Vorwerk 8, 2009) about appropriation in film and media art, and in French, *Théâtres de la mémoire. Mouvement des images* (co-edited with Sylvie Lindeperg, Michèle Lagny *et alii*, Presses Sorbonne Nouvelle, « Théorème 14 », 2011).

Alain Boillat is Professor in Film Studies at the University of Lausanne. He has authored numerous scholarly articles both in periodicals (*1895, Cinémas, Décadrages…*) and in books on audiovisual dispositives, on the relations between comics and cinema, and on issues surrounding narrative in visual medias. He published *La Fiction au cinema* ("Fiction in Film", L'Harmattan, 2001), *Du bonimenteur à la voix over* ("From the Lecturer to the Voice-over", Antipodes, 2007) and recently served as the editor for *Les Cases à l'écran. Bande dessinée et cinéma en dialogue* ("Comics Frames on the Screen", Georg, 2010) and, in collaboration with Jean Kaempfer und Philippe Kaenel, for *Jésus en représentations. De la Belle Epoque à la post-modernité* ("Representations of Jesus. From Belle Epoque to Postmodernism", Infolio, 2011).

Wolfgang Brückle trained as an art historian in Marburg, Dijon and Hamburg. His 2001 PhD thesis discusses art in fourteenth-century France. He was an Assistant Curator at the Staatsgalerie Stuttgart, and an Assistant Professor at the universities of Stuttgart and Bern. From 2007, he worked at the University of Essex; since 2010, he has been teaching art history at Zürich University as a Guest Professor for the history of photography and in other areas. Brückle's research interests focus on medieval art, early modern art theory and contemporary art.

Myriam Chermette is a Library Curator. Graduate of the Ecole nationale des Chartes and Doctor in history, she studied the photography in daily press in her doctoral thesis: *Picturing. Photography in Le Journal: discourses, practices, uses (1892-1944)*. Historian of photography and member of the Editorial board of the journal *Etudes photographiques*, she published some articles about the relationship between photography and media.

Clément Chéroux is Curator for Photography at the Centre Pompidou – Musée national d'art moderne. Photo historian, PhD in Art history, he recently published *Henri Cartier-Bresson, le tir photographique* (Gallimard, 2008) and *Diplopie, l'image photographique à l'ère des médias globalisés: essai sur le 11 septembre 2001* (Le Point du jour, 2009). He was the curator of *Mémoire des camps. Photographies des camps de concentration et d'extermination nazis, 1933-1999* (2001), *Le Troisième œil. La photographie et l'occulte* (2004), *La Subversion des images: surréalisme, photographie, film* (2009), *Shoot! La photographie existentielle* (2010), *From here on* (2011), *Brancusi, photographie, film* (2011), *Edvard Munch, l'œil moderne* (2011), *Derrière le rideau, l'esthétique Photomaton* (2012).

David Forgacs holds the Guido and Mariuccia Zerilli-Marimò Chair of Contemporary Italian Studies at New York University. He was Panizzi Professor of Italian at University College London, 1999-2011. Before that he was Reader in Film Studies at Royal Holloway (2007-2009), University Lecturer in Italian and Fellow of Gonville and Caius College, Cambridge (1989-97) and Lecturer in Italian and European Studies at Sussex (1978-89). His recent publications include *Mass Culture and Italian Society from Fascism to the Cold War* (with Stephen Gundle) (Indiana University Press, 2007); *Rome Open City* (BFI Film Classics, 2000); *Roberto Rossellini: Magician of the Real* (co-edited with Sarah Lutton and Geoffrey Nowell-Smith, BFI, 2000); *L'industrializzazione della cultura italiana, 1880-2000* (2nd edition, Il Mulino) and *The Antonio Gramsci Reader* (2nd edition, NYU Press, 2000).

Michel Frizot, photography historian, is Director of Research Emeritus at CNRS. A specialist of the work of Étienne-Jules Marey and chronophotography, he has also written on the identity of and movement in photography, the relationship of photography to cinema, the calotype, photographic magazines, amateur photography, Lartigue, Niépce, Bayard, Bonnard, Kertész, Frank, Appelt, etc. He was the leading author and editor of *A New History of Photography* (Bordas/Adam Biro, 1994, and Oxford, 2001), which has become a standard reference book for the history of the medium. Other major works include: *E.-J. Marey: The Photography of Movement* (Centre Pompidou, 1977); *Histoire de Voir* (Actes Sud, Photo Poche, 1989); *Etienne-Jules Marey: Chronophotographe* (Nathan/Delpire, 2001); *Henri Cartier-Bresson: Scrapbook* (Thames & Hudson, 2007); *Photo Trouvée* (with C. de Veigy, Phaidon, 2006); *VU: The Story of a Magazine* (with C. de

Veigy, Thames & Hudson, 2009); *André Kertész* (with A. L. Wanaverbecq, Hazan/Jeu de Paume, 2010).

Thierry Gervais is a Researcher in Residence at the Ryerson Image Centre (Toronto, Canada). He teaches history of photography at Ryerson University, and is pursuing research about the use of photography in magazines and the first photoreporters. He is the Editor in Chief of *Études photographiques* and published *La photographie. Histoire, technique, presse, art* (with Gaëlle Morel, Larousse, 2008). He was the curator of the exhibition *Léon Gimpel: les audaces d'un photographe* (Musée d'Orsay, Paris, 2008).

Tom Gunning is Distinguished Service Professor in the Department on Cinema and Media at the University of Chicago, and author of *D.W. Griffith and the Origins of American Narrative Film* (University of Illinois Press, 1991), *The Films of Fritz Lang: Allegories of Vision and Modernity* (British Film Institute, 2000), and over a hundred articles.

André Habib is Adjunct Professor of Film Studies at the Université de Montréal. He is the author of *L'Attrait de la ruine* (Crisnée, Yellow Now, 2011). He edited with Viva Paci, *Chris Marker et l'imprimerie du regard* (L'Harmattan, 2008) as well as, with Michel Marie, *L'Avenir de la mémoire: patrimoine, restauration, réemploi cinématographique* (Editions du Septentrion, forthcoming). His recent research interests have dealt with the aesthetic of ruins, archives, experimental cinema and cinephilia. He is also co-editor of the web journal *Hors champ*.

Patricia Kruth is Senior Lecturer at the Université Lille 3 where she teaches American Studies and Film. A former Cultural Delegate for the French Embassy in Cambridge, she has curated photography exhibitions (Patrick Bailly-Maître-Grand) in Great-Britain and collaborated with museums (Sainsbury Centre for Visual Arts). She is the editor of *Sound* (with H. Stobart, Cambridge UP, reprinted 2007), the author of *Figures filmiques: les mondes new-yorkais de M. Scorsese et W. Allen* (P.U. du Septentrion, 2002), and of numerous articles and book chapters on Scorsese, and on the relationships between cinema and other art forms in *Cinema and Architecture* (BFI, 1997), *Peinture et Cinéma* (*Ligeia*, n° 77-90, 2007), *Peintres cinéastes* (*Ligeia*, n° 97-98-99-100, 2010).

Samantha Lackey is a Curator at The Hepworth Wakefield, Yorkshire's major new art gallery which opened in May 2011. She worked previously at the Whitworth Art Gallery, University of Manchester as an Assistant Curator and Curatorial Research Fellow. Before this she was Senior Research Fellow for the AHRC Research Centre for Studies of Surrealism and its Legacies, The University of Manchester and a Lecturer within the Art History and Visual Studies department at The University of Manchester. Her research interests include contemporary moving image, surrealism and modes of artistic practice.

Guillaume Le Gall is Senior Lecturer in History of contemporary art at the Paris-Sorbonne University (Paris IV) and a former resident at the Villa Medicis in Rome. He defended a thesis on Eugène Atget in 2002 and has published books and articles on the photography of the 19th and 20th centuries. He has been curator of exhibitions on contemporary photography (*Fabricca dell'immagine*, Villa Médicis, Rome, 2004), Eugène Atget (*Eugène Atget: une rétrospective*, Bibliothèque Nationale de France, Paris, 2007; Martin-Gropius-Bau, Berlin, 2007-2008; Fotomuseum Winterthur, 2010), Surrealist photography (*La Subversion des images*, Centre Pompidou, Paris, 2009; Fotomuseum Winterthur, 2010; Institute de Cultura/Fundacion Mapfre, Madrid, 2010).

Barbara Le Maître is Senior Lecturer in Film Studies at the University Sorbonne nouvelle Paris 3. She has published *Entre film et photographie. Essai sur l'empreinte* (PUV, 2004, *L'Impronta. Tra cinema et fotografia*, Kaplan, 2010), and about twenty essays on theory and aesthetics of images, such as: "De l'effet cinéma à la forme tableau", in *Images contemporaines. Arts, formes, dispositifs* (Aléas, 2009), "Contemporanéité, anachronisme. Autour de quelques propositions théoriques sur la temporalité des images", in *Extended Cinema. Le Cinéma gagne du terrain* (Campanotto, 2010), and "Géographie filmique de Pierre Perrault: le Royaume, l'utopie, l'écomusée", in *Cinema & Cie. International Film Studies Journal*, vol. X, n° 14-15 (Spring-Fall 2011). Her current research deals with cinema and museology, the figure of the living dead, and the relations between films and fossils.

Viva Paci is Professor in Film Studies at the École des médias (Université du Québec à Montréal), where she is also the director of the MA program "Cinéma et images en mouvement." She is a member of the Centre for Research into Intermediality and of the Groupe de recherche sur l'avènement et la formation du spectacle cinématographique et scénique. Paci is the author of *Il Cinema di Chris Marker* (2005) and co-author with André Habib of *Chris Marker et l'imprimerie du regard* (2008); with Ronald de Rooy and Beniamino Mirisola of *Romanzi di deformazione: 1988-2010*

(2010); and with Michael Cowan and Alanna Thain of an anthology about the street in contemporary European cinema (*Cinémas*, vol. 21, no. 1, 2010). Her recent books: *La comédie musicale et la double vie du cinéma* (2011) and *La machine à voir. À propos de cinéma, attraction, exhibition* (2012).

Christel Taillibert is Senior Lecturer in Film Studies at University Nice Sophia-Antipolis (France). She is in charge of the Master "Information-communication" (First Degree). She is a member of the research Laboratory "LIRCES" (Laboratoire Interdisciplinaire Récits, cultures et sociétés). Her research focuses on the history of educational cinematography, Italian cinema, and festivals. She is the author of *Tribulations festivalières – Les festivals de cinéma et audiovisuel en France* (L'Harmattan, 2009), *L'Institut international du cinématographe éducatif. Regards sur le rôle du cinéma éducatif dans la politique internationale du fascisme italien* (L'Harmattan, 1999).

Kim Timby is a photography historian living in Paris where she teaches at the École des Hautes Études en Sciences Sociales and the École du Louvre. She is a former curator at the Musée Carnavalet in Paris, where her exhibits included *Paris in 3D, from Stereoscopy to Virtual Reality* (2000), and at the Musée Niécpe in Chalon-sur-Saône, where she curated *Sous un beau ciel bleu* (2006). Her doctoral thesis (2006) explored the history of screen photography and she is currently preparing a manuscript on the subject, tentatively titled *From Utopia to Entertainment: A History of 3D and Animated Lenticular Imagery in France*. Her research interests also include the uses of colour photography, in particular its integration into illustrated magazines in the 1950s.

Maria Tortajada is Professor in Film Studies at the University of Lausanne, president of Réseau Cinéma CH and Réseau Cinéma CH project chief, director of research at the FNS for ProDoc projects "Cinéma et dispositifs audiovisuals" (formation module) and "Epistémologie des dispositifs de vision et d'audition" (research module). She has recently published *Ciné-dispositifs. Spectacles, cinéma, télévision, littérature, (ed. with F. Albera, L'Age d'Homme, 2011)* and *Cinema Beyond Film. Media Epistemology in the Modern Era (ed. with F. Albera, Amsterdam University Press, 2010).*

Valérie Vignaux is Senior Lecturer qualified to direct research projects in Film Studies at the François-Rabelais University in Tours. The author of monographs (*Jacques Becker*, Céfal, 2001; *Jean Benoit-Lévy*, AFRHC, 2007) and of film analyses (*La Religieuse*, Céfal 2005; *Casque d'or*, Atlande, 2009), she is also the desk editor of the review *1895*, three editions of which she has overseen (*Archives*, 2001, *Emile Cohl*, 2007, *O'Galop/Lortac*, 2009). She is currently preparing a monograph devoted to the oeuvre of the critic and historian Georges Sadoul (having co-edited, with Clément Chéroux, *Portes, un cahier de collages surréalistes de Georges Sadoul*, Textuel, 2009). Her studies have appeared internationally in a number of specialized journals, including *1895*, *Archives*, *Cinémas*, *Montage A/V*, *Revue de la bibliothèque nationale de France*, and *Sociétés & Représentations*.

Index